LATINOS

IN THE MIDWEST

LATINOS

IN THE MIDWEST

EDITED BY **RUBÉN O. MARTINEZ**

Michigan State University Press • East Lansing

Copyright © 2011 by Michigan State University

⊖ The paper used in this publication meets the minimum requirements
of ANSI/NISO Z39.48-1992 (R 1997) (Permanence of Paper).

 Michigan State University Press
East Lansing, Michigan 48823-5245

Printed and bound in the United States of America.

17 16 15 14 13 12 11   1 2 3 4 5 6 7 8 9 10

LIBRARY OF CONGRESS CATALOGING-IN-PUBLICATION DATA
Latinos in the Midwest / edited by Rubén O. Martinez.
p. cm. — (Latinos in the United States series)
Includes bibliographical references.
ISBN 978-0-87013-996-3 (pbk. : alk. paper)
1. Hispanic Americans—Middle West. I. Martinez, Rubén Orlando.
F358.2.S75L37 2011
305.868'077—dc22
2010051931

Cover and book design by Charlie Sharp, Sharp Designs

g **green**
press
ɪɴɪᴛɪᴀᴛɪᴠᴇ Michigan State University Press is a member of the Green
Press Initiative and is committed to developing and
encouraging ecologically responsible publishing practices. For more
information about the Green Press Initiative and the use of recycled
paper in book publishing, please visit *www.greenpressinitiative.org*.

Visit Michigan State University Press on the World Wide Web at
www.msupress.msu.edu

Dedication

To Julian Samora, whose intellectual, professional, and community leadership set the standards for all who seek to contribute to the betterment of Chicana/o and Latina/o communities

Contents

FRANCISCO A. VILLARRUEL

Foreword

THE STUDY OF LATINOS IN THE MIDWEST IS NOT A NEW PHENOMENON, BUT one that has gained increased recognition due in part to the leadership and vision of Julian Samora. The growth in the numbers of Latinos in the Midwest, a region that is today viewed as a rust belt and a context where change is slow to occur, has become increasingly important. In many ways, Latinos can be seen as contributing to the regeneration of the vitality of communities in the heartland of the United States. Especially important is their social, political, and economic incorporation in the coming decades, when the Baby Boomers will depart from the workforce to enjoy their "golden years." Who will fill the void in the labor force left in the wake of the Baby Boomers' departure? What barriers to the incorporation of Latinos across societal sectors must be overcome? Can the incorporation of Latinos occur before it is too late to prevent economic decline due to an inadequately educated labor force? How will the United States maintain a competitive economy if its educational institutions are unable to meet the educational needs of Latino students?

These questions are not rhetorical; rather they are questions that must be addressed by political and community leaders, by researchers and political analysts and, most importantly, by Americans across the country. This volume begins the critical process of raising these questions and shedding light on Latino communities in the Midwest in the current context of extremist politics, the Great Recession, the War on Terrorism, and a multitude of "Save Our Nation" nativist efforts.

The contributors to this volume come to these issues from a diverse set of academic disciplines. Sociologists, political scientists, anthropologists, demographers, and other scholars join together here in a common goal: to advance our scholarly knowledge of the experiences and challenges facing Latinos in the Midwest and in the nation as we move further into the 21st century. Key institutional arenas are examined, including politics, economic status and employment, education, and health care. Case studies and survey data provide insight into the experiences of Latinos in a variety of social settings, from rural farm towns to midsize suburban communities. Each chapter adds important elements to our overall understanding of what it means to be Latino in the Midwest.

The next few decades will be crucial in determining the long-term outcome of the country's demographic shift, not only for Latinos, but for the nation as a whole. Policymakers, community leaders, and others who are or should be concerned with the future of this country need to familiarize themselves with these issues and utilize research such as the work presented in this volume to make informed and effective decisions regarding Latinos at the community, state, and national level.

Census 2010 will most likely show that the demographic shift is further along than we think, and that poverty among Latinos and other minorities is more widespread than we know. It should, however, generate greater awareness of these issues in the American public. Until those data are available, however, researchers such as those contributing to this volume are setting the stage for a constructive policy discourse that promotes the realignment of the nation's institutions with Latinos and other minority citizens as a means of repositioning the nation for a better future. The alternative, a nation increasingly divided by race, ethnicity, and socioeconomic and political inequality, surely cannot be sustained in a world of increasing diversity.

Acknowledgments

LIKE SO MANY OTHER THINGS IN LIFE, SCHOLARSHIP IS A VOYAGE—ONE FILLED with both excitement and difficulty—and in the end one is left with a new understanding of the issues irrespective of whether the final product under- or overshot its initial mark. I am grateful to the many persons who assisted me on the voyage of this volume, especially Catie Jo Hilbelink and Dr. Jennifer Tello Buntin. Without their assistance the voyage would certainly have been more arduous and difficult. I also am grateful to the many persons who in one way or another assisted with the manuscripts, including Sheila Contreras, Jodie O'Gorman, Ellen Hayse, Jean Kayitsinga, Jesenia Pizarro and Francisco Villarruel. I also want to thank Kristine M. Blakeslee, project editor at Michigan State University Press, who improved everyone's writing and made the entire volume more understandable and readable. The strengths of the volume are due to them and to the authors of the chapters contained herein. I take responsibility for any faults or weaknesses that characterize the volume. Finally, thanks to Gabriel Dotto, Director of Michigan State University Press, and Julie L. Loehr, Editor in Chief and Assistant Director at Michigan State University Press, for their continued encouragement and patience throughout the process of editing the volume. Their support surely made the task much more satisfying.

Introduction

THE SPANISH EXPLORERS LEFT HUGE FOOTPRINTS IN THE NEW WORLD, AND their cultural influences are widely felt today from the Canadian border with the United States to Tierra del Fuego, an archipelago off the tip of South America. The mixing of Spanish, African, and other Old World cultures in the New World over the past five hundred years has left few, if any, indigenous peoples untouched and has produced a rich cultural tapestry that has variants of the Spanish language as the major thread that ties it together. In the United States, these peoples are called Latinos. They are a heterogeneous subpopulation of the country's overall population that varies by history, culture and length of time in the geographical area known as the United States. In 1492, Cristóbal Colón, or Christopher Columbus, and his men, after visiting other islands, landed in present-day Cuba and claimed it on behalf of Spain. In 1513, Ponce de León settled the island Borinquen, known today as Puerto Rico, and in the spring of 1513 he landed on the east coast of present-day Florida near present-day San Augustine, naming it "Pascua de Florida" or "Festival of Flowers." Over the next century, the Spaniards continued to explore and spread their influence in the New World. Hernán Cortés, Cabeza de Vaca, Hernando de Soto, and Francisco Coronado are but a few of the men whose exploits would contribute to the imposition of Spain's power in the New World.

In 1539 and the early 1540s, Hernando de Soto made his way, albeit in a rather circuitous route, from Florida to the hinterlands of the southeastern region and the southern parts of the region known today as the Midwest, possibly going as far north as Indiana and Illinois, and then southwesterly to present-day Texas (Chaves Tesser and Hudson 1991; also see Clayton, Knight, and Moore 1993).[1] In June 1541, de Soto and his men discovered a muddy river with a strong current that they called the Río Grande, but which in time came to be known as the Mississippi River. De Soto made it to the Great Plains and came in contact with Comanche and Sioux Indians. That expedition turned out to be de Soto's final one, as he died of fever on June 25, 1542 (Clayton, Knight, and Moore 1993).

Around the same time as de Soto's final expedition, Francisco Vásquez de Coronado y Luján explored the southern Rockies in what is today present-day Arizona and New Mexico and made his way into the Great Plains, reaching Kansas in 1541, where he held the first Christian mass in the interior of North America. During his expedition, one of his parties discovered the Grand Canyon (Hammond 1926a). Fifty-seven years later, in 1598, Juan de Oñate established the northernmost Spanish settlement in New Spain in what is today known as the Española Valley in northern New Mexico (Hammond 1926b; Brebner 1933). In 1605, Oñate led an expedition that followed the Colorado River down to the Gulf of California (Hammond 1927). By the time that Jamestown was founded in 1607 by the Virginia Company, Spanish expeditions had traversed the hinterlands of what is today the United States from the Atlantic Ocean to the Gulf of California.

It is from these early settlements and those across Central and South America that the nation's Latino population has descended across the centuries. Some individuals are descendants of Cortés, conqueror of the Aztecs, or of Moctezuma, ruler of the Atzec Empire. These two men symbolize the worlds of the conquerors and the conquered, but their descendants blend the cultures, both as *mestizos* and *genizaros* that comprise the rich tapestry of Hispanic cultures across North and South America. It is from these broad cultural processes and groupings that Latinos in the United States are descended.

Today, Latinos are comprised of a mix of peoples who are native and foreign born. Those who are native born have historically been rooted in the Southwest, and include descendants of the Spanish colonists (from both Spain and New Spain), who at the time of the American conquest of Mexico in 1848, included three major groups: Tejanos, Hispanos, and Californios. Generations of Mexican immigrants over the past century and a half have given rise to new generations of native-born Mexican Americans, and continue to do so today. Other native-born Latinos include Puerto

Ricans, at least since 1917, when they were given citizenship. As an "unincorporated territory" of the United States, Puerto Rico's people are U.S. citizens, although they are not fully enfranchised, as are those born on the mainland. Cuban Americans also have several generations of native-born persons; the first major generation having arrived in the early 1960s, following the Cuban Revolution. More recently, the United States has seen the arrival of substantial numbers of immigrants from Central and South America. Referred to as "Other Hispanics" by the U.S. Bureau of the Census, these "Other Latinos," when lumped together, comprise the second largest Latino group in the country, following Chicanos or Mexican Americans.

The rapid growth of the Latino population since the 1980s constitutes one of the major dimensions of the demographic shift that is occurring in the country today. The other major dimension is the aging of the U.S. population, primarily White and African Americans. Taken together these two demographic processes present a major challenge, if not an impending crisis, to the nation and its future (Myers 2008). Consequently, although this volume focuses on Latinos in the Midwest, most of the issues addressed in the chapters contained in it have relevance for other regions and the nation as a whole.

Latinos in the Midwest

The systematic study of Latinos in the Midwest began with the work of George Edson and Manuel Gamio in the late 1920s and Paul Taylor in the 1930s, all of whom focused on Mexican immigration and Mexican labor, particularly farmworkers. The field then received attention by Norman D. Humphrey and John Thaden, both of whom focused on Mexicans in Michigan in the 1930s and 1940s. They were followed by Elena Padilla, who focused on Puerto Ricans in Chicago and New York in the 1940s and 1950s, and by Barbara Macklin, who at the close of the 1950s was studying Mexicans in Toledo, Ohio. During the 1960s, more and more scholars were conducting research on Latinos in the Midwest (see Choldin and Trout 1969). Lyle Shannon and his students did research on Mexican immigrants in Racine, Wisconsin, and Julian Samora and Richard Lamanna focused on Spanish Americans and Mexican Americans in East Chicago (Samora and Lamanna 1967). Samora and his students continued their work in the 1970s (Cardenas 1976a), and organized the Midwest Conference on Chicano Studies in 1974 at South Bend, Indiana. By this time several efforts were occurring simultaneously at universities in the Midwest to establish both Chicano student organizations and Chicano Studies programs.

Over the next three decades several other scholars began studying Latinos in the Midwest (Barger and Reza 1994; Millard and Chapa 2004; Valdés 2000; Vargas

1993), especially with the establishment of Chicano/Latino centers and programs at midwestern universities in the 1980s and 1990s (e.g., the Julian Samora Research Institute at Michigan State University and the Institute for Latino Studies at the University of Notre Dame). The focus has tended to be on migrant and industrial workers (Norris 2009; Valdés 2000; Vargas 1993; Wells 1976), with recent studies beginning to examine socio-economic and other aspects of the Latino population (Kayitsinga 2009; Millard and Chapa 2004). Today, the Cambio de Colores conference at the University of Missouri–Columbia and the Cumbre conference at the University of Nebraska at Omaha provide regular venues for the dissemination of scholarship on Latinos in the Midwest. Still, despite the scholarly work that has been done on Latinos in the Midwest, a coherent body of research has not yet emerged, and given the population changes of the past three decades, much more remains to be done.

Latino Demographics

The demographic shift predicted by scholars in the 1980s is now in full swing. Not only did Latinos surpass African Americans as the largest ethnic minority group in the nation in 2001, but by midcentury they are projected to be one in three of the nation's residents.[2] At that time, Latino youth are projected to surpass the number of White youth.[3] These shifts have major implications for the nation, and their importance increases when one considers the aging of the Baby Boomers, the overwhelming majority of whom are White. Why are these shifts important? Mainly, because Latinos are the most marginalized major population group in society, and this fact has considerable implications for the future of the nation's economy. As the Boomers leave the workforce and become less capable of independent living, who will replace them in the economy and who will meet their health-care needs? Already significant shortages in the heath-care services industry exist in some sections of the country, and they are expected to increase (Leutz 2007). At the same time, the number of immigrant workers is increasing, especially among nursing, psychiatric, and home health aides (Leutz 2007). As the ratio of seniors to working-age adults (25 to 64) increases—it is expected to increase from today's figure of approximately 245 per 1,000 to approximately 423 by 2030—the demands on a smaller workforce will be profound.[4]

With the majority of Latino adults being immigrants, and the majority of today's Latino children being born to immigrants, language becomes a major issue for the integration of Latinos into the core fabric of societal institutions (Fry and Passel 2009). It has implications for the education of children, for the integration of Latino workers into the workplace, and for their integration into the spheres of civic and political engagement. As the Baby Boomers reach their career and earning peaks they will move into their retirement years and their numbers will slowly begin to decline, but because they comprise approximately one-fourth of the overall population, their needs as seniors will ripple through societal institutions in significant ways over the next three decades. It is precisely during this period that Latinos will increase significantly in numbers, but while they may be positioned demographically to contribute to the nation's economy, educationally they are not. Thus, one of the great challenges for the nation is the social, economic, and political incorporation of Latinos, both native and foreign born.

Latinos in the Midwest have increased their numbers enormously since the beginning of the 20th century, when their number was a mere 1,200 (Cardenas 1976b). By the mid-twentieth century, they numbered approximately 80,000, increasing rapidly and steadily thereafter. For 1970, in the twelve states we include in the Midwest region (Illinois, Indiana, Iowa, Kansas, Michigan, Minnesota, Missouri, Nebraska, North Dakota, Ohio, South Dakota, and Wisconsin)[5] estimates set their number at just over one million (see Estrada 1976), and they were at 1.25 million by 1980, and nearly 1.5 million by 1990 (Gibson and Jung 2002). Today, they are estimated at more than 4.1 million. The total population for the 12 states is estimated at 65.8 million, with Latinos comprising approximately 6.2% of the population.

Although the six states in the Midwest with the largest populations are Illinois, Ohio, Michigan, Indiana, Missouri, and Wisconsin, slightly more than one-half (51.1%) of the region's population resides in only three states: Illinois, Ohio, and Michigan (in rank order). The majority of Latinos (approximately 64.2%), however, resides in the three states of Illinois, Michigan, and Indiana (in rank order). Illinois alone has nearly one-half (46.7% or 1.9 million) of the Latino population in the Midwest, with the majority residing in Cook County (1.2 million) or Chicago and surrounding cities, which together constitute the "Big Manzana," or the Big Apple of the Midwest. The numbers of Latinos in the other midwestern states drop off significantly from those of Illinois (or Chicago), with none yet reaching the mark of one-half million. Michigan comes closest with approximately 410,000 Latinos. In Minnesota, however, Latinos are expected to surpass African Americans in the coming decade to become the largest ethnic minority group (Peterson 2009). This scenario is likely to repeat itself in other midwestern states as well.

The majority of Latinos in the Midwest are of Mexican ancestry (75%), followed by Puerto Ricans (9.3%), Spaniards and Spanish Americans (5.5%), Central Americans (4.8%), South Americans (3.7%), Cuban Americans (1.3%) and Dominicans (0.4%). The majority (58.3%) of the 3,090,884 Mexican and Mexican American population is in Illinois (1,505,101) and Michigan (296,469). The majority (65.2%) of the 382,281 Puerto Ricans are concentrated in Illinois (170,511) and Ohio (78,549), with some in

Wisconsin (37,875), Michigan (32,884), and Indiana (26,768). The majority (58.7%) of the 226,198 Spaniards and Spaniard Americans are in Illinois (71,238), Michigan (37,029), and Ohio (24,447). The majority (59.5%) of the 197,679 Central Americans are in Illinois (66,466), Ohio (17,131), and Indiana (17,089), with a relatively sizable group in Michigan (16,867). The majority (57.3%) of the 150,500 South Americans in the Midwest are in Illinois (72,329) and Minnesota (15,888), with a sizable group in Ohio (14,938). The majority (58.0%) of the 51,948 Cuban Americans are in Illinois (21,031) and Michigan (9,143), with a sizable group in Ohio (5,823). Finally, of the 16,156 Dominicans, the majority (55.0%) are in Illinois (4,747) and Ohio (4,146), with a relatively sizable group in Michigan (2,610).

Why have the numbers of Latinos increased in the Midwest? One would think that with the deindustrialization that has gripped the Midwest, there would be little to attract them to the region. However, despite deindustrialization in the region over the past several decades, increases in service occupations have contributed to both the geographic dispersion of Latinos and the relative distribution of ethnic groups in the occupational structure (Liaw and Frey 2007; Zuñiga and Hernández-León 2005). In the Midwest, Latinos and Mexican immigrants, especially those with low levels of education, are concentrated at the lower end of the service occupation ladder, in manual labor positions in construction and in the service sector, such as the food retail industry. In other words, deindustrialization and the restructuring of the economy have created pull forces in the labor market that continue to attract manual workers from across the nation and from across the nation's southern border. In 1990, 24.1% of Mexican-origin workers (both native born and immigrants) were in service occupations, 15.0% were in precision production, craft, and repairs, and 41.6% were in fabricator, operator, and laborer positions (Saenz 1996). Similar distributions are provided for Latinos by Chapa and coauthors (2004) using 2000 census data.

Why This Book?

This volume was envisioned as part of the celebration of the Julian Samora Research Institute's 20th anniversary celebration conference on Latino/as in the Midwest, which was held in November 2009. After a call for papers, a blind peer review process of the manuscripts that were submitted, and the selection of the manuscripts for the volume, some of the authors were able to attend the conference and present their papers. The volume provides an overview of Latinos in the Midwest, focusing on their demographic characteristics, political attitudes, and experiences in the region, especially in relation to dominant group institutions such as law enforcement, U.S. Immigration and Customs Enforcement, health care, and other agencies. The volume provides studies by a mix of young, midcareer, and senior scholars who recognize the demographic shifts that are under way and the importance of the dynamics that shape the lives of Latinos in the Midwest. Of importance is the mix of case studies and quantitative studies that compare Latinos in the Midwest with Latinos in other regions of the country.

The opening essay, by Sandra M. Gonzales, reflects the search for identity through narrative connections between midwestern Latinos and prehistorical civilizations in present-day Mexico. Ancient migrations across the Bering Strait, an accepted view on the movement of humankind to the Western Hemisphere, gave rise to a multitude of civilizations that were cut off from the Eastern Hemisphere until the arrival of the Spaniards in 1492. The connections among the ethnic groups that arose in the Western Hemisphere remain under scientific study still today, and although cultural connections among the mound peoples in the Midwest and ancient Mexico have not been empirically established (or perhaps have been shown not to have existed), Gonzales argues that narrative discourses make and seek to make connections, if only as a form of solidarity with indigenous peoples subjected to conquest by European powers. An interesting shift in population movements in the Western Hemisphere is the northern migration of people in recent decades. The cultural impacts of these migrations are being felt today in the Midwest and across the United States, and they will continue to generate new discourses about ethnic and national identities in the years to come as processes of ethnogenesis meld groups into new ethnic identities.

In the next chapter, Rogelio Saenz provides a demographic overview of Latinos in the Midwest, concluding with the implications that the rapid growth of Latinos may have for their future. The status of Latinos in the Midwest is mixed with some improvements made by native-born Latinos in education and employment, while foreign-born Latinos have low rates of educational achievement and high rates of poverty. Compared to White Americans, Latinos in the Midwest continue to lag behind on major socioeconomic indicators. How the states and communities in the Midwest, and across the nation for that matter, respond to the growing population of Latinos, especially in the area of education, will have significant consequences for the region and the nation.

In the next chapter Arturo Vega, Rubén O. Martinez, and Tia Stevens provide results from secondary analyses of data from the Latino National Survey 2006, focusing on Latinos in the Midwest in comparison to their counterparts in other regions of the country. They first provide a demographic overview of the sample, which consists of 9,509 respondents in 16 states and Washington, DC, and then focus on political attitudes and perceptions, including same-sex marriage, abortion, and immigration. While Midwest Latinos are similar to Latinos in other regions of the country, the foreign born in the Midwest are more likely to have come from Mexico, particularly the states of Chihuahua, Jalisco, Michoacán, and Guanajuato, to improve their economic condition. Although some respondents in the Midwest reported slightly higher incomes than their counterparts in other regions, others reported income levels that put them below the poverty threshold at rates similar to those across other regions, which are quite high (33%). Like Latinos in other regions, Latinos in the Midwest have relatively weak partisan and political ideology identification, and a weak sense of internal political efficacy. They tend to have moderate levels of shared commonality with African Americans, and slightly lower levels of commonality with White Americans. These findings indicate that Latinos are somewhat alienated from the American political system and point to the need for their political incorporation.

Following that, Theo J. and Linda C. Majka examine the incorporation of Latino immigrants into the local institutions of Dayton, Ohio, a midsized midwestern city that has experienced deindustrialization and demographic shifts, including massive population decline, in recent decades. The influx of Latino immigrants has engendered backlashes and contentious discussions among the members of local government boards seeking to address issues such as the formal recognition of the Matricula Consular de Alta Seguridad, which is an identification card issued to Mexican nationals residing outside of Mexico by the Mexican government through its consulate offices. In West Dayton, boards representing predominantly Black communities formally supported a resolution allowing local city agencies to recognize the Matricula as a form of ID, whereas those in predominantly White communities opposed the resolution. Acceptance of the Matricula is an important step in improving relations with Latino immigrant communities. Other factors important to the incorporation of Latinos include language and cultural barriers, including gaps in knowledge among both Latino and dominant group members about each other, neglect by institutional representatives, and the racial division of labor. These factors tend to leave Latinos as marginalized communities that are relatively isolated from mainstream institutions. The authors recommend steps that can be taken by cities to promote the incorporation of Latino immigrants, and conclude with a critical discussion of assimilation models promoted by members of the dominant group.

In the next chapter, Jan L. Flora, Claudia Prado-Meza, Hannah Lewis, César Montalvo, and Frank Dunn, using a community capital framework, examine the impact of the raid by the U.S. Immigration and Customs Enforcement (ICE) agency on the Swift & Pork processing plant in Marshalltown, Iowa, on December 12, 2006. ICE raids on Latino communities and their employers have occurred across the country over the past several years and have struck terror into Latino immigrant families. The influx of Latino immigrants to small cities like Marshalltown is partly tied to the restructuring of the meat-processing industry and the movement of meat- and poultry-processing plants into the region. The restructuring of the meat-processing industries included mechanization, the deskilling of the occupations, and the lowering of wages. Together these changes in the industry ultimately led to a change from White to Latino workers, with plants recruiting Latinos when it became too difficult to employ local White workers. In 2000, Marshalltown was recognized by the governor as a model community in integrating immigrants. The carefully planned raid by ICE on the plant in Marshalltown, among other things, created a community crisis that left 90 workers in detention, many children without parents, families with fewer wage earners, and impaired relations between Latinos and White Americans. A positive externality of the raid was that it engendered increased public attention on the issue of raids on Latino communities and employers of undocumented immigrants, the conditions of detention for those taken into custody, and the need to address the institutional integration of immigrants.

As is widely known, health care and health disparities are a prominent concern and a high priority among Latino communities. Lydia P. Buki, Jennifer B. Mayfield, and Flavia C. D. Andrade focus on the need for early detection of cervical and breast cancer among Latinas and provide results from a needs assessment of 120 Latinas in four small, "new growth" communities in central Illinois. Buki, Mayfield, and Andrade provide an overview of cancer disparities in incidence, mortality, and survivor rates between Latinas and their dominant group counterparts. Their assessment findings indicate that Latinas are not screening regularly for cervical and breast cancer, that younger women and women without children are least likely to have had a Pap smear examination, and that older women are at risk of not remaining up-to-date with their Pap smear examinations. Additionally, they find that Latinas of Mexican descent were more likely to report barriers to regular screening. The authors conclude with recommendations for improving regular screening among Latinas, including increased efforts to disseminate information about screening for cervical and breast cancer and the use of *promotoras de salud* to help close the gaps in this area of health.

In the next chapter, Michael Tapia, Donald T. Hutcherson, and Ana Campos-Holland examine race and ethnic minority status as a risk factor for arrest across geographic regions using data from the National Longitudinal Survey of Youth 1997. This data set is a valuable alternative to official data, which use only racial categories and not ethnicity. The analysis of these authors shows that race and ethnic minority status are significantly related to increased risk for arrest, and that the risk is at least two times greater for Blacks than it is for Latinos, who are more at risk for arrest than Whites. Moreover, it shows that Latinos in the Midwest are more at risk of arrest than their counterparts in the southern and western regions. Finally, native-born

Latinos are more at risk than foreign-born Latinos. This study breaks new ground by estimating Latino effects as risk factors for arrest in comparison to other racial and ethnic groups across geographic regions.

The eighth chapter, by David A. Badillo, who has done substantial research on Latinos in Michigan and Illinois (2003; 2004), provides a social historical analysis of the work of the Mexican American Legal Defense and Education Fund (MALDEF), which maintains an office in Chicago, on behalf of Latinos in the Midwest. Following an overview of MALDEF's work on issues of desegregation and bilingual education, Badillo focuses on the case of *Gomez v. Illinois State Board of Education,* which resulted in a ruling favorable to Latinos in 1987. In the evolution of the federal protection of the educational rights of language-minority students, *Gomez v. Illinois* stands as an important step in the implementation of the Equal Educational Opportunities Act of 1974, which made Title VI of the Civil Rights Act of 1964 applicable to all educational institutions and required state and local educational agencies to take affirmative actions to overcome language barriers facing language-minority students. Badillo traces the difficulties inherent in the context in which the case of Margarita Gómez emerged as a class action suit charging that the state educational agency had violated federal and state laws by failing to provide uniform and consistent guidelines for local school districts to identify, place, and educate language-minority students. Although the case was dismissed by the U.S. District Court for the Northern District of Illinois, Eastern Division, in 1987, the U.S. Court of Appeals for the Seventh Circuit overruled in part the decision of the lower court and held that state educational agencies must do more than go through the motions to meet the needs of language-minority students; they must take "appropriate action" to ensure that the needs of language-minority children are met. Whether the educational needs of Latino children are being met throughout the Midwest is an important question that requires systematic research. By implication, the study raises the question of how local agencies and institutions are responding to the needs of Latino communities today, and shows that responses are not always substantive despite appearing positive.

In the next chapter, Jennifer Tello Buntin examines how Mexican transnational migration has affected public schools in Aurora, Illinois. In particular, she focuses on the "transnationalizing effect" the influx of Mexicanos had on the local school district as the latter sought to find ways by which to meet the educational needs of the newcomers. The local school district responded to the educational needs of Latino children from immigrant families in two important ways: (1) by developing a partnership with the Mexican government, among others, to provide a distance learning program that linked adult learners with teachers in Mexico via satellite, and (2) by recruiting teachers from Mexico. Both programs were short-lived, one because of a change in leadership in the district, and the other because of No Child Left Behind, which imposed English-language requirements that could not be met by teachers from Spanish-speaking countries. Tello provides an interesting perspective on how community institutions, at least those that are creative and proactive, may be reorienting themselves to demographic change. It remains to be seen how common proactive approaches are at the local level.

Maria Josefa Santos and Antonio Castro Escobar continue the focus on institutional responses to the needs of Latino communities by focusing on Latino growers in southwestern Michigan. Latino farm operators are the fastest growing population segment in the industry, yet they remain greatly underserved by the government agencies and organizations whose responsibilities are to serve agricultural operators. Much like the nation, the agricultural sector is experiencing a demographic shift in which White and Black growers are aging and Latinos are moving into the industry. Santos and Escobar emphasize the importance of building capacity among the service-delivery agencies in order to close the gaps that exist between them and Latino growers. Not only is there a dearth of services and relevant information available in Spanish, but activities across federal and state agencies lack coordination, hindering the development of sustainable educational programs for Latino agricultural producers. At this point, Latino growers are on their own, struggling to learn the best practices in their industry without much support by established agencies.

The final chapter in this volume is by George Vargas, who focuses on the importance of *CitySpirit*, Detroit's oldest outdoor Latino mural, located on a busy street corner in southwest Detroit, which is also known as Mexicantown. As Detroit experiences major economic and political problems, Mexicantown is increasingly viewed as one of the most economically vibrant areas of the city. As one of the artists who created the mural more than 30 years ago, Vargas provides an intimate view of the theory behind the image, and interprets the mural as a historical and cultural image of Detroit and the state of Michigan; one with multiple meanings expressed through signs and symbols. The mural persists as a living monument that conveys both local and universal meanings in the tradition of the great Mexican muralists. As the peoples and the communities of the Midwest seek to reposition themselves for the future, the mural reminds us, Latinos and non-Latinos, of our interconnectedness and common humanity and the promise of tomorrow.

Summary

This collection of studies and essays provides an introduction to the current status of Latinos in the Midwest across a range of life areas and contributes to our understanding of the challenges that they face where they live and work. It shows us steps that could be taken to improve and support their education and economic activity, especially the closing of gaps in the delivery of services. Particularly important is the struggle between forces that promote either the inclusion of Latinos in societal institutions or their exclusion from them. Poverty, education, and health remain looming challenges both for Latinos and for the communities in which they reside. Despite their relative alienation from the political system and the difficulties they experience with institutions, Latinos are resilient in their efforts to survive and to improve their lot in life. Although American ideology has it that individuals are to make it on their own, the historical reality is that some groups have received considerable sustained support through government-sponsored programs, such as those in agricultural production, while others not only have been left to fend for themselves, they have been systematically excluded from full participation in society through discrimination (see Fix and Struyk 1993). Still, there are proactive efforts to bring Latinos into the folds of institutional life in their communities. Such efforts require research that can enhance their effectiveness.

Much research remains to be done in order to shed light on specific localities and institutions, and their responses to the needs of Latinos. One thing is clear, however: the demographic shift will continue even if the national borders are to be sealed, and the future of the nation will increasingly be bound up with the status of Latinos (Cisneros 2009). The more the status of Latinos improves, especially in the area of education, the more Latinos will be able to contribute to the nation's economy and its future. Midwestern cities, like those in the South and other regions, are starting to move beyond initial reactions to the influx of Latinos, sometimes positively and at other times negatively. To be sure, Latinos, like their predecessors centuries ago, are leaving large footprints across the Midwest and the nation, and their greatest influence is yet to come.

NOTES

1. There is some speculation that de Soto may have made it as far north as the point of Lake Michigan near present-day Chicago. See Donald E. Sheppard's account, "American Conquest: The Oldest Written Account of Inland America" (2010) One would think, however, that such an event would have received considerable treatment in the chronicles of his men.

2. Table 4, "Projections of the Population by Sex, Race, and Hispanic Origin for the United States: 2010 to 2050," U.S. Population Projections, U.S. Census Bureau. Available online: http://www.census.gov/population/www/projections/summarytables.html.

3. Table 14, "Projections of the Non-Hispanic White Alone Population by Age and Sex for the United States: 2010 to 2050," and table 20, Projections of the Hispanic Population (Any

Race) by Age and Sex for the United States: 2010 to 2050," U.S. Population Projections, U.S. Census Bureau. Available online: http://www.census.gov/population/www/projections/summarytables.html.

4. Calculated using figures from table 12, "Projections of the Population by Age and Sex for the United States: 2010 to 2050," U.S. Population Projections, U.S. Census Bureau. Available online: http://www.census.gov/population/www/projections/summarytables.html. Also see Myers 2008.

5. There is little standardization when it comes to the states included in any given region of the United States. The inclusion of the 12 states here matches the regional boundaries of the U.S. Census Bureau's Midwest Region (which includes both the East North Central Division and the West North Central Division) and that of the U.S. Department of Agriculture's North Central Regional Center for Rural Development, which is one of four regions for rural development. The figures for this section were compiled from U.S. Census Bureau, Population Finder, American Factfinder. The figures are three-year estimates from 2006 to 2008.

REFERENCES

Badillo, D. A. 2003. *Latinos in Michigan.* East Lansing: Michigan State University Press.

———. 2004. "Mexicanos and Suburban Parish Communities." *Journal of Urban History* 31(1): 23–46.

Barger, W. K., and E. M. Reza. 1994. *The Farm Labor Movement in the Midwest.* Austin: University of Texas Press.

Brebner, J. B. 1933. *The Explorers of North America, 1492—1806.* London: A & C Black.

Cardenas, G. 1976a. "Who are the Midwestern Chicanos: Implications for Chicano Studies." *Aztlán* 7(7): 141–52.

———. 1976b. "Los Desarraigados: Chicanos in the Midwestern Region of the United States." *Aztlán* 7(7): 153–86.

Chapa, J., R. Saenz, R. I. Rochin, and E. Diaz McConnell. 2004. "Latinos and the Changing Demographic Fabric of the Rural Midwest." In *Apple Pie & Enchiladas: Latino Newcomers in the Rural Midwest*, ed. A. V. Millard and J. Chapa, 47–74. Austin: University of Texas Press.

Chaves Tesser, C., and C. Hudson. 1991. "Before Oglethorpe: Hispanic and Indian Cultures in the Southeast United States." *OAH Magazine of History* 5(4): 43–46.

Choldin, H. M., and G. M. Trout. 1969. *Mexican Americans in Transition: Migration and Employment in Michigan Cities.* East Lansing: Rural Manpower Center and Department of Sociology, Michigan State University.

Cisneros, H. G., ed. 2009. *Latinos and the Nation's Future.* Houston: Arte Público Press.

Clayton, L. A., V. J. Knight Jr., and E. C. Moore, eds. 1993. *The De Soto Chronicles: The Expeditions of Hernando de Soto to North America in 1539–1543*, vol. 1. Tuscaloosa: The University of Alabama Press.

Edson, G. T. 1927. "Mexicans in Illinois." Paul S. Taylor Collection, Bancroft Library, University of California, Berkeley.

Estrada, L. F. 1976. "A Demographic Comparison of the Mexican Origin Population in the Midwest and Southwest." *Aztlán* 7(7): 203–34.

Fix, M., and R. J. Struyk, eds. 1993. *Clear and Convincing Evidence: Measurement of Discrimination in America.* Washington, DC: Urban Institute Press.

Fry, R., and J. S. Passel. 2009. "Latino Children: A Majority Are U.S.-Born Offspring of Immigrants." Pew Hispanic Center, Washington, DC, May 28.

Gamio, M. 1930. *Mexican Immigrants to the United States.* Chicago: University of Chicago Press.

Garcia, J. R. 1996. *Mexicans in the Midwest.* Tucson: University of Arizona Press.

Gibson, C., and K. Jung. 2002. "Historical Census Statistics on Population Totals by Race, 1790 to 1990, and by Hispanic Origin, 1970 to 1990, for the United States, Regions, Divisions, and States." Population Division Working Paper No. 56, U.S. Census Bureau, Population Division.

Hammond, G. P. 1926a. "Oñate and the Founding of New Mexico." *New Mexico Historical Review* 1(1): 42–77.

———. 1926b. "Oñate and the Founding of New Mexico (cont'd)." *New Mexico Historical Review* 1(3): 292–323.

———. 1927. "Oñate and the Founding of New Mexico (cont'd)." *New Mexico Historical Review* 2(1): 37–66.

Humphrey, N. D. 1941. "Mexican Repatriation from Michigan: Public Assistance in Historical Perspective." *Social Science Review* 15: 497–513.

Kayitsinga, J. 2009. "The Well Being of Latinos in the Midwest." Paper presented at the 20th Anniversary Conference of the Julian Samora Research Institute, East Lansing, MI, November 5–7.

Leutz, W. N. 2007. "Immigration and the Elderly: Foreign-Born Workers in Long-Term Care." *Immigration Policy in Focus*, vol. 5, issue 12. Washington, DC: Immigration Policy Center, American Immigration Law Foundation.

Liaw, K-L., and W. H. Frey. 2007. "Multivariate Explanation of the 1985–1990 and 1995–2000 Destination Choices of Newly Arrived Immigrants in the United States: The Beginning of a New Trend?" *Population, Space and Place* 13: 377–99.

Macklin, B. J. 1963. "Structural Stability and Culture Change in a Mexican-American Community." Ph.D. diss., University of Pennsylvania.

Millard, A. V., and J. Chapa, eds. 2004. *Apple Pie & Enchiladas: Latino Newcomers in the Rural Midwest.* Austin: University of Texas Press.

Myers, D. 2008. "Thinking Ahead About Our Immigrant Future: New Trends and Mutual Benefits in Our Aging Society." *Immigration Policy in Focus*, vol. 6, issue 1. Washington DC: Immigrant Policy Center, American Immigration Law Foundation.

Norris, J. 2009. *North for the Harvest: Mexican Workers, Growers, and the Sugar Beet Industry.* St. Paul: Minnesota Historical Society Press.

Padilla, E. 1958. *Up from Puerto Rico.* New York: Columbia University Press.

Peterson, D. 2009. "Hispanics Expected to Become Minnesota's Largest Minority Group in 10 Years." *StarTribune.com.* Available online: http://www.startribune.com/local/38429674.html.

Saenz, R. 1996. "The Demography of Mexicans in the Midwest." ERIC Document: ED 413 159.

Samora, J., and R. A. Lamanna. 1967. "Mexican-Americans in a Midwest Metropolis—A Study of East Chicago." Mexican-American Study Project, Advance Report No. 8, Graduate School of Business Administration, University of California, Los Angeles.

Shannon, L. W., and K. Lettau. 1963. "Measuring the Adjustment of Immigrant Laborers." *Southwestern Social Science Quarterly* 44(2): 139–48.

Sheppard, Donald E. 2010. "American Conquest: The Oldest Written Account of Inland America." Available online: http://www.floridahistory.com/inset44.html.

Taylor, P. 1932. *Mexican Labor in the United States: Chicago and the Calumet Region.* Berkeley: University of California Press.

Thaden, J. F. 1942. *Migratory Beet Workers in Michigan.* Special Bulletin 319. East Lansing: Michigan State University, Agricultural Experiment Station.

Valdés, D. N. 2000. *Barrios Norteños: St. Paul and Midwestern Mexican Communities in the Twentieth Century.* Austin: University of Texas Press.

Vargas, Z. 1993. *Proletarians of the North: A History of Mexican Industrial Workers in Detroit and the Midwest, 1917–1933.* Berkeley: University of California Press.

Wells, M. J. 1976. "Emigrants from the Migrant Stream: Environment and Incentives in Relocation." *Aztlán* 7(7): 267–90.

Zuñiga, V., and R. Hernández-León, eds. 2005. *New Destinations: Mexican Immigration in the United States.* New York: Russell Sage Foundation.

SANDRA M. GONZALES

Aztlán in the Midwest and Other Counternarratives Revealed

IN THE FIELD OF CHICANO STUDIES, THE MESOAMERICAN CONNECTION TO THE southwestern United States is well documented. However, these connections have not been adequately explored for the American Midwest. An alternative perspective, however, suggests a long-standing connection between the indigenous peoples of the Midwest, the Southwest, and Mesoamerica. Examining midwestern Chicano identity through the lens of story provides an interesting counternarrative that dramatically deviates from the dominant historical narrative for the region.

Aztlán and How Stories Can Shape Identity

Storytelling and oral traditions have played an important role in the development of the field of Chicano Studies. In 1969, at the First Chicano National Conference in Denver, Colorado, "El Plan Espiritual de Aztlán" was drafted. "El Plan" highlighted building unity within the Chicano community as well as the importance of education and the perpetuation of cultural values. But the most significant result of "El Plan de Aztlán" was the crystallization of a Chicano national identity built around the story of Aztlán.

According to the Aztec narrative, Aztlán was located somewhere in the north, on an island with seven caves and a twisted hill called Colhuacan (Leal 1998). To this day, it is not clear where exactly Aztlán is located geographically, but there are theories that place its location everywhere from Nayarit, Mexico (Pina 1998), to California, New Mexico, Florida, and Wisconsin. Even China has been theorized as a possible location for the Aztec homeland (Leal 1998). It is from Aztlán that the Aztecs departed on a journey that would eventually lead them to found Tenochtitlán, or what is now known as Mexico City.

The power of the Aztlán narrative has attracted the attention of anthropologists and archaeologists on both sides of the U.S.-Mexican border. U.S. scholars largely believe that Aztlán must be located somewhere near the Four Corners region of the American Southwest, while Mexican scholars have largely settled on the Mexican state of Nayarit as the most probable location. There is no conclusive archaeological evidence to substantiate either claim, and yet the story of Aztlán lives on to be told and retold, generation after generation, century after century, creating a historical consciousness in the contemporary psyche of Chicanos today.

The significance of the story of Aztlán for the Chicano community lies not in any scientific evidence, but rather in the construction of a unifying identity that strongly suggests that Chicanos are not immigrants who steal opportunities from white Americans, but, indeed, are native to the Southwest United States and have indigenous roots in the region that go back thousands of years. As Rudolfo Anaya and Francisco Lomelí (1998, ii) argue in the introduction to the collection *Aztlán: Essays on the Chicano Homeland*: "Knowledge of the homeland provides an important element of identity. The Mexican American community in this country in the 1960s lived at the margin of the society, and thus the margin of history. . . . For Chicanos the concept of Aztlán signaled a unifying point of cohesion through which they could define the foundations for an identity."

The prevailing discourse within Chicano Studies theorizes that midwestern Chicanos are newcomers or immigrants to the Midwest, arriving around the 1900s from either the southwestern United States or Mexico, whereas Chicanos from the southwestern United States are native to that region (Cardenas 2001). Because most Chicano Studies programs concentrate on the history of Chicanos in the Southwest, very little is known about the history of Chicanos in the Midwest that predates the 1900s (Cardenas 2001). Without such inquiry, Chicanos in the Midwest are trapped at the periphery of an already peripheral discourse with regards to Chicano identity and history. Though all Chicano discourse occurs at the periphery of Western knowledge production, midwestern Chicano identities and experiences are at the margins of southwestern Chicano scholarly research. Cardenas (2001, 79) writes: "Judging by the published literature, one would hardly know that Chicanos and other Spanish-speaking ethnic populations reside outside the Southwest or East Coast since the literature ignores the Midwest despite the availability of historical documentation on the subject."

A strong argument can be made that Chicanos have a long-standing connection to the American Midwest. Just like their *hermanos* and *hermanas* (brothers and sisters) in the American Southwest, the cultural ancestry of midwestern Chicanos may be deeply intertwined with Native American history and folklore. These stories imply that midwestern Chicanos are a vibrant part of intercontinental diasporas of Mesoamerican and Native American heritage that predate the time of Christ. They have the potential to ignite a regional metamorphosis whereby midwestern Chicanos have greater access to each other, to their shared histories, and to their ancestral roots in the region, allowing them to contribute to the national level of Chicano discourse. Using oral histories to establish a link between Mesoamerica and the Midwest could liberate midwestern Chicanos from their double immigrant label—immigrant to the United States *and* immigrant to the Midwest.

As with the story of Aztlán, the recovery of Chicano pre-Columbian history requires a shift from a positivist position that relies on the scientific method to a more holistic approach, by which something can matter regardless of proof. Though the current colonial structure teaches one to think in terms of city-states and territories, these categories did not exist in the precolonial era in the same way they do today; these categories did not define a group or culture, nor did they bind people to a physical landscape. These perspectives are based on European ways of thinking and living and are not transferable to pre-Columbian native peoples because they had their own unique way of defining their world (Rodriguez 2008). Such evidence requires the ability to reenvision the Americas without borders and its people without the labels that are used today to define identity and territory, such as American Indian, Mesoamerican, Mexican, and even Chicano, because none of these identities existed during the pre-Columbian era. Geoffrey Turner (1992, 10) in *Indians of North America* suggests, "Is that famous border [the U.S./Mexican border] a natural boundary? In aboriginal times the line would have been utterly indistinguishable; one would have been more conscious of changes in language and life-style in travelling along it from east to west. From north to south across it one would have met only gradations of change."

Migrations, Mounds, and
the Mayans in the Midwest

Midwestern Chicano history typically credits the industrial and agricultural boom for driving Mexicans northward (Cardenas 2001) from the central Texas region at the turn of the 20th century. However, this trend may have begun several centuries earlier, if we credit Alfredo Chavero's work. A Mexican scholar, Chavero wrote *Historia Antigua*, the first in a five-volume set of books entitled *Resumen integral de México a través de los siglos.* These texts outline the history of Mexico from indigenous "prehistory" to the age of industrialization and political reformation. Chavero (1953) details pre-Columbian trade and migratory practices that date back to at least 2,500 B.C.E., linking indigenous communities in what is now the American Midwest with Mayan groups as far away as present-day Central America. He describes the Mayans as the same as the peoples of "the North" (Chavero 1953, 69) and intermittently defines "the North" as the regions of the Mississippi Valley up to the Great Lakes. Chavero suggests that the Nahuas may have inhabited the region, predating the Mayans.

There are many pyramid-shaped structures in the Midwest called "mounds," which Chavero argues are the remnants of the Mayans. According to Chavero, there were entire mound cities capable of defense that sustained large populations of people. The larger truncated, or flat-topped pyramids, were used as government buildings, palaces, and temples, while the smaller marked roads or trade routes that led from the lakes to the city centers. The truncated mounds were made of earth or sometimes of earth and stone mixed together; they were of various sizes and were composed of various platforms, built one on top of the other in successive stages over time (Chavero 1953). There were also animal mounds, used to revere the animal kingdom and spirits, and burial mounds for the dead.

Mounds are not native to the Midwest alone; there are mound groups in the Southeastern United States, indeed all over the globe. Some have been unearthed and restored to their original shape and luster, others are fragile and crumbling, and still others lay silent—undiscovered and undisturbed. Unfortunately, much of this history is lost, and a substantial number of the mound structures in the Midwest have been destroyed by farmers or industry.

The state of Michigan is a good example. According to Hinsdale (1931), there were once 1,068 mounds in the state. However, a small cluster of mounds in Grand Rapids, called the Norton Mound Group, are nearly all that remain. There is also one tiny mound located at Fort Wayne in the Delray neighborhood of Southwest Detroit. A rusty iron fence protects these modest remains.

FIGURE 1. Monks Mound, Cahokia State Park in Illinois. Photo by the author (2003).

Though there were once thousands of mounds dotting the midwestern land-scape, this chapter will focus on the mounds in Illinois, Wisconsin, and Ohio.

The largest mound by far in the United States is Monks Mound, one of the Cahokia Mounds (figure 1) near East St. Louis, Illinois: "It is a truncated pyramid about 1,080 feet long and 710 feet wide, raising to a maximum height of some 100 feet and covering approximately 16 acres" (Silverberg 1968, 320). A bustling city, Cahokia, included over 100 mound structures (Coe, Snow, and Benson 1986) that spanned 4000 acres "with a central urban area and suburbs" (Waldman 2000). Monks Mound is larger than the Great Pyramid of Egypt and almost equals the size of the pyramid located in Cholula, Mexico (Coe, Snow, and Benson 1986). The mound city of Cahokia was founded about A.D. 600 and began its decline after A.D. 1,250 (Coe, Snow, and Benson 1986).

Truncated mounds like the ones at Cahokia are found elsewhere in the Midwest. They are so reminiscent of the pyramids of Mexico that in 1836 Judge Nathaniel Hyer concluded that his city in rural Wisconsin was the original homeland of the Aztecs, Aztlán . He thought the stepped pyramid structures discovered in the area (figure 2) were built by the Aztecs before they began their journey south to found what we now know as Tenochtitlán. Hyer was so certain of this history that he renamed his town Aztalan, a misspelling of Aztlán (Birmingham and Eisenberg 2000).

Another important symbol that shares cultural ties with Mesoamerica is the serpent-shaped mound. Serpent effigies can be found all across the Midwest and Southeast in various forms such as winged serpent, water serpent, and egg-eating serpent. The Great Serpent Mound in Peebles, Ohio, is the largest intact animal

FIGURE 2. Truncated Pyramid, Aztalan Mound Park in Wisconsin. Photo by the author (2003).

effigy mound in the world (Ohio Historical Society 2007). It is oriented toward the sun, with the head in alignment with the setting sun of the summer solstice and the three coils of its body aligned with the sunrise of the solstices and the equinoxes. The Ohio Historical Society dates its origin back to between A.D. 1,000 and 1,650, but note that there are researchers who argue that it can be dated back to as early as 800 B.C.E. to A.D. 100. Squire and Davis (1998) believe that when it was first examined in 1848, the effigy was 1,000 feet long and was an awesome five feet in height and 30 feet wide at the center of its body.

These serpent symbols are also found in the Southwest, as illustrated by a video recorded by the Equinox Project, a group that studies Old World connections to America. The recording provides a visual representation of the relationship between the serpent symbol and the sun (Schmidt 2008). The video was filmed in Inyo County, California, just south of Yosemite National Park, where indigenous peoples etched various symbols into stone, several of them in the shape of concentric circles. While there is no serpent mound at Inyo, researchers captured on film a shadow which is reminiscent of the serpent and egg effigy at the Great Serpent Mound in Ohio (Schmidt 2008). The clip shows that when the sun rises on the morning of the equinox, a shadow is cast in the form of a serpent which appears to slither toward an egg, at which point the jaws open to consume the egg (Schmidt 2008). This is similar to the equinox celebration held at Chichen Itza, the Mayan site located in the Yucatan Peninsula, where a shadow is cast during sunrise on the equinox that makes it appear as if a snake is moving the length of the central staircase of the main pyramid.

Serpent stories and symbolism can be found throughout the United States and Mexico. Rodriguez (2008) affirms that the people of the Americas were bound together by a belief in a feathered serpent called Quetzalcoatl by the Nahua and Kukulcán by the Mayans. This connection is supported by a community of Ho-Chunk/Winnebago students and faculty who share a belief in a Mesoamerican link to the Midwest. In 2001 they received a grant through the United States Department of Education to actively study their Mayan ancestry through a partnership between Little Priest Tribal College in Winnebago, Nebraska, and Metropolitan Community College in Omaha, Nebraska. This partnership was designated "The Mayan Connection," and their purpose was to

> begin with a comparative study of the ancient Mayan Civilization of the Yucatan and Central America and Nebraska's Winnebago or Ho-chunk people who lived in the states of Kentucky, Illinois, Iowa, and Wisconsin. Little information is available to share this knowledge of U.S. Native American heritage and the roots of Midwestern Native American people who appear to be descendents of the ancient Mayan civilization. ("Mayan Connection" 2003)

The Ho-Chunk Nation have adopted many of the sacred mound sites in Wisconsin, particularly Aztalan and the effigies or animal-shaped mounds, which they claim to have built (Birmingham and Eisenberg 2000).

In chapter 10 of *Historia Antigua*, Chavero (1953) describes what may be a Ho-Chunk connection. He argues that the animal mounds of Wisconsin and Ohio are from the great civilization of the Usumacinta region, a Mayan region, which borders the southern tip of Mexico and the northernmost part of Guatemala. More specifically, he argues that the Mayans went from south to north via the Gulf of Mexico, penetrating the Mississippi Valley region as they made their way up to the Great Lakes.

Another group asserting a Mesoamerican connection is the Yuchi. David Hackett (1997), the Yuchi tribal historian, asserts that the Yuchi are of ancient mound-builder and Mayan ancestry. He believes that the Yuchi are a Mayan satellite culture; according to oral tradition, they island-hopped across the Caribbean, migrating into what is now the Southeastern United States (Hackett 2009). Though the Yuchi lived primarily in villages scattered from the Carolina coast to the Mississippi River and Florida, they could also be found as far north as Illinois (Hackett 1997).

Prior to the arrival of the Europeans, indigenous people used boats to travel great distances across the hemisphere, and they traded extensively in the Americas, quite possibly trading with Old World cultures as well (Hackett 1997). Hackett (2009) argues that, contrary to popular belief, pre-Columbian native peoples were not homogenous groups occupying discreet territories, but rather a melting pot of people, cultures and ideas; they were very mobile and multilingual. The Yuchi people were the translators because they knew many different languages (Hackett 2009). The arrival of the Europeans disturbed the delicate alliances that allowed groups to live harmoniously intermingled within each other's villages. Eventually, according to Yuchi legend, the tribe was forced to break apart, with some joining the Cherokee, some the Seminoles, and others the Creek (Hackett 1997). The fate of the rest of the Yuchi is unknown (Hackett 1997).

Remarking on the cultural divide between Native and dominant scholars, Hackett (2009) points out that the study of bones and rocks is important, but the full complexity of a living culture or civilization can only be discovered through stories. Similarly, Deloria (1997) speaks about the cultural divide between many Western and Native American academic scholars, particularly with regards to theories of pre-Columbian dispersal. He debunks the popular Bering Strait model, arguing that Native people did not need to wait for a land bridge to cross from Asia to North America because they had boats (Deloria 1997). Thus, an alternative point of connection between pre-Columbian Mesoamerica and the Midwest may have been important waterways such as the Mississippi River and the Gulf of Mexico. Boats and water travel are key to understanding the complexity and brilliance of pre-Columbian civilizations. Deloria (1997) argues that getting the Western world to realize that pre-Columbian indigenous people of the Americas were capable of building and using boats is a huge leap forward.

In 2002, the Foundation for the Advancement of Mesoamerican Studies (FAMSI) produced a report entitled "Rescuing the Origins of Dos Pilas Dynasty: A Salvage of Hieroglyphic Stairway #2, Structure L5-49" (Fahsen 2002). This report detailed an ancient Mayan trade route starting in the Pasión and Usumacinta rivers of Guatemala and "leading to the great capitals of kingdoms like Ceibal, Tres Islas, Altar de Sacrificios, Yaxchilán, Piedras Negras, and the Palenque region as it flows into the Gulf of México" (Fahsen 2002, 3). Fahsen argues that the Mayans from the Usumacinta region of Guatemala were connected to other Mesoamerican communities via a water route that led from the Mayan highlands to the Gulf of Mexico and that significantly corresponds to Chavero's (1953) assertions. Scholars such as Waldman (2000) have established that the Mayans were "a seafaring people" (11) who had "far-reaching trade routes" (11), extending into the Gulf of Mexico, as Fahsen (2002) reports. Others, such as Helen Tanner (1987), note the importance of waterways extending from the Gulf of Mexico to the Great Lakes region via the Mississippi River.

Nonetheless, many contemporary researchers are hesitant to suggest that pre-Columbian people south and north of the U.S.-Mexican border were connected. Few scholars are willing to propose that pre-Columbian people might have boated the short distance of 500 miles (Gore 1992) to travel from the Yucatan Peninsula to the mouth of the Mississippi River delta. Yet it seems reasonable to make this assumption in order to more closely examine stories of Mesoamerican and midwestern ancestry, given that the Spanish crossed an entire ocean before reaching even the Caribbean Islands. According to Eschborn (2006), modern-day scholars dismiss what Native North Americans tell us about their historical past, underestimating the power of Native peoples to have developed an engineering process for intercontinental travel and commerce.

Furthermore, the passageways of mound cities and river routes leading from the Yucatan to the Gulf Coast, penetrating the Southeastern United States via the Mississippi River, Texas, and Florida, are still in use today by Mexican and Chicano farmworkers and laborers. These ancient passageways are called migration streams.

Farmworkers generally follow three migration streams: an eastern migrant stream starts in Florida, moving north into Ohio or Maine. In the pre-Columbian era it may have linked the Yucatan to the Caribbean Islands and Florida before moving into the Midwest and eastern states. The midwestern migrant stream begins in Texas and leads workers in one of two directions, northwest toward Washington or northeast into Wisconsin, Michigan, and Ohio. The pre-Columbian midwestern stream may have begun in central Mexico or in the Yucatan, crossing the Gulf of Mexico toward Texas or the Mississippi River. And last, the Western stream follows the Pacific Coastline northward toward Washington or the Dakotas.

The work of midwestern Chicano scholars such as Gilberto Cardenas (2001), Nancy Saldaña (1969), and Dennis Valdés (1999) corroborates a strong connection between Mexico, Texas, and the Midwest, indicating that a significant number of Mexican Americans living in the region migrated north on the Midwest migrant stream. This may be the same migrant stream that the Ho-Chunk/Winnebago traversed using waterway routes such as the Gulf of Mexico and the Mississippi River to efficiently travel north to Illinois and Wisconsin by boat. The eastern migrant stream is the route that the Yuchi traveled as they "island-hopped" from the Yucatan to Florida, according to David Hackett (2009). Figure 3 illustrates the three contemporary migratory streams along with the pre-Columbian migration route as described by Hackett (2009) and Chavero (1953).

Perhaps midwestern Chicanos, mistakenly labeled new immigrants to the region, are simply following the migratory patterns established hundreds of years ago by their own indigenous ancestors at a time before the geopolitical boundaries had been drawn. Perhaps some stayed, perhaps some left, perhaps some were absorbed by other groups in the region. Perhaps we will never know, and yet this prehistory could establish that Chicanos are not new to the region but are instead returning

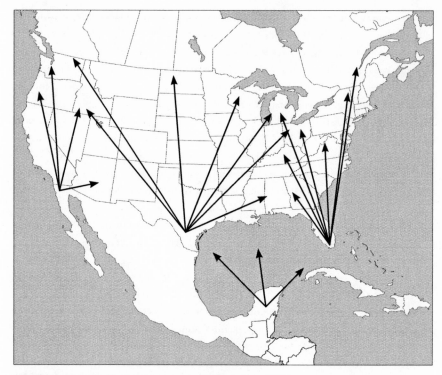

FIGURE 3. Migration Routes. Image created by the author (2009).

home. Whether it was to extract sugar beets from the earth or to work in the factories, whether Chicanos came from central Texas or central Mexico, whether they crossed the Bering Strait or the Gulf of Mexico—no matter where Chicanos migrated to or from—the Midwest is their home, and they belong.

Indigenous Connections and Chicana/o Identity

Native identity can be a prickly topic in academic scholarship. Deena J. González (2001) brings to the forefront the complexity of Chicano constructions of identity and homeland, because *Chicano*, as a contemporary term, cannot be used to describe their forefathers and foremothers in previous centuries. Though many Mexican Americans identify more with their Spanish-Mexican ancestry than with their indigenous Mexican ancestry, Rodriguez and Gonzales state that "most Chicanos and Latinos are at least part Native American and descend from such nations as Mexica, Nahua, Chichimeca, Tarahumara, Pueblo, Kikapu, Tarascan, Tlaxcalan, Mixtec, Zapotec, Maya, Quechua, Mapuche or any one of the hundreds of other Indian peoples" (1996, 2).

Nonetheless, these challenges of origins cause ruptures within the Chicano community and are apparent when Chicanos seek their native American roots in the Americas. As Kidwell and Velie put it, "In the eyes of the Indian community, it is not enough to wish oneself Indian"—you must have federal status (2005, 10). However, Kidwell and Velie also argue that native people are a diverse people whose origins reside throughout the Americas, and though Native American Studies is moving toward more openness, the federal government still determines who fits the legal definition of a native person. These dilemmas reveal that identity is not a homogenous, one-size-fits-all construct, nor is there consensus even within a single group, particularly when it comes to sensitive issues such as sacred sites and identities.

However, stories can fill in some of the gaps, bridging people and identities severed by time, conquest, and territories and establishing significant connections between groups on both sides of the U.S.-Mexican border. Archaeologist Robert Hall holds a similar belief about stories and is one of the few scholars in his field to study mound-building cultures using a Native American "frame of reference" (Birmingham and Eisenberg 2000, 66). Hall uses oral traditions, belief systems, ceremonies, and rituals to breathe life into what he calls "the soulless artifact of a dehumanized science" (via Birmingham and Eisenberg 2000, 66). However, most archaeologists believe that the use of oral traditions may lead to what Birmingham and Eisenberg (2000, 67) call "erroneous interpretations of the past" and are critical of the use of oral tradition as a source of credible information, citing such issues as reliable transmission, interpretation and translation of stories from generation to generation, recorders' biases, and heavy reliance on the interviewee. They call upon William McKern and other noted scholars who argue that archaeology should not provide "ideological motivations" but instead simply describe what people did (Birmingham and Eisenberg 2000, 67).

Thus, Aztlán as a story may not be significant within dominant discourse, yet it has enjoyed wide revolutionary appeal within the Chicano community. Many Chicanos who have been educated in a Western academic setting, which espouses certain empirical traditions, have also been raised to understand the metaphorical, cultural, and symbolic significance of stories. In her groundbreaking work *Border-lands / La Frontera*, Gloria Anzaldúa (1999, 87) writes, "Nudge a Mexican and she or he will break out with a story." She goes on to recount a story that her father told her about a giant phantom dog that would run along the side of her father's pickup truck. Though this story may not seem empirically credible or significant, it demonstrates how a story imparts a different kind of truth in the Chicano community, a folk knowledge that speaks to life's deeper meaning. Each story has a purpose: to teach survival, reverence, and respect for all things seen and unseen, understood and not understood.

Sheila Trahar (2008) observes that story shapes every culture and cultures use story to shape knowledge. Although the ways people tell and hear stories differ, stories are universal in that they attribute meaning to our experiences and demonstrate the complexity of human lives (Trahar, 2008). Yet many scholars, adhering to their understanding of Western scientific research traditions, do not consider them a valid source of data. Communities that rely on oral traditions to transfer knowledge, values, and history from one generation to another are often held at the fringes of academia.

Oral tradition is the paradigm for many Chicanos who choose to break from Western epistemological structures; it is the "visual-conceptual experience" noted by Kuhn (1970, 113) that many Chicanos bring to the table. The use of this paradigm to investigate midwestern and Mesoamerican connections could have the same kind of transformational impact on identity and thought for Chicanos in the Midwest that occurred in the 1960s and 1970s when the narrative of Aztlán galvanized a nationalistic identity for those living in the Southwest.

Conclusion

One Texas morning while sitting outside in his yard next to the pecan trees and pepper plants this author's *abuelito* looked up into the sky, and exclaimed with a smile, "Look, *mija*, it's an eagle!" He tilted his head to the side and chuckled as he broke out with a story, "*Híjole*, I remember one time I was with this rancher—it was a long time ago—and I pointed to this big eagle flying up over our heads. Oh, she was a beauty, *mija*! And do you know what he told me, that gringo? He said, 'That ain't no eagle,' as if he knew everything. *Híjole*, *mija*, you can't argue with them gringos. They got their books, their schools, and if you don't agree with them, *mija*, they'll think you ain't got nothing up there. They'll think you ain't nothing but a stupid Mexican."

With this story Abuelito taught me about the dominant culture and the harsh divide between Chicano and dominant knowledge structures. His message was simple: Chicanos are at the periphery of dominant cultural constructions of reality and knowledge, even when it comes to their own stories and experiences. In *A Geopolitics of Academic Writing* A. Suresh Canagarajah (2002) adeptly points out that it is power that differentiates who is at the center and who is at the periphery of knowledge construction. Abuelito, without so much as a middle-school education, used narrative to convey the same message. Whether the story about the rancher and the eagle is true or not, its messages are valid: trust yourself; trust your instincts; trust your own ways of knowing as you navigate the cultural divide of central and peripheral relations.

In her article "Icons of Longing: Homeland and Memory in the Sierra Leonan Diaspora," JoAnn D'Alisera quotes Pierre Nora: "When memory is no longer everywhere, it will not be anywhere unless one takes the responsibility to recapture it through individual means" (Nora 1989, in D'Alisera 2002, 73). D'Alisera describes an attempt to revive a historical image of the cotton tree for Sierra Leoneans. The revival of the story represents a wish that the cotton tree could be a unifying symbol for the community; a symbol that guides how people relate to each other; a symbol that links the past to the present and creates "an unbroken continuum of community identity" (73). This sentiment captures with words something this author has long been struggling to define, the symbolic meaning of a pre-Columbian icon to a contemporary resident. The mound structures of the American Midwest represent, for this author, what the cotton tree represents for Sierra Leoneans.

Within the Chicano community of the American Southwest, a similar need for a unifying symbol was expressed through the revival of Aztlán, the ancestral homeland of the Aztecs. For Chicanos in the Southwest, Aztlán represented a utopian space from Nahua mythology that speaks to origins, ancestors, and belonging (Anaya and Lomelí 1998).

The spirit of Aztlán does not reside in the discovery of its location; like the cotton tree—like the mounds—the spirit of Aztlán lies in its symbolism. The story of Aztlán parallels the story of the mounds in symbolic meaning because it speaks to "those who yearn to know the origins of their history on this continent" (Anaya and Lomelí 1998, iii). Just as Aztlán symbolized a return to the historical legends of its ancestors, so do the mounds. Like the cotton tree for Sierra Leoneans, like the story of Aztlán for Chicanos from the Southwest, the mounds are a symbol that links the past to the present and create "an unbroken continuum of community identity" (D'Alisera 2002, 73).

REFERENCES

Anaya, R., and F. Lomelí. 1998. "Introduction." In *Aztlán: Essays on the Chicano Homeland*, ed. R. Anaya and F. Lomelí, ii–iv. Albuquerque: University of New Mexico Press.

Anzaldúa, G. 1999. *Borderlands / La Frontera: The New Mestiza*. San Francisco: Aunt Lute Books.

Birmingham, R., and L. Eisenberg. 2000. *Indian Mounds of Wisconsin*. Madison: University of Wisconsin Press.

Canagarajah, A. S. 2002. *A Geopolitics of Academic Writing*. Pittsburgh: University of Pittsburgh Press.

Cardenas, G. 2001. "Los Desarraigados: Chicanos in the Midwestern Region of the United States." In *The Chicano Studies Reader: An Anthology of Aztlán, 1970–2000*, ed. C. Noriega, E. Avila, K. M. Davalos, C. Sandoval, and R. Perez-Torres, 79–112. Los Angeles: Chicano Studies Research Center Publications.

Chavero, A. 1953. *Resumen Integral de México: A Través de los Siglos*. Mexico City: Compañía General de Ediciones, S.A.

Coe, M. 2001. *Mexico: From the Olmecs to the Aztecs*. New York: Thames and Hudson.

Coe, M., D. Snow, and E. Benson. 1986. *Atlas of Ancient America*. Oxford: Equinox Books.

D'Alisera, J. 2002. "Icons of Longing: Homeland and Memory in the Sierra Leonean Diaspora." HYPERLINK *Political and Legal Anthropology Review* 25(2): 73–89.

Deloria, V., Jr. 1997. *Red Earth, White Lies: Native Americans and the Myth of Scientific Fact*. Golden, CO: Fulcrum.

Eschborn, A. 2006. *The Dragon in the Lake*. Philadelphia: Xlibris.

Fahsen, F. 2002. "Rescuing the Origins of Dos Pilas Dynasty: A Salvage of Hieroglyphic Stairway #2, Structure L5-49." Foundation for the Advancement of Mesoamerican Studies. Available online: http://www.famsi.org/reports/01098/index.html.

González, D. 2001. "Chicana Identity Matters." In *The Chicano Studies Reader: An Anthology of Aztlán, 1970–2000*, ed. C. Noriega, E. Avila, K. M. Davalos, C. Sandoval, and R. Perez-Torres. 411–26. Los Angeles: Chicano Studies Research Center Publications.

Gore, R. 1992. *The Gulf of Mexico*. Sarasota, FL: Pineapple Press.

Hackett, D. 1997. "Who Were the Mysterious Yuchi of Tennessee and the Southeast?" Yuchi Tribal Archive. Available online: www.yuchi.org.

———. 2009. Interview by Sandra M. Gonzales. May 10.

Hinsdale, W. B. 1931. *Archaeological Atlas of Michigan*. Michigan Handbook Series, 4. Ann Arbor: University of Michigan Press.

Kidwell, C. S., and A. Velie. 2005. *Native American Studies*. Lincoln: University of Nebraska Press.

Kuhn, T. 1970. *The Structure of Scientific Revolutions*. Chicago: University of Chicago Press.

Leal, L. 1998. "In Search of Aztlán." In *Aztlán: Essays on the Chicano Homeland*, ed. R. Anaya and F. Lomelí, 6–13. Albuquerque: University of New Mexico Press.

"Mayan Connection: Purpose/Abstract." 2003. April 23. Available online: http://resource.mccneb.edu/MAYA/purpose.htm.

Nora, Pierre. 1989. "Between Memory and History: Les Lieux de Mémoire." *Representations* 26: 7–24.

Ohio Historical Society. 2007. "Effigy Mounds of Eastern North America: Serpent Mound. A Nomination for the Tentative List of the World Heritage Program." Available online: www.ohiohistory.org.

Pina, M. 1998. "The Archaic, Historical and Mythicized Dimensions of Aztlán." In *Aztlán: Essays on the Chicano Homeland*, ed. R. Anaya and F. Lomelí, 14–48. Albuquerque: University of New Mexico Press.

Rodriguez, R. 2008. "Centeotzintli: A 7,000 year Ceremonial Discourse." Ph.D. diss., University of Wisconsin.

Rodriguez, R., and P. Gonzales. 1996. "Indigenous and Mestizos in the Americas." Available online: www.indigenouspeople.net.

Saldaña, N. 1969. *Mexican-Americans in the Midwest: An Annotated Bibliography.* East Lansing: Michigan State University, Department of Sociology, Rural Manpower Center.

Schmidt, R. 2008. "An Analysis of the Inyo Equinox Display." The Equinox Project. Available online: www.equinox-project.com.

Silverberg, R. 1968. *Mound Builders of Ancient America.* Greenwich, CT: New York Graphic Society.

Squire, E., and E. Davis. 1998. *Ancient Monuments of the Mississippi Valley.* Washington, DC: Smithsonian Institution Press.

Tanner, H. 1987. *Atlas of Great Lakes Indian History.* Norman: University of Oklahoma Press.

Trahar, S. 2008. "It starts with once upon a time . . ." *Compare: A Journal of Comparative and International Education* 38(3): 259–66.

Turner, G. 1992. *Indians of North America.* New York: Sterling.

Valdés, D. 1999. "Region, Nation, and World-System: Perspectives on Midwestern Chicana/o History." JSRI Occasional Paper No. 20, Julian Samora Research Institute, Michigan State University.

Waldman, C. 2000. *Atlas of the North American Indian.* New York: Checkmark Books.

ROGELIO SAENZ

The Changing Demography of Latinos in the Midwest

THE MIDWEST HAS ATTRACTED LATINOS SINCE THE EARLY PARTS OF THE 20TH century, when Mexicans were recruited to work in jobs in agriculture, railroads, meatpacking, stockyards, and manufacturing (Garcia 1978; Mapes 2004; Lane and Escobar 1987; Rosales 1978; Saenz 1991; Samora and Lamanna 1987; Sepulveda 1978; Valdés 1991; Vargas 1993; Wells 1978). While 90% of the Mexican-origin population in 1930 in the United States were located in five southwestern states (Arizona, California, Colorado, New Mexico, and Texas), 7% (numbering 98,122) made their home in the Midwest. At that time, Illinois had the sixth largest Mexican-origin population, with 28,906 making their home in this state. Thus, the early roots of the Mexican population in the Midwest were well established by 1930.

Over the remainder of the century, two other flows would contribute to the increasing presence of Latinos in the Midwest. First, following World War II and up to the 1960s, Mexican Americans settled out of the migrant farmworker stream and established their homes in such midwestern states as Illinois, Indiana, Michigan, Minnesota, and Ohio (Lane and Escobar 1987; Samora and Lamanna 1987; Wells 1978). Second, the most recent migrant flow of Latinos to the Midwest has been in motion since the 1980s. This movement of Latinos—primarily Mexicans—to the region has been stimulated by the restructuring of the meatpacking industry and the recruitment of Latinos to fill jobs in this sector of the economy (Baker and Hotek 2003; Cantu 1995; Dalla, Ellis, and Cramer 2005; Fink 1998; Gouveia and Saenz 2000; Gouveia and Stull 1995; Grey 1999; Guzmán and McConnell 2002; Haverluk and Trautman 2008; Lopez 2000; Millard and Chapa 2004; Saenz 2005; Stull, Broadway, and Griffith 1995; Zuñiga and Hernández-León 2005).

Three decades ago, Gilbert Cardenas (1978a) placed a call for researchers to pay more attention to the Latino population in the Midwest. While a string of articles on Latinos in the Midwest appeared in *Aztlán* (Cardenas 1978a, 1978b; Estrada 1978; Faught 1978; Garcia 1978; Kanellos 1978; Parra, Rios, and Gutiérrez 1978; Rosales 1978; Sepulveda 1978; Wells 1978, 1981) and other outlets in the 1970s and 1980s (Sena-Rivera 1979), much of the scholarship on Latinos in the Midwest has appeared in the last couple of decades (see, for example, McConnell and LeClere 2002; Villanueva 2002). Nonetheless, because of data limitations, much of this literature has been cross-sectional, community-specific, and ethnographic. There is relatively little information with which to assess the changing demographic and socioeconomic conditions of Latinos in the Midwest over an extended period of time. This chapter fills this gap in the literature. In particular, individual-level census data for four time periods (1980, 1990, 2000, and 2005–7) are used to assess the changing demographic and socioeconomic profile of Latinos in the Midwest. Before gauging these changing patterns, however, the chapter provides a brief historical overview of the roots of Latinos in the Midwest.

Historical Context

The roots of Latino migration to the Midwest extend back to the early parts of the 20th century. A series of "push" and "pull" factors worked in tandem to bring persons of Mexican origin to the Midwest (Saenz and Cready 1997). Various factors impelled Mexican Americans and Mexican nationals to migrate out of the Southwest (especially Texas) and Mexico, respectively. In the case of the former, throughout the mid-19th century and into the 20th century Mexican Americans experienced horrendous exploitation and discrimination, especially in Texas. Rodolfo Alvarez (1973) notes that Mexican Americans in the Southwest were essentially a caste group until World War II. There was hardly any social mobility for this group, which had become a landless proletariat as Texas made the transformation from a ranching to an agricultural economy in the late 19th and early 20th centuries (Acuña 1988; Barrera 1979; Montejano 1987). Mexican Americans were second-class citizens living in Jim Crow–like conditions in the Southwest, especially in Texas. Without social mobility and fair work opportunities, many Mexican Americans found it attractive to leave the region in search for better fortunes (Saenz 1991).

In the case of Mexicans, the Mexican Revolution in the second decade of the century pushed many toward the United States. Indeed, the revolution resulted in the first major wave of Mexican immigrants to the United States. The mass movement of Mexicans to Texas and other parts of the Southwest created surplus labor in the region. Thus, migration to search for better economic opportunities in areas beyond the Southwest was an attractive alternative for many Mexican immigrants (Saenz 1991).

Moreover, there were also pull factors that attracted persons of Mexican origin to the Midwest. For example, labor shortages associated with World War I and the 1921 and 1924 immigration quota acts resulted in midwestern capitalists turning to new sources of cheap labor. Recruiters—known as *enganchistas* (contractors)—made their way to the Texas-Mexico border and even further south into Mexico in search of cheap labor. Recruiters hailed the better working conditions and higher wages found in the Midwest, comparing them favorably to the working conditions and pay in the border area and in Mexico. Persons of Mexican origin were recruited to work primarily in the agricultural, railroad, and manufacturing industries (Acuña 1988; Arreola 1985; McWilliams 1948; Saenz 1991; Valdés 1991). It has been estimated that between March and August 1923, recruitment agencies contracted 34,585 persons of Mexican origin to work in the Midwest and in Pennsylvania (Acuña 1988). So many persons of Mexican origin moved to Chicago that it became known as the "Midwest Mexican capital" (Acuña 1988). Acuña points out that Mexicans comprised two-fifths of the railroad maintenance workers in Chicago in the 1920s. Other popular midwestern destinations for persons of Mexican origin included Detroit, Gary (Indiana), Kansas City, Loraine (Ohio), Saginaw (Michigan), St. Louis, St. Paul (Minnesota), and Toledo (Ohio) (Acuña 1988; McWilliams 1948; Valdés 1991).

The agricultural sector also attracted many Mexican-origin workers. This is particularly the case in the sugar beet industry, which used similar tactics as the railroad industry to bring these workers to the Midwest. Valdés (1991) points out that the state of Michigan became known as the "Michoacán del norte" ("Michoacán of the north"), a phrase that emphasized the similarity in the pronunciation of "Michigan" and the Mexican state of "Michoacán." Valdés (1991) notes that sugar beet zones existed in Michigan, Ohio, Indiana, Wisconsin, Minnesota, Iowa, and North Dakota. Mexican-origin workers came to dominate the sugar beet industry by the 1920s, with a 1927 survey reporting that these workers accounted for somewhere between 75% and 95% of sugar beet workers in the Midwest (Valdés 1991).

It is clear that Latinos, especially persons of Mexican origin, have a long history in the Midwest extending back to the early 20th century. Despite this long history, however, there is a dearth of knowledge about the social and economic conditions of Latinos in the Midwest. The chapter now turns to an examination of the earliest profile of the Latino population based on census data.

The Baseline: The Demographic and Socioeconomic Conditions of Mexican Americans in the Midwest in 1970

Although the Latino population had been in the United States for generations, the U.S. government and Census Bureau for the most part did not know how to classify the population until recently. For example, in 1930—at the height of the immigration of Mexicans to the United States due to the Mexican Revolution and the advent of the Great Depression—the Census Bureau treated Mexicans as a racial group, the first and only time that it did so. In the 1960 and 1970 decennial censuses, persons originating from Latin America were classified as "persons of Spanish surname" or "persons of Spanish language" depending on their geographic location—measures that were highly problematic because not all Latinos had Spanish surnames or spoke Spanish (see Estrada 1978). Thus, prior to the 1980 census, when the Census Bureau allowed persons of Hispanic origin to self-identify themselves, there was a dearth of information on the demographic and socioeconomic characteristics of the Latino population in the United States.

To make matters worse, the literature extending back to the 1970s hardly made reference to Mexican Americans or Latinos in the Midwest, the focus being almost exclusively on those in the Southwest. To call attention to Latinos in the Midwest, Cardenas (1978b) developed a demographic and socioeconomic profile of them. I draw on this information as a baseline for grounding a profile of this population from 1980 to the present. In particular, the following two subsections draw exclusively on the Cardenas (1978b) article to illustrate the demographic and socioeconomic characteristics of the Latino population in the Midwest in 1970.

DEMOGRAPHIC PROFILE OF THE SPANISH-ORIGIN POPULATION IN THE MIDWEST IN 1970

According to Cardenas (1978b), in 1970 there were slightly over one million persons of Spanish origin in the Midwest. As today, Illinois was the midwestern state with the most members of this group, with 393,204. Three other states (Michigan, Ohio, and Indiana) also had more than 100,000 persons of Spanish origin. The Spanish-origin population was significantly different at that time in nativity. Indeed, 85% of

Spanish-origin individuals in the region were born in the United States. This period corresponded to the early immigration shift from Europe to Latin America and Asia that began in 1965.

The roots of persons of Spanish origin living in the Midwest in 1970 ran deep to the Southwest (Arizona, California, Colorado, New Mexico, and Texas) (see also Saenz and Cready 1997). At that time, about 1 of every 11 Spanish-origin persons living in the Midwest was born in the Southwest. Among persons of Spanish origin born in the Midwest, 66,141 were living in the Southwest in 1970 with most living in California (54.1%) and Texas (30.3%). Comparison of the state of birth and state of residence in 1970 among native-born persons of Spanish origin indicates that the Midwest had a net gain of approximately 83,000 people—that is, the Midwest gained 83,000 more people born in states outside of the region than it lost to such states. The greatest benefactors of net migrants from outside of the region were Illinois (net gain of 34,490) and Michigan (net gain of 25,506). In contrast, Iowa, Kansas, Missouri, and Nebraska were net exporters of native-born Latinos to states outside of the Midwest.

SOCIOECONOMIC PROFILE OF THE SPANISH-ORIGIN POPULATION IN THE MIDWEST IN 1970

Because of limits to data on the socioeconomic status of Latinos in the Midwest in 1970, Cardenas (1978b) used data based on persons of Spanish language (or Spanish-speaking individuals) to develop a socioeconomic profile of the Latino population. Again, this section describes the socioeconomic characteristics of the Latino population at that time, drawing from the profile that Cardenas developed.

In general, the Spanish-speaking population in the Midwest had relatively low socioeconomic status in 1970. For example, relatively few (about 15%) were employed in professional, technical, managerial, and administrative occupations, with Spanish-language persons lagging behind whites in these occupations (22.3%) but ahead of blacks (7.3%). Spanish-language workers were more likely to be crafts-men and operatives, service workers, laborers, farmworkers, or to have jobs in sales and clerical occupations. In particular, they were most likely to work as operatives (about 33%), more so than blacks (28%) and whites (18%). The high frequency of Spanish-speaking operatives was especially apparent in Chicago and Detroit.

Overall, the income of Spanish-language families was higher than that of black families but lower than that of white families. The gap between the income of Spanish-language families and white families was greatest in Illinois, where the median income of the former was 16% lower than that of the latter. Cardenas (1978b) observed that the median income of Spanish-speaking families actually surpassed the median income of white families in Iowa, Minnesota, Missouri, and Nebraska. Black families had the highest poverty rate in the Midwest at 21.3%, followed by Spanish-language families (11.6%) and white families (7.1%).

Spanish-speaking individuals 25 years of age and older had a lower level of education than whites and blacks. Indeed, 42% of Spanish-language individuals had no high school education in 1970, compared to 33% of blacks and 26% of whites. Spanish-speaking persons 25 and older had the lowest level of education in Illinois, where nearly half did not have a high school education.

The socioeconomic profile that Cardenas (1978b) developed from census data suggests that in some dimensions—occupation, income, and poverty—Latinos fared fairly well in 1970. Nonetheless, given the relatively low educational standing of Latinos, it may be that the standing of the group with respect to occupation, income, and poverty may have not been adequately captured in the 1970 census through the Spanish-language designation. On the other hand, one can argue that the socioeconomic position of the Spanish-speaking population—that is, between whites and blacks—in the Midwest in 1970 reflected its relatively small size, as well as the low percentage of foreign-born persons among the group. Research has shown that minority groups fare better in areas where they account for a smaller share of the area's population (Blalock 1967; Saenz 1997; Tienda and Lii 1987).

The chapter now turns to its major objective, which is to present a demographic and socioeconomic profile of the Latino population across various time periods (1980, 1990, 2000, and 2005–7). The data are obtained from the 5% Public Use Microdata Surveys (PUMS) from the 1980, 1990, and 2000 decennial censuses and for the three-year 1% pooled data from the 2005, 2006, and 2007 American Community Surveys (ACS).

The Demographic and Socioeconomic Profile of Latinos in the Midwest Since 1980

The Latino population has grown tremendously in the Midwest since Cardenas (1978a) called for social scientists to pay more attention to the region. In this section, I draw on data from the 1980, 1990, and 2000 decennial censuses and from the 2008 American Community Survey to illustrate the change in the Latino population in the Midwest over the 28-year period from 1980 to 2008. The Latino population in the region more than tripled, from nearly 1.3 million in 1980 to nearly 4.3 million in 2008 (table 1). By way of contrast, the overall population in the Midwest grew by a mere 13% between 1980 and 2008, increasing from 58.9 million in 1980 to 66.6 million in 2008. Thus, despite their relatively small share of the region's population,

TABLE 1. Latino Population in Selected Geographic Areas, 1980–2008

	1980	1990	2000	2008
United States	14,608,673	22,354,059	35,305,818	46,891,456
Midwest	1,276,545	1,726,509	3,124,532	4,247,973
States in the Midwest				
Illinois	635,602	904,446	1,530,262	1,967,568
Indiana	87,047	98,788	214,536	328,725
Iowa	25,536	32,647	82,473	123,895
Kansas	63,339	93,670	188,252	254,297
Michigan	162,440	201,596	323,877	413,286
Minnesota	32,123	53,884	143,382	215,821
Missouri	51,653	61,702	118,592	186,829
Nebraska	28,025	36,969	94,425	139,771
North Dakota	3,902	4,665	7,786	13,286*
Ohio	119,883	139,696	217,123	299,778
South Dakota	4,023	5,252	10,903	18,605*
Wisconsin	62,972	93,194	192,921	286,112

Sources: 1980 to 1990 data are from Hobbs and Stoops, 2002; 2008 data are from the 2008 American Community Survey.

*Population estimates for North Dakota and South Dakota are not available directly from the 2008 American Community Survey because of small populations. The entries shown in the table are estimates computed by the author, obtained by distributing the difference between the Midwest Latino population and the sum of the Latino population in the other 10 midwestern states and distributing this difference on the basis of the proportion of Latinos in North Dakota and South Dakota living in each state in 2000.

Latinos accounted for two of every five persons added to the Midwest population between 1980 and 2008. Because of the disproportionate influence of Latinos on the region's overall growth, they increased their relative share of the Midwest population from 2.2% in 1980 to 6.4% in 2008.

Over the period from 1980 to 2008, the growth in the number of Latinos has been concentrated in a handful of states. Nearly 45% of the Latino growth in the Midwest between 1980 and 2008 occurred in Illinois alone, with an additional 24% taking place in three other states (Michigan, Indiana, and Wisconsin). While Latinos in the Midwest have tended to be concentrated in four states (Illinois, Michigan, Indiana, and Ohio), the percentage living in these states slipped somewhat from 79% in 1980 to 71% in 2008. This change is due to the increasing movement of Latinos to "new destination" areas where they have historically been relatively rare. The Latino population grew nearly sixfold in Minnesota and nearly fourfold in Nebraska and Iowa between 1980 and 2008.

FIGURE 1. Age-Sex Pyramid of the Latino Population in the Midwest, 2005–07

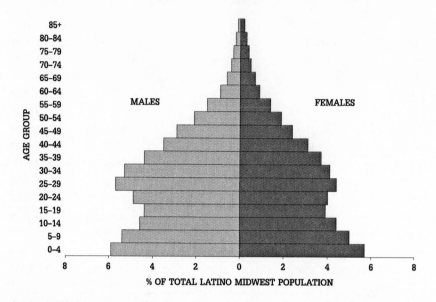

FIGURE 2. Age-Sex Pyramid of Non-Hispanic White Population in the Midwest, 2008

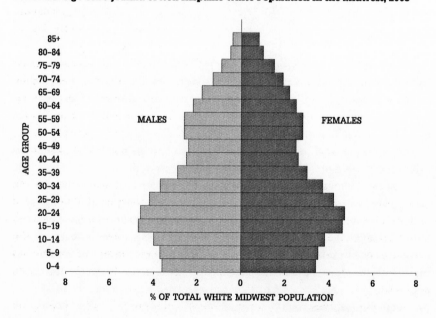

A DEMOGRAPHIC PROFILE OF LATINOS
IN THE MIDWEST SINCE 1980

This section presents an overall demographic profile of the Latino population across four time periods using data from the 1980, 1990, and 2000 PUMS and from the pooled 2005, 2006, and 2007 ACS (Ruggles et al. 2009). The rapid pace at which the Latino population is growing relative to the rest of the region is due largely to the young age structure of the Latino population, fueled by a significant level of immigration and a relatively high fertility rate. Figure 1 shows the age-sex pyramid of the Latino population in the Midwest in the 2005–7 period. Note that the pyramid provides a graphic illustration of the age structure of a given population. The vertical axis is associated with age groups, from 0–4 years to 85 years and older. The horizontal axis indicates the relative percentage of a given age group. Males appear on the left-hand side and females on the right-hand side. Thus, for example, males 0 to 4 years of age accounted for nearly 6% of the Latino population in the Midwest in 2005–7. The wide base of the age-sex pyramid indicates the heavy presence of youth in the Latino population. In addition, bulges at ages 25 to 34 reflect the presence of a young workforce. Moreover, it is apparent that for the working ages, there are more males than females, a pattern associated with the presence of immigrants, a disproportionately male segment. Indeed, there were about 124 males per 100 females among persons 25 to 44 years of age in 2005–7. Finally, the very narrow bars at the older ages reflect the relative absence of elderly among the population. In contrast, the white population in the Midwest is much older than the Latino population (see figure 2).

Over time, between 1980 and the 2005–7, there has been some transformation in the age structure of the Latino population in the Midwest. Overall, however, the population continues to be very young, with the largest share of the age group being among children (i.e., under 18 years of age) (figure 3). Still, the percentage in this age group has decreased somewhat over time, as has the percentage of persons 18 to 24 years of age. In contrast, the percentage of persons 25 to 44 years of age (and those 45 to 64 to a certain degree) has risen over time.

In 1980, Latinos were much more likely to have been born outside of the United States than they were in 1970, when Cardenas (1978b) developed his demographic profile. However, the percentage of Latinos who are foreign born has increased noticeably since then, rising from 26% in 1980 to 39% in 2005–7 (figure 4). The percentage of native-born Latinos in the Midwest who were born in the region has remained fairly stable over time, ranging from 44% in 2000 to 50% in 1990 (data not shown).

As a result of these demographic transformations in the Latino population

FIGURE 3. Age Distribution of the Latino Population in the Midwest by Period

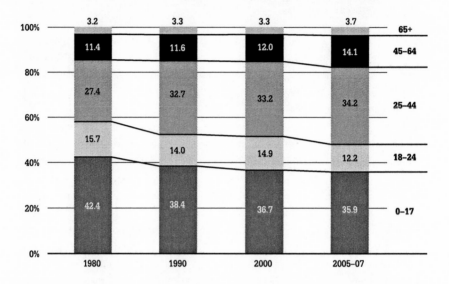

FIGURE 4. Percentage of Latinos in the Midwest Who Are Foreign-Born by Period

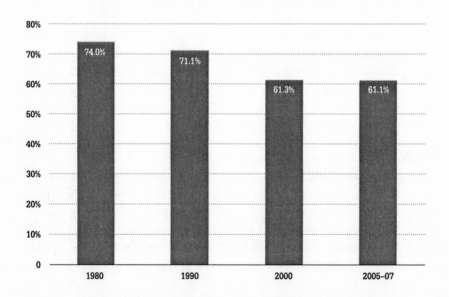

FIGURE 5. Nation-Origin Distribution of Latinos in the Midwest by Period

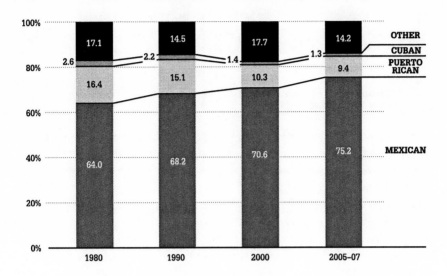

FIGURE 6. Distribution of Language Spoken among Latinos in the Midwest by Nativity and Period

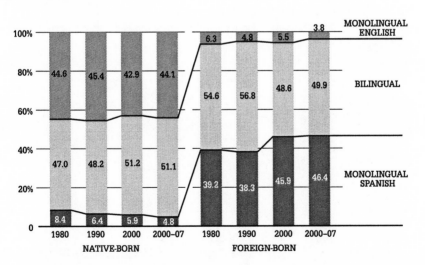

between 1980 and 2005–7, the national-origin of the population has changed accordingly. In particular, while Mexicans have been the dominant population within the Latino population in each time period, their percentage has risen progressively, increasing from 64% in 1980 to 75% in the 2005–7 (figure 5). Accordingly, the percentage of non-Mexicans has slipped over the period.

A SOCIOECONOMIC PROFILE OF LATINOS IN THE MIDWEST SINCE 1980

I now examine changes in the socioeconomic profile of Latinos over time. Regardless of time period or nativity status, the majority of Latinos in the Midwest are bilingual, that is, they speak Spanish at home and speak English "well" or "very well" (figure 6). Among those that are not bilingual, native-born Latinos are almost exclusively monolingual English speakers (i.e., they speak English at home) while foreign-born Latinos are almost exclusively Spanish speakers (i.e., they speak Spanish at home and speak English "not well" or "not at all"). For the most part, there has not been much change in the distribution of Latinos across the three language categories.

The educational levels of Latinos vary significantly by nativity status with noticeable progress in the educational patterns of the native born and fairly stagnant patterns among the foreign born. For instance, the percentage of persons 16 to 24 years of age who have not completed high school and who are not currently enrolled

FIGURE 7. Percentage of Latinos 16 to 24 Years of Age in the Midwest Who Are Dropouts by Nativity and Period

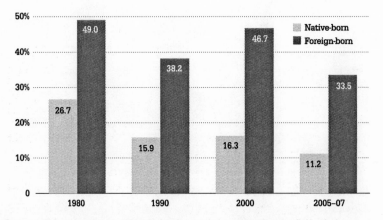

Note: Dropouts include persons who are not high school graduates and who are currently not enrolled in school.

in school (an indicator of the dropout rate) has dropped significantly among native-born Latinos, declining from 26% in 1980 to 11% in 2005–7 (figure 7). In contrast, the dropout rate continues to be elevated among the foreign born, with individuals 16 to 24 years of age being nearly three times more likely than their native-born counterparts to have not completed high school. Note that some foreign-born persons 16 to 24 years of age may not be technically high school dropouts because they may have never enrolled in high school in the United States. Furthermore, similar distinctions between the native born and the foreign born are found among Latinos 25 years of age and older in terms of the percentage of persons who are high school graduates or college graduates (table 2).

TABLE 2. Percentage of Latinos 25 Years of Age and Older in the Midwest by Educational Level Completed and by Nativity Status and Period

	NATIVE BORN				FOREIGN BORN			
	1980	1990	2000	2005–7	1980	1990	2000	2005–7
High School	47.9	67.3	75.8	80.3	37.3	45.6	45.7	51.6
College	6.5	10.4	13.7	16.8	10.6	9.8	8.3	9.3

Sources: 1980 to 1990 data are from Hobbs and Stoops, 2002; 2008 data are from the 2008 American Community Survey.

FIGURE 8. Unemployment Rates for Latinos in the Midwest by Nativity, Sex, and Period

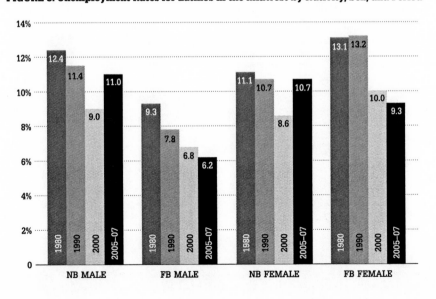

FIGURE 9. Median Hourly Wages in 2006 Constant Dollars for Latino Workers in the Midwest by Nativity, Sex, and Period

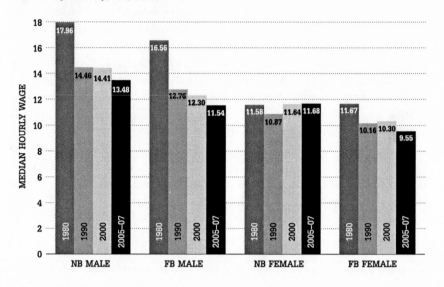

FIGURE 10. Percentage of Latinos 25 to 44 Years of Age in the Midwest Who Are in Poverty by Nativity and Period

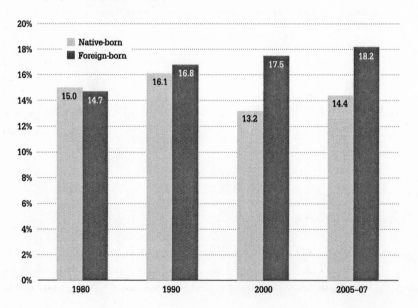

There have been significant changes over time in the unemployment rate, with the foreign-born unemployment rate declining significantly and that of native-born remaining relatively high (figure 8). However, it has been foreign-born male Latinos who have enjoyed the greatest improvements in their job prospects, with their unemployment rate falling by one-third, from 9.3% in 1980 to 6.2% in 2005–7.

However, native-born Latinas are the only group that has been able to maintain fairly stable hourly wages (measured in 2006 constant dollars) between 1980 and 2005–7 (figure 9). In contrast, males have experienced significant drops in their hourly wages over time, with the wages of the foreign born declining by 30% and those of the native born slipping by 25% between 1980 and 2005–7.

The economic fortunes of native-born and foreign-born Latinos have shifted across time. Indeed, the poverty rates of these two groups (among those 25 to 44 years of age) were relatively similar in 1980 and 1990, but they have diverged since then (figure 10). In 2005–7, foreign-born Latinos 25 to 44 years of age were one-fourth more likely than their native-born counterparts to be in poverty. Children tend to be the most vulnerable to poverty. The poverty rate of Latino children has hovered around 25% across the four time periods in the analysis (data not shown).

Latinos have made some progress in attaining the "American dream" of owning their own home, rising from 45% in 1980 to 54% in 2005–7 (figure 11). Nonetheless, we suspect that given the housing and economic crisis of the last few years, the progress of Latino homeownership may well be reversed. Indeed, research shows that Latinos were more likely than whites to have subprime loans for purchasing their homes (see McConnell 2008).

Finally, intermarriage has historically represented the most intimate indicator of boundary reduction between racial and ethnic groups. Native-born individuals have experienced significant increases in the degree to which they marry non-Latinos over time (figure 12). By the 2005–7 period, approximately half of native-born Latino men and women were married to someone who was not Latino, with most of these spouses being non-Hispanic whites. In contrast, relatively few foreign-born Latinos (about 1 in 10) marry outside of the Latino group, and the trend has been toward foreign-born persons being less likely to marry outside of the Latino group.

Intergroup Comparisons: Latinos Compared to Whites and Blacks

Having examined the changing demographic and socioeconomic characteristics within segments of the Latino population across four time periods, I now turn attention to a broad assessment of how Latinos fare relative to whites and blacks

FIGURE 11. Percentage of Latino Householders in the Midwest Who Are Homeowners by Period

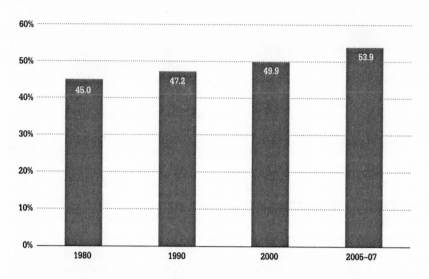

FIGURE 12. Percentage of Latino Husbands and Wives with Non-Latino Spouse by Nativity, Sex, and Period

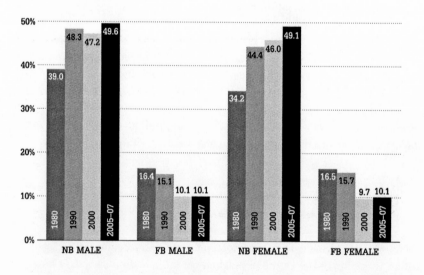

in the Midwest. One major difference between the three groups is their varying age structures. In particular, as observed above, the Latino population is much younger than are the white and black populations. The age differences between Latinos and whites are especially noticeable (figure 13). Children less than 18 years of age account for 36% of the overall Latino population, while they comprise only 23% of the white population in the Midwest. In fact, persons less than 45 years of age make up a larger share of the Latino population than they do in the white and black populations. These differences reflect the relatively large share of Latinos in the K–12 school-age population and in the workforce as well and portend a workforce in the coming decades that will be increasingly Latino. In contrast, whites and blacks have larger shares of the population that are elderly or will reach retirement age in the near future.

Despite these demographic trends, it is obvious that Latinos continue to lag behind whites and to a certain extent blacks as well with respect to a variety of socioeconomic indicators. Table 3 presents data showing the standing of Latinos, whites, and blacks on a variety of socioeconomic measures over time. Rather than provide detailed analysis of the observed patterns, I describe the broad patterns revealed in the table. First, whites consistently have a more favorable position than Latinos and blacks on all the socioeconomic indicators examined. In particular, whites enjoy the highest levels of education, lowest unemployment rates, highest wages, lowest rates of poverty, and highest homeownership rates. Second, in some dimensions Latinos have more favorable socioeconomic standing than blacks,

FIGURE 13. Age Distribution of Latinos, Whites, and Blacks in the Midwest, 2005–07

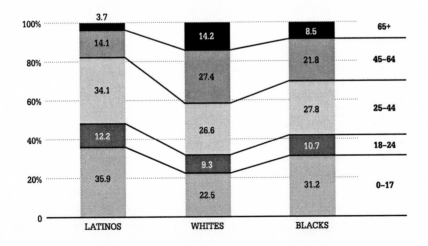

TABLE 3. Comparison of Latinos, Whites, and Blacks in the Midwest on Selected Socioeconomic Indicators by Period

	1980	1990	2000	2005–7
Percentage age 16–24 who are dropouts				
Latinos	33.0	23.1	29.2	19.4
Foreign-born Latinos	49.0	38.2	46.7	33.5
Native-born Latinos	26.7	15.9	16.3	11.2
Whites	11.6	7.2	6.3	5.2
Blacks	21.4	14.0	13.7	10.6
Percentage age 25+ who are high school graduates				
Latinos	43.7	57.9	59.2	63.7
Foreign-born Latinos	37.3	45.6	45.7	51.6
Native-born Latinos	47.9	67.3	75.8	80.3
Whites	69.4	81.5	88.5	91.1
Blacks	55.0	71.9	80.6	83.6
Percentage age 25+ who are college graduates				
Latinos	8.1	10.2	10.7	12.5
Foreign-born Latinos	10.6	9.8	8.3	9.3
Native-born Latinos	6.5	10.4	13.7	16.8
Whites	15.2	19.1	23.9	26.9
Blacks	7.9	10.5	13.2	15.7
Unemployment rate				
Latino males	11.1	9.8	7.8	8.1
White males	6.8	5.3	4.2	5.9

specifically in unemployment, poverty, and homeownership. Third, however, Latinos lag behind blacks on other socioeconomic dimensions, specifically in education and wages.

The gap between Latinos and whites on the various socioeconomic measures has changed between 1980 and 2005–7. Latinos made modest progress relative to whites with respect to the percentage of persons 25 and older who have graduated from high school, the unemployment rates of males, and the percentage of householders who own their homes. However, the gap between Latinos and whites has expanded or remained unchanged on all other socioeconomic indicators. Particularly disturbing is the widening chasm between Latinos and whites on two measures of education (the dropout rate and the percentage of persons 25 and older who have completed

	1980	1990	2000	2005–7
Black males	17.7	18.4	14.6	18.3
Latino females	11.7	11.6	9.2	10.1
White females	6.0	4.7	3.8	5.4
Black females	14.0	15.1	12.2	15.0
Median hourly wage (2006 constant $)				
Latino males	17.36	13.68	13.03	12.16
White males	20.24	17.84	18.11	17.77
Black males	18.86	14.85	15.13	13.75
Latino females	11.58	10.57	11.09	10.45
White females	11.75	11.72	13.15	13.59
Black females	13.36	12.51	13.38	12.94
Percentage of persons in poverty				
Latinos	19.1	21.1	18.4	19.7
Whites	8.2	9.2	7.5	8.9
Blacks	27.5	31.8	26.4	28.3
Percentage of householders who are homeowners				
Latinos	45.0	47.2	49.9	53.9
Whites	72.2	72.2	75.0	76.1
Blacks	45.0	43.7	45.3	43.6

Sources: 1980, 1990, and 2000 data are from 5% Public Use Microdata Samples (PUMS) and 2005-7 from 1% American Community Survey (ACS).

college) and the increasing gap between the wages of Latino workers and the wages of white workers.

Conclusion

Latinos have a long history of living in the Midwest. Indeed, throughout the 20th century, it has been the region outside of the Southwest that has had the most Latinos. Nonetheless, for most of the 20th century relatively little attention was paid to the Latino population in this region. Three decades ago Gilbert Cardenas (1978a) called on social scientists to give more attention to Latinos in the Midwest. In the last two decades, there has been a significant increase in the amount of research generated on them. This increase is due primarily to the major increase of Latinos in this region, much of it driven by the recruitment of Latinos to work in the meatpacking industry. This pattern is reminiscent of the recruitment that took place early in the 20th century, when recruitment agencies lured persons of Mexican origin to work in agriculture, railroads, and manufacturing.

Because of data limitations, however, there has been little research that provides a broad overview of the demographic and socioeconomic changes that Latinos in the Midwest have experienced over time. This chapter has sought to fill this gap. It is clear that Latinos have become a crucial part of the demography of the region. Latinos, in fact, have been the engine propelling population growth in the Midwest. Two out of every five individuals added to the Midwest between 1980 and 2005–7 have been Latino. Indeed, were it not for Latinos, the Midwest region would have grown much more slowly than it has. The future of the Midwest will increasingly be tied to the Latino population, given the group's youthfulness. Today's K–12 students in the Midwest are increasingly Latino, and tomorrow's workforce in the region will be increasingly Latino.

However, the findings show mixed results in how well Latinos are doing in the areas of social and economic integration. For example, native-born individuals have made significant gains in education, with the dropout rate falling significantly, alongside steady increases in the rate of completion of high school and college. Similarly, foreign-born Latinos have made significant progress in the workforce, with their unemployment rates dropping significantly over the last three decades. Moreover, the majority of Latinos speak English, either as their only language or alongside Spanish. Finally, native-born Latinos have increasingly married outside of the Latino group.

Still, Latinos have not made much progress in other dimensions. For instance, foreign-born Latinos continue to lag significantly behind in the area of education. In addition, native-born Latinos continue to have high levels of unemployment and Latino men have experienced significant erosion in their wages. Furthermore, poverty levels have increased noticeably among foreign-born individuals. Finally, while Latinos have made steady progress in homeownership, data in the near future may well show that this progress has been reversed, as many Latinos are likely to have lost their homes to foreclosure. The ongoing economic crisis provides major challenges for Latinos in the Midwest.

The analysis comparing the standing of Latinos relative to whites and blacks on a variety of socioeconomic dimensions clearly shows that major gaps continue to exist, especially in the areas of education and wages. All demographic measures indicate that the economy of the Midwest will become increasingly dependent on today's Latino youth. Latinos in new destinations of the Midwest are not a sojourner population. Rather, they are establishing roots in these new destinations (see Saenz 2006). Latino youth will be called upon to compete and perform effectively in an increasingly technological and global workforce. Moreover, it will be today's Latino youth who will be called upon to provide the economic support for an aging population, one comprised disproportionately of whites. Socioeconomic gaps between Latinos and whites will undoubtedly widen in the face of the current economic crisis. The failure to educate and train Latino youth today will likely have daunting long-term economic implications. As we invest in the future of Latino youth, these individuals must be seen as an asset rather than a liability.

REFERENCES

Acuña, R. 1988. *Occupied America: A History of Chicanos.* 3rd ed. New York: HarperCollins.

Alvarez, R. 1973. "The Psychohistorical and Socioeconomic Development of the Chicano Community in the United States." *Social Science Quarterly* 53: 920–42.

Arreola, D. D. 1985. "Mexican Americans." In *Ethnicity in Contemporary America: A Geographical Appraisal,* ed. J. O. McKee, 77–94. Dubuque, IA: Kendall/Hunt.

Baker, P. L., and D. R. Hotek. 2003. "Perhaps a Blessing: Skills and Contributions of Recent Mexican Immigrants in the Rural Midwest." *Hispanic Journal of Behavioral Sciences* 25(4): 448–68.

Barrera, M. 1979. *Race and Class in the Southwest.* Notre Dame, IN: University of Notre Dame Press.

Blalock, H. M. 1967. *Toward a Theory of Minority-Group Relations.* New York: Wiley.

Cantu, L. 1995. "The Peripheralization of Rural America: A Case Study of Latino Migrants in America's Heartland." *Sociological Perspectives* 38(3): 399–414.

Cardenas, G. 1978a. "Who are the Midwestern Chicanos: Implications for Chicano Studies." *Aztlán* 7(2): 141–52.

———. 1978b. "Los Desarraigados: Chicanos in the Midwestern Region of the United States." *Aztlán* 7(2): 153–86.

Dalla, R. L., A. Ellis, and S. C. Cramer. 2005. "Immigration and Rural America: Latinos' Perceptions of Work and Residence in Three Meatpacking Communities." *Community, Work and Family* 8(2): 163–85.

Estrada, L. F. 1978. "A Demographic Comparison of the Mexican Origin Population in the Midwest and Southwest." *Aztlán* 7(2): 203–34.

Faught, J. D. 1978. "Chicanos in a Medium-Size City: Demographic and Socioeconomic Characteristics." *Aztlán* 7(2): 307–26.

Fink, D. 1998. *Cutting Into the Meatpacking Line.* Chapel Hill: University of North Carolina Press.

Garcia, J. R. 1978. "History of Chicanos in Chicago Heights." *Aztlán* 7(2): 291–306.

Gouveia, L., and R. Saenz. 2000. "Global Forces and Latino Population Growth in the Midwest: A Regional and Subregional Analysis." *Great Plains Research* 10(2): 305–28.

Gouveia, L., and D. D. Stull. 1995. "Dances with Cows: Beefpacking's Impact on Garden City, Kansas, and Lexington, Nebraska." In *Any Way You Cut It: Meat Processing and Small Town America,* ed. D. D. Stull, M. J. Broadway, and D. Griffith, 85–107. Lawrence: University Press of Kansas.

Grey, M. A. 1999. "Immigrants, Migration, and Worker Turnover at the Hog Pride Pork Processing Plant." *Human Organization* 58(1): 16–27.

Guzmán, B., and E. D. McConnell. 2002. "The Hispanic Population, 1990–2000: Growth and Change." *Population Research and Policy Review* 21: 109–28.

Haverluk, T. W., and L. D. Trautman. 2008. "The Changing Geography of U.S. Hispanics from 1990–2006: A Shift to the South and Midwest." *Journal of Geography* 107: 87–101.

Hobbs, F., and N. Stoops. 2002. *Demographic Trends in the 20th Century.* U.S. Census Bureau Special Reports, CENSR-4. Washington, DC: U.S. Census Bureau.

Kanellos, N. 1978. "Fifty Years of Theatre in the Latino Communities of Northwest Indiana." *Aztlán* 7(2): 255–65.

Lane, J. B., and E. J. Escobar, eds. 1987. *Forging a Community: The Latino Experience in Northwest Indiana.* Chicago: Cattails Press.

Lopez, D. A. 2000. "Attitudes of Selected Latino Oldtimers toward Newcomers: A Photo Elicitation Study." *Great Plains Research* 10(2): 253–74.

Mapes, K. 2004. "'A Special Class of Labor': Mexican (Im)Migrants, Immigration Debate, and Industrial Agriculture in the Rural Midwest." *Labor: Studies in Working-Class History of the Americas* 1(2): 65–88.

McConnell, E. D. 2008. "U.S. Latinos/as and the 'American Dream': Diverse Populations and Unique Challenges in Housing." In *Latinas/os in the United States: Changing the Face of América,* ed. H. Rodríguez, R. Sáenz, and C. Menjívar, 87–100. New York: Springer.

McConnell, E. D., and F. B. LeClere. 2002. "Selection, Context, or Both? The English Fluency of Mexican Immigrants in the American Midwest and Southwest." *Population Research and Policy Review* 21: 179–204.

McWilliams, C. 1948. *North from Mexico: The Spanish-Speaking People of the United States.* Philadelphia: J. B. Lippincott.

Millard, A. V., and J. Chapa, eds. 2004. *Apple Pie & Enchiladas: Latino Newcomers in the Rural Midwest.* Austin: University of Texas Press.

Montejano, D. 1987. *Anglos and Mexicans in the Making of Texas, 1836–1986.* Austin: University of Texas Press.

Parra, R., V. Rios, and A. Gutiérrez. 1978. "Chicano Organizations in the Midwest: Past, Present and Possibilities." *Aztlán* 7(2): 235–53.

Rosales, F. A. 1978. "The Regional Origins of Mexicano Immigrants to Chicago during the 1920s." *Aztlán* 7(2): 187–201.

Ruggles, S., M. Sobek, T. Alexander, C. A. Fitch, R. Goeken, P. Kelly Hall, M. King, and C. Ronnander. 2009. *Integrated Public Use Microdata Series: Version 4.* Machine-readable database. Minneapolis: Minnesota Population Center.

Saenz, R. 1991. "Interregional Migration Patterns of Chicanos: The Core, Periphery, and Frontier." *Social Science Quarterly* 72(1): 135–48.

———. 1997. "Ethnic Concentration and Chicano Poverty: A Comparative Approach." *Social Science Research* 26: 205–28.

———. 2005. "Latinos and the Changing Face of America." In *The American People: Census 2000,* ed. R. Farley and J. Haaga, 352–79. New York: Russell Sage Foundation.

———. 2006. "Latino Births Increase in Nontraditional Destination States." February 13. Available online: www.prb.org/Articles/2006/LatinoBirthsIncreaseinNontraditionalDestinationStates. aspx.

Saenz, R., and C. Cready. 1997. "The Southwest-Midwest Mexican American Migration Flows, 1985–1990." JSRI Research Report No. 20, Julian Samora Research Institute, Michigan State University.

Samora, J., and R. A. Lamanna. 1987. "Mexican Americans in a Midwest Metropolis: A History of East Chicago." In *Forging a Community: The Latino Experience in Northwest Indiana*, ed. J. B. Lane and E. J. Escobar, 215–25. Chicago: Cattails Press.

Sena-Rivera, J. 1979. "Extended Kinship in the United States: Competing Models and the Case of La Familia Chicana." *Journal of Marriage and the Family* 41(1): 121–29.

Sepulveda, C. 1978. "Una Colonia de Obreros: East Chicago, Illinois." *Aztlán* 7(2): 327–36.

Stull, D. D., M. J. Broadway, and D. Griffith, eds. 1995. *Any Way You Cut It: Meat Processing and Small Town America*. Lawrence: University Press of Kansas.

Tienda, M., and D. Lii. 1987. "Minority Concentration and Earnings Inequality: Blacks, Hispanics, and Asians Compared." *American Journal of Sociology* 93: 141–65.

Valdés, D. N. 1991. *Al Norte: Agricultural Workers in the Great Lakes Region, 1917–1970*. Austin: University of Texas Press.

Vargas, Z. 1993. *Proletarians in the North: A History of Mexican Industrial Workers in Detroit and the Midwest, 1917–1933*. Berkeley: University of California Press.

Villanueva, M. A. 2002. "Racialization and the Latina Experience: Economic Implications." *Feminist Economics* 8(2): 145–61.

Wells, M. 1978. "Emigrants from the Migrant Stream: Environment and Incentives in Relocation." *Aztlán* 7(2): 267–90.

———. 1981. "Oldtimers and Newcomers: The Role of Context in Mexican American Assimilation." *Aztlán* 11(2): 271–95.

Zuñiga, V., and R. Hernández-León. 2005. *New Destinations: Mexican Immigration in the United States*. New York: Russell Sage.

ARTURO VEGA, RUBÉN O. MARTINEZ, and TIA STEVENS

Cosas Políticas: Politics, Attitudes, and Perceptions by Region

THE U.S. LATINO POPULATION IS NOT ONLY THE NATION'S LARGEST ETHNIC minority group, it is also the fastest growing group in the country, making up "more than half of the overall population growth in the United States" since 2000 (Passel and Cohn 2008). Indeed, Latinos are expected to more than double their numbers by 2050 and comprise 30% of the nation's population. Accompanying this growth, unfortunately, is a fear of its impact on the "conventional tapestry" of the nation. Samuel Huntington, for example, in his 2004 book *Who Are We: The Challenges to America's Nation Identity*, argued that Latinos threaten the ethos of the nation because of an inability or resistance to assimilate into American life (see also Huntington 2004b). This fear is exacerbated by the increasing globalization of the nation's economy and workforce and by a lack of understanding of the diversity and complexity that makes up Latinos as a group.

Despite accounting for approximately 15% of the U.S. population and having a presence across the nation, especially in the Southwest, that dates back centuries, U.S. Latinos as a group are not well known. Latinos are still less known in the Midwest, where, having increased substantially in the last two decades, they comprise slightly over 6% of the population, a percentage that will grow in the coming years. What are their views on social and political issues? What political resources do they possess, represent, or portend? Are there differences within subgroups that fracture this pan-ethnic group? And, if so, how are these differences manifested? Or, if not, then what are the commonalities of this group?

Take Latinos in Michigan and Maryland, for example. According to the U.S. Census Bureau, the states have a similar number of Latinos (406,000 and 359,000, respectively), comprising a similar percentage of each state's population (4.0% and 6.4%, respectively). However, compared to Latinos in Maryland, Michigan Latinos are younger, poorer, and more likely to be native born and of Mexican origin (Pew Hispanic Center 2010). Moreover, despite aggregate summaries, there are few studies that compare the characteristics of Midwest Latinos, for example, in relation to Latinos living in other regions of the United States (see Longoria 2000). If Latinos throughout the Midwest are similar to Michigan Latinos, for instance, one might nonetheless find important differences between Latinos of this region and those in other parts of the country.

This chapter explores some of these differences by examining U.S. Latinos by region of the country through a secondary analysis of the Latino National Survey (LNS) 2006 dataset. The LNS 2006[1] was a nationwide telephone survey with a sample of Latino adults from 16 states and Washington, DC, that was conducted from November 17, 2005, to August 4, 2006.[2] The instrument contained "approximately 165 distinct items," ranging from demographic information to political attitudes and policy preferences.[3] This chapter reports the survey findings on items ranging from nativity and birthplace to political interest and partisan and political ideology. In addition, Latino perceptions of commonality with African Americans, whites, and other Latinos and their attitudes and perceptions on same-sex marriage, abortion, and immigration are examined.

These analyses are driven by the following questions: In what ways are Latinos across the country the same? And in what ways are they different? Our principal objective is to compare the responses of midwestern Latinos to Latinos in the South, Southwest, East, and West, with a focus on political resources, attitudes, and perceptions.

First, an overview of the sample is in order, as are a few words on how respondents were coded into regions (the appendix provides a list of the "variables of interest," the coding strategy, and the foci of this work). The LNS 2006 polled Latinos from 16 states and the District of Columbia. The sample of 9,509[4] comprised 5,049 (53.1%) females and 4,460 (46.9%) males. The overall average age was 37, with females (38.0 years) being slightly older than males (36.0 years). Overall, 40% of respondents were older than the average age of 37 years. In addition, two-thirds (66%) of the respondents were foreign born, and a majority identified their ancestral ethnicity as Mexican (69.9%), indicated that they were Catholic (71.5%), and had incomes between $15,000 and $34,999 (54.2%). Finally, a large percentage (40.8%) had less than a high school education.

Using the respondent's state variable (RSTATE), each state was recoded into one of five regions (1 = South, 2 = Southwest, 3 = West, 4 = Midwest, and 5 = East). Southern states included the District of Columbia, Florida, Georgia, North Carolina, and Virginia (n = 2,329). Southwestern states included Arizona, California, Colorado, New Mexico, and Texas (n = 3,723).[5] Respondents from Nevada and Washington were coded as western (n = 944), while respondents from Illinois and Iowa were coded as midwestern (n = 1,168). Finally, New Jersey, New York, and Maryland were coded as East respondents (n = 1,346). The LNS 2006 covered approximately 87.5% of the U.S. Hispanic population and, despite limitations, provides an important resource for comparative analyses.

This chapter proceeds by reporting responses to five areas covered in the LNS 2006: nativity; select demographic characteristics; politics; commonality with other groups; and social issues. Simple descriptive statistics and one-way analysis of variance (ANOVAs) are reported, followed by short summaries for each section.[6] The chapter concludes with an overall review and discussion of the findings and their implications.[7]

Nativity

LNS respondents were asked to indicate their birthplace. Here possible responses were "mainland United States," "Puerto Rico," or "some other country." Overall, two-thirds of the respondents indicated that they were born in another country (see table 1). While significant variations exist by region, the highest concentration of foreign-born Latinos was in the South (78.8%), and the lowest concentration was in the Southwest (59.4%). Approximately two-thirds (64.3%) of the midwestern Latinos indicated that they were born in another country, which nearly equals the percentage of foreign born among all respondents.

Nativity is further illuminated by contingency questions and responses. Respondents who were born in another country were next asked "where were you born?" (B6), and if they answered "Mexico," they were asked, "In what state in Mexico?" (B7). Responses to these questions provide an interesting context in which to view Mexico-born Latinos in the United States. Of the 751 midwestern Latinos who responded that they were born in another country, 91.3% indicated they were born in Mexico. This is the largest percentage of Mexican-born respondents in any of the five regions (see table 2). In contrast, 63% of the southern Latinos and only 26% of

TABLE 1. Cross-Tabulations of Birthplace by Region, 2006

Place of birth	South f	South %	Southwest f	Southwest %	West f	West %	Midwest f	Midwest %	East f	East %	Total f	Total %
Mainland U.S.	**346**	**14.9**	**1,492**	**40.1**	**249**	**26.4**	372	31.8	**326**	**24.2**	2,785	29.3
Puerto Rico	**147**	**6.3**	**20**	**0.5**	**22**	**2.3**	45	3.9	**210**	**15.6**	444	4.7
Other country	**1,835**	**78.8**	**2,211**	**59.4**	**672**	**71.3**	751	64.3	**810**	**60.2**	6,279	66.0
Total	2,328	100	3,723	100	943	100	1,168	100	1,346	100	N=9,508	100

Notes: Chi-square = 931.2; $p < 0.001$; Cramer's $v = 0.22$. Values in bold are statistically significant ($p < 0.05$).
Source: Latino National Survey (LNS) 2006.

TABLE 2. Cross-Tabulations of Nativity by Region, 2006

	South f	South %	Southwest f	Southwest %	West f	West %	Midwest f	Midwest %	East f	East %	Total f	Total %
Mexico	1,151	62.8	1,932	87.4	596	88.6	686	91.3	207	25.5	4,572	72.8
Chihuahua	30	2.6	324	16.8	26	4.4	21	3.1	8	3.8	409	8.9
Federal District	77	6.7	87	4.5	22	3.7	52	7.6	15	7.2	253	5.5
Guanajuato	129	11.2	134	6.9	44	7.4	93	13.6	2	1.0	402	8.8
Jalisco	79	6.9	198	10.2	106	17.8	90	13.1	2	1.0	475	10.4
Michoacán	104	9.1	188	9.7	115	19.3	88	12.8	7	3.4	502	11.0
Other country	419	36.4	931	48.2	313	52.5	344	50.1	34	16.4	2,041	44.6
Total	1,835	100	2,211	100	672	100	751	100	810	100	N=6,279	100

Source: Latino National Survey (LNS) 2006.

TABLE 3. One-Way ANOVA of Mean Years in US by Region, 2006

Region	f	Mean	Std. Deviation
South	1,982	15.5	12.8
West	694	16.0	10.5
Midwest	796	17.2	12.0
Southwest	2,231	17.9	12.3
East	1,019	20.7	15.1
Total	N = 6,723	17.4	12.8

$F = 31.3; p < 0.001$

Note: Latinos in the South were significantly different than those in the Midwest, Southwest, and East; Latinos in the East were significantly different than Latinos in all other regions (Tukey's HSD, $p < 0.05$).

the eastern Latinos were born in Mexico. One must keep in mind that Florida has a high concentration of Cuban Americans and that New Jersey and New York have high concentrations of Puerto Ricans.

Further, of the midwestern respondents who indicate that they were born in Mexico, the states of Chihuahua, Guanajuato, Jalisco, and Michoacán and the Federal District were the five most frequently cited birthplaces. Interestingly, Guanajuato, Jalisco, and Michoacán are in the center of the country, while Chihuahua is a northern state.

One additional contingency question assists in contextualizing Latinos who were born in another country. When asked how many years they had been in the United States, midwestern Latinos' responses matched the average of foreign-born Latinos across the country (see table 3). Midwestern Latinos born in another country have been in the United States an average of 17.2 years. This is slightly less than eastern Latinos, who average 20.7 years in the United States (the longest among Latinos by region), and more than Latinos in the South, who report 15.5 years (the shortest average time among the five regions).

Examining nativity by region is also revealing. Again, while two-thirds of the midwestern Latinos (64.2%) are foreign born (see table 4), they make up the smallest percentage (11.9%) of all foreign-born Latinos among the five regions (calculation not shown in table 4). In contrast, nearly 8 in 10 (78.8%) of Latinos in the South are foreign born and represent nearly 3 in 10 (29.2%) of all foreign-born Latinos in the United States.

Similar patterns emerge among other generational cohorts by region.[8] The West, for example, has the smallest percentage of first-generation Latinos (8.9%), while the South has the smallest percentage of second-generation (5.8%) and third-generation (4.6%) Latinos. In contrast, the East has the largest percentage of first-generation Latinos (24.1%), while the Southwest has the largest percentage of second-generation (11.8%) and third-generation (17.2%) Latinos. The proportions of first-, second-, and third-generation Latinos in the Midwest fall in between the other regions, with 1 in 6 (15.4%) first-generation and 1 in 10 second- and third-generation Latinos (10% and 10.4%, respectively).

Ancestral identification by region demonstrates the overall influence of Mexican ancestry (see table 5). Ancestry was collapsed into eight categories: Mexican, Cuban, Dominican, Puerto Rican, Salvadoran, Central American, and Hispanic (which includes South Americans, Spaniards, and "other" responses). Overall, 7 in 10 Latinos in the United States trace their ancestry to Mexico. Regional variations are notable. Midwestern, southwestern, and western Latinos, for example, have very high percentages of Mexican ancestry (85%). Only 1% of the midwestern Latinos identified Cuban or Dominican ancestries. In contrast, eastern Latinos

TABLE 4. Cross-Tabulations of Generational Cohort by Region, 2006

	South		Southwest		West		Midwest		East		Total	
	f	%	f	%	f	%	f	%	f	%	f	%
Foreign born	1,835	78.8	2,211	59.4	672	71.3	751	64.2	810	60.2	6,279	66.0
1st generation	254	10.9	433	11.6	84	8.9	180	15.4	325	24.1	1,276	13.4
2nd generation	134	5.8	438	11.8	91	9.7	117	10.0	144	10.7	924	9.7
3rd generation	106	4.6	642	17.2	96	10.2	121	10.4	67	5.0	1,032	10.9
Total	2,329	100	3,724	100	943	100	1,169	100	1,346	100	N=9,511	100

Notes: Chi-square = 570.8; $p < 0.001$; Cramer's v = 0.14. Values in bold are statistically significant $p < 0.05$.
Source: Latino National Survey (LNS) 2006.

TABLE 5. Cross-Tabulations of Ancestral Identification by Region, 2006

	South		Southwest		West		Midwest		East		Total	
	f	%	f	%	f	%	f	%	f	%	f	%
Hispanic*	205	8.8	90	2.4	33	3.5	47	4.0	252	18.7	627	6.6
Mexican	1,317	56.5	3,290	88.4	816	86.6	993	85.0	230	17.1	6,646	69.9
Cuban	270	11.6	20	0.5	18	1.9	11	0.9	86	6.4	405	4.3
Dominican	82	3.5	0	0	1	0.1	1	0.1	258	19.2	342	3.6
Puerto Rican	245	10.5	44	1.2	28	3.0	72	6.2	443	32.9	832	8.8
Salvadoran	59	2.5	196	5.3	22	2.3	15	1.3	30	2.2	322	3.4
Central American	151	6.5	83	2.2	24	2.5	29	2.5	46	3.4	333	3.5
Total	2,329	100	3,723	100	942	100	1,168	100	1,345	100	N=9,507	100

Notes: Chi-square = 4226.5; $p < 0.001$; Cramer's v = 0.33. Values in bold are statistically significant ($p < 0.05$).
*Includes South Americans, Spaniards, and "other" responses.
Source: Latino National Survey (LNS) 2006.

are more diversified, with the highest percentage (32.9%) identifying a Puerto Rican ancestry.

When asked to indicate the reasons they came to the United States, nearly two-thirds (65.1%) of the midwestern Latinos who were born in another country cited "to improve economic condition" (see table 6). This percentage compares to 56% of all foreign-born Latinos and 58% among southwestern Latinos—the second highest percentage among the five regions. The next most frequent response from midwestern Latinos and respondents overall was that their parents brought them to the United States as children. For midwestern Latinos, these two responses cover 80% of the reasons they came to the United States.

Finally, table 7 reports the percentage of Latinos who were born in another

TABLE 6. Cross-Tabulations of Reasons Respondents Came to United States by Region, 2006

	South		Southwest		West		Midwest		East		Total	
	f	%	f	%	f	%	f	%	f	%	f	%
Education	142	7.2	157	7.0	**62**	**8.9**	**35**	**4.4**	58	5.7	454	6.8
Family reunification	189	9.5	218	9.8	53	7.6	72	9.0	**132**	**13.0**	664	9.9
Escape political turmoil	**193**	**9.7**	**55**	**2.5**	**18**	**2.6**	**11**	**1.4**	57	5.6	334	5.0
Parents brought as a child	**258**	**13.0**	346	15.5	118	17.0	113	14.2	175	17.2	1,010	15.0
Improve economic situation	1,063	53.6	1,305	58.5	387	55.8	**518**	**65.1**	**515**	**50.5**	3,788	56.3
Other	137	6.9	151	6.8	56	8.1	47	5.9	82	8.0	473	7.0
Total	1,982	100	2,232	100	694	100	796	100	1,019	100	N=6,723	100

Notes: Chi-square = 212.7; $p < 0.001$; Cramer's v = 0.09. Values in bold are statistically significant ($p < 0.05$).
Source: Latino National Survey (LNS) 2006

TABLE 7. Cross-Tabulations of Citizenship among Foreign Born by Region, 2006

	South		Southwest		West		Midwest		East		Total	
	f	%	f	%	f	%	f	%	f	%	f	%
Naturalized	528	26.6	663	29.7	195	28.1	222	27.9	268	26.3	1,876	27.9
Noncitizen	1,455	73.4	1,569	70.3	499	71.9	574	72.1	751	73.7	4,848	72.1
Total	1,983	100	2,232	100	694	100	796	100	1,019	100	N=6,724	100

Notes: Chi-square = 6.5; p = 0.163; Cramer's v = 0.03.
Source: Latino National Survey (LNS) 2006.

country and whether they are naturalized American citizens, by region. Overall, 7 in 10 (72.1%) indicate that they are not naturalized citizens. Latinos in the Midwest report the identical percentage (72.1%), with southwestern Latinos having the smallest percentage (70.3) and eastern Latinos the largest (73.7).

SUMMARY

The LNS 2006 data are revealing on questions of nativity, citizenship, and diversity across the United States and by region. Overall, according to the LNS sample, two-thirds of Latino adults in the nation are *not* U.S.-born. Midwestern Latinos not born in the United States are predominantly from Mexico, and half are from a handful of

TABLE 8. Cross-Tabulations of Education by Region, 2006

	South		Southwest		West		Midwest		East		Total	
	f	%	f	%	f	%	f	%	f	%	f	%
Less than high school	968	41.6	1,511	40.6	413	43.8	498	42.6	**490**	**36.4**	3,880	40.8
High school	574	24.7	958	25.7	246	26.1	301	25.8	344	25.6	2,423	25.5
Some college	405	17.4	741	19.9	178	18.9	219	18.8	279	20.7	1,822	19.2
Four-year degree and above												
	381	**16.4**	513	13.8	**106**	**11.2**	150	12.8	**232**	**17.2**	1,382	14.5
Total	2,328	100	3,723	100	943	100	1,168	100	1,345	100	N=9,507	100

Notes: Chi-square = 40.4; $p < 0.001$; Cramer's v = 0.04. Values in bold are statistically significant ($p < 0.05$).
Source: Latino National Survey (LNS) 2006.

TABLE 9. Cross-Tabulations of Household Income by Region, 2006

	South		Southwest		West		Midwest		East		Total	
	f	%	f	%	f	%	f	%	f	%	f	%
< $15,000	385	16.5	546	14.7	132	14.0	**154**	**13.2**	**262**	**19.5**	1,479	15.6
$15,000–34,999	**1,340**	**57.6**	2,025	54.4	494	52.3	610	52.2	685	50.9	5,154	54.2
$35,000–54,999	**304**	**13.1**	626	16.8	**173**	**18.3**	198	16.9	188	14.0	1,489	15.7
$55,000 +	**299**	**12.8**	526	14.1	145	15.4	**207**	**17.7**	210	15.6	1,387	14.6
Total	2,328	100	3,723	100	944	100	1,169	100	1,345	100	N=9,509	100

Notes: Chi-square = 67.2; $p < 0.001$; Cramer's v = 0.05. Values in bold are statistically significant ($p < 0.05$).
Source: Latino National Survey (LNS) 2006.

TABLE 10. Cross-Tabulations of Poverty Status by Region, 2006

	South		Southwest		West		Midwest		East		Total	
	f	%	f	%	f	%	f	%	f	%	f	%
In poverty	605	26.0	895	24.0	206	21.8	263	22.5	351	26.1	2,320	24.4
Near poverty	**230**	**9.9**	301	8.1	85	9.0	119	10.2	**84**	**6.2**	819	8.6
Income between "near poverty" and median												
	1,075	46.2	1,747	46.9	430	45.6	499	42.7	634	47.7	4,385	46.1
Income above median												
	419	**18.0**	780	21.0	223	23.6	**288**	**24.6**	277	20.6	1,987	20.9
Total	2,329	100	3,723	100	944	100	1,169	100	1,346	100	N=9,511	100

Notes: Chi-square = 50.8; $p < 0.001$; Cramer's v = 0.04. Values in bold are statistically significant ($p < 0.05$).
Source: Latino National Survey (LNS) 2006.

Mexican states in the interior of the country. In short, they in general are different ethnically from eastern or southern Latinos and more akin to their southwestern and western counterparts.

On average, foreign-born midwestern Latinos have been in the country for 17 years, comparable to foreign-born Latinos across the five regions. Two-thirds of all foreign-born midwestern Latinos came to this country to improve their economic condition—the largest percentage among the five regions—and yet despite their longevity in the country, only 3 in 10 midwestern Latinos have attained U.S. citizenship—an important step to developing political resources.

Demographic Characteristics: Education, Income, and Religious Affiliation

In terms of educational achievement, 41% of the LNS 2006 respondents indicated that they had less than a high school education, while one in seven (14.5%) had at least a college degree (see table 8). A slightly higher proportion (42.6%) of midwestern Latinos have less than a high school education than Latinos overall (40.8%), and a slightly lower percentage (12.8% compared to 14.5% across all five regions) have a college degree. Approximately two-thirds of Latinos across the five regions have low educational attainment, defined as high school or less. Nearly 7 in 10 (68.4%) of respondents in the Midwest indicated that they have a high school education or less—the second highest rate in the five regions. Although the relationship between education and region is statistically significant, the measure of association is extremely weak.

Table 9 reports household income by region. Midwestern Latinos have the smallest percentage of respondents with household incomes less than $15,000 annually (13.2% compared to 15.6% overall) and the largest percentage reporting household incomes of $55,000 or more (17.7% compared to 14.6% overall). Seven out of 10 (69.8%) Latinos across the five regions report household incomes of less than $35,000 a year. As a point of reference, the median household income for non-Hispanic whites in 2004 was $50,546 (DeNavas-Walt, Proctor, and Lee 2005).

Table 10 reports poverty status by region. Overall, nearly one-quarter (24.4%) of the respondents were below the poverty line. The highest concentrations of Latinos below the poverty line were in the East (26.1%) and in the South (26.0%), and the lowest concentration was in the West (21.8%). Among midwestern Latinos, 22.5% reported incomes below the poverty line. Latinos in the Midwest were significantly more likely than Latinos in other regions to report household incomes greater than the median household income in the United States ($44,389). In total, 33% of Latinos

TABLE 11. Cross-Tabulations of Religious Affiliation by Region, 2006

	South		Southwest		West		Midwest		East		Total	
	f	%	f	%	f	%	f	%	f	%	f	%
Non-Catholic	**740**	**31.8**	1,059	28.4	270	28.6	**264**	**22.6**	378	28.1	2,711	28.5
Catholic	1,589	68.2	2,664	71.6	674	71.4	**904**	**77.4**	967	71.9	6,798	71.5
Total	2,329	100	3,723	100	944	100	1,168	100	1,345	100	N=9,509	100

Notes: Chi-square = 32.3; $p < 0.001$; Cramer's v = 0.06. Values in bold are statistically significant ($p < 0.05$).
Source: Latino National Survey (LNS) 2006.

in the United States have household incomes that put them either below or near the poverty threshold (near poverty is defined as a household income below 125% of the poverty threshold). As point of reference, the poverty threshold for a family of four in 2004 was $18,850.

Finally, 7 in 10 Latinos in the survey identify with Catholicism (see table 11). Midwestern Latinos have a higher percentage (77.4%) of Catholic identification than their counterparts in any other region; the overall rate among respondents is 71.5%.

SUMMARY

Latinos are very undereducated, have relatively low incomes, and are predominantly Catholic. Midwestern Latinos exhibit typical patterns in educational attainment and religious affiliation but report higher household income and lower rates of poverty. For midwestern Latinos. low educational attainment may be offset by higher wages in industrial, agricultural, and services work than in other regions of the country.

The combination of low income and educational attributes with extremely low levels of citizenship, despite long residence in the United States, results in weak political resources.

Cosas Políticas / Political Characteristics

When asked, "Generally speaking, do you usually consider yourself a Democrat, a Republican, an Independent, some other party, or what?" respondents indicated a primary preference for the Democratic Party (33.8%), independence (17.7%), and then the Republican Party (10.8%; see table 12). More than one-third (37.7%) of the respondents gave "don't care" or "don't know / other" responses to this question. If we compare partisan identification by region, midwestern Latinos follow the national

TABLE 12. Cross-Tabulations of Latino Partisan Identification by Region, 2006

Political Party	South f	South %	Southwest f	Southwest %	West f	West %	Midwest f	Midwest %	East f	East %	Total f	Total %
Democrat	507	21.8	1387	37.3	284	30.1	421	36.0	616	45.8	3,215	33.8
Republican	347	14.9	389	10.4	91	9.6	91	7.8	110	8.2	1,028	10.8
Independent	436	18.7	663	17.8	180	19.1	194	16.6	208	15.5	1,681	17.7
Don't care	457	19.6	533	14.3	200	21.2	215	18.4	175	13.0	1,580	16.6
Don't know/Other	581	25.0	751	20.2	189	20.0	247	21.1	237	17.6	2,005	21.1
Total	2,328	100	3,723	100	944	100	1,168	100	1,346	100	$N=9{,}509$	100

Notes: Chi-square = 314.1; $p < 0.001$. Cramer's v = 0.09. Values in bold are statistically significant ($p < 0.05$).
Source: Latino National Survey (LNS) 2006.

TABLE 13. Cross-Tabulations of Political Ideology by Region, 2006

	South f	South %	Southwest f	Southwest %	West f	West %	Midwest f	Midwest %	East f	East %	Total f	Total %
Conservative	497	21.3	804	21.6	200	21.2	**208**	**17.8**	296	22.0	2,005	21.1
Liberal	**240**	**10.3**	482	12.9	132	14.0	170	14.6	**204**	**15.2**	1,228	12.9
Middle of the road	**352**	**15.1**	679	18.2	168	17.8	199	17.0	231	17.2	1,629	17.1
Don't think of self in these terms	803	34.5	1,157	31.1	292	30.9	384	32.9	427	31.7	3,063	32.2
Don't know	**436**	**18.7**	602	16.2	152	16.1	207	17.7	**187**	**13.9**	1,584	16.7
Total	2,328	100	3,724	100	944	100	1,168	100	1,345	100	$N=9{,}509$	100

Notes: Chi-square = 55.8; $p < 0.001$; Cramer's v = 0.04. Values in bold are statistically significant ($p < 0.05$).
Source: Latino National Survey (LNS) 2006.

pattern, with 36% identifying themselves as Democrats and 16.6% as independents, but they were significantly less likely than Latinos in other regions to identify themselves as Republican (7.8%). Nearly 4 in 10 (39.5%) of the respondents in the Midwest gave "don't care" or "don't know / other" as an answer. Latinos from the South identified themselves far less frequently as Democrats (21.8%) and far more frequently as Republicans (14.9%) then their counterparts in other regions.

To illustrate partisanship "ambivalence," respondents who identified themselves as either Democrats or Republicans were also asked, "Would you consider yourself a strong Democrat/Republican [dependent upon their previous response] or not a very strong Democrat/Republican?" Overall, responses were split: 49.6% indicated they were "strong" partisans; 50.4% were "not very strong." There were no substantial

TABLE 14. Cross-Tabulations of Midwest Latinos' Political Ideology by Party Identification, 2006

	Democrat		Republican		Independent		Don't care		Don't know/other		Total	
	f	%	f	%	f	%	f	%	f	%	f	%
Conservative	87	20.7	**37**	**40.7**	35	18.0	**23**	**10.7**	**26**	**10.5**	208	17.8
Liberal	**95**	**22.6**	8	8.8	34	17.5	**13**	**6.0**	**20**	**8.1**	170	14.6
Middle of the road	77	18.3	21	23.1	**55**	**28.4**	**18**	**8.4**	**28**	**11.3**	199	17.0
Don't think of self in these terms												
	136	32.3	22	24.2	57	29.4	**91**	**42.3**	78	31.6	384	32.9
Don't know	**26**	**6.2**	**3**	**3.3**	**13**	**6.7**	**70**	**32.6**	**95**	**38.5**	207	17.7
Total	421	100	91	100	194	100	215	100	247	100	*N*=1,168	100

Notes: Chi-square = 263.9; $p < 0.001$; Cramer's v = 0.24. Values in bold are statistically significant ($p < 0.05$).
Source: Latino National Survey (LNS) 2006.

TABLE 15. Cross-Tabulations of Political Interest by Region, 2006

	South		Southwest		West		Midwest		East		Total	
	f	%	f	%	f	%	f	%	f	%	f	%
Not sure/don't know	109	4.7	146	3.9	40	4.2	51	4.4	**39**	**2.9**	385	4.0
Not interested	**762**	**32.7**	**1,042**	**28.0**	278	29.5	350	29.9	**448**	**33.3**	2,880	30.3
Somewhat interested												
	1,060	45.5	1,765	47.4	479	50.8	552	47.2	581	43.2	4,437	46.7
Very Interested	**398**	**17.1**	**770**	**20.7**	**146**	**15.5**	216	18.5	277	20.6	1,807	19.0
Total	2,329	100	3,723	100	943	100	1,169	100	1,345	100	*N*=9,509	100

Notes: Chi-square=48.8; $p < 0.001$. Cramer's v = 0.04. Values in bold are statistically significant ($p < 0.05$).
Source: Latino National Survey (LNS) 2006.

differences in partisanship by region. Midwestern Latinos, for example, followed the national pattern—48% "strong" partisans, 52% "not very strong."

Respondents were next asked to indicate their political ideology ("Generally speaking, in politics do you consider yourself as conservative, liberal, middle-of the-road or don't you think of yourself in these terms?"; see table 13). Here, nearly half gave the answer "don't think of self in these terms" (32.2%) or "don't know" (16.7%). More midwestern Latinos identified themselves as conservatives (17.8%) and "middle of the road" moderates (17.0%) than identified themselves as liberals (14.6%), which also follows the national pattern.

Contrasting political ideology with partisan identification is also informative.

Midwestern Democrats, for example, were evenly distributed in terms of political ideology (see table 14). Twenty-one (20.7) percent identified their political ideology as conservative, 22.6% as liberal, and 18.3% as "middle of the road." One-third (32.3%) of these Democrats indicated that they "don't think of themselves in these terms," and an additional 6.2% indicated that they "didn't know." Finally, of the nearly one-fifth (18.4%) of midwestern Latinos who indicated that they "did not care" about a political party affiliation, nearly three-quarters either indicated that they don't think of themselves in these terms of political ideology (42.3%) or "didn't know" (32.6%).

Midwestern Republicans, on the other hand, exhibited less ambivalence regarding political ideology, with approximately 4 in 10 (40.7%) identifying themselves as conservatives and nearly 1 in 4 (23.1%) as "middle of the road." One-quarter (24.2%) gave a "don't think of themselves in these terms" response, and an additional 3.3% gave a "don't know" response.

When asked about their political interest ("How interested are you in politics and public affairs?"), one-third of all Latinos (34.3%) responded that they were either "not interested" in politics (30.3%) or were "not sure / don't know" (4%) (see table 15). In contrast, nearly one in five (19%) of the Latino respondents indicated that they were politically "very interested." Midwestern Latinos followed the national trend closely—34.3% indicated that they were either "not interested" in politics (29.9%) or were "not sure / don't know" (4.4%), while 18.5% were very interested.

LNS respondents were asked to indicate their level of agreement (strongly agreed; agreed; disagreed; strongly disagreed) with four statements about their political efficacy:

1. Government is pretty much run by just a few big interests looking out for themselves.
2. Sometimes politics and government seem so complicated that a person like me can't really understand.
3. People like me don't have any say in what the government does.
4. People are better off avoiding contact with government.

Responses to these statements are examined here by region as well as by generational cohort.

Overall, the vast majority of Latinos can be characterized as looking with a jaundiced eye on their political efficacy, with very few variations across region but important variations by generational cohort (see tables 16 through 19). For example, when asked whether they believed statement 1, "Government is pretty much run by just a few big interests looking out for themselves," more than 7 in 10 (72.7%) either

TABLE 16. One-Way ANOVA of Mean Political Efficacy as Measured by Responses to Statement 1 by Region, and Generational Cohort, 2006

	Somewhat or strongly disagree		Somewhat or strongly agree			Somewhat or strongly disagree		Somewhat or strongly agree	
	f	%	f	%		f	%	f	%
South	718	30.8	1,611	69.2	Foreign born	1,875	29.9	4,405	70.1
West	268	28.4	676	71.6	2nd generation	224	24.3	698	75.7
Midwest	309	26.4	860	73.6	1st generation	295	23.1	981	76.9
Southwest	964	25.9	2,759	74.1	3rd generation	87	19.8	828	80.2
East	339	25.2	1,006	74.8					
Total	2,598	27.3	6,912	72.7	Total	2,598	27.3	6,912	72.7

$F = 5.5; p < 0.001$ $\qquad$ $F = 19.0; p < 0.001$

Note: Statement 1 is "Government is pretty much run by just a few big interests looking out for themselves." Latinos in the South were significantly different from those in the Midwest, Southwest, and East; foreign-born Latinos were significantly different from first-, second-, and third-generation Latinos; second-generation Latinos were significantly different from third-generation Latinos (Tukey's HSD, $p < 0.05$). Source: Latino National Survey (LNS) 2006.

TABLE 17. Political Efficacy as Measured by Responses to Statement 2 by Region, and Generational Cohort, 2006

	Somewhat or strongly disagree		Somewhat or strongly agree			Somewhat or strongly disagree		Somewhat or strongly agree	
	f	%	f	%		f	%	f	%
West	320	33.9	623	66.1	3rd generation	396	38.4	636	61.6
East	437	32.5	909	67.5	1st generation	478	37.5	798	62.5
South	781	33.5	1,548	66.5	2nd generation	318	34.5	604	65.5
Midwest	367	31.4	801	68.6	Foreign born	1,893	30.1	4,386	69.9
Southwest	1,180	31.7	2,542	68.3					
Total	3,085	32.4	6,423	67.6	Total	3,085	32.4	6,423	67.6

$F = 0.7; p = 0.602$ $\qquad$ $F = 38.8; p < 0.001$

Note: Statement 2 is "Sometimes politics and government seem so complicated that a person like me can't really understand." No main effect for geographic region; third-generation Latinos were significantly different from second-generation and foreign-born Latinos; foreign-born Latinos were significantly different from all others (Tukey's HSD, $p < 0.05$). Source: Latino National Survey (LNS) 2006.

somewhat agreed or strongly agreed (see table 16). While no significant differences in these views were found by region, foreign-born Latinos were least likely to agree with the statement, while subsequent generational cohorts were more likely to agree with the statement, suggesting that over time they develop a more cynical view of government.

When asked to consider whether politics seemed too complicated to understand

TABLE 18. Political Efficacy as Measured by Responses to Statement 3 by Region, and Generational Cohort, 2006

	Somewhat or strongly disagree		Somewhat or strongly agree			Somewhat or strongly disagree		Somewhat or strongly agree	
	f	%	f	%		f	%	f	%
South	968	41.5	1,361	58.4	3rd generation	87	19.8	828	80.2
West	365	38.7	579	61.3	1st generation	295	23.1	981	76.9
Southwest	1,412	37.9	2,311	62.1	2nd generation	224	24.3	698	75.7
East	498	37.0	848	63.0	Foreign born	1,875	29.9	4,405	70.1
Midwest	417	35.7	752	64.3					
Total	3,660	38.5	5,852	61.5	Total	2,598	27.3	6,912	72.7

$F = 4.3; p < 0.01$ $F = 15.4; p < 0.001$

Note: Statement 3 is "People like me don't have any say in what the government does." Latinos in the South were significantly different from Latinos in the East and the Midwest; foreign-born Latinos were significantly different from third- and first-generation Latinos (Tukey's HSD, $p < 0.05$).
Source: Latino National Survey (LNS) 2006.

TABLE 19. Political Efficacy as Measured by Responses to Statement 4 by Region, and Generational Cohort, 2006

	Somewhat or strongly disagree		Somewhat or strongly agree			Somewhat or strongly disagree		Somewhat or strongly agree	
	f	%	f	%		f	%	f	%
South	1,601	68.7	728	31.3	3rd generation	701	75.9	350	37.9
Southwest	2,474	66.4	1,190	32.0	1st generation	744	72.1	456	44.2
Midwest	796	68.1	374	32.0	2nd generation	886	69.4	544	42.6
East	894	66.4	452	33.6	Foreign born	4,136	65.9	2,308	36.8
West	645	68.3	300	31.7					
Total	6,469	68.0	3,044	32.0	Total	6,467	68.0	3,658	38.5

$F = 0.6; p = 0.661$ $F = 26.9; p < 0.001$

Note: Statement 4 is "People are better off avoiding contact with government." No main effect for geographic region; second-generation Latinos were significantly different from first-generation and foreign-born Latinos; foreign-born Latinos were significantly different from all others (Tukey's HSD, $p < 0.05$).
Source: Latino National Survey (LNS) 2006.

(table 17), two-thirds (67.6%) of the respondents and a similar proportion of mid-western Latinos (68.6%) somewhat agreed or strongly agreed. Here, however, foreign-born respondents were more likely to agree with the statement, while later generations were somewhat more likely to disagree with it.

A similar pattern emerged with the statement "People like me don't have any say in what the government does" (see table 18). Here, midwestern Latinos exhibited the largest percentage of agreement (64.3%), in comparison to 58.4% of southern Latinos and to 61.5% overall. Again, third-generation Latinos were the most likely to agree with this internal political efficacy statement, with 8 in 10 (80.2%) agreeing or strongly agreeing with the statement. Foreign-born Latinos, in contrast, were the least likely to judge themselves inefficacious. In combination, tables 16 and 18 demonstrate a consistency in responses both by region and by generational cohort.

A similar pattern emerged when respondents were asked to consider the statement that "people should avoid contact with government." More than two-thirds (68%) of all respondents strongly disagreed or somewhat disagreed, and there were no significant differences by region. However, when this same question is examined by generational cohort, foreign-born respondents expressed less agreement (65.9%) with it than did their first- (69.4%), second- (75.9%), and third-generation (72.1%) counterparts.

SUMMARY

Politically, Latinos in general, and Midwest Latinos in particular, exhibit mixed perceptions of politics. Large proportions of the respondents have a weak sense of partisanship and political ideology; others indicate that they simply do not think of themselves in such terms or just "don't know." On the other hand, of those who have partisan identification, midwestern Latino Republicans exhibit much less ideological ambivalence than their Democratic counterparts. In addition, one-third of the respondents indicated that they are simply not interested in politics, and only one in five is "very interested." Finally, while large percentages exhibit weak internal political efficacy ("hard for a person like me to understand" and "people like me don't have a say"), foreign-born Latinos were more likely to agree with these sentiments than the native born. On the other hand, in terms of external political efficacy ("government run by a few big interests" and "people are better of avoiding contact with government"), foreign-born Latinos were in less agreement and tended to have a stronger sense of their efficacy than did the native born.

The previous points of nativity, diversity, lack of citizenship, low incomes and educational attainment, combined with a partisan and ideological ambivalence and mixed political efficacy, suggest a population that has few political resources.

Commonality with Others: African
Americans, Other Latinos, and Whites

LNS 2006 respondents were asked to consider their commonality not only with other Latinos but also with African Americans and whites. Two questions ("Thinking about the political situation in society, how much do you have in common with [other Latinos / African Americans / whites]?" and "Thinking about issues like job opportunity, educational attainment or income, how much do you have in common with [other Latinos / African Americans / whites]?") were scaled to measure "shared commonality." Responses ranged from "nothing" and "some" to "a little" and "a lot." Combining the two variables yielded scales with values that ranged from 2 (meaning low commonality) to 8 (meaning high commonality). Analysis of variance was employed to examine averages across regions of the country.

When asked to consider their shared commonality with African Americans, LNS 2006 respondents had a 5.24 average on the scale and a modal value of 6, suggesting that they have a moderate sense of commonality with African Americans. Slightly less than one in seven (13%) respondents expressed "low shared commonality" scores (2 or 3), while nearly one in five (18.8%) expressed "high shared commonality," with scores of 7 or 8. These scores reveal statistically significant differences by region (see table 20). Midwestern Latinos exhibited the middle average (5.17), with western and southern Latinos having lower averages (5.09 and 5.11, respectively), and Latinos from eastern states having the highest average (5.53). Southwestern Latinos also had a middle average (5.27).

TABLE 20. One-Way ANOVA of Commonality with Others by Geographic Region, 2006

	f	Mean	SD		*f*	Mean	SD		*f*	Mean	SD
*Commonality with African Americans**				*Commonality with Other Latinos†*				*Commonality with Whites‡*			
West	944	5.09	1.54	East	1,346	6.11	1.47	Midwest	1,168	4.90	1.62
South	2,829	5.11	1.58	Southwest	3,723	6.15	1.48	East	1,346	5.00	1.54
Midwest	1,168	5.17	1.57	South	2,829	6.17	1.51	West	944	5.00	1.60
Southwest	3,723	5.27	1.57	Midwest	1,168	6.19	1.43	Southwest	3,723	5.00	1.61
East	1,346	5.53	1.50	West	944	6.28	1.35	South	2,829	5.01	1.57
Total	9,509	5.24	1.57	Total	9,509	6.17	1.47	Total	9,509	4.99	1.59

$F = 18.11; p < 0.001$ $\quad\quad$ $F = 2.30; p = 0.069509$ $\quad\quad$ $F = 1.19; p = 0.31$

* In their perceptions of commonality with African Americans, Latinos in the Southwest were significantly different from those in the West, South, and East; Latinos in the East were significantly different from those in all other regions.
† In their perceptions of commonality with other Latinos, Latinos in the East were significantly different from those in the West.
‡ In their perceptions of commonality with whites, there was no main effect for geographic region (Tukey's HSD, $p < 0.05$).
Source: Latino National Survey (LNS) 2006.

When asked the same questions, this time as applied to other Latinos, again statistically significant difference emerged across the nation. Overall, Latinos had a 6.17 average and 6.0 modal score of commonality with other Latinos. In contrast to their sense of shared commonality with African Americans, only 4.1% of respondents expressed "low shared commonality" scores (2 or 3) with other Latinos, and nearly 4 in 10 (38.7%) had "high shared commonality" scores (7 and 8). Midwestern and western Latinos had the highest average scores of commonality with other Latinos (6.19 for midwestern and 6.28 for western Latinos; again see table 20).

Finally, when the same questions were applied to white Americans, respondents exhibited the least sense of commonality, while tending toward the positive. Overall, when considering their commonality with white Americans, Latinos had an average and modal score of 5. Here, again, Latinos were evenly distributed in their perceptions. For example, nearly one in six (15.7%) exhibited "low commonality" scores (2 and 3) with white Americans, while a nearly similar percentage (15%) exhibited "high commonality" scores (7 and 8) with white Americans. Midwestern Latinos had the lowest commonality averages (4.90), while southwestern Latinos had the highest average (5.01).

SUMMARY

Latinos perceive far greater commonality with other Latinos than they do with African Americans and non-Hispanic whites. In addition, Latinos feel more commonality with African Americans than with whites. The sense of commonality with African Americans exhibited statistically significant differences by region, with the Midwest and the West having the highest averages. On the other hand, there were no statistically significant differences by region in perceptions of commonality with whites.

These findings suggest that Latinos are somewhat group or ethnic-centric. Given the low levels of political resources that Latinos in general exhibit, ethnic centrism portends a pan-ethnic identity politics built on a sense of shared fate. On the other hand, it may also suggest a "go-it alone" politics, or may be a reflection of relative isolation in society (i.e., marginalization and segregation).

Views on Social Issues: Abortion, Same-Sex Marriage, and Immigration

The social views of Latinos relative to the issue of abortion and same-sex marriage were examined with a split sample (see table 21). Respondents were asked to

TABLE 21. Cross-Tabulations of Views on Abortion and Same-Sex Marriage by Region, 2006

	South		Southwest		West		Midwest		East		Total	
	f	%	f	%	f	%	f	%	f	%	f	%
Abortion												
Always legal	**88**	**7.7**	210	11.3	55	11.7	64	9.8	78	12.1	495	10.4
Mostly legal	69	6.0	135	7.3	37	7.9	55	8.4	50	7.8	346	7.3
Legal to save the life of the woman or in cases of incest												
	590	51.7	886	47.6	201	42.8	324	49.8	319	49.6	2,320	48.7
Always illegal	231	20.2	376	20.2	102	21.7	114	17.5	127	19.8	950	19.9
Unsure	164	14.4	255	13.7	75	16.0	94	14.4	**69**	**10.7**	657	13.8
Total	1,142	100	1,862	100	470	100	651	100	643	100	N=4,768	100

Chi-square = 31.7; $p < 0.001$; Cramer's v = 0.04.

	South		Southwest		West		Midwest		East		Total	
Same-Sex marriage												
Legal marriage	**170**	**14.9**	380	20.4	82	17.4	145	22.3	**154**	**23.9**	931	19.5
Civil unions	90	7.9	107	5.7	34	7.2	49	7.5	51	7.9	331	6.9
No legal recognition	383	33.5	619	33.3	148	31.4	**169**	**26.0**	204	31.6	1,523	31.9
No opinion	500	43.7	755	40.6	207	43.9	288	44.2	**236**	**36.6**	1,986	41.6
Total	1,143	100	1,861	100	471	100	651	100	645	100	N=4,771	100

Notes: Chi-square = 46.4; $p < 0.001$; Cramer's v = 0.06. Values in bold are statistically significant ($p < 0.05$).
Source: Latino National Survey (LNS) 2006.

consider the circumstances of legal abortion ("Generally speaking, do you think abortion should be legal in all circumstances; legal in most circumstances; legal only when necessary to save the life of the woman or in cases of incest; illegal in all circumstances; or unsure). Overall responses approximate a normal distribution. Nearly one in five (17.7%) expressed the view that abortion should be always legal or mostly legal. Nearly one in five (19.9%) expressed the view that abortion should be illegal in all circumstances, while nearly one-half (48.7%) believed that abortion should be legal only when necessary to save the life of the woman or in cases of incest. Finally, 13.8% expressed uncertainty in responding to this question.

While the differences across the regions are statistically significant ($p < 0.001$), the measure of association is quite weak (Cramer's v = 0.04), with the views of midwestern Latinos, for example, not differing substantively from the national trends.

However, views on abortion varied by generational cohorts. Here, for example, while only 11% of the foreign born believed abortion should be "always legal" (6.4) or "mostly legal" (4.6), the percentages of subsequent generations holding the same views more than doubled (27.7%) for second-generation and more than tripled (37.5%) for third-generation Latinos.

When asked to consider whether same-sex couples should be allowed to marry, respondents expressed socially conservative views. Here, again, the differences across regions are statistically significant ($p < 0.001$) but the overall measure of association is weak (Cramer's $v = 0.06$). In the aggregate, nearly one-third of the respondents expressed the view that same-sex relationships should not receive legal recognition (31.9%). In contrast, one in five (19.5%) respondents replied that same-sex couples should be allowed to marry legally. Next, 1 in 14 respondents (6.9%) expressed the view that same-sex couples should be allowed to enter into civil unions. Finally, over 4 in 10 (41.6%) had no opinion or could not provide an answer to this question. Midwestern Latinos were significantly less likely than those in other regions to believe that same-sex couples should not receive legal recognition. In other words, they (and their eastern counterparts) tended to be more accepting of legal marriage and civil unions than their counterparts in other regions.

When the issue of same-sex marriage is examined by generational cohort of the respondents, a pattern similar to the issue of abortion emerges. Slightly less than one in six (16%) of the foreign-born Latinos expressed support for same-sex marriage. In contrast, 1 in 4 first- and second-generation Latinos and 3 in 10 third-generation Latinos held the same view.

Latino views on immigration and immigration policy, while statistically significant by region, are weak in association (see table 22). Overall, Latinos have positive views of immigration. They were asked, "Which comes closer to your own views? Immigrants today strengthen our country because of their hard work and talents; or immigrants today are a burden on our country because they take our jobs, housing, and health care." Over 9 in 10 (91.2%) viewed immigrants as strengthening the country. Only slight variations in this view were found among Latinos across the regions, and midwestern Latinos were significantly less likely than those in other regions to believe that immigrants are a burden (5.9% compared to 8.8% nationally).

In contrast, there was far less agreement on the "preferred policy on undocumented or illegal immigration." Here, roughly 4 in 10 (42.4%) of the respondents expressed the view that undocumented or illegal immigrants should be allowed immediate legalization. Roughly another 3 in 10 (31.6%) expressed the view that legalization should be permitted through a guest worker program. One in nine (11.8%) indicated that their preference was to have a guest worker program without a legalization process. Finally, 4.6% of the respondents expressed preference for "closing" or "sealing" the border as a public policy response. Latinos in the East were the least likely to support immediate legalization (38.7% compared to 42.4% nationally) and the most likely to support sealing off the border (6.5% compared

TABLE 22. Cross-Tabulations of Views on Immigration by Region, 2006

	South		Southwest		West		Midwest		East		Total	
	f	%	f	%	f	%	f	%	f	%	f	%
Immigrants today ...												
Strengthen our country												
	2,193	94.2	3,318	89.1	863	91.4	1,100	94.1	1,200	89.2	8,674	91.2
Burden our country	136	5.8	405	10.9	81	8.6	69	5.9	146	10.8	837	8.8
Total	2,329	100	3,723	100	944	100	1,169	100	1,346	100	*N*=9,511	100

Chi-square = 64.8; $p < 0.001$; Cramer's v = 0.08.

	South		Southwest		West		Midwest		East		Total	
Preferred policy for undocumented immigration												
Immediate legalization												
	1,032	44.3	1,548	41.6	417	44.2	517	44.3	521	38.7	4,035	42.4
Guest worker program leading to legalization												
	685	29.4	1,203	32.3	303	32.1	381	32.6	428	31.8	3,000	31.6
A temporary guest worker program												
	305	13.1	457	12.3	90	9.5	121	10.4	145	10.8	1,118	11.8
Seal off / close border	88	3.8	183	4.9	32	3.4	42	3.6	88	6.5	433	4.6
None of these	219	9.4	332	8.9	101	10.7	106	9.1	163	12.1	921	9.7
Total	2,329	100	3,723	100	943	100	1,167	100	1,345	100	*N*=9,507	100

Chi-square = 57.6; $p < 0.001$; Cramer's v = 0.04.
Source: Latino National Survey (LNS) 2006.

to 4.6% nationally) or chose "none of these" (12.1% compared to 9.7% nationally). Midwestern Latinos did not differ significantly from the national trends.

SUMMARY

In terms of social issues, Latinos in the United States exhibit mixed views on abortion, conservative views on same-sex marriage, and consistent affirmative views on immigration. Significant but weak associated variations on the issues of abortion and same-sex marriage were also found by region and generational cohort, with the foreign born expressing the least support for the legality of abortion and for same-sex marriage. Generational views are notable, with second and third generations exhibiting views more akin to national averages than to their foreign-born or first-generational counterparts. These findings point to assimilation in political beliefs from generation to generation, but decreased commonality in perceptions and attitudes with earlier generational cohorts.

Conclusion

So what are we to make of these findings? In what ways are Latinos across the country the same? In what ways are they different? In addition, how do midwestern Latinos compare to Latinos in the South, Southwest, East, and West? At first glance, there seem to be more similarities than differences. Taken together, Latinos in many ways appear similar in their patterns of nativity, demographic characteristics, views on politics and policies, and perceptions of shared commonality with other groups. In the aggregate, Latinos in this study were about 37 years of age, foreign born, Catholic, married, and had approximately five children.

Latinos in the United States are generally undereducated, and many reported incomes below the poverty level. Those Latinos who were not born in the United States reported largely Mexican ancestry, with important variation across regions; Latinos in this survey were generally not naturalized U.S. citizens and not recent arrivals, having lived in the United States an average of 17 years.

On the other hand, significant differences exist among Latinos by region, subgroup, and generational cohort. These differences make it risky to speak of "a U.S. Latino" or of "Latinos in the U.S. experience." Nativity is representative of the difficulty in thinking of Latinos as a homogenous group who share a pan-ethnic identity. Eight in 10 Latinos from the Southwest and West and slightly over 9 in 10 from the Midwest are of Mexican origin. On the other hand, only 1 in 4 eastern Latinos and slightly over 6 in 10 southern Latinos are of Mexican origin. In addition, half of midwestern Latinos are from central parts of Mexico, compared to only 16% of eastern Latinos who are from Mexico. One-third of eastern Latinos identify ancestral roots in Puerto Rico, while over a third (34.5%) of southern Latinos identify Cuban and Central American ancestries.

Adding variations by generational cohort contributes further diversity. While two-thirds of the respondents indicate that they are foreign born, this ratio rises to nearly 8 in 10 (78.8%) for Latinos from the South and 7 in 10 for Latinos in the West, but recedes to 6 in 10 for southwestern and eastern Latinos, with midwestern Latinos nearly at the national average (64.2%). The other side is also important to note. Overall, only 11% of the respondents were third-generation Latinos. Across regions, only 5% of southern Latinos and eastern Latinos are third generation. This compares to over three times that percentage of southwestern Latinos (17.2%), and twice as many western and midwestern Latinos (10.2 and 10.4, respectively)—still relatively small percentages.

Other important differences were found in the reasons foreign-born Latinos came to the United States and in educational attainment, household income, poverty, and views on politics. Overall, Latinos exhibit a belief in an insular shared common fate with other Latinos, and a less shared fate with African Americans and whites. Large percentages of Latinos in the United States and by region are not naturalized, and, unfortunately, sizable numbers are disengaged politically—given their socioeconomic status, the opportunity costs to political participation appear too high. Latinos have mixed views on social issues (abortion and same-sex marriage) but express empathy for the highly visible and controversial issue of immigration, with many of these views varying by generational cohort.

Acculturative and assimilative elements are evident in comparisons of the foreign born with first-, second-, and third-generation native-born Latinos. How these acculturation patterns unfold will determine the social and political influences that Latinos contribute to the tapestry of their region and the United States as a whole.

Of course, additional analyses, including gender and age, are warranted, but the overall portrait here is Picasso-esque or disjointed and fragmented. There are, however, significant implications for the nation and its institutions in the large number of foreign-born Latinos. How the United States incorporates Latinos, both native born and immigrants, in light of the fact that the nation's seniors (the majority of whom are white) are becoming one of the largest population segments, will define social and economic relations and the cultural milieu of the country. As the baby boomers move out of the economy and become dependent on the productivity of others, their well-being becomes more directly tied to that of Latinos. It comes as no surprise that as these population shifts continue to unfold, the nation's future will increasingly be defined by the diversity and complexity that characterize Latinos in the United States (see Cisneros 2009). How social and political institutions integrate them and their children foreshadows the capacity of the nation to meet tomorrow's challenges.

Latinos in the Midwest face similar challenges. Whether the immigration pipeline continues or contracts in relation to the nation's economy will determine the political and social resources of midwestern Latinos relative to their counterparts in other regions. Low educational attainment in a deindustrialized region and an increasingly service-oriented and changing economy cannot bode well for the long-range aspirations of midwestern Latinos. Increasing levels of political resources—citizenship, higher educational attainment, and increased civic engagement—are directly linked to increased levels of social and political integration among midwestern Latinos and their counterparts across the country.

NOTES

1. The sample was drawn from Geoscape International, of Miami, Florida, and covered 15 states and the District of Columbia. The margin of error is approximately plus or minus 1.05%. State-level results are computed using state-level weights. See Fraga et al. 2006.

2. The Latino National Survey (LNS) 2006 was funded by the Ford Foundation, Russell Sage Foundation, National Science Foundation, Irvine Foundation, Hewlett Foundation, Carnegie Foundation, Joyce Foundation, W. K. Kellogg Foundation, Texas A&M University, the Annie E. Casey Foundation, and the Inter-University Program for Latino Research.

3. Latino National Survey (LNS), 2006, Codebook, ICPSR 20862, Inter-university Consortium for Political and Social Research.

4. These data represent the original data weighted by state proportions.

5. While Texas is usually included in the South, especially by federal agencies, we include it in the Southwest since it is one of the traditional homeland states of Mexican Americans, with past civil rights struggles oriented to the Southwest rather than the South. This gap in perspectives between white Americans and Latinos with regard to where Texas belongs regionally reflects a fundamental difference in orientation, both historically and culturally.

6. Missing values were imputed prior to the construction of scales and indices. Modal values were substituted for the missing values for categorical variables, and mean values were substituted for continuous variables (again, detailed descriptions of the variables and coding schemes are included in the appendix).

7. All analyses were conducted with weighted data.

8. For analytical purposes, respondents were coded into separate generational cohorts—foreign born and first, second, and third generations. The placements were constructed from the following questions: B5, Were you born in the mainland U.S., Puerto Rico, or some other country? (BORNUS = 1) and PARBORN (Where were your parents born, were they both born in the U.S., was one born in U.S., and were both born in another country; B11b (GRANBORN2), How many of your grandparents were born in the U.S.A.? (0 = none; 1 = one; 2 = two; 3 = three; 4 = all). If, for example, respondent was born in the United States, had a parent who was also born in the United States, but did not have any grandparents born in the United States, the respondent was coded second generation; similarly, if a respondent was born in the United States, had at least one parent and grandparent also born in the United States, the respondent was coded third generation. Other literature combines foreign born and first generations; here we seek analytical differences.

REFERENCES

Cisneros, H. G. 2009. *Latinos and the Nation's Future*. Houston: Arte Público Press.

DeNavas-Walt, C., B. D. Proctor, and C. H. Lee. 2005. *Income, Poverty, and Health Insurance Coverage in the United States: 2004*. Current Population Reports, P60-229. Washington, DC: U.S. Census Bureau.

———. 2006. *Income, Poverty, and Health Insurance Coverage in the United States: 2005*. Current Population Reports, P60-231. Washington, DC: U.S. Census Bureau.

DeNavas-Walt, C., B. D. Proctor, and J. Smith. 2007. *Income, Poverty, and Health Insurance Coverage in the United States: 2006.* Current Population Reports, P60-233. Washington, DC: U.S. Census Bureau.

Fraga, L. R., J. A. Garcia, R. H. Hero, M. Jones-Correa, V. Martinez-Ebers, and G. M. Segura. 2006. Latino National Survey. Inter-university Consortium for Political and Social Research, 26 ICPSR 2862.

Huntington, S. P. 2004a. *Who Are We? The Challenges to America's Identity.* New York: Simon and Schuster.

————. 2004b. "The Hispanic Challenge." *Foreign Policy* 141: 30–45.

Longoria, T. Jr. 2000. "Context, Identity, and Incorporation—Are Latinos in the Midwest Different?" In *Minority Politics at the Millennium,* ed. R. Keiser and K. Underwood, 179–201. New York: Garland.

Passel, J. and D. Cohn. 2008. "Trends in Unauthorized Immigration: Undocumented Inflow Now Trails Legal Inflow." Pew Hispanic Center. Available online: pewhispanic.org/files/reports/94.pdf.

Pew Hispanic Center. 2010. "Demographic Profile of Hispanics in Michigan, 2008." Available online: pewhispanic.org/states/index.php?stateid=MI.

U.S. Census Bureau. 2008. "Poverty Thresholds 2006." Available online: www.census.gov.

APPENDIX. VARIABLES USED AND CODING STRATEGY

VARIABLE	MEASUREMENT	RESPONSES
REGION	Recoded respondents' state: 1 = Arizona, District of Columbia, Florida, Georgia, North Carolina 2 = Arkansas, California, Colorado, New Mexico, Texas 3 = Nevada, Washington 4 = Illinois, Iowa 5 = Maryland, New Jersey, New York	1. South 2. Southwest 3. West 4. Midwest 5. East No missing values
PLACE OF BIRTH AND NATIVITY	B5. Were you born in the mainland U.S., Puerto Rico, or some other country? B6. Where were you born? B7 (if Mexico). In what state you were born?	1. Mainland 2. Puerto Rico 3. Some other country No missing values
YEARS IN THE UNITED STATES	If foreign born, constructed from: B9. When did you first arrive to live in the U.S. [mainland]?	1–85 Missing values replaced with the mode

GENERATIONAL COHORT	Constructed from: B5. Were you born in the mainland U.S., Puerto Rico, or some other country? (BORNUS = 1) and PARBORN (Where were your parents born, were they both born in the U.S., was one born in U.S., or were both born in another country?); B11b (GRANBORN2). How many of your grandparents were born in the U.S.? (0 = none; 1 = one; 2 = two; 3 = three; 4 = all) (e.g., if BORNUS = 1 and PARBORN =1 and GRANBORN2 = 0, cohort = 2nd generation; if BORNUS = 1 and PARBORN = 1 and GRANBORN2 = 1, cohort = 3rd generation).	0. Foreign born 1. First generation 2. Second generation 3. Third generation Missing values replaced with the mode prior to variable construction
ETHNICITY	Constructed from: B4. From which country do you trace your Latino heritage?	1. Hispanic (includes South Americans, Spaniards, and "other" responses) 2. Mexican 3. Cuban 4. Dominican 5. Puerto Rican 6. Salvadoran 7. Central American No missing values
REASON CAME TO U.S.	If foreign born: B8. What would you say is the main reason you came to live in the United States?	1. Education 2. Family reunification 3. Escape political turmoil 4. My parents brought me as a child 5. Improve economic situation 6. Other Missing values replaced with the mode
CITIZENSHIP	If foreign born: B10. Are you a naturalized American citizen?	1. Yes 2. No Missing values replaced with the mode

EDUCATION	D12. What is your highest level of formal education completed?	0. None 1. Eighth grade 2. Some high school 3. GED 4. High school graduate 5. Some college 6. 4-year college degree 7. Graduate or professional degree Missing cases replaced with the mode
INCOME	N5. Which of the following best describes the total income earned by all members of your household during 2004?	1. Below $15,000 2. $15,000–24,999 3. $25,000–34,999 4. $35,000–44,999 5. $45,000–54,999 6. $55,000–64,999 7. Above $65,000 Missing values replaced with the mode
POVERTY STATUS	Constructed from income, household size (SUPPINC), the U.S. census 2006 poverty thresholds, and the 2006 U.S. median household income (DeNavas-Walt, Proctor, and Smith 2007 and 2006)	1. In poverty 2. Near poverty (income within 125% of the poverty threshold) 3. Income between "near poverty" and the median U.S. household income ($48,201) 4. Income higher than the median U.S. household income ($48,201) Missing values replaced with the mode (income) and mean (household size) prior to variable construction
AGE	Respondent's age	0–97 Missing values replaced with the mean
RELIGION	E17. With what religious tradition do you most closely identify? (recoded and dichotomized)	1. Non-Catholic 2. Catholic Missing values replaced with the mode

PARTY IDENTIFICATION	J1. Generally speaking, do you usually consider yourself a Democrat, a Republican, an independent, some other party, or what?	1. Democrat 2. Republican 3. Independent 4. Some other party 5. Don't care 6. Don't know / other No missing values
IDEOLOGY	J6. Generally speaking, in politics do you consider yourself as conservative, liberal, middle-of-the-road, or don't you think of yourself in these terms?	1. Conservative 2. Liberal 3. Middle of the road 4. Don't think of self in these terms 5. Don't know No missing values
POLITICAL INTEREST	A6. How interested are you in politics and public affairs?	1. Not sure / don't know 2. Not interested 3. Somewhat interested 4. Very interested Missing values replaced with the mode
POLITICAL EFFICACY	K3A. Government is pretty much run by just a few big interests looking out for themselves. K3C. Sometimes politics and government seem so complicated that a person like me can't really understand. K3B. People like me don't have any say in what the government does. K3D. People are better off avoiding contact with government.	1. Strongly disagree 2. Disagree 3. Agree 4. Strongly agree Missing values replaced with the mode
PERCEPTION OF COMMONALITY WITH AFRICAN AMERICANS	G2a (AAPOLCOM). Thinking about the political situation in society, how much do you have in common with African Americans? G1a (AFCOMM). Thinking about issues like job opportunity, educational attainment, or income, how much do you have in common with African Americans?	1. Nothing 2. Little 3. Some 4. A lot Scale ranges from 2 (nothing) to 8 (a lot); Cronbach's alpha = 0.581. Missing values replaced with the mode prior to variable construction

PERCEPTION OF COMMONALITY WITH WHITES	G2b (WHIPOLCOM). Thinking about the political situation in society, how much do you have in common with whites? G1b (WHICOMM). Thinking about issues like job opportunity, educational attainment, or income, how much do you have in common with whites?	1. Nothing 2. Little 3. Some 4. A lot Scale ranges from 2 (nothing) to 8 (a lot); Cronbach's alpha = 0.628. Missing values replaced with the mode prior to variable construction
PERCEPTION OF COMMONALITY WITH OTHER LATINOS	G2b (LATPOLCOM). Thinking about the political situation in society, how much do you have in common with other Latinos? G1b (LATICOMM). Thinking about issues like job opportunity, educational attainment, or income, how much do you have in common with other Latinos?	1. Nothing 2. Little 3. Some 4. A lot Scale ranges from 2 (nothing) to 8 (a lot); Cronbach's alpha = 0.648. Missing values replaced with the mode prior to variable construction
ABORTION	L22. Generally speaking, do you think abortion should be . . .	1. Legal 2. Mostly legal 3. Legal only to save the life of the woman or in cases of incest 4. Always illegal 5. Unsure No missing values
SAME-SEX MARRIAGE	L21 What is your view on same-sex couples? Should they be permitted to . . .	1. Legally marry 2. Form civil unions 3. Receive no legal recognition 4. No opinion / NA No missing values
IMMIGRATION I	L25. Which comes closer to your own views? Immigrants today . . .	1. Strengthen our country because of their hard work and talents. 2. Are a burden on our country because they take our jobs, housing, and health care. No missing values

| IMMIGRATION II | L26. What is your preferred policy on undocumented or illegal immigration? | 1. Immediate legalization
2. Guest worker program that leads to legalization
3. Guest worker program that permits immigrants to be in the country only
4. An effort to seal or close off the border to stop illegal immigration
5. None

No missing values |

THEO J. MAJKA and LINDA C. MAJKA

Institutional Obstacles to Incorporation: Latino Immigrant Experiences in a Midsized Rust-Belt City

THIS CHAPTER EXPLORES THE INCORPORATION OF RECENT LATINO IMMIGRANTS into local primary institutions in a medium-sized metropolitan area in the Midwest. Institutional incorporation is one dimension of what Portes and Rumbaut (2006) term "context of reception," situations in the host nation and its communities that can both facilitate and inhibit the successful integration of newcomers and their ability to use whatever opportunities or resources are available. As Portes and Rumbaut (2006, 92) describe it, "Individuals with similar skills may be channeled toward very different positions in the labor market and the stratification system, depending on the type of community in which they become incorporated." While some aspects of the context of reception, such as the state of the economy, are national or international in scope, many other factors are dependent on local conditions and situations. The dimensions of incorporation in the local region are what we wish to explore.

During the past two decades, there has been a well-documented expansion of Latino immigrants into the Midwest, particularly in states and locales that as recently as 20 or 30 years ago had very small numbers of foreign-born residents. The growth of the Latino population has occurred in places that during the previous half century have not had much experience responding to an influx of foreign-born persons, especially those without high levels of education and professional qualifications. These locations lacked preexisting ethnic communities that could integrate the new residents and help them adapt. Newcomers, then, have essentially been pioneers in many of the places they have located in the Midwest. Under these circumstances, key questions concern whether native-born residents will accept the newcomers, and more importantly, whether local institutions will make necessary adaptations to accommodate them.

Compared with those of the 19th and early 20th centuries, recent immigrants depend on a wider range of institutions for their well-being. For example, health care is more regulated, and education is far more essential to occupational achievement for the 1.5 generation and second generation. In addition, the mediating institutions that assisted immigrant incorporation in the past, such as large manufacturing enterprises, labor unions, and urban schools, have declined in vitality. The federal government continues to lack a center or agency or even set of coherent policies that facilitate immigrants' adaptation and integration. As a consequence, social and political incorporation of recent immigrants has become an important challenge for midwestern communities. How they respond will be crucial for the future life circumstances of many of the newcomers and their children.

We focus on the process of institutional accommodation in the Dayton metropolitan region in southwest Ohio. In particular, we explore the adaptations, or in many cases the failures to adapt, to the growing number of Latino immigrants and their children.

The focus on immigrants' experiences with organizations is based on the understanding that a society's institutions shape the kind and extent of incorporation. Institutional incentives are important in channeling the actions of individuals and groups. The speed, trajectory, and extent of incorporation of contemporary immigrants are functions of the interplay between the purposive actions of immigrants (and their descendants) and the institutional structures, cultural beliefs, and social networks that set the context for and shape immigrants' experiences. We wish to argue that mainstream institutions through their policies, as well as actions by their staff, can either facilitate the incorporation of newcomers or create unnecessary obstacles that push some toward the margin. For immigrants themselves, and for their communities and the larger society, the disadvantage of not becoming sufficiently incorporated is likely to be blocked opportunities and prolonged marginalization, circumstances that may be passed on to children and future descendants.

How accessible to immigrants are the organizations that most of us deal with routinely in the course of our lives: public education, hospitals and health-care agencies, banks and other financial institutions, law enforcement and the courts, public transportation, churches and other faith-based organizations, and libraries?

What can be said about opportunities for employment and job advancement and access to the housing market? What have been the experiences with interpreters and bilingual staff in those organizations which have them? These are the day-to-day experiences that can facilitate, postpone or prevent immigrants' incorporation into community institutional life.

The Dayton Region: Deindustrialization and Increasing Disparities

Dayton historically has been a center of invention and manufacture. However, beginning in the 1970s, deindustrialization and corporate outsourcing, a response to expanding global competition, decimated the local economic order. A third of manufacturing jobs (about 50,000) were lost by the mid-1980s (Rimmer 1996), and further losses continue to the present. From 2001 to 2008, Montgomery County (Dayton) lost 42% of its manufacturing jobs (from 52,974 to 30,766), Clark County (Springfield) lost 38% of its manufacturing employment (from 11,647 to 7,188), and the three other counties comprising the Dayton Metropolitan Statistical Areas lost 22% (from 21,373 to 16,747) (Zeller 2009). In parallel to labor market decline were losses in union membership. Decades of economic uncertainty led to a fall in expectations of stability, security, and a dependable economic future both in Dayton and in all of Ohio. Decent-paying jobs have always been a crucial source of identity and self-worth, personal dignity and social participation (Hacker 2006). Dayton has become a prime example of trends that by now have reached other similar cities in the rust belt of the upper Midwest (Kuttner 2007). Economic restructuring has sharpened disparities in socioeconomic status that increasingly correspond to residential patterns manifested in urban sprawl. Mergers, layoffs, job shuffling, and ad hoc attempts at a development strategy based on services and new technologies expanded regional disparities in income and many public services between city and suburbs and between Montgomery County (Dayton) and much of the rest of the Dayton region. As industrial decline continued for decades, the demographic proportions in the city of Dayton shifted, with a decrease in the higher-waged, mostly white population and an increase in lower-waged racial-ethnic minorities. Overall, the city's population declined from a peak of around 265,000 in the mid-1960s to 166,210 in 2000 and 154,200 in June 2008. The city lost 20% of its population during the 1970s alone. Projections that this decline has bottomed out have not yet proved accurate.

The loss of manufacturing jobs disrupted not only lives and jobs but also the business of banks, other large corporations, schools, and religious, cultural, and other institutions. Voluntary organizations had been a real part of the social safety net in the era after World War II. Under repeated episodes of economic distress, corporations spent less on local community initiatives, and membership losses in voluntary organizations weakened the civic capacity to solve problems. In 2009, the NCR Corporation, a global technology firm, moved its corporate headquarters from Dayton to a suburb of Atlanta, the latest manifestation of withdrawal of elite support.

The income gap in Dayton became a gap in access to social institutions and the civil society itself. An unwritten social contract formed from local shared expectations was significantly based on the underlying existence of jobs and profits of corporations with ownership and corporate control ties to Dayton. Losses in corporate sponsorship, partially as a result of mergers and takeovers, increased the perception of vulnerability of the community itself. The further expectations that more jobs could leave at any time weakened the ties between hard-pressed individuals and their community.

Dayton is similar to many cities in that demographic change becomes contentious during times of economic change. In Dayton, the debate over immigration in part reflects the rise in long-term unemployment, insufficient job creation at adequate income levels for those without professional credentials, and the declining health of the economy locally and statewide. Structural strains reflecting corporate responses to global competition increase the likelihood that new immigrants, especially working-class ones, will be regarded as threats. The question of how much impact the recent arrival to the area of lower-skilled and less-educated immigrants poses to other low wage workers is not a trivial one under these circumstances. Anxieties about livelihood are easily transferred to those about neighborhoods. Historically, Dayton has been one of the more residentially segregated cities. In addition, the influx of Latinos has the potential of altering long-standing, relatively stable patterns of racial-ethnic residential segregation. These changes expand the potential of increased polarization among racial-ethnic groups, particularly since economic change has eroded the belief that the community shared a cooperative civil society with the ability to work out solutions.

These patterns were illustrated by an attempt to persuade the city of Dayton to accept the Matricula Consular as a recognized form of identification. The Matricula is an ID card issued to Mexican nationals living in the United States by Mexican consulate offices. During this decade, the Mexican Consulate office in Indianapolis visited Dayton one day a year and took applications for and issued Matricula cards. During their 2004 and 2005 visits, over 600 of the cards were issued to people living in the Dayton area. In Ohio, Cleveland, Toledo, Columbus, and Cincinnati were among over 900 municipalities nationwide that accepted the consular cards, but Dayton was not among them. When an organization chaired by one of us, the

Ethnic and Cultural Diversity Caucus of the Community Summit on Eliminating Racism, decided to campaign for the city to accept the cards as a recognized form of ID, the mayor strongly advised that we seek support for the Matricula from the city's Priority Boards. The city is divided geographically into seven of these boards, which are made up of elected members. The boards act as the primary avenues for citizen input and participation for the neighborhoods they represent with respect to city policies, agencies, and officials. After hearing our presentations and requests for their endorsements, the two priority boards in predominately white and working-class east Dayton, where most Latino immigrants in the city live, decided to oppose the resolution. The discussions were quite contentious. While racism and xenophobia were evident in many of the comments made at the meetings, these patterns were heightened by periods of economic uncertainty and decline. In contrast, two of the three priority boards in west Dayton, which is predominantly black, formally supported the resolution (the third never voted on it as far as we are aware), as did 11 local civil rights, faith-based, advocacy, human relations, and social service organizations. Despite the polarization that our campaign encountered, a formal resolution authorizing city agencies to accept the Matricula was unanimously passed by the City Commission in March 2005.

Particularly under circumstances like those in Dayton, local institutions can inhibit polarization between newcomers and long-term residents. Institutional incorporation acts as a strong proactive measure against prolonged marginalization and the scapegoating that often accompany disadvantaged and separated groups that are situated in a community but not of it. Few communities would consciously choose a trajectory toward greater polarization, but many institutional leaders may overlook the implications of not accommodating new groups of immigrants. The context of reception is crucial not only for immigrants themselves but also for the future of the communities in which they reside.

Growth of Latinos in Dayton and Ohio

The numbers and percentage of Latinos in Ohio and in the two major counties in the Dayton area have grown significantly during the past two decades. Table 1 shows that between 1990 and 2009, the number of Latino residents of the state more than doubled. Much of this recent increase has occurred among the Mexican community, which grew by more than half between 2000 and 2009. The number of Latino Ohioans with an ancestral link to Mexico is more than 137,000, or about 42% of the total Latino population. Even though more than two-thirds of those with Mexican ancestry were born in the United States, recent immigration from Mexico has been

TABLE 1. Growth of the Latino Population in Ohio, 1990–2009

	1990	2000	Increase 1990–2000	2009	Increase 2000–2009	Increase 1990–2009
Population	139,696	217,123	55.4%	326,413	50.3%	134%
	(1.3%)	(1.9%)		(2.8%)		

Note: Figures in parentheses represent the proportion of Latinos in the total state population.
Source: U.S. Census 1990 and 2000; Ohio Department of Development; Migration Policy Institute.

TABLE 2. Growth of the Foreign-Born Latino Population in Ohio, 1990–2007

	1990	2000	Increase 1990–2000	2007	Increase 2000–2007	Increase 1990–2007
Population	18,154	47,124	160.0%	76,000	61.3%	319.0%
	(13.0%)	(21.7%)		(27.0%)		

Note: Figures in parentheses represent the proportion of foreign born among all Latinos in the state.
Source: U.S. Census 1990 and 2000; Migration Policy Institute.

TABLE 3. Growth of the Latino Population in Montgomery and Clark Counties, 1990–2009

County (largest city)	1990	2000	2009 (projected)	Increase 1990–2000	Increase 2000–2009	Increase 1990–2009
Montgomery (Dayton)	4,539	7,096	11,958	56.3%	56.4%	145%
	(0.8%)	(1.3%)	(2.1%)			
Clark (Springfield)	970	1,699	2,812	75.2%	65.5%	190%
	(0.7%)	(1.2%)	(2.0%)			

Note: Figures in parentheses represent the proportion of Latinos in the total county population.
Source: U.S. Census; American Fact Finder; American Community Survey.

an important factor in the growth in Ohio's Latino population. For example, more than 20,000 residents have arrived in Ohio from Mexico since 2000. Reflecting this recent influx, as of 2006 the median age of Latinos was 27 years, compared to 38 years for Ohioans as a whole (Ohio Department of Development 2007).

Table 2 shows the numbers and percentage of foreign-born Latinos in Ohio. Their growth rate is over three times that of Latinos as a whole. Even though most of Ohio's Latinos were born in the United States or Puerto Rico, the percentage of foreign born among them has increased from 13% to 27% between 1990 and 2007.

Table 3 shows the numbers and percentage of the Latino population in the two largest counties in the Dayton area: Montgomery and Clark. Because the boundaries of the Dayton Metropolitan Statistical Area changed in 2005, adding a largely-rural county and eliminating Clark County, home of the region's other major city of Springfield, we have focused on data for the counties rather than the metropolitan area as a whole. The figures are for Latino residents, regardless of place of birth.

Data on foreign-born Latinos in the Dayton area show an increase comparable to Ohio as a whole. Montgomery County's foreign-born Latino population increased 48% between 2000 and 2005–7, from 1,790 (0.3%) to 2,651 (0.5%). For the old Dayton-Springfield Metropolitan Statistical area, the number of foreign-born Latinos increased by 20% between 2000 and 2004, from 2,796 to 3,359.

Even though the numbers are relatively small, these are significant increases. In fact, many of those knowledgeable about Latino immigrants believe some of these numbers are significant undercounts. For example, according to the 2000 census, Latinos comprise only 2.3% of those living in two particular east Dayton zip codes where Latino residents in the city tend to live, not much greater than 1.6% for the city as a whole for that year. In contrast, according to a social service agency operating in this area, 20% of the children in an after-school tutoring program and 12% of the students in a charter elementary school were Latinos by roughly 2005. Based on these data, surveys of the area the agency has done, and their knowledge of the area, staff members estimated that around 10% of the residents of these zip codes are Latinos (Stough and Silva 2006).

Research Methodology

In order to explore institutional incorporation, six focus groups with recent Latino immigrants were conducted in the Dayton area from October 2006 to April 2007. In addition, in spring 2006 and 2007 interviews were conducted by students in several of our classes with leaders of 11 local organizations, 10 of which either represent or serve immigrant populations, with the 11th becoming increasingly involved in issues involving immigrants as part of its broader focus on minority group relations. Both the focus groups and interviews were composed of standardized questions that probed the accessibility of local organizations for immigrants, including barriers or obstacles to their use. At the conclusion of the focus groups, participants filled out a questionnaire that asked them for personal information and what they personally thought were the "two biggest difficulties or obstacles that immigrants like yourself in the Dayton area have in adjusting to and being integrated into our communities." Both the focus group discussion and the questionnaire were in Spanish.

The limitations of focus group research are well known. Since they usually are not random samples of their respective populations, one cannot generalize any statistical analyses to the larger population. In addition, it is difficult to check on the accuracy of participants' descriptions of their experiences. However, as sociologists often note, people's perceptions of their experiences and the ways they interpret and understand them are crucial in defining their reality. Focus groups are a particularly good methodology for identifying significant issues and patterns, which is the primary goal of this research.

Organizations that arranged the focus groups were ones that have worked with Latino immigrants for many years and were trusted by them. Leaders of these organizations also acted as facilitators of the focus group they had organized. They were instructed to invite participants who had lived in the Dayton area long enough to have had significant contact with local institutions. They also attempted to balance gender and have a range of ages of the participants. The facilitators were trained by two methodologists in our department. Two of the organizations were the only nongovernmental social service agencies in the area that focus exclusively on Latino immigrants and their children. Four others were faith-based organizations whose primary purpose is working with the Latino population.

There were 43 total participants in the six Latino immigrant focus groups. Their characteristics are as follows:

- Median year for first living in the United States was 2000, with the range from 1977 to 2007, with 93% coming after 1992.
- 57% were females, and 43% were males.
- Ages ranged from 21 to 56, with a median age of 37.
- Median years of school completed was 8.5, with 30% completing less than six years, 10% completing high school, and another 12% having some post-high school education (including 5% with college degrees).
- 93% were born in Mexico.
- 75% were currently employed, with 83% employed full time.
- Median individual income for previous year was in the $10,000–$15,000 category, with none above $30,000.
- 54% were referred to their current job by a relative, friend, or workmate, while 14% were recruited by the employer or their agent.
- The most common employers were manufacturing (29%), restaurant/food (26%), and nursery/agriculture (24%).
- The most common occupations were farm or field worker (includes nursery worker), (27%), assembly or materials worker (15%), and cook (12%).
- The median time with their current employer was one to two years, with 18% five years or more.

- Two-thirds drove their own cars to work. Most (69%) get to their jobs in 30 minutes or less.
- 29% lived in Dayton, while the rest lived in other cities and towns in the Dayton area.
- Few had developed functional use of English; 29% indicated they could not speak English at all, while another 56% indicated they could speak English "a little." For reading English, the percentages were 38% (not at all) and 47% (a little); 55% had taken or were taking ESL classes.

Leaders of organizations were selected for interviews based on their history and experiences of working with Latino immigrants. They represented a variety of social service, advocacy, legal, and faith-based organizations. All were interviewed using a standardized questionnaire. Among other questions, they were asked to rate the accessibility of specific kinds of local institutions for Latino immigrants on a scale of 1 to 4. They also were asked what they thought were the "major problems, difficulties, or obstacles that immigrants in the Miami Valley [Dayton area] face in becoming better integrated into our communities."

Results

For both the focus group participants and leaders interviewed, language issues and barriers were the most frequently mentioned source of difficulties that Latino immigrants experienced in becoming incorporated into the larger community. The language category includes comments about both obstacles created by a lack of English language fluency and the inability or unwillingness of local institutions to adapt. In the written questionnaires filled out by focus group participants, 35% indicated this was the most important issue, and another 12% said it was the second most important. Additionally, 5 of the 11 leaders interviewed (45%) indicated that language issues were the most important difficulty that immigrants experienced, while two others (18%) gave it as the second most important difficulty, and one other leader gave it as the third most important.

The following are comments made in one of the focus groups by a Latina in her mid-fifties with three sons, all living in Dayton.

> We cannot integrate ourselves well into the community because . . . we cannot communicate, specifically about what we even feel. Take me, for example, sometimes at work I have some . . . grievance . . . [But I am going to say] that everything is okay. Some [English-speaking employees] are given more priority, and [our work] is not compensated.

. . . We dedicate ourselves to our work . . . [but] they don't compensate us anything. Or they don't recognize it. For example, I have realized that we Latinos work and we give all that we can give. . . . [Native-born Americans] earn more than us simply because they have a good Social [Security number], because they have good language, because they understand perhaps. And us, since they don't understand us and they know that we can't make a complaint . . . they're going to pass us by. . . . We cannot be well integrated with the community, that they would know that we, as well, as human beings, we also feel and we also realize that things are hurting us, but we don't say anything because we cannot express what we feel. Sometimes, I have had to cry.

Some consequences of institutions not accommodating those not yet fluent in English are illustrated by the following comment from a focus group participant concerning the lack of ready access to interpreters in some hospitals.

Sometimes you go to the hospital and they won't do anything for you because they don't have the papers in order. One time I was at the hospital, and there was a woman [non-English speaking Latina] giving birth. She was there for about five hours, and no one approached her but the nurses. The nurses kept telling her the doctors only come by for 15 minutes during the birth. At the end of the day, the doctor came by finally and said he would have to operate. My daughter was translating between the women and the doctor. But my daughter was a minor, so he had to use simple words with her. They could really use interpreters.

Beyond language matters, the second most important concerns mentioned by focus group participants were those involving transportation and immigration status and laws. Transportation problems were listed as one of the top two issues by 38%, most of which involved difficulties in obtaining a drivers license (30% overall). Immigration issues were listed by 30%, with 21% overall specifically mentioning a lack of legal status. Other areas listed included schools (18%), health care, including hospitals and health clinics (18%), and job issues (15%).

In contrast, six (55%) of the leaders interviewed cited cultural barriers or a lack of awareness about how institutions work as one of the three most important issues, although none believed it was the most important. Five (45%) cited prejudice, skin color, racism, xenophobia, or anti-immigrant attitudes as the first or second most important issue.

Although many difficulties that Latino immigrants experienced with specific institutions were a consequence of language issues, most institutions maintained their own distinct set of obstacles. When asked about the accessibility of specific kinds of organizations, such as health care, law enforcement, education, and public

TABLE 4. Evaluation of Institutional Accessibility by Leaders of Organizations That Serve or Represent Latino Populations

	Very accessible	Accessible	Not very accessible	Very inaccessible	Mean*
Institution					
Law enforcement	0	2	4	6	3.33
Emergency services	0	2	6	3	3.09
Public transportation	1	3	1	6	3.09
Housing and utilities	1	1	6	3	3.00
Media organizations (TV, newspapers, etc.)	1	4	1	5	2.91
Employment and knowledge of job availability	0	4	6	2	2.83
Legal system and courts, including access to legal services					
	2	2	6	3	2.77
Health-care organizations, including hospitals and clinics					
	0	6	7	0	2.54
Education from preschool to college	0	5	5	0	2.50
Banking and financial services	2	5	3	1	2.27
Services					
Proof of personal identity (e.g., an ID card like a driver's license)					
	0	0	5	6	3.55
Translation of documents and forms (e.g., those used by hospitals, courts, and banks)					
	1	1	4	5	3.18
Interpreters (persons translating conversations, e.g., with doctors)					
	2	2	6	2	2.67
Using bilingual staff of organizations that have them					
	1	3	2	2	2.63
English-language classes	2	4	5	0	2.27
Other†	0	0	1	1	3.50

Note: In some cases the number of responses is greater than 11 because respondents gave more than one answer, for example by comparing two locations for which there are different evaluations. In other cases, the number is less than 11 because respondents gave no answer or did not think the institution or service was applicable.

* Calculated by assigning these scores to responses: 1 = very accessible; 2 = accessible; 3 = not very accessible; 4 = very inaccessible.
† Two respondents voluntarily brought up the handling of domestic violence.

transportation, most focus group participants judged these institutions to be less than adequate. Although the lack of interpreters, bilingual staff, and translated documents and forms were judged to be a major concern, respondents overall thought the use of bilingual staff by agencies that had them were generally fine. ESL classes were also judged to be adequate or better, although some commented that they were held at times inconvenient for them, with several noting the lack of coordination among ESL providers. Leaders also evaluated most institutions as significantly less than fully accessible. Since many of them have worked with immigrants daily as part of their positions, they were especially critical of institutional inadequacies.

Neither group believed immigrants have major access problems with banking and financial institutions, libraries, and religious organizations. In fact, in line with other research, churches and other faith-based organizations were frequently praised by immigrants as offering social support and assisting adaptation (e.g. Zhou and Bankston 1998; Zhou, Bankston, and Kim 2002; Portes and Rumbaut 2006).

Leaders were asked to rate the accessibility of local institutions to Latino immigrants on a scale of 1 to 4, from very accessible to very inaccessible. Table 4 presents the results.

When we compared the results of the six of those interviewed who work primarily in Dayton with the results of the five who work primarily in smaller towns outside the city, there were several differences in their perceptions. Those working in Dayton judged the following institutions to be more accessible: the legal system and the courts, banking and financial services, public transportation, and the media. They judged interpreters and English-language classes more positively. The differences in scores between Dayton and outlying smaller towns were greatest for the legal system, interpreters, and, understandably, public transportation, but urban transportation was still judged less than adequate. These differences confirm what many of those who work with Latinos locally have observed. For example, courts in Dayton and Montgomery County now have interpreters readily available, and banks located within the city have made substantial efforts to encourage Latinos to open accounts, with many having bilingual tellers at their downtown and nearby branches. But in adjacent counties and smaller towns, there has been little effort to make these accommodations.

When taken as a whole, our results suggest that many immigrants are not assisted in making use of mainstream institutions and seeking services because of a language barrier. This disadvantage suggests specific steps or innovations that institutions could make, including some or more bilingual staff, availability of interpreters, and translated versions of forms and documents.

Below are summaries of discussions by focus group participants and leaders' comments about specific institutions and the accessibility of services. Since jobs and education are the most important institutions if immigrants and their children are to be successfully incorporated, we will describe them first.

JOBS AND EMPLOYMENT

Most focus group participants had working-class jobs, with nursery worker, assembler, restaurant cook, and laborer being the most frequent. All 32 respondents to the questions on employment were either currently employed (24) or expected to work again (8). In general, they discussed themes that relate to job discrimination and low pay. The work world described in focus groups confirms the prevalence and persistence of discriminatory attitudes and exploitative practices.

During one focus group in an outlying small town, at least four participants reported they worked two to three weeks for the same local employer and received no compensation. They said once the employer discovered that most of them were not authorized to be in the United States, all were dismissed without pay for the weeks they had worked, including one person who was a U.S. citizen. In general, participants reported supervisors denying them proper benefits because of their immigration status. They believed that employers assume undocumented immigrants are unaware of many benefits. In addition, some said they experienced discrimination for being Hispanic. Several commented that Mexicans are given the worst jobs with the worst working conditions, or are paid less than others doing comparable work. They connected this discrimination not only with their undocumented status, but also with their inability to speak English. This theme was echoed by other participants in different focus groups.

Leaders also noted employment injustices. Several also commented on the more positive dimension of the informal job networks among Latino immigrants:

- There are a lot of places that will take advantage of them or will not pay well. There is one factory known for hiring them and firing them before a two-year period because that is when they will have to start providing benefits. [It] rehires them [undocumenteds] again a few months later.
- There is a network within ethnic communities so we know who's in the kitchens of these restaurants and so forth, but as far as the larger economic opportunities I'm not sure there's really adequate—or I'm not sure they're really taking advantage of the [Montgomery County] Job Center, the kinds of opportunities they might. Maybe information isn't getting out there as it should be.
- There is a remarkable word-of-mouth job network among Latino immigrants.
- In restaurants, people apply through others who already have jobs. Knowledge and acquisition of jobs often occurs through networks. When they fill out applications for jobs they can list a reference who is already working at the place where they're applying.

Employment experiences suggest that at least some Latino immigrants are being negatively typified by employers; that is, they are thought to be able to perform menial work only. They are channeled into low-wage jobs and not given chances for advancement. As the above examples illustrate, some have been denied payment for work completed or discharged before employers were obliged to pay for benefits.

Job networks appear to be strong and are buffers against prolonged unemployment. Over half of the focus group participants found their present job through a relative, friend, or workmate. However, these networks do not overcome negative typification by employers. Compared to ethnic communities with established businesses, job networks by themselves tend to provide fewer options, and they are limited to what relatives and friends know.

Several focus group participants reported that there is a compelling need for presentations about jobs and companies, along with the rights people possess, regardless of immigration status. They believed that many immigrants are scared because they do not know their rights and are not aware of what resources are available.

EDUCATION

Ethnicity is a demographic feature that links many public schools and challenges many educators. Schools have a critical role to play in analyzing and deflecting stereotypes and cultivating respectful relationships. Nurturing aspirations is difficult when students not yet fluent in English are not accommodated or when parental involvement and concerns are deflected.

Respondents reported an array of difficulties with public schools, both for their children and themselves. Experience with public schools is regarded as a bumpy path. Below are some of the comments made by focus group participants in a small town:

- When the children arrived here, in the United States, they had to speak English. For example, they were in the first and the second grades because they didn't speak English. They would be at home crying, traumatized, they didn't want to go to school because they would have to speak English but they didn't know it. We've been here two years now and the children have learned English, but when we first arrived we felt that it was a really serious problem.
- The kids in primary school or junior high have to speak English and they feel traumatized because they don't understand the language.
- They walk around not knowing what is going on or what the teachers are saying.
- Recently the schools have been helpful. They have helped to explain things in Spanish to the mothers.
- The schools discriminate against Latinos.

One woman talked at length about the frustration she experienced trying to communicate with the staff at the high school her son was attending.

> For the first two years, they [school administrators] said they sent home the grades. I told them that I hadn't received them in the mail. They stopped sending the grades and [I] tried to make an appointment, but they wouldn't give me one. A whole year passed, until a year ago I was able to talk to the office about what had happened with the grades the first year. I told them I wanted to know what kind of grades he [the son] was getting and how he's doing. They knew I didn't speak English and they needed someone to translate. They got a Spanish teacher to translate and we made an appointment. They told me that they had sent all the grades, even though I never received them. [I told them] I have my mail key; no one else checks our mail besides me and I hadn't received anything, so you must not have sent me anything. I kept checking and nothing arrived. If you don't tell me and the teachers [don't] send me anything to tell me if my son's doing well or if he's doing badly, I'm not going to know how he is, if he's taking his courses. If he's trying to deceive me or if he's doing what's right, I won't know. So the teacher told me that they couldn't let us know how he's doing because we don't speak English. She said, "You don't know how to speak English, so you won't understand what we tell you, but *you* can send us a note or call to make an appointment." If I don't understand English, who do I look for to talk to?

She concluded: "No nos toman cuenta en las escuelas!" (They don't pay attention to us in the schools!)

A common observation was that all of the school calendars, newsletters, grade reports, and other communication from schools are in English. Many of the younger children know English but not well enough yet to translate newsletters to their parents. Some commented that this situation is very frustrating and makes communicating with the school difficult.

Even though leaders in Dayton did not rank the accessibility of education any higher than those in the surrounding towns, most did comment favorably on the availability of interpreters in some public schools, particularly in one PK–8 school where 16.5% of the students are Latino. In addition, a bilingual approach is available at a Head Start program in Dayton.

HEALTH CARE

Although judged by leaders as more accessible than some other institutions, health care was the area that elicited the most discussion and sharing of experiences by both leaders and focus group participants. The expense of health care and the reluctance and frequent refusal to treat those without money or documentation were common themes. Only 9 of 36 focus group participants indicated they worked or had worked at a job where the employer provided a health-care plan or paid for their health care.[1] One participant in a focus group held in a smaller town mentioned that a particular clinic does not want "to take care of pregnant Hispanic women, especially those without papers, so these women are sent to Dayton," 20 miles away.

Hospitals received mixed evaluations. Several participants in the focus groups held in Dayton commented that hospitals generally do not have interpreters on staff or even readily available, let alone bilingual medical staff. Most have to wait several hours, and in some cases interpreters never come.

Nevertheless, there was considerable variation among particular health-care organizations. One Dayton hospital was judged to be quite accessible to non-English speakers, and several health-care clinics in Dayton have bilingual staff or interpreters regularly present. A few clinics in outlying towns periodically have bilingual staff, for example, weekly or monthly. Focus group participants commented that they very much appreciate the bilingual physicians when they are there.

Much of the time non-English-speaking adults need to have their English-speaking children with them in order to understand what medical personnel are saying. An ever-present risk with children as interpreters is that they may not be able to translate medical terms accurately, and some feel intimidated in a hospital environment.

One of the more poignant stories was from a woman who began to experience bad headaches when she was pregnant.

> I was seven months pregnant [in 2002] and . . . told the doctor [at a local hospital] that my head hurt a lot. It was what was most bothering me. And he gave me medicine [and said to come back in two weeks. She continued to feel bad but was told to wait until her appointment.] I arrived there at the hospital. They did the ultrasound, they took x-rays, and [told her] the baby was already dead. They no longer could do anything. . . . They went and put me in bed, and there they left me. All night, there I stayed. The only thing that they did was give me . . . an injection in order to provoke the delivery, and I [had been] there from, like, from two in the afternoon. They put me in bed around eleven o'clock at night; at eight in the morning was when I gave birth to the baby, but alone, without anyone. . . . The only one that was there was [her partner]. . . . Afterwards, I was also sick for a long time because it gave me a lot of depression. And that's up to today.

Leaders also concurred with the judgment of enormous variations in accessibility among hospitals and clinics. Several commented that the more accessible ones were sometimes overwhelmed with non-English-fluent patients.

The head of the local chapter of a national Latino civil rights organization captured the overall sense that although there remain many inadequacies, accessibility in health care is improving.

> There is frustration in this area. On the one side, the caregiver tries to communicate the system and the person being helped is trying to communicate their needs. The frustration goes both ways when they can't communicate. The caregiver's role has changed in the last five years. Before, they [Latinos] were turned away because of the frustration of not being able to communicate. Families would leave because they couldn't communicate. This is getting better. The translation services and written forms have improved, although they're not there yet. Education and literacy are still a concern because even now some still cannot read and sign their name.

HOUSING

Most of the focus groups had participants who mentioned a variety of difficulties with housing. Issues included negligent landlords, cost of rent for those with minimum wage jobs, and discrimination against them because they are Hispanic. One person had to live two months without water in her apartment, until finally someone other than the landlord corrected the problem. A person in a focus group in a medium-size town commented that it is hard to find a landlord who will rent to his family because they are Hispanic. They are turned away, he commented, "as soon as they are looked at" because they "are not Americans." The prevalence of difficulties implies considerable discrimination in housing matters and awareness of the status of Latinos as a "second-class" ethnic group.

Several leaders also mentioned housing discrimination and negligent landlords. One added the following:

> There are often 10–16 people renting a house. They're almost never homeless because of this. It's illegal to have so many people renting a house, but they are often unaware that it's illegal. Some people rent out their place to others in order to made house payments. This is done without any contract or official agreement. They often don't have knowledge of Ohio housing laws and therefore don't have concern for them.

LAW ENFORCEMENT AND THE COURTS

Not unexpectedly, interviews with leaders and especially the focus groups suggested that there is a general distrust of police, and not only because of fear of arrest and possible deportation. Some focus group participants related incidents when the police acted in ways that would be unacceptable for most other people, including confiscation of Mexican driver's licenses and ID cards. Like most countries, the U.S. government has a policy that it will accept the driver's licenses of other countries, but the police often do not abide by that policy. One man had his car taken from him by the police without reason when he was in an accident that he said was not his fault. Another person mentioned that when the police are called in a domestic violence incident and one person speaks English, without an interpreter the police favor the English speaker's interpretation and act accordingly. Several participants said that, because of the language barrier, they were scared when police called or came to the house.

Below are summaries of representative comments made at one of the focus groups held in Dayton.

- A participant was pulled over for going through what he claimed was a nonexistent stop sign. The officer that came to translate told the participant to take the ticket and leave because it was easier.
- A participant was searched with his hands up after he did a U-turn.
- Two years ago, four policemen entered the participant's house without a search warrant, "pointing guns and shouting, banging the door down, saying, 'Don't move!'"
- A participant remarked that he was treated like a criminal during a minor encounter with the police.
- A participant observed, "They know you don't want to defend yourself and cause problems."
- One woman told a story about her experience when she went to renew her license at a DMV office. The official took away her Social Security card because her maiden name was still listed and not her married name.

In a focus group held in a medium-sized town, a woman mentioned that her son was currently in jail. However, because of a lack of interpreters, she did not know for how long or what would happen to him. The son originally got into trouble because of a misinterpretation by an interpreter. He was put on probation, but he claimed he was not told that he was on probation. After being found in violation of probation, he was jailed. The mother felt that she could not do anything and was neglected by criminal justice system because of the language barrier and her status as a Mexican. She felt that she had no way to communicate with officials and said she does not know what is going on.

Leaders generally corroborated these patterns. The following are several of their comments:

- There is not a decent relationship that exists between the police and the Hispanic population. There need to be more minorities within law enforcement—probations detention officers, FBI, and the police. If this country wants to slow down racism, the law enforcement must reflect the population that is not all white by including all populations.
- We need more interpreters; 911 has a line they [Spanish speakers] can call. The [Dayton] police department has four police officers that speak Spanish, but they are underpaid and overworked. Plus, police tend to confiscate their [Latino] IDs.
- They [Latinos] often don't know why they are stopped.
- Police don't take into account cultural or language difficulties. They allow children to interpret.
- It is beginning to get better, with training of personnel in handling people of different cultures.
- Hispanics don't even call the police for fear of being deported. Domestic violence is a problem, but the women don't call because of this fear. [This leader told a story about the neighbors calling the police on a man for domestic violence because he was beating his wife. The man got deported, and his wife felt guilty for it afterward.]

An attorney with a nonprofit regional law firm that assists low-income individuals and groups recounted a story that illustrates the connectedness among these various institutional spheres: "[Some Latino males] were pulled over after leaving work at 3:00 A.M. from a place where undocumented workers were often hired. [Because of] language misunderstanding, they were held for drinking, but they weren't [drinking], so they [the police] had to let them go. But then they were fired because the police threatened to raid the company where they worked."

With respect to the courts, the availability of interpreters was again a primary issue. Several leaders observed that Montgomery County (Dayton) courts have a permanent bilingual staff and supply interpreters when immigrants need an attorney. But adjacent counties lag far behind.

BANKS

Both focus group participants and leaders interviewed commented that frustration with banks stemmed primarily from English-only forms and the lack of interpreters or bilingual staff in most branches, except for many located downtown. In addition, some complained about the kinds of identification required to conduct banking.

In accordance with their corporate policies, most banks in the Dayton area accept the Matricula Consular for the purposes of opening an account, cashing checks, and related business. We found that many bank officials were not aware of this policy and had to be educated about the Matricula by members of advocacy groups. Personnel at some bank branches, however, continue to be unaware of this policy and lack knowledge of the Matricula card.

One focus group participant mentioned that without access to banking, many immigrants keep their money in their houses. One of his friends had a lot of money stolen from his home, but because of the distrust of the police, he did not report the crime. Vulnerability to theft emerged as a common pattern of concern in several of the focus groups.

LIBRARIES

Both focus group participants and those interviewed had overwhelmingly positive comments on libraries. Libraries were judged to be especially helpful. The Dayton Metro Library system was one of the first local organizations to accept the Matricula Consular card. Focus group participants commented that it is easy to get library cards, and many library branches have books and other material in Spanish.

CHURCHES

The comments on churches and faith-based organizations were overwhelmingly positive. The churches participants used were very supportive. With no preexisting ethnic community, churches have a particularly important function in creating cohesion among groups of immigrants. Several churches offer Spanish-language masses and other services. Some have ESL classes, individual tutoring in English, and social events after their services. Hirschman's comments that "immigrants become American by joining a church and participating in its religious and community life" seem to fit our observations (2004, 1212). In general, respondents appear to place a high level of trust in their churches and in individuals involved in pastoral care. Indicative of the concerns and involvements of some local faith-based organizations, four of our six focus groups were arranged by them.

INTERPRETERS

One of the common themes throughout the focus groups was the lack of sufficient numbers and availability of interpreters in most institutions. For example, 9 of the 11 participants in one of the focus groups in a small town said they have needed an interpreter when dealing with an organization, but only three participants actually received them.

Since most of the leaders interviewed act as interpreters themselves on a regular basis and provide training for other interpreters, they were particularly aware of the need for interpreters specifically trained in areas such as medical and legal work. They also emphasized the need for interpreters trained in cultural sensitivity and believed this training to be particularly important in family counseling and criminal investigation.

The president of the local chapter of a national Latino civil rights organization elaborated: "There are different kinds of interpreters needed for the different kinds of Spanish that are spoken. There is a difference between people from Colombia, Puerto Rico, and Mexico. This is especially necessary in the medical field and in the legal system where a language misunderstanding could be very damaging."

Because of the relatively recent nature of Latino migration to places like Dayton, it is too early for the development of an adult second generation with familial or emotional ties to the first generation. The result is too few persons at present who would seek formal training as interpreters. This lack of availability of trained interpreters is a dilemma for local organizations.

ESL CLASSES

More than half (55%) of the focus group participants have been in ESL classes. In part, this is because sponsoring organizations host ESL classes. Interestingly, none of the 11 participants in one of the focus groups, disproportionately composed of people working in nurseries, indicated they had been in an ESL class. Yet there was no significant difference between them and other focus groups in length of time in the United States.

Common difficulties included the inconvenient time when ESL classes are offered and the lack of transportation to get to them. The head of a Latino-oriented social service organization strongly encouraged work-site ESL classes, since, as she commented, "immigrants have a busy workweek."

Discussion

Language issues emerged in both the focus groups and the interviews as the most frequently identified obstacle to better incorporation into the institutional structures of the wider community. The lack of fluency in English affected the ability of a sizable proportion of Latino (and other) immigrants to make effective use of nearly every kind of institution, from health care to financial services to public education. Since the Dayton region is typical of places that until the last couple of decades have not had to adjust to large numbers of non-English speakers, its mainstream institutions did not devise policies and practices to accommodate them.

It would be obvious to recommend that learning English should be a top priority. Unlike some places where adult ESL classes are offered by public schools and community colleges, most local classes are provided by nonprofit community and faith-based organizations, a more difficult situation for responding to demands and coordinating efforts. A recent study of immigrants' incorporation and integration in Los Angeles and in California overall discusses several methods to facilitate English language acquisition that are relevant for our case. Media outlets and community organizations may be used systematically to publicize the availability of adult English language classes and their enrollment procedures. The level of classes can be adjusted for the different proficiencies of participants. Programs of self-study can be created to complement classes (Fix et al. 2008). While our findings do not directly address the process of English language acquisition, the results suggest what many other studies have concluded (Portes and Rumbaut 2006; Alba and Nee 2003). With few exceptions, immigrants who foresee their future in the United States do acquire at least a functional use of English, although doing so usually takes some years, and the extent of fluency varies widely. Moreover, their children, whether born in the United States or coming to the United States as children, not only grow up fluent in English but actually prefer it to the first language of their parents (Hakimzadeh and Cohn 2007).

For many non-English-speaking immigrants, the period when interpreters, translated material, and bilingual staff would be the most needed is during their early transitory period. Notably, these first years or first decade after arrival are crucial for immigrants to get established, find an occupational niche, get their children situated in schools, and build relationships with teachers and administrators. In other words, for working-class immigrants, the early years in their new country set the context for a trajectory toward either incorporation and generational mobility, or marginalization and prolonged, and possibly intergenerational, disadvantage. As with other subordinated populations, continued marginalization is the consequence of the interplay between individual and group characteristics on the one hand (concentration of poverty, lack of marketable skills, low levels of human capital), and the context set by institutional patterns (lack of employment opportunities, inadequate economic development, struggling school systems, withdrawal of support systems, etc.).

While some of the leaders interviewed commented that there have been improvements among some institutions in their accessibility to Latino and other immigrants, the overall perception is that too many organizations still seem to be unable or unwilling to accommodate non-English speakers. The following are some of their comments to a question concerning what institutions locally "could do or change in order to improve their accessibility to immigrants and to serve them better."

- First, recognize that this population exists, and local institutions need to accommodate it. For example, there is a genuine need for Spanish-speaking bank tellers. The Ethnic and Cultural Diversity Caucus helps, and so do various religious organizations. More broadly, there is a need for "reciprocity" in immigrant-employer and immigrant–local business relations. Local businesses need to quit thinking about how they can extract something from immigrants and begin to think a bit more about how they could benefit immigrants. (Head of one of the two Latino social service agencies in the Dayton area.)
- Promote hiring of bilingual staff. ESL classes on site, because immigrants have a busy workweek. Both these are directed at the private sector. Bilingual signage is a huge necessity. Employers should pay them as an American would be paid. ... A key to bilingual staff, especially with the police, on a domestic violence call, is that the bilingual staff be bicultural. This way, they can pick up on cultural clues, such as a woman not speaking, because as a Latina she is not allowed to speak up over her husband. (Head of the second of the two Latino social service agencies in the Dayton area.)
- Look at every point of entry from their shoes. Outreach, helping to change telephone lines to provide Spanish, checking for language accessibility, make yourself known in their community and their events so they come to trust you. (A bilingual professional who has worked for several local agencies: social service, civil rights, and family violence.)
- Hire more bilingual persons who are in touch with their communities. Provide translation services that are more inclusive. For instance, in the courts translate and help fill out paperwork for public defenders and for probation services. At hospitals, make sure that forms that are needed for medical financial assistance are filled out. Stop charging so much for services. They need to have forms in Spanish, have sensitivity training for their staff, and provide a hospitable welcoming environment for immigrants. (A Protestant minister who is head of a Dayton-area Hispanic Ministry organization.)
- Institutions should educate their workers. Often institutions have a system set in place to help immigrants, but the everyday workers who are low in the hierarchy know nothing about it. For example, of the institutions that accept the Matricula card, many of the employees don't know that they accept it. (Staff member of a local social service agency.)

• In general institutions need to relook at what they are doing to provide services to the Hispanic community. They need to have options that are accessible to those who need them. Programs need to be arranged around the working class of Hispanics. For example, one Hispanic priest holds church on Friday nights. He does this to get the Hispanic population to attend church on Friday nights instead of taking their paychecks to the bars. Institutions also need to be aware of the language barrier that exists for the Hispanic populations. (President of the local chapter of a national Latino civil rights organization.)

• The biggest thing would be the language barrier, to have a good interpreting service. Forms need to be in foreign languages. Stores need to have signs in other languages. As far as the language barrier, we need to understand that to be American does not mean you have to speak English. (Professional staff member of the local chapter of a national civil rights and antidiscrimination organization.)

• Have bilingual employees to help overcome the language barrier. (Bilingual professional staff member of a county public health clinic.)

• Hospitals need to have permanent interpreters on staff. (Hispanic ministry pastor of a local church.)

Local leaders regard much of the disadvantage that Latinos experience in employment, health care, housing, and law enforcement as the result of institutional practices. Further, they believe that these disadvantages can be reduced or eliminated by changes in practices with tandem changes in cultural and social attitudes toward Latinos.

MODELS OF ASSIMILATION

Immigrants' incorporation into American culture and institutional life has been a contentious issue, not only among the public but also among scholars, since it raises the more general issue of assimilation. *Incorporation* is often the term preferred to *assimilation*, and we have used the former throughout this chapter since it is a more appropriate term for the specific issue we have addressed.

For many scholars and activists, *assimilation* implies a negative association with the experiences of earlier immigrants, particularly those from eastern and southern Europe. The belief was that in order to become fully incorporated without disadvantage, immigrants needed, and were often pressured, to divest themselves of non-English language use and their cultural attributes crucial to sustaining an identity as a distinct group. The assumption was that maintenance of any ethnic cultural distinctiveness or attachments was an obstacle to individual and group integration. Although assimilated descendents of European immigrants may still practice "symbolic ethnicity" on special occasions or when it is appropriate to do so, these practices usually are not central to their identities, perspectives, or major life decisions (Alba 1990). They are for all practical purposes Americans.

The "older" assimilation model is most frequently associated with this process of "Americanization" (sometimes critically called "homogenization"). The work of Milton Gordon is often used as representative of this model. Alba and Nee (2003) term Gordon's work the "Canonical Synthesis" of previous studies of immigrants' incorporation, especially those of the "Chicago School." However appropriate Gordon's description of the process of assimilation for pre-1965 European immigrants might be, it did place cultural assimilation as the first of the seven stages. The process that Gordon described was that immigrants first needed to learn the culture of the host society and conform their behavior to that of the dominant group before the other stages of assimilation could unfold. Significant immigrant and ethnic cultural characteristics were jettisoned in the process, undermining the possibility of cultural pluralism and resulting in "Anglo-conformity," although Gordon himself did not endorse the latter (Gordon 1964). Current attempts at forced assimilation in states and localities include the elimination of bilingual education and the designation of English as the official language. These cultural displacements in the assimilation process are the target of current debates and criticisms.

In contrast, multiculturalism as an ideal and cultural pluralism as a description have emerged in more recent U.S. immigration studies as part of something like a dominant or preferred model (e.g., Portes and Stepick 1993; Rumbaut and Portes 2001). It is, nevertheless, hazardous to write of a dominant model today, given the diverse origins, backgrounds, and experiences of contemporary (post-1965) immigrants.

Some immigration scholars, however, contend that assimilation is continuing for contemporary immigrants, although in altered forms that place more importance on selective acculturation (Portes and Rumbaut 2001 and 2006) and institutional incorporation (Alba and Nee 2003) than did the older model. With respect to institutional incorporation, it is important to recall that *structural assimilation* was identified as the second stage of the assimilation process by Gordon. By this term Gordon meant social acceptance by dominant group, and he thought it was the key stage since, once achieved, all the other states of assimilation, such as intermarriage and decline of prejudice and discrimination, would naturally follow. Structural assimilation was controlled by influential members of the dominant group, and without it, the other stages could only be transcended incompletely. Although Gordon conceptualized structural assimilation in part as the opening of social clubs and similar organizations to participation by immigrants and minorities, one might redirect the emphasis to more formal institutions, such as those in the educational, financial, and legal spheres.

Richard Alba and Victor Nee (2003) update the assimilation approach. Like many other scholars, they understand that assimilation can occur without complete cultural absorption. They discuss studies that document different dimensions of assimilation across the first and second generations: English language acquisition, socioeconomic mobility, dispersal in residential patterns, and increasing social relations outside one's ethnic group. They define assimilation as "the decline of an ethnic distinction and its corollary cultural and social differences" (Alba and Nee 2003, 11). They emphasize the transcending of social boundaries where ethnic identity becomes less relevant for key aspects of a person's life, and individuals on both sides of ethnic boundaries come to "see themselves as more and more alike" and "perceive themselves with less and less frequency in terms of ethnic categories" (Alba and Nee 2003, 11). Such a definition is compatible with our emphasis on formal institutions, since institutional incorporation sets the context for increasing opportunities and expanding relationships.

INSTITUTIONAL OR STRUCTURAL ASSIMILATION

The need for immigrants to be integrated into institutional spheres has been a critical factor in both the older and newer models of assimilation. For Gordon, structural assimilation was the key barrier to surmount. For Alba and Nee, institutional assimilation has been eased in the post-civil rights era, as enforcement of federal rules increases the costs of discrimination. More important, mechanisms for enforcing equal rights help give different groups socioeconomic and residential opportunities that previously were denied minority group members.

One consequence of our focus on practices of local institutions is the recognition that institutional incorporation or assimilation can vary across a society given local or regional differences in the ways new immigrants are received. Regrettably, both the older and newer models do not operationalize institutional assimilation (or institutional incorporation, as we use it here) very well. In other words, there is little analysis of how this incorporation works in practice and thus little ability to assess local and regional variations. In addition, discussion of barriers or obstacles—lines of resistance to incorporation, whether intentional or not—are largely absent. In contrast, most writers on institutional assimilation emphasize either smaller, intimate organizations, like private clubs, or large-scale institutional sectors, like the job market or the economy. Both these foci seem to us to be misplaced. On the one hand, integration into more intimate contexts within the larger community is irrelevant for the incorporation of many if not most recent working-class immigrants.

Their concerns are stable employment, decent housing, good schools, and, for some, avoiding arrest and deportation. On the other, immigrants themselves do not experience the job or housing market or educational system directly. Instead, they have experiences with particular organizations, specific employers, and individual landlords, schools, teachers, and administrators.

There are several patterns that may limit the extent of institutional incorporation. One is the current economic recession. Antidiscrimination and similar laws work best during periods of economic expansion. It is no coincidence that sentiments scapegoating undocumented Latinos and demanding their removal have sharpened during the past decade of economic stagnation. In addition, immigrants enter a nation with a relatively stable racial-ethnic hierarchy. Some Latino immigrants become "racialized": they are designated as having a racial status. As was the case with earlier immigrants from South and East Asia, southern and eastern Europe, and Ireland, phenotypes play key roles in "racialization" and inhibit the ability of those so designated to overcome disadvantages.

Further, we believe most contemporary writers on assimilation do not give sufficient attention to the impact of immigration status, something far less relevant for 19th- and early 20th-century immigrants, but certainly very relevant for contemporary ones. For example, Alba and Nee (2003) only briefly mention that the unauthorized status of some immigrants may complicate their efforts to assimilate, yet this group comprises 30% of all foreign-born persons in the United States (Passel 2009). The experience with legalizing the status of almost 3 million undocumented residents under the provisions of the 1986 Immigration Reform and Control Act (IRCA) suggests that those legalized had little difficulty in taking advantages of any opportunities their newly legalized status opened up. Still, it has been over 20 years since legalization under IRCA ended in 1989. Future research will need to focus on the long-term impact of an unauthorized status on both the first generation and their children.

Conclusion: Human Rights, Mobilization, and Institutional Change

This chapter has explored the incorporation of recent Latino immigrants into local primary institutions. Our perspective is that the incorporation experience is central to the well-being and civic participation of immigrants and their children. It is also important for the nation at a time when the white population is aging, the native-born workforce is not growing at a rate sufficient to meet future labor needs, and the baby boomer generation is nearing retirement. These patterns will create workforce shortages and reduce the ranks of middle-class taxpayers even as entitlement expenditures increase. A well-integrated first generation and well-educated second would increase the numbers of workers, taxpayers, homeowners, and professionals (Myers 2007). A coordinated strategy that engages both immigrants and other stakeholders would address opportunities and challenges that are created by efforts at integration.

While we have observed mixed reactions to their presence and considerable variation in the ability and willingness of local institutions to adapt, new immigrants offer a substantial promise of local revitalization by creating immediate economic activity and vibrant cultural infusions. In places such as Dayton, many occupy housing that would otherwise be vacant, and some open businesses along streets where many previous businesses have closed. Their children bolster the numbers in a declining enrollment in public schools. As we have come to appreciate more fully during the course of this research and our involvement with immigration in the Dayton area, the incorporation of immigrants and their families is not just about their well-being and their futures but, perhaps more significantly, about the future cohesiveness and vitality of the communities in which they reside.

As with many other places, debates in the Dayton area about demographic change tend to be shaped by issues of citizens' rights that sometimes pit different groups against each other. This approach stresses individual rights and focuses only on the type of rights that nation-states permit their citizens. The result has often been polarization of contentious groups based on individual differences. Some of the conflicts are also implicitly expressed as ethnic issues, as the latter continue to be salient because of the socioeconomic gap that is correlated with ethnicity.

In contrast, human rights perspectives challenge members of civil society to cultivate intergroup trust in order to build communities around the principles of social justice and the well-being of the human person. It is particularly appropriate since the process of economic globalization has stimulated an unprecedented migration of peoples, and nation-states must find better ways to respond to that flow, including the movement of transnational labor and the well-being of families.

The Universal Declaration of Human Rights affirms the priority of personhood rights: "All human beings are born free and equal in dignity and rights." Article 2 stresses the universality of the rights: "Everyone is entitled to all the rights and freedoms set forth in this Declaration, without distinction of any kind, such as race, color, sex, language, religion, political or other opinion, national or social origin, property, birth or other status." An example relevant for our respondents is Article 26, which states in part, "Everyone has the right to education . . . Education shall be directed to the full development of the human personality and to the strengthening of respect for human rights and fundamental freedoms. It shall promote understanding, tolerance and friendship among all nations, racial or religious groups" (United Nations 1948). Such a perspective would emphasize steps to better integrate immigrant children into their schools.

Some issues and obstacles that immigrants face, including many discussed by the focus groups and in interviews, can only be addressed on the federal level. An obvious one is the lack of documents or the undocumented status of some. Legal status is a pivotal resource to racial and ethnic groups in solving some of the problems associated with class and status inequalities where they live and work. Those without a legal status have few resources in resolving their grievances. Other obstacles can be addressed on the state level, such as permitting foreign-born residents without Social Security cards to obtain driver's licenses. Labor and job standards are enforceable at the federal and state levels, regardless of the immigration status of workers. Advances in labor standards and their enforcement remain important because class inequalities themselves provide a vehicle for racial-ethnic status inequalities.

Many other obstacles, moreover, are those that institutions at the local level can reduce or eliminate. As Fix and coauthors (2008, 63) conclude, "Decisions are made every minute of every day . . . by key government administrators, elected officials, foundation officers, employers, and many other stakeholders that could be harnessed to achieve integration goals."[2] Suggestions concerning improvements in accessibility were made throughout the focus groups and interviews. The results of our study suggest that a general strategy of making organizations accessible to those not yet fluent in English would be a good starting point for many institutions that might then explore ways to confront more specific issues and obstacles relevant for immigrants' incorporation.

Some of those interviewed mentioned gradual improvements in accessibility and integration in particular areas. However, such changes have not come easily. Most have resulted from the deliberate work of local advocacy, civil rights, faith-based, and social service organizations. Together, they have made useful contacts with organizational leaders, particularly in health care and law enforcement, made repeated requests for accommodation, appealed to the self-interest of organizations, and brought to bear initiatives including training interpreters; holding educational and cultural sensitivity sessions for service providers; offering ESL and Spanish-language classes; translating documents; educating immigrants in the ways institutions work; making referrals to medical, legal, and interpreter services, family counseling centers, and battered women's shelters; sponsoring health promotion and after-school tutoring programs; offering college scholarships; and organizing social events for immigrants and long-term residents. The organizations have also served as liaisons to public health and other agencies, coordinated volunteers from local colleges, nurtured grassroots leadership among immigrants, and worked with the Mexican consulate office to promote the Matricula Consular, among other initiatives. Particularly in the absence of a preexisting ethnic community, these organizations serve as important buffers against the overt anti-immigrant prejudice and racism expressed by some residents. Some even have successfully confronted local law enforcement agencies about the apparent targeting of Latinos for arrest and deportation. As we have observed them, the local organizations have been crucial in obtaining whatever improvements have been achieved.

With the encouragement and involvement of many of the leaders of the organizations, the focus groups and interviews became the impetus for two daylong "Forums on Immigration" sponsored by our organization and held in 2008 and 2009 at the University of Dayton. The themes were institutional accessibility and the second generation respectively. Both forums integrated concerns about human rights. The target audiences were professionals in education and social services and public officials. Speakers addressed the kinds of issues and obstacles discussed in this chapter. The evaluations of both forums by those attending were overwhelmingly positive, and stimulated the hope that further changes in institutional practices will result.

The Dayton region is similar to many areas without a continuous tradition of incorporating newcomers. Different from places like New York City, Los Angeles, Miami, and Chicago, local institutions have not until recently had to adjust to people who lack knowledge of institutional patterns and English fluency. Dayton and places where significant Latino immigration is a recent phenomenon still lack a sizable number of second-generation college graduates whose parents' struggles helped inform their outlooks and who now are in professional positions in education and human services. Latino working-class immigrants are not yet in circumstances to advocate effectively for their interests, at least not on a continuous basis.

As a consequence, institutional incorporation of recent immigrants has been a piecemeal process. Organizational change has tended to involve one entity at a time. Our experiences have suggested that it is essential to mobilize a variety of groups and individuals around specific regional issues in order to produce needed change. Actions to create a more favorable institutional context for the integration of some of the most vulnerable members of the community significantly help to minimize the extent of marginalization and polarization that result from exclusion.

NOTES

We would like to thank the many individuals and organizations without whose cooperation this research would not have been possible. Among the organizations whose officials were interviewed or arranged a focus group are Artemis Center, Attorneys for Basic Legal Equality, Casa Amiga, College Hill Community Church, Del Pueblo, East End Community Services, Hispanic Catholic Ministry of Dayton, Hispanic Ministry of Miami Presbytery, League of United Latin American Citizens, National Conference for Community and Justice, and Reach Out Montgomery County (health-care clinic). We would also like to thank our students who conducted interviews with organizational leaders and helped arrange and then observed the focus groups. Finally, our thanks to Bob Stoughton of the Brother Raymond Fitz Center for Leadership in Community at the University of Dayton for his assistance in gathering the population data.

1. A social service agency in east Dayton reported that 46% of the Latino families they serve have difficulties accessing health-care resources, while 80% do not have health insurance and do not qualify for public assistance (East End Community Services 2006).

2. Other recommended works on immigrant integration include Bean et al. 2007; Fix 2007; and a publication by the Catholic Legal Immigration Network (2007).

REFERENCES

Alba, R. D. 1990. *Ethnic Identity: The Transformation of White America*. New Haven: Yale University Press.

Alba, R. D., and V. Nee. 2003. *Remaking the American Mainstream: Assimilation and Contemporary Immigration*. Cambridge: Harvard University Press.

Bean, F. D., S. K. Brown, M. A. Leach, and J. Bachmeier. 2007. *Becoming Stakeholders: The Structure, Nature and Pace of US Integration among Mexican Immigrants and their Descendants*. Washington, DC: Merage Foundation for the American Dream Symposium on Immigrant National Leaders.

Catholic Legal Immigration Network. 2007. *A More Perfect Union: A National Citizenship Plan*. Washington, DC: Catholic Legal Immigration Network. Available online: cliniclegal.org.

Fix, M., ed. 2007. *Securing the Future: US Immigrant Integration Policy. A Reader*. Washington, DC: Migration Policy Institute.

Fix, M., M. McHugh, A. M. Terrazas, and L. Laglagaron. 2008. *Los Angeles on the Leading Edge: Immigrant Integration Indicators and their Policy Implications*. Washington, DC: Migration Policy Institute.

Gordon, M. M. 1964. *Assimilation in American Life: The Role of Race, Religion, and National Origins*. New York: Oxford University Press.

Hacker, J. 2006. *The Great Risk Shift*. New York: Oxford University Press.

Hakimzadeh, S., and D. Cohn. 2007. *English Usage among Hispanics in the United States*. Washington, DC: Pew Hispanic Center. Available online: pewhispanic.org.

Hirschman, C. 2004. "The Role of Religion in the Origins and Adaptation of Immigrant Groups in the United States." *International Migration Review* 38(3): 1206–33.

Kuttner, R. 2007. *The Squandering of America: How the Failure of Our Politics Undermines Our Prosperity*. New York: Alfred A. Knopf.

Migration Policy Institute. N.d. MPI Data Hub. Available online: migrationpolicy.org.

Myers, D. 2007. *Immigrants and Boomers: Forging a New Social Contract for the Future of America*. New York: Russell Sage Foundation.

Ohio Department of Development. 2007. "Ohio Hispanic Americans." Available online: development.

ohio.gov.

Passel, J. S. 2009. "Recent Trends in Immigration: 1980s to 2009." Presentation at the conference "Immigration Reform: Implications for Farmers, Farm Workers, and Communities," Washington, DC, May 21–22.

Portes, A., and R. G. Rumbaut. 2001. *Legacies: The Story of the Immigrant Second Generation.* Berkeley: University of California Press.

———. 2006. *Immigrant America: A Portrait.* 3rd ed. Berkeley: University of California Press.

Portes, A., and A. Stepick. 1993. *City on the Edge: The Transformation of Miami.* Berkeley: University of California Press.

Rimmer, S. 1996. "A Hometown Feels Less Like Home." *New York Times,* March 6.

Rumbaut, R. G., and A. Portes, eds. 2001. *Ethnicities: Children of Immigrants in America.* Berkeley: University of California Press.

Stough, G., and C. Silva. 2006. "The Latino Community and East End Community Services Corporation." Presentation for East End Community Services, Dayton, Ohio.

United Nations. 1948. Universal Declaration of Human Rights. Available online: un.org.

Zeller, G. 2009. "Economic Indicators: Jobs and Earnings Trends in Ohio Counties, Second Quarter 2008 Update." February. Available online: www.n2net.net.

Zhou, M., and C. Bankston. 1998. *Growing Up American: How Vietnamese Children Adapt to Life in the United States.* New York: Russell Sage Foundation.

Zhou, M., C. Bankston, and R. Kim. 2002. "Rebuilding Spiritual Lives in the New Land: Religious Practices among Southeast Asian Refugees in the United States." In *Religions in Asian America: Building Faith Communities,* ed. P. D. Min and J. K. Min, 37–70. New York: AltaMira Press.

JAN L. FLORA, CLAUDIA PRADO-MEZA, HANNAH LEWIS, CÉSAR P. MONTALVO, and FRANK DUNN

The Impact of an Immigration and Customs Enforcement Raid on Marshalltown, Iowa

EARLY ON TUESDAY, DECEMBER 12, 2006, IMMIGRATION AND CUSTOMS ENFORCE-
ment (ICE) entered the Swift & Company pork-processing facility in Marshalltown,
Iowa.[1] Federal agents blocked the exits and began checking identification, sorting
workers into groups of citizens, legal residents, and those without legal documentation. Using handcuffs, they arrested 90 people, loaded them into three buses with
opaque windows, and drove them to Camp Dodge, in Johnston, Iowa, a National
Guard facility. Families, lawyers, and members of clergy struggled to get straightfor-
ward information from ICE officials about detainees' whereabouts. After 72 hours,
the arrested workers were deported or transferred to out-of-state federal detention
centers. A few were charged with identity theft, and the majority with being in the
country illegally. Five other Swift plants around the nation were raided on the same
day for a total of 1,282 workers arrested. It was the largest immigration raid on a
single company in U.S. history (Hisey 2006).

A Latino leader from Marshalltown remembers that day clearly.

> Past Christmases were really nice for Hispanics. December 12 was a really big day—it
> was memorable and a sad day because, in the night, we congregated in the church and

. . . Oh, my God, the pastor couldn't speak. Everybody was kind. It was like many people died. Everybody was crying and you saw kids crying and saying, "I want my mama." They were crying and yelling and you said, "O my God, why did they take them during this season? Why didn't they come in November or some other day? In other years I'm the one who has done the Posadas. That year, nobody wanted to attend it because everyone was so sad and so mad. . . . I don't think the people had enough money for Christmas. They had the worst Christmas in their lives. . . . We got presents for kids in the church and we tried to distribute them and we also had a lot of rallies. One Des Moines station came and gave kids presents. The kids were so happy, but later said, "I wish my mom or my dad could be here."

Background on Marshalltown, Meatpacking, and Immigration

The meatpacking industry in Marshalltown originated with a small locally owned shop, at the site of the present much larger facility. Today the Marshalltown plant is owned by JBS, a Brazilian company that purchased Swift in July 2007. The plant employs 2,400 workers and slaughters 19,000 pigs a day, according to field notes from an August 2008 tour of the Swift & Company plant by coauthors Lewis and Prado. It is the most significant employer in town. Lennox Manufacturing and Fisher Controls are two other major employers.

The growth of meatpacking in Marshalltown and associated growth of the Latino population has been repeated in localities throughout Iowa and the Midwest. The Latino population in Iowa, which was 25,500 in 1980, increased nearly fivefold to 126,500 by 2008 (State Data Center of Iowa 2009). This growth is partly related to changes in the meatpacking industry, which moved its core of operations from former urban hubs like Chicago, St. Paul, and Kansas City, to the rural Midwest, and later began recruiting low-wage workers from Mexico, the Texas border, California, and elsewhere.

The restructuring of meatpacking in Iowa originated with the founding of Iowa Beef Packers (IBP) in 1960 (Fink 1998; Broadway 1995). IBP set a precedent for a "new breed" of plant that increased mechanization, deskilled labor, and established an industry standard of packaging cuts of meat in boxes instead of shipping carcasses to retail butchers. This concentrated the work of meat fabrication on assembly lines in large plants, rather than in decentralized butcher shops. IBP is also responsible for the innovation of locating operations near feedlots to save money by purchasing livestock directly instead of through stockyards. Rural plants save the owners money on labor, too, because a rural workforce is less likely than an urban one to be unionized and more likely to accept lower wages. A series of mergers and buyouts in the 1980s consolidated the transition to this new breed of meatpacking, which is now dominated by such firms as Tyson, Cargill, Smithfield, and JBS. Swift & Company was owned by ConAgra before its purchase by JBS.

These structural changes resulted in the creation of an abundance of deskilled jobs in sparsely populated rural areas of the Midwest. As meatpackers' salaries declined precipitously, it became more and more difficult to recruit local Anglo workers. Rather than raise wages, the industry chose to recruit workers from a distance. Figure 1 shows the changes in real (inflation-adjusted) annual income per worker in the Iowa meatpacking sector plotted against changes in the Hispanic population of the state of Iowa. Clearly, the decline in meatpackers' earnings was largely completed by 1991—before recruitment of Latino workers to the Swift & Company plant in Marshalltown began to bear fruit.

In 1989, Swift began to bus Latino men into Marshalltown from Waterloo to work at the plant (Griffith 2004). This brought the first handful of Mexican meatpacking workers to Marshalltown, who in turn recruited their own friends and relatives. Thus, in 1990, there were 291 Hispanics in Marshalltown, which had a total population of 25,178. They were just over 1% of the population. By 2000, the population of the city had increased modestly to 26,009 inhabitants, but there were 3,265 Latinos, which represented 12.6% of the population (U.S. Census Bureau 2003). In 2007, the city's total population was estimated at 25,619 (State Data Center of Iowa 2009), and we estimate the Latino population at around 5,000[2]—nearly 20% of the total.

The December 2006 raid was not the first in Marshalltown. A previous raid by the Immigration and Naturalization Service (INS), also on the Swift & Company plant, occurred in 1996 and was the largest such raid in Iowa at the time. A total of 148 workers were arrested. A few months before the raid, the Marshalltown Diversity Committee (MDC) had been established. Grey (2000) chronicled the responses to the raid:

> Plant management fully cooperated with the INS and identified 300 illegal immigrants on the workforce. In order to facilitate the raid the plant even made arrangements to call in suspected employees to work on Saturday afternoon. After they were gathered in the cafeteria, detainees were taken for processing to a National Guard armory in another town. The raid caused a great deal of stress and confusion among Latinos. Families were divided. Some spouses were unable to see each other before one or the other was deported. Children found themselves stranded without either parent. Even Latinos who were in the country legally feared deportation. The raid generated a good deal of controversy in Marshalltown and around the state.

FIGURE 1. Latino Population in Iowa (1999–2008) and Average Annual Salary (in 2008 Dollars) of Meatpacking Plant Workers in Iowa (1978–2008)

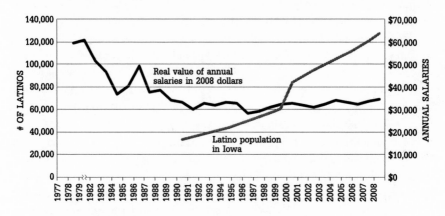

Sources: U.S. Census Bureau, 1980, 1981, 1984–1994, 2010a, 2010b; State Data Center of Iowa 2010.

Methods

The purpose of this research is to assess the effects on the community of the 2006 ICE raid on Swift & Company in Marshalltown. We collected data through structured key informant interviews, a focus group with families of persons detained or deported in the raid, and secondary sources such as local newspapers and governmental and administrative data. The key informant interviews employed the community capitals (social, human, financial, built, cultural, and political) as an organizing framework (see Flora and Flora 2008). Each interview question was linked to a community capital.

We selected subjects for key informant interviews based on their position or role in particular community institutions, such as a hospital, school, church, or city government. We were unable to secure an interview with current management of JBS Swift. For interviews and focus groups with members of families directly affected by the raid, subjects were selected through referrals from trusted leaders in the Latino community. Qualitative and quantitative analysis techniques were used to measure changes to the community capitals after the raid as compared to before the raid.

The research team was composed of an Iowa State University (ISU) sociologist as principal investigator, three ISU graduate student researchers, one Department of Sociology staff research sociologist, and two volunteers from AMOS (A Mid-Iowa

Organizing Strategy). Three pairs of interviewers conducted a total of 41 in-depth structured interviews, 10 short structured interviews with businesses, and one focus group. Two bilingual graduate students, one from Mexico and one from Ecuador, conducted five interviews and one focus group in Spanish and seven in English. Nine of the 10 interviews with local businesses were in Spanish. The rest of the interviews were in English. The Institutional Review Board of the university approved the project and all data collection instruments.

Background on the December 12 Raid

A DESCRIPTIVE CHRONOLOGY

The owners and upper management of Swift & Company knew for months a raid was likely to occur at the plant, and actively tried to prevent it (SEC 2006). ICE had subpoenaed the work documents of all Swift employees the previous March, retaining 665 belonging to Marshalltown employees. Swift claimed that an Immigration and Customs Enforcement action would violate the company's longtime participation in a federal program to verify employment documents. Attempting to clear its files of potentially false documents, Swift began interviewing its employees at several plants about their work documents in September and October. This action caused 400 to quit or be terminated. In November, Swift filed an injunction in federal court against a pending raid, which was denied. ICE had the names and addresses of all the suspected undocumented workers they sought to arrest.

On the morning of Tuesday, December 12, employees arrived before sunrise for the early shift. At about 7:30 A.M., six ICE buses pulled up to the plant and quickly secured all the exits. They entered with a warrant to arrest workers on charges of administrative immigration violation and, in some cases, identity theft. Word spread quickly through town because of the presence of the buses and a flurry of phone calls for family members to bring IDs to detainees in the plant and to family and friends to pick up children from school.

ICE never visited the schools, but there was great fear that it would. To dispel such rumors, the police chief asked for confirmation from ICE that agents would not go to the schools. He also asked for confirmation that ICE had a plan for preventing the stranding of kids and dependent adults whose caregivers were arrested. ICE's plan was to ask detainees if they had a dependent, and to release those who did if they were the only caregiver. But employees were uncertain of ICE's intentions and thought that if they mentioned their kids, they would arrest them too. So many said nothing and in cases where both parents were arrested, neither was released that day to take care of the children.

Workers were initially separated by race and nationality. Those who appeared to be American citizens were moved into the cafeteria and held there for questioning, while legal immigrants and persons suspected of being unauthorized were held separately. The ICE agents did not always guess right who was a native-born citizen and who was not. Here is part of the story of Michael Graves, a United Food and Commercial Workers' Union member, a long-term employee at the plant, a former student at Iowa State University, and an African American whom we interviewed and who also testified at the UFCW hearing in Des Moines:

> [M]e and two other coworkers . . . [were] going our normal route to the cafeteria. . . . ICE agents that [were] heavily armed met us at the door and asked us where we [were] going. We told him we were going to the cafeteria as we were instructed to go. He asked us, did we have any weapons on us and did I have any identification? I told him I had [my identification] in my locker. He told us to get against the wall and handcuffed us from behind.
>
> So then he escorted us to the locker room . . . and asked me where my locker was . . . he took me to my locker and asked me for my combination. . . . I gave him my combination, he opened my locker, and he asked me, did I have any weapons in my locker? And I said no, I don't have any weapons. So he searched my locker, he went through my clothes and my equipment and everything and found no weapons. He asked me, where's my identification? I told him it was in my pants pocket. So he went in my pants pocket, pulled out my identification, and questioned me about [it.] He asked me where I was living and I told him I was living in Waterloo, Iowa. And he questioned me, why was I working in Marshalltown? I said, well, this is the place I wanted to work and I've been working here, at that time, for 20 years.
>
> [H]e questioned me about my status as a U.S. citizen and I said my mother and father were born and raised in Mississippi. He questioned me about that and asked me, did I know my route to Mississippi? And I said no, but I can find my way there because I had been there a lot of times with my parents. He looked at my ID again, told me to sit down with my hands behind my back, still handcuffed. (Michael Graves, quoted in United Food and Commercial Workers 2009, 16)

Graves was still handcuffed an hour later when he was taken to the cafeteria where other citizens were being held. He was not allowed to use the bathroom until he finally arrived at the cafeteria. He was released eight hours after he had been detained. Manuel Vedínez, also a U.S. citizen, was handcuffed and taken with other detainees to Camp Dodge, the National Guard facility some 60 miles from Marshalltown in the afternoon because ICE could not find a match for the Social Security number he gave them:

They found my record . . . and said they had made a mistake. Then [the ICE agent] finally took off my handcuffs . . . [T]hey called a cab for me and I had to pay $90 for the cab ride back. I was not allowed to leave that place until 8 P.M. I was detained by the ICE agents for more than 12 hours. During that time I was not able to move around anywhere without permission from ICE agents. . . . I had even been handcuffed for about 9 hours. I had done nothing wrong that would give . . . ICE agents any reason to believe I had done anything wrong, or that I deserved to be handcuffed. (Manuel Vedínez, quoted in UFCW 2009, 19)

ICE asked Swift & Company for a blueprint of the building so agents could thoroughly search the premises; they asked managers to show them through the building to find anyone who might have tried to hide to avoid arrest. In midafternoon, three buses filled with 90 detainees pulled out of Marshalltown for Camp Dodge for further processing.

On Thursday, a small group of single mothers was released to return to Marshalltown to care for their children. Legal advocates and clergy had lobbied ICE to release single mothers. On Friday, all the detainees were moved from Camp Dodge to federal prisons around the country, or they were deported. The people held in prison (principally one outside of Atlanta) awaited trial. Family, clergy, and counsel of the detainees say ICE would not tell them where family members had been moved. Immigration lawyers that were involved claim ICE violated detainees' rights to due process by limiting their access to legal counsel. ICE said people were moved so far away from home because that's where there was space in federal facilities (Rood 2006).

A couple of days after December 12, ICE returned to Marshalltown with a list of six identity-theft suspects that were not arrested in the raid. Officers in plainclothes went to these houses and found and arrested one person (Black 2006). Several months later, on September 28, 2007, local police (including the Marshalltown police) conducted a raid at a Monsanto plant in Grinnell, in a neighboring county. They arrested 16 people on forgery and identity theft charges. Marshalltown residents had been subcontracted by Manpower to work at Monsanto. ICE assisted in checking identities but did not participate in the raid, but the Marshalltown police initiated and conducted the raid (Burke 2007a and 2007b).

INITIAL COMMUNITY RESPONSE TO THE RAID

The immediate concern in the community the day of the raid was to identify children whose parents had been detained, and to ensure and coordinate their care. To do so, a list of detainees was needed. Many people disappeared that day, but not all were detained. Some left town and some went into hiding. A list of detainees would help responders identify which households to visit or call to check that children had not been stranded. Several parties requested this information from ICE, including the local chapter of the Red Cross, Mayor Gene Beech, and Police Chief Lon Walker. ICE was unwilling to release a list, however, so the community assembled one on its own based on whatever local information could be gathered.

In addition, the school district helped identify all possible households with dependent children of detained parents. Each school was instructed to account for all of its own students. Counselors, teachers, and others used a list of emergency contacts to contact each household and determine who was there and would be responsible for providing care for the students. In some cases, schools had to send children home with unauthorized caregivers, in which case they called third parties to verify the relationships. (For the longer term, power-of-attorney forms were provided to detained and deported parents through ICE and the Mexican Consulate, respectively, to be signed and faxed back to caregivers. These forms would enable guardians or caregivers to get medical care for children and pick students up from school.)

Two other critical needs were to coordinate financial assistance for families that had lost one or more wage earners, and to get information about detainees. In particular, family members needed to find out where detainees had been taken, how to contact them, what was happening to them, where they were going to be moved, and what legal recourse families could take. To find out whether a particular person was in custody and how to get in touch with him or her, people were instructed to call ICE's family hotline. Because of the high volume of calls, though, people were put on hold for long periods, and a second hotline was eventually established (on December 14). Family members, clergy, and lawyers reported difficulty getting information about, and getting in touch with, detainees.

The Hispanic Ministries at St. Mary's Catholic Church became the central place for people seeking information and solace, and it was also the hub for coordinating a collaborative response among local service organizations. The first of three meetings was called at St. Mary's on Wednesday, December 13, for community leaders to figure out how to respond to the emergency. It was established that the Red Cross would coordinate information flow among the key organizations and individuals helping or supporting affected families and the community as a whole. The Red Cross received all relevant information (the family hotline number, visitation hours, how attorneys could gain access to detainees, when community response meeting would be, etc.), verified it, and packaged it in daily emails to community leaders. Multiple emails per day were sent in the first days after the raid. Hispanic Ministries disseminated this information to the immigrant community.

On Friday, December 15, the church hosted a town hall meeting, which was coordinated by the Iowa Division of Latino Affairs. Those present included state and local officials, Latino community leaders, school representatives, and pro bono lawyers, who explained the deportation process. The lawyers met with families to assess their situation and immediate needs (Pierquet 2006).

The church received donations that flowed in unsolicited from individuals and organizations in Marshalltown and throughout Iowa and beyond. More than $100,000 was received and distributed to families through the church. This included a contribution of a few hundred dollars per family from Swift, $20,000 from a local foundation, and $5,000 from a foundation in Minnesota. Other companies contributed gift cards for food and gasoline, and the LIHEAP (low income heating assistance) program was used to reduce the heat bills for households of people not working because of the raid. The United Way received Swift's donation to affected families, and funneled money to Hispanic Ministries to disburse, keeping a tab of each payment.

In addition to a coordinated response between St. Mary's Church, the Red Cross, and other leadership and service organizations, there was a range of individual demonstrations of support or assistance. Many community members volunteered to take in children, and a list of volunteers was provided to Hispanic Ministries. The offers were generally not taken up, though, because extended family members took on responsibility for care of children of detainees. A few days after the raid, a service organization that administers programming to families visited homes to check on financial and other needs. Many community and service organizations with regular contact with immigrants made an effort to reassure people that certain places were safe and would not be visited by ICE, and by answering questions and directing people to resources they needed.

Library attendants assisted people in faxing paperwork and finding information on the Internet (such as legal services). A realty firm offered to help people stuck with a house if their name was on the mortgage of a house being paid for by somebody who was deported. They advertised the house for free and basically did all the work of selling the house at a break-even rate. In addition, everyone in that real estate office contributed money to send to St. Mary's.

The media helped by putting a human face on the story of the raid (see Jacobs 2006). This may have increased pressure on ICE to release single mothers to care for kids. Later, in February 2007, the *Marshalltown Times-Republican* held a summit on immigration to help people understand immigration issues and policy and to make a unified call for reform. This was held at Marshalltown Community College.[3] The newspaper sent tapes and transcripts to several U.S. senators and representatives. In April 2008, the United Food and Commercial Workers (UFCW) held a public hearing in Des Moines to investigate ICE misconduct, which featured testimony of people from Marshalltown and outside volunteers involved in the raid response.

Impact of the Raid: A Community Capitals Analysis

All communities have resources of various kinds. If those resources or assets are invested to create new resources, then they become *capital.* One kind of capital, whether social, human, cultural, or financial may be transformed into another kind of capital. One capital can also detract from another, particularly when one capital is emphasized over all others. In this chapter, we will assess the short-term and longer-term impacts of the ICE raid of December 12, 2006, in terms of the following capitals: social, financial, human, political, and cultural.

SOCIAL CAPITAL

Social capital is often defined to include the networks, norms of reciprocity, and mutual trust that exist among and within groups and communities. It contributes to the formation of groups, a sense of a common identity, a shared future, and ultimately to groups working together for a common purpose (collective action). Of particular relevance to this study is the distinction between bonding social capital (multiple linkages to enforce norms and encourage trust, usually among individuals and organizations that are similar to one another in background, experience, and outlook) and bridging social capital (single-purpose linkages between individuals and groups that are different from one another) (Flora and Flora 2008, 18, 125–31). We will examine bonding social capital within the Anglo and Latino communities and bridging between the two groups and how those patterns were affected by the raid to assess whether the ability of the entire community to engage in collective action has been enhanced or hampered by the raid.

THE BACKGROUND LEVEL OF COMMUNITY SOCIAL CAPITAL

Generally, Marshalltown is viewed as a friendly community by Latino newcomers and long-term European American residents alike. Over 90% of each group of interviewees disagreed with the statement, "It is hard to make good friends in Marshalltown." When we asked them to respond to the statement, "Marshalltown is welcoming to newcomers," there was a slight difference between the two groups: 95% of Anglos agreed, but only 84% of Latinos did. Even those who consider relations between Latinos and European Americans (or Anglos, as we will refer to them from here on) to be fair or poor, still consider it to be a friendly town. Some emphasize that it is a community of many civic organizations and churches.[4]

It is likely that the level of bonding social capital among Latinos has increased over the past decade or more. One thoughtful young Latino stated that before the raid, "Parks were always full. Always, public places, as they say, bars were always full on weekends." Others cited strong church attendance, the constitution of a 16-team soccer league (organized by Latinos in Action), the existence of a Latino activist organization (Latinos in Action), and the establishment of a Hispanic Festival two years ago. With respect to school involvement, a religious leader observed,

> I would say that as more and more [Latino] parents have kids who are involved in sports, they go to those things. I think they are feeling more and more welcomed to the school events. I know a lot of parents who will go when there is a concert for the kids. The kids are not real [sic] into band or anything like that but the grade school kids—when they have their little programs, the parents go. And that is a tradition in Mexico. They have those kinds of things.

A Latina social service provider stated, "I have noticed that in the last 10 years . . . everyone is related to everyone pretty much here in Marshalltown." The Latino population of Marshalltown, like many other meatpacking communities in the Midwest, has followed a "maturing" process whereby individual men were first attracted to work in the plant, and in time they brought their families. A substantial number bought homes, and increasingly they began participating in community life.

BONDING SOCIAL CAPITAL

■ *Impact of the raid on bonding social capital among Latinos.* Many Latino leaders felt that trust among immigrants had increased subsequent to the raid. A majority of Anglo leaders were reluctant to venture an opinion on the effect on Latino immigrant solidarity, and those who did were likely to see little change in immigrants' trust of one another (see figure 2). A couple of people mentioned that immigrants who are documented are more concerned for those who are undocumented than they were before. The more activist Latinos tended to see an increase in group solidarity. Although there was less participation in day-to-day public activities such as going to church, the reduction in public engagement did not lead informants to argue that bonding among Latinos had decreased. The effort by the police chief to get the city council to pass an ordinance so that the police could act on behalf of ICE in arresting people suspected of being unauthorized (known as a 287(g) agreement) led to a protest by some 175 people, organized by Latinos in Action in April 2007. One person remarked that persons with and without documents participated in the protest. In addition, business leaders were apparently active behind the scenes in opposing the ordinance.

FIGURE 2. "Following the ICE raid on December 12, 2006, would you say that the level of trust among immigrants increased, stayed the same, or decreased?"

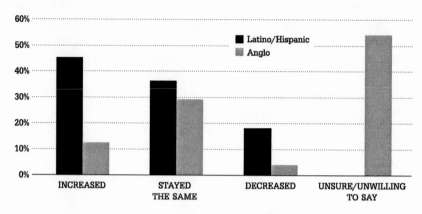

Note: 11 Latinos and 24 Anglos responded.

■ *Impact of the raid on bonding social capital among Anglos.* Anglo and Latino leaders were similar in their views on the impact of the raid on Anglo solidarity: a plurality of Anglos (40%) and a majority of Latinos (60%) felt that trust among Anglos had not changed because of the raid. Anglos were more likely to indicate either an increase or decrease in trust among Anglos than were Latinos. Perhaps Anglos viewed their own group through slightly more discerning eyes than Latinos saw them. A couple of people felt the raid increased solidarity among Anglos who were active in support of Latino families. Another small number indicated that Anglos were divided, as did this Anglo leader:

> I think that the neighbor versus neighbor . . . came out after [the raid.] Both sides showed
> up and I think that among themselves, the bickering may have decreased the trust level
> a little bit. . . . I know of two [Anglo] neighbors who don't like to talk to each other now
> because of it, which is sad. The raids don't actually even directly impact them, and they
> allowed it to come between them.

Marshalltown is a community that over more than a decade leading up to the ICE raid had made great strides in encouraging Latinos to feel like members of the community, and to gradually engage along with their Anglo counterparts in public activities for the common good. There is no doubt that the ICE raid brought at least a temporary halt, and perhaps a sharp reversal, to the construction of bridging social capital between Latinos and Anglos in Marshalltown. It gave license to

FIGURE 3. "How would you describe relations between recent immigrants and persons born in Marshalltown?"

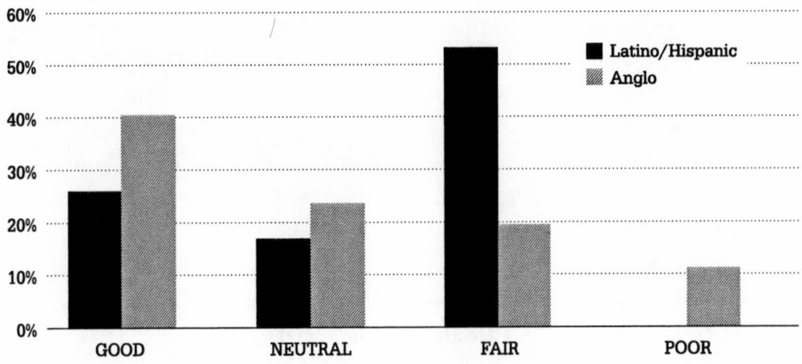

Note: 11 Latinos and 24 Anglos responded.

those who held views opposing the presence of unauthorized immigrants—with spillover effects on documented immigrants and, indeed, Latino citizens—to engage in anti-immigrant statements, and at least in some instances, to actively insult or discriminate against Latino residents. On the other hand, the raid generated bonding social capital among Latinos and bridging social capital with a small, but important number of Anglo social service providers and community leaders who pitched in to ameliorate the effects of this "unnatural" disaster. The long-term effects of the raid on community social capital are still not clear.

BRIDGING SOCIAL CAPITAL BETWEEN ANGLOS AND LATINOS

■ *The background level of bridging social capital.* While Marshalltown is viewed by most, regardless of ethnicity, as a town where one can easily make friends, when respondents were asked "How would you describe relations between recent immigrants and persons who were born in Marshalltown?" the modal response of Anglo leaders was "Good," while the majority of Latino leaders said relations were only "Fair" (see figure 3). No one chose "Excellent." It is interesting that three Anglos chose the "Poor" response; none of the Latinos did.

Interviews with Anglos and Latinos suggest that discrimination and exclusion still exist. Anglos are featured in the following quotes (statements by Latinos experiencing discrimination are in a later section):

I think there are a lot of misconceptions . . . that a lot of the "old school" Marshalltown people think that immigrants brought all of the drugs and the raids and everything with them. (Social service provider)

I've been in Wal-Mart with my wife and we have watched as someone would walk up to the cashier, take one look at the cashier, and realize that she's Hispanic and then move over an aisle. (Media person)

We have had people who left our parish because of the Hispanics. We have had people complain that they don't think the Hispanics are paying their fair share—assuming their fair share of the responsibility financially—and have left. I don't see a whole lot of crossover. Language is obviously a problem. There probably are more Hispanics who come to the English Mass than vice versa, which means that the Hispanics are learning English and the Anglos are not learning Spanish, or they just don't feel comfortable in that situation, or there is no need to go. (Religious leader)

An astute Anglo observer summarizes the situation as follows:

In Marshalltown I feel there are still two distinctive communities, and I don't feel the two communities are fully interfaced. . . . My sense is that this is evolutionary and it takes a while and if you look back at the history of any immigrant [group]—there was a large Polish community at the turn of the century in here and very similar sorts of things happened. They were in a certain part of town and they worked in a certain industry and they had certain kinds of places that they were more likely to organize themselves and get together. Over time, that changed. So I don't know enough to know if we are on the same course with the newest wave of immigration into this community or not. It seems to be like that is happening. But again if I go to a party at a friend's house, there is not likely to be a whole bunch of immigrants there. I have relationships with some folks, but they tend not to be social relationships. But I don't see in certain institutions that there is full melding. (Social service provider)

■ *Impact of the raid on bridging social capital among Latinos and Anglos.* Two thirds of Latino leaders felt that trust between Latinos and Anglos after the raids had decreased following the raid (see figure 4). However, most Anglos, in about equal proportions, believed trust had either remained the same or decreased. A few Anglo leaders felt that trust between the two groups had actually increased. (We address that sentiment later in this section.) Clearly, the group most directly affected by the raid was less sanguine about the raid's effect on intergroup trust.

Many who believed that trust had decreased thought that it was a short-term phenomenon, but a few Latino and Anglo leaders said that the raid had done such

FIGURE 4. "Following the ICE raid/Swift raid on December 12, 2006, would you say that the level of trust between immigrants and long-term residents increased, stayed the same, or decreased?"

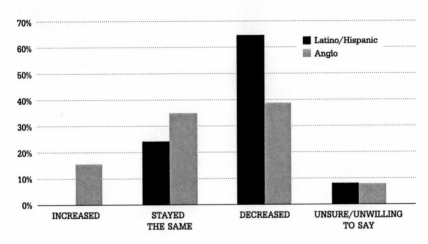

Note: 12 Latinos and 25 Anglos responded.

damage that relations would take many years to recover. A Latino leader stated, "What happened was that, with the raids, everything was thrown out the window, what had calmed began all over again. We lost all the work we had done." An Anglo media person echoed some of the same sentiments:

> The sad part is that when you look around, [Latinos] are buying homes, they are buying cars, they are buying groceries; they are integrated 100% that way, but the animosity in the community is stronger than it has ever been before. The day those raids came through, it kicked it up a notch back to earlier levels. People crawled out of the woodwork like you wouldn't believe. We ran a special section a year after the raids, and the number of comments—we actually had to disable comments on our website because of the problems we had with people complaining: "All you people do is write about the sad, sad story. Have you forgotten what the word 'illegal' means?" Well, actually, if you look, the people we wrote about weren't illegal. We wrote about the impact it had on those who are here legally. So that has been tough.
>
> I think we took 20 years of stepping forward and in one hour on that morning, we went back 20 years right away. I think it took that little of time to take a massive step backwards.

The impact on immigrants, whether documented or not, was palpable. It is most notable in the case of this worker who was arrested at the Swift plant and later released. A year and a half later, she is still anxious:

> For me everything changed as a result of the raid, because now I live in fear. I don't feel secure in my own house . . . and even when I just see a policeman, he arouses fear in me.

A Latina professional explains the climate following the raid and how her job changed as a result of it:

> Yet again, when this immigration thing happened at Swift, they [immigrant Latinos] were kind of staying low for awhile. They wouldn't go to church as much. You wouldn't see them out—most of the time you would see families out at McDonald's or Hardees, but you didn't for quite some time. I think they are just now starting to come out [again] but with a little bit of fear. So there has been a big difference—I mean even with just me. Everybody in Marshalltown knows me, and if it is a new family that I need to enroll, it's hard because if you go nicely dressed, they won't open the door for you. Even [especially if] you are wearing black or dark blue, they won't open the door for you. You have to wear different colors just because they relate that with immigration, and you don't want that.

Some Latinos reported instances of discrimination that they believed resulted from the raid:

> I think that some people took a great dislike to us, based on an incident that occurred to me several months ago. I go to the House of Compassion [a soup kitchen and emergency relief agency] occasionally, and in this instance I took my children. We set out walking and when the children and I arrived, according to my son the person in charge asked if we wanted coffee and crackers and if we did, invited us to sit down. Since we were pretty hot, I said to my son, "Let grab some water." There were some *gabachos* [slang for North Americans or Anglos] who were playing dominos, and I felt uncomfortable because they turned around and stared at me and my children and then said something. I asked my son what they were saying and he told me they asked what are we doing here. And wasn't it true that we just came to ask for what really belonged to *them*? I said, "Why are they bothering us if they came for the same reason?" So I felt very badly because never before in my life had I had *gabachos* be so ugly to me. So I said to my children, "No, we had better go," and I grabbed them and we left. My daughters left their glasses on the table, and they [the domino players] said to the children that they should not leave the glasses there, and that we should wash them carefully because they could infect someone. My son took the

glasses back and said, "Ay, Mommy! They are saying we must wash the glasses so that we won't infect anyone." I had never had something happen like what occurred that day.

Following the raid, another Latina professional noted that clerks asked her more frequently for her driver's license. She also experienced an instance of harassment in a retail establishment:

Actually, I was being served and then that person just got close to me and put his hands on me a little bit and pushed and I said, "Excuse me, I was here first." He was just making faces, no words, and that is the first time—and I had been in Iowa for 21 years—and that is the first time that I have ever experienced something like that.

There is another side of the solidarity or trust question that involves collaboration of Latinos and Anglos in organizations that were central to developing collaborative responses to the raid. Figure 4 shows that none of the Latino leaders interviewed felt that intergroup trust had increased, while 16% of the Anglos did. An Anglo leader explains:

What I saw was sort of the disaster phenomenon, this outpouring of compassion. People in this area really care about other people, and they really respond when they know that people are hurting and it has been caused by some event. . . . so there was a strong wave of compassion and community, and "these are our people too." And the whole method—ICE probably couldn't have engineered any better to create negative feelings toward ICE and empathy toward those rounded up. I think just like the patriotism and the sense of unity we saw after September 11, a huge outpouring of support and compassion that we saw after Hurricane Katrina, it was that same kind of thing. (Director of social service agency)

While the raid caused great suffering, community disruption, and some enmity, a keen observer of the situation, taking the long view, has an optimistic assessment of bridges that are being built between Latinos and long-term residents. When asked whether trust between the two groups had increased or decreased over the years, she stated,

I would say that generally it has probably increased because people have more neighbors who are Hispanics. They have worked with them and their kids are friends with them. They see them on the street; they go to church with them. They work next to them, so I think in that way they have become more than just these people who are foreigners here who don't speak the language. They have become real people to a lot of them. And I think a lot of them have heard people's stories too after the raids. They heard stories about, "This is why we came and this is why we are here and this is our situation." So, like I say, it kind of put a human form to this immigration thing.

FINANCIAL CAPITAL

Financial capital consists of money or financial instruments used for investment, but not for consumption. Financial capital is the easiest of all capitals to measure, and is thus most frequently used as a yardstick for progress, although often it is not the most appropriate measure. Financial capital can be measured at the individual, family, organizational, firm, community, or other levels beyond the community (Flora and Flora 2008, 18, 175–79).

The ICE raid affected the economic environment and the performance of both consumers and businesses in Marshalltown. This section examines the economic effects of the raids, with a special emphasis on variables such as retail sales based on sales taxes, employment change, and labor turnover. The last section analyzes some of the perceived effects from Latino businesses in Marshalltown based on a set of interviews conducted with the owners of the businesses from January to April 2008.

Marshalltown is the primary economic center within Marshall County, Iowa. In 2007, the U.S. Census Bureau estimated that Marshalltown had a population of 26,073 inhabitants, with 12,817 persons (63% of all adults) in the labor force. The median income of a household in Marshalltown is $35,688 annually. At least 12.5% of the population lives below the official poverty level, and during 2007 unemployment for the Marshall County as a whole was estimated at 4.1%.

The major industries and leading employers in the city of Marshalltown include JBS Swift, Lennox Manufacturing (heating units and air conditioners), and Emerson Process Management Fisher Division (divisional headquarters of a control valves and systems company) among others. JBS Swift (Swift & Company at the time of the raid), a company dedicated to meat processing, is the largest employer in Marshalltown. JBS is considered the largest beef producer in the world. The plant in Marshalltown possesses a pork-processing capacity of 17,200 head per day (SEC 2005).

EFFECTS OF THE RAID ON FINANCIAL CAPITAL

We did not have sufficient funds to carry out a study showing overall employment effects of the raid in Marshalltown, so we have relied on secondary data collected for other purposes, and on the interviews we conducted, which must remain anecdotal. Still, it is evident that the raid contributed to an economic slowdown, although the length of that slowdown is not clear. We begin the analysis of financial capital with an assessment of the raid's effect on Swift and Company.

Representatives of Swift & Co. reported losses of approximately $50 million as a direct result of the raids conducted by ICE in six of their meatpacking plants, including the processing plant in Marshalltown. The estimated costs of the raid included losses in operating efficiency, since new employees had to be trained, and a package of $10 million to maintain current workers and offer incentives for new hires. According to Swift authorities, the pork plant based in Marshalltown returned to normal production levels after March 2007 (Storck 2007). Additionally, the company expressed concerns for the negative third-quarter earnings. It had lost $9 million before interest payments, taxes, amortization, and depreciation were calculated.

Employment within the food industry in Marshalltown (a sector dominated by Swift and Company) decreased by more than 150 employees in the quarter following the raid, but within six months employment had returned to the pre-raid level. Swift and Company lost production time and, as indicated above, encountered additional training expenses following the raid. The average monthly earnings of new hires at the Marshalltown plant increased substantially in the quarter in which the raid occurred and then receded to a level only slightly higher than before the raid (Iowa Workforce Development, 2009). The immediate increase in wages was an effort to attract new employees to bring the operations of the plant back to normal.

We learned the following regarding financial capital from the interviews:

From one of the banks we learned that at least 20 Latino families with accounts in that bank left town following the raid. About half returned later. New people came into town and the persons who left were eventually replaced by new accounts, but the new people were often not Latinos.

It was estimated by a knowledgeable person that balances in the bank accounts of Latinos declined by some 15% due to the raid.[5] It was estimated to have taken eight or nine months for the balances to return to previous levels.

This bank handles half a dozen accounts for Latino businesses. In visiting with the proprietors, the interviewee indicated that all had experienced sharp declines in their business following the raids. The interviewee believed that their businesses had not yet fully recovered more than a year later. This conforms to the interviews conducted with 10 Latino businesspersons reported on in the next section.

A realtor who handles the Hispanic clients for one agency sold 15 fewer houses in 2007 than in 2006. The value of sales to Hispanics fell by one-third. In addition, there were about a dozen foreclosures on homes owned by Latinos; two-thirds involved families that were deported or left following the raid. Foreclosures on Latino families increased 50% over 2006, although part may have been due to the overall mortgage crisis.

The administrator of a low-income nutrition program indicated having lost Latino clients as a result of the raid, and found it difficult to recruit new ones. It was necessary to ask a number of personal questions in order to determine eligibility and to get them enrolled. People were afraid to provide the information because they feared it might be used against them. Initially, the clientele dropped to half its usual number and it took about six months to get back to the number of clients the administrator had prior to the raid.

Hispanic Ministries raised $120,000 in donations from both inside and outside the community to cover emergency needs of the families affected by the raid. The monetary losses of those families were much greater than the funds donated through the United Way and dispensed by Hispanic Ministries.

Business performance was negatively affected by the decrease of consumer purchases in the city of Marshalltown in the period in which the raid occurred. The main indicators used to assess such a decline are retail sales per capita and changes in real retail sales. The Regional Capacity Analysis Program (ReCAP) at Iowa State University has calculated real per capita sales over time for cities in Iowa and makes comparisons by category of city.

Fiscal year 2007 ran from July 2006 to June 2007. Thus, the raid occurred near the middle of FY2007. Marshalltown had experienced declines in real sales since 2003. In FY2006, a negative growth of only 0.5% perhaps signaled a leveling off after this continuous period of sales decrease. However, an important decrease in real sales (−3.2%) was once more recorded in FY2007, which encompassed the ICE raid (see figure 5). The decline, however, was less than in four of the previous six years. In FY2008 sales recovered 2.3% from the previous year.

The quantitative data just presented is inadequate to prove by itself that the raid of the Swift plant in December 2006 was the primary factor affecting taxable sales. From the interview data we know that immediately after the raid, there was a sense of fear among the Latino population that constrained families from engaging in grocery shopping, dining out, or even visiting the downtown, which, at least temporarily, reduced the demand for goods and services in the city.

FINANCIAL CAPITAL CASE STUDY: EFFECTS ON LATINO BUSINESSES

The following are comments by Latino business owners:

In January 2007 we did not sell anything.
I will also have to leave the town because this town has not stabilized yet.
I am traveling to sell my merchandise to other towns, even going to Missouri.
I have almost seven years in business, but after the raids I lost all sales.
My sales in the business were very low all the year. We say that even if it is a bad year, people do not stop eating. But this year was bad for businesses.

FIGURE 5. Annual Percentage Change in Real Retail Sales: Marshalltown, Iowa

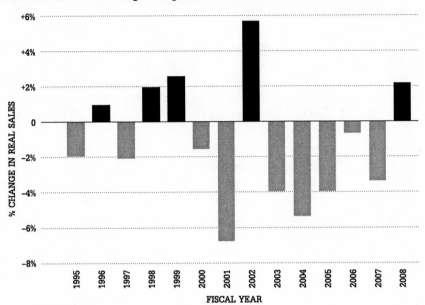

Source: Regional Capacity Analysis Program 2009.

> I have my business in front of the Swift Company. Sales decreased a lot.
> Economically, we lost a lot. A lot of people left.
> It took two or three months to come back to normality.

According to the Iowa Department of Revenue (2008), Marshalltown generated $320.1 million in sales during 2006. In the same year, a survey conducted by the Marshalltown Hispanic Business Development (Cardenas 2006) determined that Marshalltown possessed 55 Latino businesses in different sectors, including retail services (29%), auto repairs (18%), restaurants (16%), food products (11%), and construction and painting (5%). Eleven food-related businesses reported sales of $3.1 million during that year, which represents 21% of total sales in the food sector in Marshalltown.

During the first quarter of 2008, our team interviewed 10 Latino business proprietors in Marshalltown. These businesses are in four different sectors, including food sales (grocery stores and restaurants), retail clothing sales, liquor store retailing, and auto repair services. The majority of businesses were restaurants, and their main clientele is the Latino population. Additionally, businesses like clothing stores and liquor stores provide money-wiring services as a complementary activity to increase their sales.

Businesses that offered goods and services to the Latino community declared significant drops in sales after the period of the raid. The base of customers of Latino businesses was undermined as people left, were deported, or returned to Mexico to join members of their families who were detained. Latino customers refrained from making purchases in order to save money in case of future economic hardship or a need to leave Marshalltown. As indicated earlier, one respondent said there was a steep decline in housing sales to Latino clients.

Several Latino businesses, especially clothing stores, reported losses due to people leaving the city without paying some debts. Some owners commonly offer informal credit to regular customers. One of the owners interviewed reported $70,000 in losses due to families that left Marshalltown without canceling their debts. The value of remittances, if calculated according to the commissions obtained by merchants from wiring money internationally, dropped suddenly by 70%. Sales decreased for these businesses by nearly two-thirds, according to the rough estimates of the interviewees.

Latino businesses in the food and beverage sector reported a sharp decrease in the number of customers per week after the raids. During interviews, every proprietor mentioned having lost at least 50% of his or her customers immediately after the raids. A year after the raid, several of the Latino business owners indicated that their sales had still not returned to previous levels.

These losses by Latino businesspersons were not shared by Anglo proprietors. In FY 2007 and 2008 eating and drinking establishments and food stores showed a modest overall increase in real sales over the previous two years, while apparel sales held steady (Regional Capacity Analysis Program 2009). The different patterns for Latino and Anglo businesses indicates that the ethnic economy is not well integrated into the larger economy of the community.

HUMAN CAPITAL

Human capital is the skills, abilities, and experience of each individual within a community. Human capital was first popularized by T. W. Schultz, who received the Nobel Prize in Economics for his development of the concept in 1979. Schultz considered human capital to consist of education, training, work experience, migration, and health. Leadership skills are also part of human capital (Flora and Flora 2008, 18).

The general economic slowdown in the first years of the twenty-first century seems to have affected Marshalltown, as measured by retail trade, but also by

FIGURE 6. Population Estimates, Marshalltown, Iowa, 2000–2008

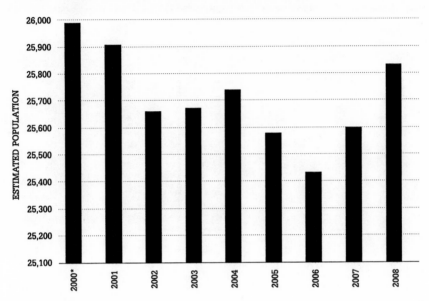

*2000 Census figure, not an estimate.
Source: State Data Center of Iowa 2009.

population. As figure 6 shows, the population of the city began declining in 2001. According to Census Bureau estimates, the city's population showed a modest downward trend from 2001 to 2006 and then began recovering in 2007.

Marshalltown's general economic and population stagnation during much of the past decade was not due to a decline in the Latino population. Figure 7 shows a steady increase in Latino population in Marshall County (more than 90% of Latinos in the county live in Marshalltown). While there is reason to be skeptical about the Census Bureau population estimates, the consistent growth in Latino population is reinforced by an equally robust growth in Latino school enrollment in the Marshalltown Community (public) schools[6] – until the ICE raid. Figure 8 shows that Latino public school enrollment in fall 2007 grew only 4.6%, the slowest rate of growth since the end of the 1980s, when there were fewer than fifty Latino students in school. In the fall of 2008, Latino student enrollment barely grew at all (less than 1% over the previous fall). Total enrollment of all students in the district (PreK–12) declined nearly 2% or 90 students, although the loss was recuperated in Fall 2009. From 2008 to 2009 there was an increase in total enrollment of 97 students and in Latino enrollment of 172. While the ICE raid clearly disrupted the educational

FIGURE 7. Latino Population (Marshall County, Iowa), Employment in Food Manufacturing, and Latino School Enrollment (Marshalltown, Iowa), 2000–2008

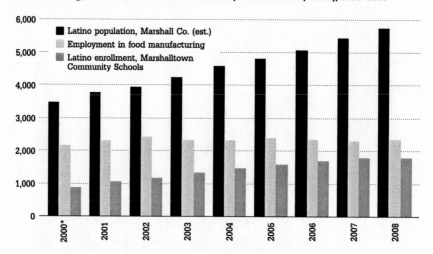

Sources: State Data Center of Iowa 2010, Iowa Workforce Development 2009, Iowa Department of Education 2010.
Note: For the 2000–2001 school year, enrollment occurs in fall 2000 and appears above "2000" in the figure.

FIGURE 8. Change in Latino/Hispanic School Enrollment from the Previous Year, PreK–12, Marshalltown Community (Public) Schools, 2002/03 to 2009/10

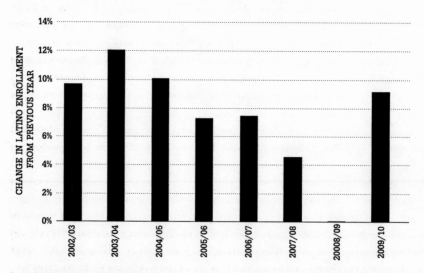

Source: Iowa Department of Education 2010.
Note: Enrollment is reported in the fall of the year.

process for a time, in less than three years after the raid Latino enrollments had surged once more, exceeding 40% of total enrollment. The raid (apparently) did not slow the growth in Latino population in Marshall County.

The rather steady employment level in the meatpacking plant (figure 7) throughout the past decade (apart from a dip in employment of 150 workers in the quarter following the raid), coupled with the continued increase in the Latino population, suggests that Latino residents are diversifying their livelihood strategies to depend on less on meatpacking, although JBS/Swift is still the largest employer of Latinos in Marshalltown. This diversification offers the opportunity for Latinos and immigrants in Marshalltown to develop a more diverse set of skills, strengthening their collective capacity to contribute to the community as a whole.

In order to use existing quantitative data in assessing the effect of the ICE raid on human capital associated with the meatpacking sector of Marshall County we had to use data from the food-processing sector as a whole. JBS Swift is by far the biggest food-processing company in Marshalltown, with approximately 2,200 to 2,400 employees. Perhaps 100 or so of the workers in that sector are not employed by JBS Swift.

Swift & Company makes up nearly the entire private food-manufacturing subsector in Marshall County.[7] Based on the information from Iowa Workforce Development, figure 9 shows annual turnover percentages from 1999 through 2005 and quarterly turnover percentages for the period 2006 to 2009. The turnover rate is the number of persons hired during the quarter divided by average employment during the same period times 100. While the turnover for this industry is always high[8] compared to other manufacturing subsectors, the level reached in the last quarter of 2006 (19.8%) cannot be considered normal. This contrasts with turnover rates of around 6% from 2004 to the middle of 2006 and in the 7% to 9% range from 1999 to 2003 (Iowa Workforce Development 2009). The turnover rate has slowly declined, but remained at or above 10% for the three quarters following the raid and above 8% until the third quarter of 2009 when it dropped to 7.3%. The turnover rate rose to 8.5% in the quarter preceding the raid, perhaps because of anticipatory firings of suspected undocumented workers by the company, which at the time was in negotiation with ICE in an attempt to avoid a raid. The high turnover rate the quarter that preceded the raid could also be due to job abandonment by some workers because rumors of a possible raid were circulating through the plant and the community.

Another way of looking at the impact of the raid on the plant is as follows: in the nine quarters preceding the raid the number of separations per quarter averaged around 260. In the quarter that included the raid (fourth quarter of 2006), that number rose to 1,022, even though only 90 persons were detained and deported. Separations were about double the pre-raid period for nearly a year, and by the

FIGURE 9. Quarterly Turnover Rate in the Private Food-Manufacturing Sector, Marshall County, Iowa

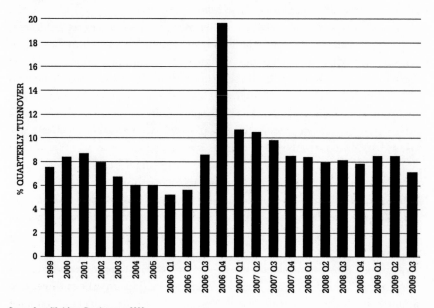

Source: Iowa Workforce Development, 2009.

fourth quarter of 2008—two years after the raid—they were still more than 50% greater than the pre-raid level. This suggests a continuing challenge for the company to find reliable and productive documented or native workers.[9] Since most workers have families, this turning over of employees suggests an even larger "churning" of community residents. Schools and other community helping organizations and agencies such as the police are faced with an expanding numbers of newcomers. This greater turnover of residents likely makes it more difficult to maintain previous levels of social capital, although we were not able to gauge that change.

POLITICAL CAPITAL

Political capital is the ability of a group to influence the distribution of resources by determining what resources are open to consideration, what governs the distribution of those resources, and what incentives and disincentives will apply to their investment. Organization, connections, voice, and power are among the components of political capital (Flora and Flora 2008, 18).

As in other rural communities in the Midwest and South with new immigrant populations, Latinos in Marshalltown generally lack political capital. The fact that most are not citizens reduces their options for formal participation in representative democracy (voice). Perhaps more important is the fact that a substantial unauthorized population makes many people reticent to participate in government-sponsored activities, and even activities in civil society. This reticence extends to many individuals with legitimate documents who are also Latino, particularly if they are part of a "blended" family (a family that includes members at different stages in the documentation process). They are full participants in the market and are more likely to shop locally than are European American residents. However, Latinos may encounter barriers to starting a business. A few of the Latino professionals we interviewed serve on civic boards and as officers of organizations, but most have been in the United States for some time or were born here. No Latino serves as an elected government official in Marshalltown.

What effects did the raid have on political capital of Latinos and immigrants? Interestingly one respondent indicated that the raid had spurred some immigrants to seek the help of Hispanic Ministries in obtaining U.S. citizenship, but that option is open to only certain immigrants. The immediate effect of the raid was to reduce participation in community affairs. However, there was an important exception—opposition to the request by the police chief that his department be authorized to request proof of authorization to be in the United States, and to turn persons without proof over to ICE (a so-called 287g agreement between ICE and local or state law-enforcement units). Latinos in Action organized a demonstration of 175–200 people to oppose such an ordinance, and it did not even reach a vote by the city council.

CULTURAL CAPITAL

Cultural capital determines how we see the world, what we take for granted, what we value, and what things we think possible to change. Important "filters" that shape cultural capital include race, class, gender, religion, ethnicity, and national origin. It includes one's *cosmovisión* (worldview), common symbols, ways of knowing, language, and ways of acting, and a common definition of what is problematic (Flora and Flora 2008, 18, 53–81).

The church—whether Catholic or Protestant—plays a central role in the lives of Latinos in Marshalltown. A Latino leader points out the central role of the Virgin Mary in various manifestations in the lives of Hispanic Catholics in Marshalltown:

> From a religious point of view, it goes without saying that the church has been an active participant, because people bring their traditions. One could say that the nun who is

in charge of Hispanic Ministries explains that there are two images, right?—one of the Virgin of the [Immaculate] Conception, who is the patron saint of the parish, one of the oldest parishes in this area, and the other is that of the Virgin of Guadalupe, placed there in the entrance to the church. And the sister says, "I will not be content until this image of the Very Holy Virgin is there in the center." And she succeeded. It has been there for quite some time in place of the image of the Immaculate Virgin, which was moved to the side. The Virgin of Guadalupe is now permanently in the front [of the church]. In sum, I think that the immigrant community has given this community [of Marshalltown] a great deal of dynamism.

Perhaps the most poignant example of cultural insensitivity was ICE's choice of the date of the raid, the Day of the Virgin of Guadalupe, as is explained by a Latina leader in the quote at the beginning of this chapter.

Anglos and Latinos in Marshalltown (and in other rural communities in Iowa) share many values: a love of small towns (many immigrants lived in metropolitan areas—Chicago and Los Angeles, prior to arriving in Marshalltown), family, community festivals, and in many cases an appreciation of agriculture. Many of the Latino immigrants come from rural parts of Mexico—particularly the *ranchito* (small agricultural community) of Villachuato, Michoacán—or from Central America. There is an appreciation among both groups of crops and animals. However, these similarities are manifested in culturally different ways, as is evidenced from the discussion of an interviewer with a city official.

INTERVIEWER: In terms of ordinances, are there any ordinances that restrict, such as chickens, poultry?

OFFICIAL: We do, we have an ordinance that restricts poultry/fowl. It came about—we were getting complaints about chickens, roosters in the morning, things like that. So we adopted that. It has been relatively recent that we adopted that. Maybe two to three years ago, that they not be allowed in residential—

INTERVIEWER: In city limits?

OFFICIAL: Right, in residential zones. All farm animals are part of this same section. We have regulations about horses, with that, one, you can keep them but there are some restrictions: so many acres and so many feet from the house. If you go under the code of ordinances, it—there is a chapter on animals.

INTERVIEWER: Do you get a request for horses across a variety of ethnic groups?

OFFICIAL: No, mostly Anglos, but we only get a couple of requests a year.

For a number of years, the Fourth of July was a multicultural celebration, with food, fashion shows, and music that featured the diverse cultural heritages of the current residents of the town. More recently a Hispanic Heritage Festival was initiated by Latinos. It is held in late spring. In addition, as one Anglo observer indicates,

> Even Oktemberfest, which is purely an excuse to bring marching bands to town and have fun and have a parade and have a blast, has become very cultural. You will find food vendors . . . I would say they almost outnumber your traditional food vendors, the Hispanic vendors and they are awesome food. I gain 10 pounds that weekend usually, every year. You know from that end of things on the social part of it, they [Latinos] are very, very good at getting involved in those types of events. Oktemberfest is not *their* Hispanic Heritage Festival, but you will see them around the courthouse. You will see them at our downtown Christmas event—you will see them there with food booths or even dancing demonstrations. At Oktemberfest they will do dancing demonstrations up on the stage, which is fun to watch. So, as far as social networking goes, they integrate themselves very well, I think. At least I think they offer to be involved, which is really neat.

Language and nationality are also important parts of culture—and create misunderstandings between Anglos and Latinos. Regarding nationality, a Latina businessperson remarked lightheartedly,

> The people don't make distinction. Everybody thinks that they [immigrants] are Mexican. . . . The other day somebody told my husband—and it is so funny because this guy says, "This Mexican from Puerto Rico. . ."
> My husband was laughing and said, "Oh, do you know geography?
> And they say, "Yeah."
> "Well, Mexico is not in Puerto Rico. Do you know that Puerto Rico is part of the United States and they are citizens and this 'Mexican' is a citizen and he is not a Mexican?"

Other misunderstandings are more consequential. The chief of police participated in one of several trips taken by groups from Marshalltown trip to the city's "sister" community in Mexico: Villachuato, Michoacán and as a result made—and acted on—the following observations:

> When I came back from my Mexican trip, one of the issues that we saw was that a lot of people don't know what the laws are and we created a "Welcome to Marshalltown" video in Spanish . . . because when I was being interviewed by a reporter in Morelia, the reporter asked, "Mr. Police Chief, why are you here?" "By understanding the cultural barriers I can do a better job at establishing a better working relationship and trust between new immigrants, the police department, and the city of Marshalltown." I thought I answered it fairly well, and the reporter had a real quizzical look on her face and said, "I don't

understand: why do you need to have trust?" And I thought about wow, there are more cultural barriers than I ever imagined.

Most of the immigrants felt that there was a mistrust of government officials, in particular police, particularly as they had to pay bribes to the Mexican police just to get to the border to get here. Most people will obey most of the laws most of the time if they know them. So this video is short and amateurish as it was made on zero dollars budget. We explained the facts that cops don't take bribes, talk about the laws that may be unique to Iowa or Marshalltown. You can't park in the front lawn because there is a new law that prohibits that. You can't drink in the parks. What a tornado siren is, because that is probably a pretty scary sound to an immigrant. That was something we did to improve relations.

Language poses greater difficulties. Several Latinos indicated or provided illustrations that suggest that those who do not speak English well experience greater discrimination and will have more problems accessing services, particularly local governmental services. Following the 1996 raid, the community college established the Education and Training Center in downtown Marshalltown to encourage the acquisition of English-language and other skills.

In short, Marshalltown is becoming a multicultural town. Latinos and immigrants are learning to fit in, to participate in community life, but they also seek to maintain—or reinvent—cultural capital from their places of origin. This sometimes separates them from their Anglo neighbors, but it also offers those neighbors the opportunity to experience new food, customs, and ideas—if they choose to take advantage of the opportunity.

Conclusion and Summary

In 2000, former governor Tom Vilsack named Marshalltown one of three model communities because of its success in integrating immigrants into the community (Woodrick 2006, 291). The police chief, the mayor, and several others visited Mexico to learn more about the new members of the Marshalltown community. Although rarely has there been mixing of Latinos and Anglos in intimate settings like each other's houses, other events, such as citywide festivals, parks, and school sporting events have drawn a brown and white tapestry of family participation. Best of all, kids have been learning each other's language at a premier bilingual elementary school, blazing a bicultural path for future leaders. In spite of a murmuring in quiet corners of anti-immigrant sentiment, the official face of Marshalltown has been consciously painted as a welcoming place, and perhaps hearts have been slowly following suit.

The 2006 raid in many ways pushed this pattern (of progress in bridging social capital) into disarray, and gave voice to suppressed resentment among a minority of Anglos unwilling to accept the fact of immigration. Distrust between Anglos and Latinos increased, according to the perception of many. Attitudes were similar following the INS raid in 1996, after a community forum organized by the Marshalltown Diversity Committee between residents and the head of the INS office in Omaha:

> The meeting was well attended with more than 100 people present.... the INS official ... was very careful to explain the plant's cooperation and how the civil rights of detainees were ensured by the presence of members of the Iowa Commission on Latino Civil Rights.
> ... Some anger was expressed by both Anglos and Latinos, and the union accused the INS of discrimination because Anglo workers had passed through the checkpoint on the basis of skin color alone. Union leaders were also angry that they were not allowed access to their members who were in detention.
> ... As long as civil rights were ensured, many in Marshalltown (both Anglo and Latino) were willing to make distinctions between deserving and undeserving immigrants. This attitude clashed with the point of view of most Latinos and some service providers, to whom such distinctions were fundamentally irrelevant. To them, the INS raid made it clear that the central question was not legal but concerned human rights. As a poster in one Latino restaurant read, "No Human Being Is Illegal." (Grey 2000, 95)

The ICE raid resulted in a localized economic recession for at least a half-year after the raid. Based on the high turnover rate at JBS Swift into the first quarter of calendar year 2008, it is likely that the plant has not yet returned to the level of efficiency in the period prior to the raid in 2006. Compounding these local effects are the effects of the mortgage crisis and the recession, which began to be felt in rural Iowa in late 2008.

At the same time, however, the situation threw people and groups together as a disaster sometimes does. Anglo- and Latino-led community organizations and individuals rolled up their sleeves and figured out how to rescue children, families, and the community in the immediate aftermath of the raid. The community came together with leaders from around the state in an immigration summit for a group learning and strategy session on how to improve immigration policy. Recently, in a yearlong effort, service agencies and organizations, local authorities, and other immigrant-serving organizations that responded during the raid, developed a raid preparedness plan should another raid occur.

Among Latinos, the perceived increase in bonding social capital has mobilized people to find their voice politically, as demonstrated by the protest against the proposal to initiate a program whereby local law enforcement personnel would be trained to check the papers of persons stopped for other reasons and to arrest and hold them for ICE if they lack documents. In addition, authorized immigrants are diligently pursuing their citizenship.

The raid prompted the Marshalltown community as a whole to engage in a conversation about immigration and community that it might not otherwise have had. New relationship and new alliances have developed, particularly among social service agencies and organizations that represent Latinos. There is a greater awareness of what can be done collaboratively at a local level to protect families and the community as a whole from the damage wrought by immigration enforcement actions. The new bridging social capital and political capital embedded in those new alliances will need to be nurtured.

Still, as in the earlier wave of INS raids in the late 1990s, the fundamental issues have not been addressed by most people in Marshalltown, nor by the state or nation as a whole. Quoting Grey after the 1996 raids:

> INS raids across the state revealed how deeply dependent packing plants are on Latino immigrants. Most criticism in the state and local press, however, targeted the immigrants and not the plants.... Very few openly acknowledged that meatpacking could not survive without immigrants, even though immigrants in general took the political heat when so many were discovered to be in the country illegally. Most critics sought deportation for the illegal immigrants. Very few believed settlement of immigrants was the answer. (Grey 2000, 96)

Regarding changes in policy today, the good news is that workplace raids have been stopped by the Obama administration. However, there is increased emphasis on arresting persons at their places of residence who, early in their stay in the United States, knowingly or unwittingly failed to appear in court when summoned. The threat of having ICE agents show up at their homes is just as scary for immigrants as is a workplace raid. (At least one home raid occurred in Marshalltown the weekend of March 20–21, 2009.)

Even if ICE raids were to stop, the fact that many immigrants lack proper documents means that they and family members, regardless of status, will remain on the margins of community life rather than feeling comfortable contributing fully to their communities. With greater emphasis by the Obama administration on employer sanctions, it becomes increasingly difficult for unauthorized immigrants to obtain formal-sector jobs and accompanying employer-provided benefits (Rood 2009).

Increasingly, in meatpacking communities like Marshalltown, as immigrant children pass through the K–12 system and graduate from high school, the prohibition against undocumented youth paying in-state tuition at the postsecondary level will prevent them from acquiring the formal skills that would make it easier for them to fulfill the American dream of intergenerational social mobility. However, it is estimated at the national level that nearly three-fourths of children with at least one unauthorized parent were born in the United States and are therefore citizens. This group represents 20.5% of all Hispanic children in the United States (Fry and Passel 2009). Children of immigrants, whether citizens or not, can serve as a strong magnet for keeping their parents in this country. When parents are deported, minor children often stay to be educated, creating a difficult family situation.

Apart from the economic contribution of immigrant workers (see Pearson and Sheehan 2007; a number of other studies are cited in Immigration Policy Center 2007), there are powerful humanitarian reasons for immigration reform that would allow unauthorized immigrants already in this country to regularize their status. They are already contributing considerable financial capital to our country and the communities in which they live. Immigration reform would also strengthen human, social, environmental, and political capital in communities where new immigrants live. Immigration reform that regularizes the status of unauthorized residents is urgent.

Short of comprehensive immigration reform, important policy changes would be to pass the DREAM Act (which gives undocumented youth in-state tuition). It would also be fair for the states and the federal government to compensate community schools more fully for the extra expenses incurred in teaching English as a second language classes and encourage school districts to adopt voluntary dual-language programs. The federal government receives billions of dollars in unclaimed Social Security taxes and withholding taxes from unauthorized immigrant workers. Those funds could be provided to communities to educate children of unauthorized immigrants and to otherwise integrate the newcomers into the community. Other policy changes that could be taken while waiting for Congress to act on comprehensive immigration reform include cessation by ICE of writing 287(g) agreements with local law enforcement agencies. These agreements allow officers to check documents of individuals suspected of a crime or a traffic violation and to turn the individuals over to ICE if they do not produce appropriate documentation. This program can easily encourage law officers to engage in racial profiling. Employer sanctions for hiring unauthorized workers should be sharply curtailed while sanctions for violation of labor standards involving vulnerable workers (including immigrant workers in low skilled positions) should be intensified.

Much can be done at the state and local level. In packing-plant communities, it is imperative that new job alternatives be made available to immigrants and others who are injured or "worn out" by work on the disassembly line (Fink 1998; Nebraska Appleseed 2009). Under Governor Vilsack, Iowa established New Iowans Centers across the state in communities where there are large numbers of immigrants.[10] These centers are administratively under Iowa Workforce Development and help immigrant workers to diversify their employment opportunities.

In Marshalltown, a coalition of organizations including MCC, Iowa State University Extension, the Leopold Center, Iowa Rivers Resource Conservation and Development, the National Center for Appropriate Technology, and the Marshalltown Chamber of Commerce are developing a local food system that includes a beginning farmer training program and farm incubator, so that immigrants and others can become vegetable and fruit farmers and supply locally grown food to retail and other outlets in the community (Kilen 2009; Black 2009). In addition, research is being conducted in Marshalltown and five other packing plant communities on Latino and female retail entrepreneurship so that effective Extension and other outreach programs can be devised for these "minority" entrepreneurs. ICE raids, whether at the workplace or in people's homes, are at least a temporary setback to these efforts to improve community and family quality of life.

NOTES

The authors are grateful to Sheryl Rippke and Jan Gray, volunteers from A Mid-Iowa Organizing Strategy (AMOS) in Ames, Iowa, for conducting several of the interviews. The research was funded by the Northwest Area Foundation, St. Paul, Minnesota.

1. On the same day, ICE raided Swift & Company plants in Greeley, Colorado; Cactus, Texas; Grand Island, Nebraska; Worthington, Minnesota; and Hyrum, Utah. A total of 1,282 persons were arrested and charged. Most were charged administratively with being in the country without legal documentation; 67 were charged with identity theft, including two in Marshalltown (Hisey 2006).

2. The Census Bureau estimates Marshall County's Hispanic population at 5,455 in 2007 (Regional Capacity Analysis Program 2008). No estimate was made for the city, but if Marshalltown continues to have 92.4% of the Latino population, as it did in 2000, we extrapolate the city's Hispanics to number 5,040.

3. MCC is a branch of the Iowa Valley Community College. The two are referred to interchangeably.

4. These questions about whether Marshalltown is a welcoming community were asked at the beginning of the interview, that is, prior to discussing the raid, and were designed to gauge the level of community social capital from the point of view of both Anglos and Latinos without explicitly taking into account the effect of the raid.

5. The interviewee estimated that half of Latino (personal, not business) bank accounts experienced a decline and that the decline for that half of savers was about 30%.

6. Annual Latino/Hispanic public school enrollment in the Marshalltown public schools grew at an even faster rate in the 1990s, ranging between 20% and 52% (Iowa Department of Education 2010).

7. Knowledgeable persons in Marshalltown indicate that the plant in recent years has employed between 2,200 and 2,400 persons. The private sector employment in "food manufacturing" since 2004 has ranged between 2,300 to nearly 2,500. Thus the numbers of food-manufacturing workers employed somewhere other than at JBS/Swift probably ranges around 100.

8. Personal interview with a former employee in the management of Swift.

9. The pattern with respect to new hires was similar to that of separations. For the period 2000–2005, new hires averaged 280 per quarter, while in the two years following the raid, nearly 500 new hires had to be trained each quarter. This suggests lowered productivity as new workers struggle in the first few months to gain the proficiency of their more experienced co-workers (Iowa Workforce Development 2009).

10. "Anyone new to Iowa, whether they arrived from Honduras or New York City, can also find assistance and help using IWD services at the New Iowan Centers. The centers are designed to support workers, businesses, and communities with information, community service referrals, job placement, translations, language training, and resettlement assistance, as well as technical and legal assistance concerning forms and documentation. There are 12 New Iowan Centers located in: Muscatine, Ottumwa, Mount Pleasant, Storm Lake, Iowa City, Mason City, Des Moines, Sioux City, Council Bluffs, Denison, Orange City and Marshalltown" (Iowa Workforce Development 2009, 8).

REFERENCES

Black, K. 2006. "ICE Returns to Marshalltown as Investigation Continues." *Marshalltown Times-Republican,* December 16.

———. 2009. "Local Foods System the Subject of Grassroots Effort." *Marshalltown Times-Republican,* September 15.

Brasher, P. 2006. "Swift Raids Largest in American History." *Des Moines Register,* December 14. Available online: www.dmregister.com.

Broadway, M. J. 1995. "From City to Countryside: Recent Changes in the Structure and Location of the Meat- and Fish-Processing Industries." In *Any Way You Cut It: Meat Processing and Small-Town America,* ed. D. D. Stull, M. J. Broadway, and D. , 17–40. Lawrence: University Press of Kansas.HYPERLINK "http://www.amazon.com/Any-Way-You-Cut-Processing/dp/0700607226/ref=sr_1_1?ie=UTF8&s=books&qid=1235587697&sr=1-1"

Burke, A. 2007a. "Grinnell Seed Company Workers Jailed in Marshall County." *Iowa Independent,* September 29.

———. 2007b. "Marshalltown Police Jail 16 Workers Arrested in Grinnell." *Iowa Independent,* October 2.

Cardenas, M. 2006. "Marshalltown Hispanic Business Development Project." Unpublished study conducted for the Marshalltown Chamber of Commerce.

Fink, D. 1998. *Cutting into the Meatpacking Line: Workers and Change in the Rural Midwest.* Chapel Hill: University of North Carolina Press.

Flora, C. B., and J. L. Flora. 2008. *Rural Communities: Legacy + Change.* 3rd ed. Boulder, CO: Westview Press.

Fry, R., and J. S. Passel. 2009. "Latino Children: A Majority Are U.S.-Born Offspring of Immigrants." Pew Hispanic Center, Washington, DC, May 28. Available online: pewhispanic.org.

Galinsky, S. 2007. "We're Workers, Not Criminals!" *The Militant,* May 7.

Grey, M. A. 2000. "Marshalltown, Iowa and the Struggle for Community in a Global Age." In *Communities and Capital: Local Struggles against Corporate Power and Privatization*, ed. T. W. Collins and J. D. Wingard, 87–100. Athens: University of Georgia Press.

Grey, M., and A. Woodrick. 2002. "Sister Cities: Meatpacking Labor Migration between Villachuato, Mexico, and Marshalltown, Iowa." *Human Organization* 61: 364–76.

Griffith, D. 2004. "'It's All Right to Celebrate': Latino Immigration into Marshalltown, Iowa." Project Report for Towards a New Pluralism: New Immigration into Rural America, Fund for Rural America, U.S. Department of Agriculture in Cooperation with Aguirre International.

Hisey, P. 2006. "Nearly 1,300 Swift Workers Detained; Company Returns to Operation." December 14. Available online: www.meatingplace.com.

Immigration Policy Center. 2007. "The Economic Impact of Immigration." Available online: http://www.tindallfoster.com/ImmigrationResources/policypapers/TheEconomicImpactOfImmigration2.pdf.

Iowa Department of Education, 2010. "Iowa Public School PreK–12 Enrollments by District, Grade, Race and Gender," Basic Educational Data Survey. Available online: www.iowa.gov/educate/index.php?option=com_docman&task=cat_view&gid=391&Itemid=1563.

Iowa Department of Revenue. 2008. Statistical Reports of Sales Taxes. Available online: http://www.iowa.gov/tax/taxlaw/taxlawst.html.

Iowa Workforce Development. 2009. "LEHD State of Iowa County Reports: Quarterly Workforce Indicators." Available online: www.iowaworkforce.org/lmi/lehd.html.

Jacobs, J. 2006. "Mom, Kids Spend 3 Days in Agony." *Des Moines Register,* December 16. Available online: www.dmregister.com.

Kilen, M. 2009. "Latino Farmers Remember Their Roots." *Des Moines Register,* September 13. Available online: www.dmregister.com.

Nebraska Appleseed. 2009. "'The Speed Kills You': The Voice of Nebraska's Meatpacking Workers." Nebraska Appleseed Center for Law in the Public Interest, Lincoln. Available online: www.neappleseed.org.

Pearson, B., and M. F. Sheehan. 2007. "Undocumented Immigrants in Iowa: Estimated Tax Contributions and Fiscal Impact." October. Iowa Policy Project, Mount Vernon. Available online: www.iowapolicyproject.org.

Pierquet, G. 2006. "Church Packed for Town Hall Meeting." *Marshalltown Times-Republican*, December 17.

Potter, A. 2007. "Latino Businesses Felt Long-Term Effects from Raids." *Marshalltown Times-Republican*, December 12.

Regional Capacity Analysis Program. 2008. "Hispanic/Latino Population Estimates." Available online: www.recap.iastate.edu.

———. 2009. "Retail Sales Analysis & Report for Marshalltown, Iowa: Fiscal Year 2008." Iowa State University Retail Trade Analysis Program, ISU Extension. Available online: www.recap.iastate.edu.

Rood, L. 2006. "Stop Aggressive Raids, Advocates Plead." *Des Moines Register*, December 16. Available online: www.dmregister.com.

———. 2009. "Obama's Immigration Policy Targets Employers." *Des Moines Register,* May 2. Available online: www.dmregister.com.

Securities and Exchange Commission (SEC). 2005. "S&C Holdco 3, Inc." Annual Report Pursuant to Section 13 or 15(D) of The Securities Exchange Act of 1934 for the Fiscal Year Ended May

29, 2005. Available online: www.secinfo.com.

——. 2006. Press releases exv99w3 and exv99w4. Available online: www.secinfo.com.

State Data Center of Iowa. 2009. "Population and Numerical and Percent Change for Iowa's Incorporated Places: 2000–2008." Available online: www.data.iowadatacenter.org.

State Data Center of Iowa. 2010. Race and Hispanic or Latino Origin in Iowa's Counties: 2000–2009," State Library of Iowa, State Data Center Program (released June 10). Available online: http://data.iowadatacenter.org/datatables/CountyAll/coracehispanic20002009.xls.

State Data Center of Iowa and the Iowa Division of Latino Affairs. 2009. "Latinos in Iowa: 2009." State Library of Iowa, Des Moines. Available online: www.iowadatacenter.org.

Storck, A. B. 2007. "Swift Returns to Standard Staff Levels, Revises ICE Raids' Financial Impact." May 14. Available online: www.meatingplace.com.

United Food and Commercial Workers. 2009. "Raids on Workers: Destroying our Rights" Available online: www.icemisconduct.org.

U.S. Census Bureau. 2010a. "1998–2008 County Business Patterns (NAICS): State data." CenStats Databases, last updated July. Available online: http://censtats.census.gov/.

U.S. Census Bureau. 2010b. "1993–1997 County Business Patterns (SIC): State data." CenStats Databases, last updated July. Available at: http://censtats.census.gov.

U.S. Census Bureau. 1980, 1981, 1984–94. "County Business Patterns1978, 1979,1982–92." Washington, DC: U.S. Government Printing Office.

U.S. Census Bureau. 2003. *U.S. Census of Population, 1990, 2000.* American Factfinder. Available online: factfinder.census.gov.

Woodrick, A. C. 2006. "Preparing the Way: Hispanic Ministry and Community Transformation in Marshalltown, Iowa." *Urban Anthropology* 35(2–3): 265–94.

LYDIA P. BUKI, JENNIFER B. MAYFIELD, and FLAVIA C. D. ANDRADE

Health Needs of Latina Women in Central Illinois: Promoting Early Detection of Cervical and Breast Cancer

LATINOS NOW CONSTITUTE THE LARGEST ETHNIC MINORITY GROUP IN THE United States (U.S. Census Bureau 2008b). As such, they have contributed more than half of the population growth (50.5%) in the United States in the 21st century (Fry 2008). Although most of the growth has taken place in geographical areas that historically have been home to a large Latino population, fast growth has occurred in smaller urban and rural areas in which the Latino influx is a relatively new phenomenon (Cunningham et al. 2006). With increased geographic dispersion of the Latino community, attention has been drawn to health coverage and access of Latinos in "new growth" communities (Cunningham et al. 2006). In this chapter, we focus on central Illinois, an area that has seen significant growth in the last decade. Specifically, we present a needs assessment addressing issues of health coverage, access, and psychosocial factors influencing cervical and breast cancer screening in Latina women residing in two central Illinois counties. Seventy percent of the data (n = 85) was collected in Champaign County, one of the 148 counties in the United States that experienced slow Latino growth in the 1990s but above average growth in the 2000s (52% growth 2000–2007; Fry 2008). The remainder of the data (n = 35) was collected in Vermillion County, a county directly east of Champaign that is home to a population of Latinos clearly on the rise (19% growth 2000–2007), though growing at a slower rate than in Champaign (Pew Hispanic Center 2009b). Local institutions in these areas are just beginning to grapple with public health issues experienced by the growing Latino population. One such issue that requires attention is cancer prevention and control.

Among Latinas, cancer disparities are evident in incidence, mortality, and survivorship (American Cancer Society 2006). Latina women have higher incidence and mortality rates from cervical cancer, and lower five-year survivorship rates from breast cancer, than non-Latina white women (Edwards et al. 2005; Jemal et al. 2008). For both of these cancers, early detection procedures are the best strategy to ensure cervical and breast health (U.S. Preventive Services Task Force 2002a; 2002b). Despite the existence of these procedures, data show that late detection contributes to health disparities in this population; Latinas are not screening according to the recommended guidelines (American Cancer Society 2006). For instance, data from 2003 show that prevalence of cervical cancer screening in the last three years is lower for Latinas (74.7%) than for non-Latina white women (80.2%), with women of Mexican descent and immigrant women having the lowest rates of screening (American Cancer Society 2006). Therefore, it is critical to promote regular screening in this population.

To increase rates of screening, scholars have proposed that in the design of interventions, we need to incorporate women's cultural, psychosocial, psychological, and geographical realities if we are to influence their screening behaviors (Buki, Salazar, and Pitton 2008; MacKinnon et al. 2007; Rajaram and Rashidi 1998). However, to date, there has not been an investigation of how these contextual factors may influence Latina women's screening rates in central Illinois. In this effort, we report on a needs assessment conducted with 120 women from four small urban and rural areas in central Illinois: Champaign, Danville, Hoopeston, and Rantoul. Because of the fast Latino growth experienced in the area and the fact that most newcomers are primarily Spanish speaking, the infrastructure is not available yet to serve the health needs of newcomers effectively (Champaign County 2003). Therefore, data from this needs assessment are needed to tailor educational interventions and prioritize efforts, thereby optimizing the use of resources while improving health outcomes.

Growth of the Latina/o Population in Central Illinois

Latinas constitute 11% of the women in the United States. It is projected that this figure will increase to 16% in 2020 and 24% in the year 2050 (U.S. Census Bureau 2008b). Overall, 12% of residents in the United States identify as Latina/o, with 77% of Latinos residing in seven states, namely Illinois, Arizona, New Jersey, California,

Texas, New York, and Florida (U.S. Census Bureau 2008b). Illinois, which is home to 4% of the country's Latino/a population, has emerged as a fast growth state. Latinos in Illinois are expected to represent 9% of the U.S. Latina/o population by the year 2025, increasing at a faster rate than that expected for Latinos in New York or Texas (Champaign County 2003; Waterman 2001). Consistent with the fast growth of the Latino population seen so far in the 21st century, there has been an influx of Latinos into small urban and rural areas (Cunningham et al. 2006). Within Champaign County in Illinois, Latinos comprise at least 4% of the population in the city of Champaign and 3% in the city of Rantoul (Champaign County 2003). In Vermillion County, just east of Champaign County, Latinos comprise at least 5% and 8% of the cities of Danville and Hoopeston, respectively (U.S. Census Bureau 2008b; Warner and McLaughlin 2002). These statistics probably do not fully reflect the presence of Latinos in the area (Champaign County 2003). Many Latino residents, in particular migrant workers, have been hesitant to either participate in the census data collection or to fully disclose their household numbers (Amaro and Zambrana 2000), possibly because fear of negative repercussions from the government.

The fast-paced growth of the Latina/o community has placed significant strain on the social infrastructure of many cities in Illinois (Champaign County 2003). A critical needs analysis performed by the Champaign County Regional Planning Commission found that enhanced service delivery was needed in Champaign County in health care, employment, and education (Champaign County 2003). Relocating to work in low-skill labor sectors, Latinos enter a new system of health provision that is ill equipped to meet their needs. The fact that at least 35% of Latinos in fast-growing communities are primarily Spanish speaking (Fry 2008) creates a new need for Spanish-language service provision. For instance, the majority of hospitals and clinics in Champaign County do not have bilingual personnel for their reception areas and information services desks, and professional medical interpreter services are provided by telephone (Champaign County 2003). Within the Champaign County Planning Board analysis, participants reported feeling distanced from their health-care providers and perceived receipt of lower quality of care (Champaign County 2003). Their sense of isolation may have been compounded by the fact that a third of Latinos coming into these areas are not U.S. citizens (Fry 2008), posing additional barriers to health-care access.

Factors Influencing Cancer Screening

There are several factors that may contribute to low cancer screening rates in new growth areas, particularly those such as central Illinois that are geographically isolated from major metropolitan centers: (1) approximately a third of Latinos in these areas are uninsured, (2) lack of health insurance could foster overreliance on service providers that do not address breast and cervical health as a routine matter, such as emergency room doctors, (3) safety net providers are in shorter supply than in larger urban areas, (4) bilingual professionals (Spanish/English) are in very limited supply and are more likely to present dual role and confidentiality issues, (5) there may be lack of cultural awareness, skills, and knowledge on the part of service providers working with the population, and (6) providers may specifically lack information about the breast and cervical health needs of Latina women in these areas (Cunningham et al. 2006; Doty 2003). In this context, low rates of early screening are likely to occur, despite having the technology available to find cancers at earlier, less critical stages.

Cancer Statistics and Screening Guidelines

As the population increases, a greater number of Latinos will be diagnosed with cancer. Using cancer prevalence rates for Latinos of 1.06% for 2008, at least 471,035 Latinos have been diagnosed with invasive cancer in the last 15 years, a number that will increase to at least 1.1 million by the year 2050 (National Cancer Institute, n.d.b; U.S. Census Bureau 2008a). For certain cancers, Latinos have disproportionately worse outcomes than the majority population. In this article, we focus on two such female cancers: cervical and breast.

CERVICAL CANCER

Across all types of cancer, incidence for this cancer is ranked number 4 and mortality at number 10 among Latina women (13.8 and 3.3 per 100,000, respectively; Edwards et al. 2005; Jemal et al. 2008). Overall, Latina women have the highest incidence rate of cervical cancer of all major racial/ethnic groups, up to three times higher than the non-Latina white population (National Cancer Institute 2005; Trapido et al. 1995). Approximately 99.7% of cervical cancers are caused by human papillomavirus (HPV) infection (Walboomers et al. 1999). Latin American countries vary in their rates of HPV infection, which results in differential rates of cervical cancer by ancestry in the United States (Clifford et al. 2005). Women of Mexican and Puerto Rican descent, for example, have higher rates of cervical cancer than women of Cuban ancestry (Trapido et al. 1995). Given that cervical cancer is 100% preventable through Pap smears, it is critically important that providers and researchers empower women to obtain this screening at intervals recommended by the national screening guidelines. The U.S. Preventive Services Task Force recommends cervical cancer screenings through Pap smears at least every three years for women who are sexually active or over the age of 21 (2002b). Similarly, the American Cancer Society recommends that all women begin cervical cancer screening about three years after they begin having vaginal intercourse, but no later than 21 years old. However, they specifically recommend that women obtain yearly Pap smear screenings until at least age 30 (American Cancer Society 2008). Beginning at age 30, women who have had three normal Pap test results in a row may get screened every two to three years. For the purposes of this chapter, in light of screening guidelines and the high incidence rate of cervical cancer in the population, we will consider a woman to be up to date with screening if she is over the age of 18 and has screened once in the last 12 months.

BREAST CANCER

Across all types of cancer, incidence and mortality rates for breast cancer are ranked number 1 among Latinas (89.3 and 16.1 per 100,000, respectively; Edwards et al. 2005; Jemal et al. 2008). In addition, in comparison with non-Latina whites, Latinas are less likely to live five years beyond diagnosis. For example, in the state of New Mexico, the five-year survivorship rate for Latinas is 76%, compared with 85% for their non-Latina white counterparts (Gilliland, Hunt, and Key 1998). This difference is due to the disease being diagnosed at later stages among Latinas (Li, Malone, and Daling 2003). Late detection may be a result of lower rates of screening as well as genetic and environmental factors that may influence Latinas' being diagnosed with a more aggressive form of breast cancer at younger ages (Biffl et al. 2001; Shavers, Harlan, and Stevens 2003). Among screening tools for breast cancer, mammography screening has received the most attention in the literature, although breast self-exams (BSE; i.e., a woman performing a systematic exam to note changes in her breast) and clinical breast exams (CBE; i.e., a breast exam performed by a doctor or nurse) are also tools for detection (American Cancer Society 2008). We acknowledge that there has been some debate concerning the effectiveness of breast self-examinations as a screening tool since Kosters and Gotzsche (2003) reported that breast self-examination does not suggest a beneficial effect. Their conclusions were largely drawn from two large investigations of female factory workers in Russia and Shanghai who were trained in breast self-examinations; women who received the training were just as likely to die of breast cancer as those who did not receive this training. However, there are great concerns about the validity and generalizability of these findings, given that women who were taught BSE did not always perform it at recommended intervals, with compliance being as low as 56% in some cases. In addition, a large proportion of participants was drawn from medical clinics or otherwise had access to health care, compromising its generalizability to Latina women in the United States without access to care, especially given the complexity of the U.S. health-care system. Therefore, we contend that regular BSE is still valuable for Latina women to detect changes in their breasts, and we present information about BSE screening in this chapter. With respect to mammography, which is considered the best tool for early detection (Centers for Disease Control and Prevention 2007), the U.S. Preventive Services Task Force (2002a) recommends mammography screening for women over 40 years of age every one to two years, whereas the American Cancer Society recommends that women obtain annual mammography starting at age 40 (Smith et al. 2003). For the purposes of this chapter, we will consider a woman to be up to date with screening if she is over the age of 40 and has screened once in the last 12 months.

Needs Assessment: Rationale and Purpose

The culture of health service delivery in the United States is largely structured according to a Western medical model. According to this model, individuals are expected to take responsibility for their own care by asserting their needs, asking questions, and taking the lead in seeking follow-up care (Pescosolido 1992). This process assumes that people have ample access to information and resources to promote their health, regardless of the local context. In addition, it assumes that an assertive, individualistic stance will be embraced by all health-care consumers, ignoring the fact that behaviors, beliefs, attitudes, and knowledge about aspects of health are culturally bound (Rajaram and Rashidi 1998). In fact, health services designed according to a Western medical model largely ignore relevant cultural variables that influence health-care use and satisfaction, such as ethnic ancestry, immigration status, cultural and conceptual knowledge, and English-language proficiency (Alegría et al. 2007; Institute of Medicine 2004). In this needs assessment, an effort was made to describe the larger population trends in the area, as well as to measure cultural aspects that have been shown to influence cancer screening behaviors such as beliefs, knowledge, language, access to health care, income, and formal education levels (Ashing-Giwa et al. 2004; Buki et al. 2004; Buki et al. 2007; McMullin et al. 2005). To this end, a sample of Latina women from various areas in central Illinois provided information about individual, psychosocial, and cultural factors that may affect their screening behaviors.

Method

PARTICIPANTS

A total of 120 self-identified Latina women were recruited from four towns in central Illinois: Champaign (n = 54), Rantoul (n = 31), Hoopeston (n = 14), and Danville (n = 21). Their ages ranged from 18 to 71 years (mean = 35, SD = 11). The majority of participants were born in Mexico (64%), with smaller percentages born in the United States (22%) and other Latin American countries (14%). Twelve participants (10%) reported a family history of cervical cancer, and 10 participants (8%) reported a family history of breast cancer. Several participants reported not knowing whether they have a family history of cervical cancer (n = 6) or breast cancer (n = 5). No participants with a personal diagnosis of cervical or breast cancer were included in the study, as this needs assessment was designed to obtain information about women whose screening needs are not influenced by a previous diagnosis.

MATERIALS

A 62-item questionnaire was used to collect information about sociodemographic characteristics (e.g., age, education), participants' use of early screening methods (i.e., Pap smears, BSE, CBE, and mammograms), time elapsed since their last screening, and reasons for obtaining the screenings. In addition, the questionnaire included questions to measure participants' knowledge, beliefs, and attitudes about cervical and breast cancer on a Likert-type scale (1 = *completely agree*, 9 = *completely disagree*). Sample items include "A woman who is past menopause does not need to get a Pap smear" and "It is difficult to get a mammogram." The survey was available in both Spanish and English, yet virtually all women chose to fill it out in Spanish.

Level of acculturation was measured through a shortened version of the Acculturation Rating Scale for Mexican Americans (ARSMA; Cuellar, Harris, and Jasso 1980). This five-item acculturation scale has been used in the past with Latino samples in cancer-related studies, yielding moderate alpha coefficients of 0.70–0.80 (Buki et al. 2004; Elder et al. 1991). Consistent with other studies (Buki et al. 2004), the ARSMA wording was changed to make it applicable to Latinos of various ancestries. For example, instead of asking women if they had spent most of their childhood and adolescence in "Mexico," they were asked if they had spent it in their "country of origin." With these modifications, the ARSMA in this study yielded an internal consistency coefficient of 0.81.

PROCEDURE

We recruited participants through community outreach at health fairs, churches, and street outreach. The principal investigator, who is fully bilingual in Spanish and English, attended various events along with 1–3 fully bilingual research assistants, depending on the size of the event. Women were asked to voluntarily participate in filling out a survey about women's health. The surveys were anonymous and included a short explanation about the study and women's rights as participants at the top of the first page. Filling out the survey implied consent to participate in the study. Depending on their literacy level, women took between 20 and 40 minutes to fill out the questionnaire. Participants with low health literacy were assisted by a member of the research team in filling out the materials.

Results

PARTICIPANT INFORMATION

Only 20% of participants had lived in the United States all their lives. They varied widely in their language use: 25% of participants were bilingual Spanish/English speakers, 67% were primarily Spanish speakers, and only 8% were primarily English speakers. Forty-five percent of women reported that nearly all their friends are Latinos, whereas only 2% reported that nearly all their friends are non-Latina/os born in the United States. Consistent with these findings, over 50% of participants reported low levels of acculturation. In addition, they reported high levels of cultural pride, with 92% feeling proud or very proud to identify as Latina.

Three-quarters (74%) of participants identified themselves as married or cohabiting, 19% as single, 5% as divorced, and 2% as widowed. Over three-quarters of women (80%) reported having children; the number of children ranged from 1 to 12 (mean = 3.31, SD = 2.09). Overall, women in the sample had low levels of formal education: half of the participants reported less than 12 years of formal education, 18% had a high school diploma or equivalent, and 17% had an undergraduate degree or higher. Not surprisingly, given their low levels of educational attainment, participants reported low annual household incomes: approximately a third of the sample earned less than $10,000, another third earned between $10,001 and $15,000, and the highest group earned between $15,001 and $40,000. Compared to average statistics for Latinos in the state of Illinois, our sample has lower levels of acculturation and higher poverty levels (Pew Hispanic Center 2009a).

Table 1 shows the participants' demographic characteristics by ancestry. Among participants, women born in Mexico reported the lowest levels of formal education,

TABLE 1. Background Characteristics of Participants by Country of Origin (n = 120)

Variable	Mexico (n=77)				USA (n=26)				Other (n=17)			
	M	SD	Range	%	M	SD	Range	%	M	SD	Range	%
Age	36.81	11.94	19–71		31.54	9.33	18–50		35.12	10.45	18–56	
Marital status												
Single or divorced				23				27				24
Married or cohabitating				74				73				76
Widowed				3				0				0
Children				84				73				71
Number of children	3.64	2.28	1–12		3.00	1.56	1–6		2.00	0.78	1–4	
Education	8.47	4.55	0–17		12.08	3.11	5–17		14.12	4.53	3–18	
Income	12,615	6,310	1,118–40,000		14,906	10,033	850–37,000		19,948	10,617	4,680–36,000	
Acculturation	1.26	0.48	0.80–2.60		2.46	0.69	0.80–3.60		1.51	0.42	0.80–2.40	
Insurance												
Private				15				23				81
Medicare or Medicaid				13				19				0
No insurance				72				58				19

TABLE 2. One-Way ANOVA Summary Table Examining Number of Children as a Function of Formal Education ($n = 82$)

	Sum of Squares	df	Mean Square	F
Between group	115.54	2	57.77	19.33*
Within group	239.09	80	2.99	
Total	354.63	82		

*$p < 0.0001$.

income, and acculturation, as well as the highest number of children. Participants born in the United States were the youngest and had the highest levels of acculturation, whereas women born in other Latin American countries had the highest levels of formal education, income, and private health-care insurance.

To further understand potential screening correlates, we conducted one-way analyses of variance (ANOVAs) and Pearson correlations using demographic variables associated with screening behaviors in previous studies (Buki et al. 2007; Coughlin and Wilson 2002; Gorin and Heck 2005). We found that participants who had completed less than a 6th-grade education had more children (mean = 5.39, SD = 2.99) than participants who had completed between a 6th- and 11th-grade education (mean = 3.16, SD = 1.39) or a 12th-grade education or higher (mean = 2.26, SD = 0.93), $F(2,80) = 19.33$, $p < 0.0001$ (see table 2). Having more children was also associated with older age ($r = 0.62, p < 0.0001$). Moreover, older age was associated with lower reported proficiency in spoken English ($r = -0.28, p = 0.002$) and written English ($r = -0.27, p = 0.004$) and lower levels of formal education ($r = -0.38, p < 0.0001$). Higher levels of formal education were associated with having always lived in the United States ($r = 0.24, p = 0.008$), speaking English ($r = 0.64, p < 0.0001$), and having higher incomes ($r = 0.32, p = 0.002$).

CERVICAL CANCER

SCREENING BEHAVIOR

Eighty-four percent of the women reported having had a Pap smear at some point in their lives. Among them, 74% reported having had a Pap smear in the past year, primarily as part of a regular medical checkup; 10% indicated obtaining one more than a year ago, and 16% left the field blank. We suspect that they could not remember when they had obtained the last Pap smear, which may suggest over a year had

TABLE 3. Cervical Cancer Screening Data by Country of Origin (%)

	Mexico (*n*=77)	United States (*n*=26)	Other (*n*=17)
Ever had a Pap	86	81	82
Pap is up to date[1]	62	72	57
Regular screening[2]	39	56	50

(1) Data reported for women at least 19 years old. (2) Data reported for women at least 23 years old.

elapsed since the exam. Overall, for women who reported information, time since last Pap smear ranged from less than one month to 10 years.

To examine differences by country of origin, we computed screening rates separately for women born in the United States, Mexico, and other Latin American countries (see table 3). We calculated three different rates: (1) ever having screened for women ages 18 and older, (2) Pap screening is up to date, which shows the percentage of women over the age of 19 who had received a Pap smear in the last 12 months, and (3) regular screening, which shows the percentage of women age 23 and older who reported obtaining five Pap smears in the last five years. As table 3 shows, women born in Mexico had the highest rates of ever having been screened but the lowest rates of regular screening. In contrast, participants born in Latin America were the least likely to be up to date with screenings.

We conducted logistic regressions to model women's adherence to screening for cervical cancer. Four sequential levels of the adherence variables (initial screening, overdue screening, up to date with rescreening, and regular screening) were used to form continuation ratios. Three logistic models were fitted to examine the relationship between several predictors and cervical cancer screening behaviors. On the basis of past studies conducted with Latina samples, and given the limitations of sample size, the following predictors were considered: age, education, having had a child, having health insurance, and country of origin (Mexico vs. other). The three models are presented next.

■ *Ever versus never screened.* A total of 111 women's responses were used in modeling the probability of a woman ever having had a Pap smear. We computed odds ratios and 95% confidence interval for all variables. Having a child and age emerged as significant predictors of the probability of a woman having had a Pap smear (Hosmer-Lemeshow Chi^2(8) = 12.33; BIC = −428.94). The odds that a woman had a Pap smear given she had a child were 9.97 times larger than the odds for a woman who did not have one (p = 0.001). With respect to age, the odds that a woman ever had a Pap smear increased with age (p = 0.092). For instance, the predicted probability of having had a Pap smear is 80% for a woman age 20 and 89% for a woman 10 years older, while other variables are held constant at their mean value.

■ *Up-to-date versus overdue repeat screening.* We conducted the second analysis to model the probability of women being up to date with rescreening compared to women being overdue for rescreening (n = 98). We computed odds ratios and 95% confidence intervals for all the variables. Age was a significant predictor of being up to date with rescreening (Hosmer-Lemeshow Chi^2(8) = 11.53, BIC = −314.50). The odds that a woman was up to date with her Pap smear decreased with age (p = 0.038). For instance, the predicted probability of being up to date with rescreening is 87% for a woman aged 20 and is 80% for a woman 10 years older, while the other variables are held constant at their mean value. The predicted probability of being up to date with rescreening decreases to 60% at age 50.

■ *Regular screening versus nonregular screening.* The last model predicted women's probability of having engaged in regular screening (n = 79). We define a woman who has screened regularly as a woman who is at least 23 years old who reports obtaining at least five Pap smears in the last five years. None of the variables yielded significance for this model.

SOCIOCULTURAL FACTORS

Approximately two-thirds of participants (64%) reported preferring that a female health care provider perform their Pap smear, with 35% reporting no gender preference, and only one participant (0.8%) indicating a preference for a male provider. A third of the participants reported that no one had encouraged them to have a Pap smear, and 12% did not know where they could obtain one. Among those who had obtained a Pap smear, 60% were encouraged by a doctor or nurse, 15% by a friend, and 6% by a son or daughter. Among women who were married or cohabiting, almost 7 in 10 participants (69%) reported that they had not been encouraged by their husband or partner to receive a Pap smear. Approximately 17% of the women reported feeling low or no risk of cervical cancer. When asked how often a healthy woman their age needs to obtain a Pap smear, 82% of participants indicated once a year.

A fourth of the sample (26%) was unsure whether Pap smears are expensive. Whereas 29% of the participants believed that Pap smears are painful, 38% were certain that they are not. As table 4 shows, at least one-quarter of participants endorsed erroneous knowledge in three items related to cervical cancer, such as "A healthy woman your age should get a Pap smear only when she has a gynecological problem." However, for one of the items related to cervical cancer, "A healthy woman your age should get a Pap smear only when a doctor or a nurse recommends one," a higher proportion of women (38%) endorsed it. This higher endorsement may be due to the fact that there is some ambiguity in this item, in that some women may have interpreted it to mean that they should not obtain a Pap smear more often than indicated by the doctor or the nurse. In addition, about one-quarter (28%) of women agreed that cervical cancer definitely can occur without symptoms; however, an even larger percentage of women, 37%, did not know whether this was the case and 12% erroneously believed that cervical cancer always has symptoms. Furthermore, a third of participants reported being unsure about the risk of fatality, whereas 17% believed that cervical cancer is always fatal. Pearson correlation analyses revealed an association between older age and the belief that a Pap needs to be done only when a doctor or nurse recommends one ($r = 0.28$, $p = 0.002$). Women who reported a misconception were likely to hold more than one misconception. For instance, participants who believed that women should get a Pap smear only when a doctor or nurse recommends one were also likely to believe that women should get Pap smears only when they have a gynecological problem ($r = 0.56$, $p < 0.0001$), only when they are pregnant ($r = 0.62$, $p < 0.0001$), or only before menopause ($r = 0.35$, $p < 0.0001$).

BREAST CANCER

SCREENING BEHAVIOR

Among the 35 women over 41 years of age, all of whom would be expected to have obtained a mammogram, 84% reported having obtained one and 8% reported never having had one, with missing data for 8% of the sample. No substantive differences were noted in screening rates by ethnicity, with 83% of women born in Mexico, 83% of women born in the United States, and 80% of women born in other countries reporting ever having had a mammogram. Of 12 women age 45 and older who had screened before, 42% had obtained only one mammogram in the last five years, and 33% had obtained at least five. Time since last mammogram ranged from one month to 10 years. Eighty-two percent of the women reported that someone had taught them how to perform BSE, and 72% reported having performed this exam at least once in their lives. Eighty-eight percent of participants reported having had a CBE, with 60% among this group getting the exam as part of a regular checkup, and 25% because of a breast problem. We were unable to examine predictors of mammography screening using logistic regression analysis because the small sample size.

SOCIOCULTURAL FACTORS

Among women 40 and older, who are expected to have screened regularly, 24% believed that it is difficult to obtain a mammogram and 27% believed that if diagnosed with breast cancer they would die, with an additional 16% being unsure whether they would die or not if diagnosed. In addition, 86% endorsed the belief that trauma to the breast can cause cancer (which is inaccurate) or were unsure whether this is the case (see table 4). Only 3 out of 37 respondents believed that breast cancer is definitely not caused by being hit in the breast. More than a third of participants believed that younger women may be at higher risk of breast cancer than older women, when the opposite is true. Over half the sample (53%) either believed that they were not at risk for breast cancer, or were unsure about their risk. Five percent of participants reported a family history of breast cancer, with 15% of women age 40 and older reporting that they are definitely at risk for breast cancer. Fourteen percent of participants age 40 and older did not know how often they should obtain a mammogram. Of those who reported knowing how often they should obtain one, 65% of participants indicated once a year.

The majority of women reported a gender preference for a female provider to perform the CBE (58%). We did not inquire about preferred gender of the provider performing the mammogram, as these radiology technicians are usually female. Of women who reported having had a mammogram, 70% were encouraged by a doctor or a nurse to have the screening.

Discussion

As the Latino population continues to increase, we are challenged to develop culturally congruent programs and practical solutions to address their health needs. To enhance success of these efforts, scholars advocate the use of community-based approaches that are specific to a given geographic region (Barry and Breen 2005; Lawlor 2006; Vega and López 2001). Therefore, the main contribution of the present study is that it extends our knowledge of cervical and breast cancer screening correlates of Latinas in central Illinois, and it is the first investigation of the kind in this geographic area. Data from this needs assessment have great potential to assist in the planning of regional efforts in cancer education. Specifically, the data suggest that efforts are needed to ensure that a greater number of Latinas (*a*) obtain first time screening, (*b*) stay up to date with screening, and (*c*) screen regularly. Based on our findings, we provide specific recommendations to enhance screening rates at the end of the section.

TABLE 4. Participants' Knowledge about Cervical and Breast Cancer (*n* = 120)

	% of Participants Who Endorsed Item or Were Unsure	Facts*
Cervical Cancer		
A healthy woman your age should get a Pap smear only when a doctor or nurse recommends one.	38	Pap smears are necessary, whether a doctor or nurse advises it.
A healthy woman your age should get a Pap smear only when she has a gynecological problem.	28	Pap smears are necessary, even in the absence of gynecological problems.
A healthy woman your age should get a Pap smear only when she is pregnant.	25	Pap smears are necessary, even in the absence of pregnancy.
A woman who is past menopause does not need to get a Pap smear.	28	It is important to have Pap smears beyond menopause since risk of cervical cancer increases with age.
Breast Cancer†		
A healthy woman could suffer from breast cancer after being hit in her breast.	87	There is no empirical evidence to support the belief that trauma to the breast is a cause or risk factor for breast cancer.
Young women are at higher risk of getting breast cancer than older women.	38	Breast cancer is most common among post-menopausal women. Only 1 out of 8 women diagnosed with breast cancer is under the age of 45.

* Information presented in this column was retrieved from the American Cancer Society (2009).
† Information provided for women age 40 and older.

With respect to cervical cancer, it is encouraging that more than 8 in 10 women had obtained a Pap smear at some point in their lives, yet it is concerning that almost 20% had not screened, and participants were not screening consistently. In fact, one participant in the sample had obtained her last Pap smear 10 years prior to data collection. Consistent with previous findings, our results show that women without children were at greater risk of never having obtained a Pap than those with children (Buki et al. 2007). However, we depart from the literature in our finding that older women were more likely than younger women to have ever obtained a Pap smear. Typically, older women are less likely to have had a Pap smear, particularly in immigrant samples (Buki et al. 2007; Gorin and Heck 2005). We explain this finding by virtue of older women's longer exposure to the U.S. health-care system, especially given the composition of our sample: 20% of women had lived in the United States all their lives, and of participants who were born abroad, 25% had lived in the United States between 20 and 45 years. In addition, 80% of women in the sample reported having children, with older participants reporting a greater number of children than younger participants. Given that Latina women are likely to obtain their initial screening in conjunction with childbirth, it is not surprising that older women were more likely to have ever obtained a screening. However, among women who had screened before, those who were older were at greatest risk of not being up to date with screenings. This is consistent with previous findings focused on repeat screening (Bazargan et al. 2004; Buki et al. 2007; Coughlin and Uhler 2002). These patterns suggest that it is possible that in the process of pregnancy care, childbirth, and postnatal care, women are screened but are not informed about the importance of regular screening. This would suggest that family doctors and obstetricians can play an influential role in ensuring women obtain not only a first-time screening but also that they stay up to date with screening. In addition, older participants in our sample were more likely than their younger counterparts to believe that women should obtain Pap smears only when a health-care professional recommends one, which could act as a barrier to screening if they are not interfacing regularly with the health-care system or are not referred for screening when they go to the doctor.

We also found that almost half of the women who had obtained a Pap smear before had not screened regularly in the past five years. It is possible that some women had received normal Pap smears for three years in a row and were screening at intervals greater than one year, but it is also possible that women did not know how important it is to engage in regular screening. In fact, we found that at least one in five participants held beliefs that indicate lack of information about the need for regular screening, such as the belief that women only need Pap smears when they are pregnant or before menopause. Moreover, women were not receiving much encouragement to screen, which made it even more critical for them to schedule their screenings through self-motivated behavior, based on an understanding that regular screening is critical for cervical health. Also of concern is the fact that half of the sample was unsure whether, or believed that, cancer is fatal, because women may be less willing to screen regularly if they do not think it will make a difference in their prognosis. In fact, women who hold fatalistic beliefs may avoid screening purposefully to avoid being told they will die. Finally, half the sample was either unsure or endorsed the notion that cervical cancer is symptomatic. The fact that Latina women may believe that cervical cancer is fatal and symptomatic has been reported consistently in the literature (Borrayo and Jenkins 2001; Buki et al. 2004; McMullin et al. 2005; Ramírez et al. 2000), and suggests the need to educate women about their risk of developing cancer even when they feel healthy. Therefore, it is critical that health professionals ensure that Latina women in central Illinois understand the importance of regular screening, especially given that larger health disparities are noted with respect to cervical cancer precisely because of late detection in the context of nonregular screening.

Our findings also brought to light differences among participants born in various countries. Women born in Mexico were older, had the lowest levels of acculturation, education, income, and health insurance, as well as the greatest number of children among women in the sample. These findings are consistent with those in previous studies in that women from Mexico consistently emerge as having the greatest barriers to screening of all ethnic groups examined in multiethnic samples (Buki et al. 2004; Ramírez et al. 2000; Zambrana et al. 1999). However, our findings suggest that access to health care, higher levels of education, and higher incomes are not always associated with higher screening rates. In fact, women born in other Latin American countries were the least likely to be up to date with their cervical cancer screening of all participants. We suspect this is due to the fact that Champaign is home to an internationally renowned university that attracts international students from Latin America. It is likely that the majority of immigrant women from other Latin American countries were undergraduate and graduate students at the university, which would account for the high educational level of that group. In addition, as college students these participants had private health insurance and access to the student health center. It seems counterintuitive that this population was the least likely to be up to date with Pap smear screening despite having greater overall literacy and easy access to screenings. To explain this finding, we draw from another study of Latina college students in the Midwest that found students were not screening regularly (Schiffner and Buki 2006). In that study, participants reported that they were reluctant to go to the student health center for screenings, as they felt their confidentiality was compromised at an institution with a low proportion of Latina students. It is also possible that these were international students who prioritized their studies over their health, given an environment focused on high scholarly standards, constant deadlines, and financial pressure for timely completion of their degrees.

With respect to breast cancer, our information is limited given the small number of participants over the age of 40. However, we note that the Latino population in Illinois is a young population, such that the fact that older Latinas are underrepresented in the study is consistent with local population trends (Pew Hispanic Center 2009a). Of particular concern is the fact that at least 8% of women over the age of 41 had never obtained a mammogram before, and that among women over the age of 45 who had obtained one, two-thirds had not done so on a yearly basis in the previous five years. Moreover, the majority of women reported at least one erroneous belief about breast cancer etiology, which may also lead them to stop screening if, for example, they have not experienced trauma to the breast and feel they are not at risk of developing breast cancer as a result. On the other hand, it is encouraging that the majority of participants reported medical personnel had encouraged them to obtain a screening previously, as researchers have found that Latina women who have a physician's recommendation are more likely to obtain breast cancer screenings than those who have not been given this recommendation (Bazargan et al. 2003).

Two limitations of this study deserve mention. First, some participants were recruited at health fairs, which could result in a sample of women who are more likely to screen given their interest in health promotion. If this was the case, our data could possibly overstate the screening rates of women in the area, as well as understate the prevalence of inaccurate knowledge about cervical and breast cancer in the population. The second limitation is our low sample size, which precluded us from carrying out certain statistical analyses such as logistic regressions to identify predictors of mammography screening. Despite these limitations, we uncovered information that has potential to increase the rates of screening in Latina women in central Illinois. Based on our findings, we make the following five recommendations:

- For both cervical and breast cancer, there is a great need to (1) increase screening rates among women who are overdue for screening, and (2) increase rates of regular screening. Given the relatively large percentage of women who had been encouraged to screen by health-care professionals, doctors and nurses serving the Latina population in the Champaign County area need to be advised that in addition to promoting first-time screening, they also need to inform women about the importance of screening at regular intervals to ensure early detection of cancer.
- Because of the low levels of acculturation reported by participants, particularly by women with low levels of formal education, low incomes, and limited access to health care, the use of bilingual *promotoras de salud* to impart educational messages is likely to be particularly effective in Champaign County. *Promotoras de salud*, trusted members of the community who can help women navigate an unfamiliar health-care system, have been found to increase rates of screening in other geographic areas given their ability to reach women at the community level, in their own language, and within a familiar cultural framework (Hunter et al. 2004; Navarro et al. 1998).
- In all interventions, whether by health-care professionals or *promotoras de salud*, our findings suggest the need to inform women about cervical and breast

cancer, such as the fact that (1) these cancers are not fatal when detected in the early stages, (2) screenings are needed in the absence of symptoms because cancer can grow without symptoms, and (3) women need screenings even when the doctor does not recommend one. Specifically regarding cervical cancer, women need information about the fact that women should get Pap smears (1) when they are pregnant as well as when they are not, (2) whether they have gone through menopause or not, and (3) whether they have a gynecological problem or not. Women need to know that cervical cancer, of all cancers, provides a long window of opportunity to screen and even prevent progression of the cancer (National Cancer Institute, n.d.a). With respect to breast cancer, health care providers and *promotoras* can dispel the myth that breast cancer can be caused by bruising, as well as inform women that their risk of breast cancer increases as they get older.

• In outreach efforts, older women as well as women who do not have children need to be recruited as a priority population. Educational interventions need to also target women's male partners, as they can be a great source of support and encouragement for screenings, yet the vast majority of women reported not being encouraged to screen by them. It is imperative that interventions are conducted in Spanish, given the high proportion of women with low levels of acculturation in the area.

• It is concerning that 12% of participants did not know where they could obtain a Pap smear, and 24% of participants 40 and older felt that getting a mammogram is difficult. In Illinois, women without health insurance who meet certain guidelines qualify for free screenings though the Illinois Breast and Cervical Cancer Early Detection Program. It is possible that some women do not qualify, or that information about this program is not reaching the women who need it most. In the latter case, health-care providers and *promotoras* can play an important role in disseminating this information, as well as the Champaign-Urbana Public Health District, which administers this program.

NOTE

This research was funded in part by the Center for Democracy in a Multiracial Society at the University of Illinois at Urbana-Champaign. We would like to especially thank D. Marcela Garcés, M.D., M.S.P.H., for her invaluable assistance in the design of the survey and in the data collection process, and Youngshin Chi for her assistance with earlier versions of the data analyses. We dedicate this article to the memory of M. Carolina Hinestrosa, M.A., M.P.H., a dear colleague and friend whose unparalleled leadership in health-care disparities will continue to inspire us for years to come.

176 ■ Buki, Mayfield, and Andrade

REFERENCES

Alegría, M., N. Mulvaney-Day, M. Woo, M. Torres, S. Gao, and V. Oddo. 2007. "Correlates of Past-Year Mental Health Service Use among Latinas/os: Results from the National Latina/o and Asian American Study." *American Journal of Public Health* 97: 76–83.

Amaro, H., and R. E. Zambrana. 2000. "Criollo, Mestizo, Mulato, LatiNegro, Indígena, White or Black? The US Hispanic/Latino Population and Multiple Responses in the 2000 Census." *American Journal of Public Health* 90(11): 1724–27.

American Cancer Society. 2006. "Cancer Facts and Figures for Hispanics, 2006–2008." American Cancer Society. Available online: www.cancer.org.

———. 2008. American Cancer Society guidelines for the early detection of cancer. Available online: www.cancer.org.

———. 2009. "Detailed Guide: Breast Cancer. WHAT Are the Risk Factors for Breast Cancer?" Available online: www.cancer.org.

Ashing-Giwa, K. T., G. Padilla, J. Tejero, J. Kraemer, K. Wright, A. Coscarelli, S. Clayton, I. Williams, and D. Hills. 2004. "Understanding the Breast Cancer Experience of Women: A Qualitative Study of African American, Asian American, Latina and Caucasian Cancer Survivors." *Psycho-Oncology* 13(6): 408–28.

Barry, J., and N. Breen. 2005. "The Importance of Place of Residence in Predicting Late-Stage Diagnosis of Breast or Cervical Cancer." *Health & Place* 11: 15–29.

Bazargan, M., R. S. Baker, S. Bazargan, and B. A. Husaini. (2003). "Mammography Screening and Breast Self-Examination among Minority Women in Public Housing Projects: The Impact of Physician Recommendation." *Cellular & Molecular Biology* 49(8): 1213–18.

Bazargan, M., S. Bazargan, M. Farooq, and R. Baker. 2004. "Correlates of Cervical Cancer Screening among Underserved Hispanic and African-American Women." *Preventive Medicine* 39(3): 465–73.

Biffl, W. L., A. Myers, R. J. Franciose, R. J. Gonzalez, and D. Darnell. 2001. "Is Breast Cancer in Young Latinas a Different Disease?" *American Journal of Surgery* 182: 596–600.

Borrayo, E. A., and S. R. Jenkins. 2001. "Feeling Healthy: So Why Should Mexican-Descent Women Screen for Breast Cancer?" *Qualitative Health Research* 11: 812–23.

Buki, L. P., E. A. Borrayo, B. M. Feigal, and I. Y. Carrillo. 2004. "Are All Latinas the Same? Perceived Breast Cancer Screening Barriers and Facilitative Conditions." *Psychology of Women Quarterly* 28: 400–411.

Buki, L. P., J. Jamison, C. J. Anderson, and A. M. Cuadra. 2007. "Differences in Predictors of Cervical and Breast Cancer Screening by Screening Need in Uninsured Latina Women." *Cancer* 110: 1578–85.

Buki, L. P., S. I. Salazar, and V. O. Pitton. 2008. "Design Elements for the Development of Cancer Education Print Materials for a Latina/o Audience." *Health Promotion Practice* DOI: 10.1177/1524839908320359.

Centers for Disease Control and Prevention. 2007. "Breast Cancer: Understanding Mammograms." Available online: www.cdc.gov.

Champaign County. 2003. *Snapshot of the Latino Population in Champaign County.* Urbana: Champaign County Regional Planning Commission.

Clifford, G., S. Gallus, R. Herrero, N. Munoz, P. Snijders, S. Vaccarella, et al. 2005. "Worldwide

Distribution of Human Papillomavirus Types in Cytologically Normal Women in the International Agency for Research on Cancer HPV Prevalence Surveys: A Pooled Analysis." *Lancet* 366(9490): 991–98.

Coughlin, S. S., and R. J. Uhler. 2002. "Breast and Cervical Cancer Screening Practices among Hispanic Women in the United States and Puerto Rico, 1998–1999." *Preventive Medicine* 34: 242–51.

Coughlin, S. S., and K. M. Wilson. 2002. "Breast and Cervical Cancer Screening among Migrant and Seasonal Farmworkers: A Review." *Cancer Detection and Prevention* 26: 203–9.

Cuellar, I., L. C. Harris, and R. Jasso. 1980. "An Acculturation Scale for Mexican American Normal and Clinical Populations." *Hispanic Journal of Behavioral Sciences* 2: 199–217.

Cunningham, P., M. Banker, S. Artiga, and J. Tolbert. 2006. "Health Coverage and Access to Care for Hispanics in 'New Growth Communities' and 'Major Hispanic Centers.'" Kaiser Commission on Medicaid and the Uninsured. Available online: www.kff.org.

Doty, M. M. 2003. *Hispanic Patients' Double Burden: Lack of Health Insurance and Limited English.* New York: Commonwealth Fund.

Elder, J. P., F. G. Castro, C. Demoor, J. Mayer, J. I. Candelaria, N. Campbell, et al. 1991. "Differences in Cancer Risk-Related Behaviors in Latino and Anglo Adults." *Preventive Medicine* 20(6): 751–63.

Edwards, B. K., et al. 2005. "Annual Report to the Nation on the Status of Cancer, 1975–2002, Featuring Population-Based Trends in Cancer Treatment." *Journal of the National Cancer Institute* 97(19): 1407–27.

Fry, R. 2008. *Latino Settlement in the New Century.* Washington, DC: Pew Hispanic Center.

Gilliland, F. D., W. C. Hunt, and C. R. Key. 1998. "Trends in the Survival of American Indian, Hispanic, and Non-Hispanic White Cancer Patients in New Mexico and Arizona, 1969–1994." *Cancer* 82: 1769–83.

Gorin, S. S., and J. E. Heck. 2005. "Cancer Screening among Latino Subgroups in the United States." *Preventive Medicine* 40: 515–26.

Hunter, B., Jr., J. Guernsey de Zapien, M. Papenfuss, M. L. Fernandez, J. Meister, and A. R. Giuliano. 2004. "The Impact of a *Promotora* on Increasing Routine Chronic Disease Prevention among Women Aged 40 and Older." *Health Education & Behavior* 31(4): 18S–28S.

Institute of Medicine. 2004. *Health Literacy: A Prescription to End Confusion.* Washington, DC: National Academies Press.

Jemal, A., R. Siegel, E. Ward, Y. Hao, J. Xu, T. Murray, and M. J. Thun. 2008. "Cancer Statistics, 2008." *CA: A Cancer Journal for Clinicians* 58: 71–96.

Kosters, J., and P. Gotzsche. 2003. "Regular Self-Examination or Clinical Examination for Early Detection of Breast Cancer."? *Cochrane Database of Systematic Reviews* 2: 1–20.

Lawlor, E. F. 2006. "Diversity or Disparity in Health Services." In *Our Diverse Society: Race and Ethnicity—Implications for 21st Century American Society,* ed. D. W. Engstrom and L. M. Piedra, 183–200. Washington, DC: NASW Press.

Li, C. I., K. E. Malone, and J. R. Daling. 2003. "Differences in Breast Cancer Stage, Treatment, and Survival by Race and Ethnicity." *Archives of Internal Medicine* 163(1): 49–56.

MacKinnon, J. A., R. C. Duncan, Y. Huang, D. J. Lee, L. E. Fleming, L. Voti, M. Rudolph, and J. D. Wilkinson. 2007. "Detecting an Association between Socioeconomic Status and Late Stage Breast Cancer Using Spatial Analysis and Area-Based Measures." *Cancer Epidemiology, Biomarkers and Prevention* 16: 756–62.

Mcmullin, J. M., I. De Alba, L. R. Chavez, and A. F. Hubbell. 2005. "Influence of Beliefs about Cervical Cancer Etiology on Pap Smear Use among Latina Immigrants." *Ethnicity & Health* 10: 3–18.

National Cancer Institute. 2005. "Cancer Health Disparities: Fact Sheet." Available online: www.cancer.gov.

———. N.d. "Cervical Cancer." Available online: www.cancer.gov.

———. N.d. "Surveillance Epidemiology and End Results: Fast Stats. Statistics Stratified by Race/Ethnicity." Available online: seer.cancer.gov.

Navarro, A. M., K. L. Senn, L. J. McNicholas, R. M. Kaplan, B. Roppé, and M. C. Campoa. 1998. "*Por La Vida* Model Intervention Enhances Use of Cancer Screening Tests among Latinas." *American Journal of Preventive Medicine* 15(1): 32–41.

Pescosolido, B. A. 1992. "Beyond Rational Choice: The Social Dynamics of How People Seek Help." *American Journal of Sociology* 97(4): 1096–1138.

Pew Hispanic Center. 2009a. "Data and Resources: Demographic Profile of Hispanics in Illinois, 2007." Available online: pewhispanic.org.

———. 2009b. "Data and Resources: Vermilion County, Illinois." Available online: pewhispanic.org.

Rajaram, S. S., and A. Rashidi. 1998. "Minority Women and Breast Cancer Screening: The Role of Cultural Explanatory Models." *Preventive Medicine* 27(5): 757–64.

Ramirez, A. G., L. Suarez, L. Laufman, C. Barroso, and P. Chalela. 2000. "Hispanic Women's Breast and Cervical Cancer Knowledge, Attitudes, and Screening Behaviors." *American Journal of Health Promotion* 14(5): 292–300.

Schiffner, T., and L. P. Buki. 2006. "Latina College Students' Sexual Health Beliefs about Human Papillomavirus Infection." *Cultural Diversity and Ethnic Minority Psychology* 12: 687–96.

Shavers, V. L., L. C. Harlan, and J. L. Stevens. 2003. "Racial/Ethnic Presentation, Treatment and Survival from Breast Cancer among Women under Age 35." *Cancer* 97(1): 134–47.

Smith, R. A., D. Saslow, K. A. Sawyer, B. Wylie, M. E. Costanza, W. P. Evans III, R. S. Foster Jr., E. Hendrick, H. J. Eyre, and S. Sener. 2003. "American Cancer Society Guidelines for Breast Cancer Screening: Update 2003." *CA: A Cancer Journal for Clinicians* 53: 141–69.

Trapido, E., R. B. Valdez, J. L. Obeso, N. Strickman-Stein, A. Rotger, and E. Pérez-Stable. 1995. "Epidemiology of Cancer among Hispanics in the United States." *Journal of National Cancer Institute Monographs* 18: 17–28.

U.S. Census Bureau. 2008a. Population projections. Available online: www.census.gov.

———. 2008b. "U.S. Hispanic Population Surpasses 45 million: Now 15 Percent of Total." Available online: www.census.gov.

U.S. Preventive Services Task Force. 2002a. "Screening for Breast Cancer." Available online: www.ahrq.gov.

———. 2002b. "Screening for Cervical Cancer." Available online: www.ahrq.gov.

Vega, W. A., and S. R. Lopez. 2001. "Priority Issues in Latino Mental Health Services Research." *Mental Health Services Research* 3(4): 189–200.

Walboomers, J. M., M. V. Jacobs, M. M. Manos, F. X. Bosch, J. A. Kummer, K. V. Shah, et al. 1999. "Human papillomavirus is a Necessary Cause of Invasive Cervical Cancer Worldwide." *Journal of Pathology* 189(1): 12–19.

Warner, J., and W. McLaughlin. 2002. *Rural Community and Professional Practice Profile: Hoopeston, Illinois, Vermillion County.* Chicago: Illinois Center for Health Workforce Studies.

Waterman, R. 2001. *Latinos in the Heartland: A Look at the Latino Community of Bloomington-Normal, Illinois.* Normal, IL: Women's Wellness Initiative.

Zambrana, R., N. Breen, S. A. Fox, and M. Lou Gutierrez-Mohamed. 1999. "Use of Cancer Screening Practices by Hispanic Women: Analyses by Subgroup." *Preventive Medicine* 29(6): 466–77.

MIKE TAPIA, DONALD T. HUTCHERSON, and ANA CAMPOS-HOLLAND

Latinos and the Risk of Arrest: National and Regional Effects

THE U.S. CENSUS BUREAU ESTIMATES THAT FROM 2000 TO 2007, THE SIZE OF THE Latino population grew by 10 million people, an increase of 27%, making them, by far, the nation's largest minority group. The Latino population in the midwestern states grew by 30% over this time frame, adding about 1 million inhabitants. Crime and justice research has not kept pace with this regional and national population growth. Research on racial minorities and crime is largely a comparison of blacks' and whites' offense levels and justice outcomes (Hawkins 1995; Hebert 1997; Kaufman 2005; Martinez 2002; Russell 1998; Walker, Spohn, and DeLone 2003; Zatz 1984). This is also true of research on juvenile delinquency and system processing. For example, much prominent delinquency research using survey data fails to sample enough Hispanic youth to generalize to the population, resulting in their omission from study results (Elliott and Ageton 1980; Farrington et al. 1996; Farrington, Loeber, and Stouthamer-Loeber 2003; Lynam et al. 2000; Simcha-Fagan and Schwartz 1986; Wikstrom and Loeber 2000). Official data have even more serious limitations for studying Hispanics and crime. While numerous scholars have expressed the need for more crime and justice research on Hispanics (Hagan and Coleman 2001; Hagan and Palloni 1999; La Free 1985; Martinez 2002;

Sissons 1979; Spohn and DeLone 2000; Tonry 1997; Walker et al. 2004), this subfield faces these and other hurdles

Hispanic Crime and Arrest

Virtually any research on Hispanics and crime covers new ground, despite the notable presence of Hispanics in the criminal justice system (Tonry 1997; Walker et al. 2004). Because of data limitations, one area of race or ethnicity and crime that scholars know little about is Hispanic offending and arrest. Official crime-reporting systems do not record offense or arrest information on Hispanics, creating a major void in the race-ethnic literature. The reasons for this lacuna are varied (e.g., race politics in America, issues of data validity, a general neglect of the topic by the research community), but the most problematic is indeed the official data collection mechanisms, the FBI's Uniform Crime Report (UCR) and the National Incident-Based Reporting System (NIBRS). Since their inception, these sources of crime data have collected the race of criminal suspects and arrestees in incidents recorded by law enforcement, but not the offender's ethnicity.[1] The racial categories used in these aggregate data are white, black, Asian / Pacific Islander, and Native American / Alaskan Native. As an *ethnic* group, Hispanics may theoretically be distributed across these racial categories;[2] therefore offender data are not available for this population designation (Morenoff 2005; Sissons 1979; Walker, Spohn, and DeLone 2003). Currently, researchers interested in official rates of Latino offending must study them on a case-by-case basis, examining data for particular cities, counties, and states when they are available (Bell and Lang 1985; Cicourel 1976; Dannefer and Schutt 1982; Martinez 2002; Martinez 2003; McEachern and Bauzer 1967; Nielsen, Lee, and Martinez 2005; Terry 1967).

THE MERITS OF SURVEY DATA FOR STUDYING LATINO ARREST

In the absence of official data to assess the risk of arrest for Hispanics, a viable and perhaps superior alternative is self-report survey data. As is well noted in crime research, there are generally two types of crime estimates; one derived from incidents known to the police, that is, "official" data, as reported in UCR and NIBRS, and estimates of the "dark figure" of crime, which includes unreported incidents as well. Since most crime and delinquency goes undetected by police (Dunford and Elliott 1984; Elliott, Huizinga, and Morse 1987; Elliott and Voss 1974; Empey 1982; Farrington et al. 1996; Hirschi 1969; Huizinga and Elliott 1987; Morenoff 2005; Sampson 1986;

Williams and Gold 1972), estimates obtained from self-report data are a better depiction of the total amount of crime in a sampling area.

Much research on individual-level arrests uses survey data (Brownfield, Sorenson, and Thomson 2001; Curry 2000; Elliott and Voss 1974; Hindelang, Hirschi, and Weiss 1981; Hirschfield et al. 2006; Hirschi 1969; Sampson 1986; Sealock and Simpson 1998; Shannon 1991; Simcha-Fagan and Schwartz 1986; Williams and Gold 1972). The universe for arrest risk with survey data are typically all subjects in a given sampling area, both arrested and nonarrested (see Lattimore et al. 2004 for a focus on paroled youth). With regard to the "dark figure," for a representative sample of the U.S. juvenile and young adult population, the concept of "all crime and delinquency" is synonymous with the sample's self-reported illegal behavior. Arrests are also self-reported in this type of data. At a minimum, these are the two components necessary for computing the chances of arrest in terms of odds or some other risk indicator. Survey data also contain various demographic and social risk factors that may be exogenous to subject interactions with police.

Sources of the "no arrest" outcome in survey data are rather varied. In addition to verbal warnings for minor incidents, subjects may simply not have committed a delinquent act during the survey period, or may have avoided police detection or apprehension for their misdeeds. Moreover, with the survey method, the contribution of each risk item to the chance for arrest is more reliably quantified in a multivariate framework because of wider variability on items and the larger number of cases than studies using official arrest data on Hispanics gathered for individual cities.[3]

THE RESEARCH ON HISPANICS AND ARREST

There is a small body of research on Hispanic involvement in the early stages of processing, all on specific cities, and all on juveniles. Of the few studies that assess the arrest risk of Hispanics, most are rather dated, and findings from the more recent studies deviate from these earlier ones. While no real benchmark exists to compare against our current findings, these few studies are worth summarizing, as they help to inform our hypothesis.

Terry (1967) found that Mexican Americans were no more likely to be arrested than whites in one medium-sized midwestern city in the 1950s. McEachern and Bauzer (1967) and Cicourel (1976) also failed to observe a pattern in decisions to file petitions for Mexican, black, and white youth in various Southern California cities. In a study of two New Jersey counties, Dannefer and Schutt (1982) found that Hispanic youth experienced a higher risk of arrest than white youth, but a lower risk than black youth. This midrange arrest penalty was also recently observed by Huizinga and coauthors (2007) for Hispanic youth in Rochester, and by Tapia (2010), using youth data for the nation. In their examination of postarrest intake decisions for youth in Los Angeles, Bell and Lang (1985) found that intake officers filed petitions for blacks and Mexican Americans at a similar elevated rate, relative to white youth. Finally, one recent study using Rochester data takes a less informative approach by combining blacks and Hispanics to find general "minority" effects (Hirschfield et al. 2006).

HISPANIC CRIME AND PUNISHMENT

Most of the literature on Hispanic involvement with the criminal justice system is sentencing research. Where Hispanics appear in studies that compare them against major race groups, the general observation is that Hispanics and blacks are sentenced more harshly than whites (Hebert 1997). The extent of these penalties was comparable by some estimates (Brownsberger 2000; Petersilia 1985; Spohn and DeLone 2000; Unnever 1982), while others suggested Hispanics experience midrange penalties relative to blacks and whites (California Administrative Office of the Courts 2001; Hebert 1997; Mustard 2001; Royo-Maxwell and Davis 1999; Tapia and Harris 2006). There are also nuances that are place dependent, where blacks and Hispanics will switch rank or where race-ethnic effects are absent. Spohn and DeLone (2000), for example, found no race or ethnic effects in Kansas City, but did observe minority effects in Chicago and effects for Hispanics only in Miami.

Correctional data more convincingly inform the expectation of midrange justice penalties against Hispanics. Table 1 contains national incarceration rates per 100,000 by race-ethnicity and region in the year 2000.[4] It shows that all regions incarcerate blacks at a much higher rate than any other group. While considerably below the black rate, the national Latino incarceration rate is 63% higher than the white incarceration rate and 20% above the national rate. The Midwest is the most punitive region for blacks and the least punitive for Hispanics. In terms of minority threat theory, this is interesting given the rather substantial "browning of the Midwest" that is discussed here and in other chapters of this volume. In the minority threat framework, one would expect to see a higher incarceration rate in reaction to the rapid growth the Latino population.

A similar pattern extends to other correctional settings as well. In 1999, 16% of the parolee population was Hispanic, 47% were black, and 35% were white (U.S. Department of Justice 2008b). The proportion of probationers in the United States that is Hispanic remained steady at about 13% from 1995 to 2005. Blacks consistently comprised 31% over this time frame, and whites have hovered around 54% of the total (Glaze and Bonczar 2008). Altogether, these correctional figures depict a midrange

TABLE 1. U.S. Incarceration Rates per 100,000 in Year 2000

Region	White	Black	Hispanic	All
Northeast	102	1,346	680	320
Midwest	192	1,775	325	363
South	244	1,480	422	517
West	226	947	470	426
U.S. Total	214	1,694	576	463

Sources: U.S. Census Bureau. 2000. *American FactFinder* fact sheet: http://factfinder.census.gov/ (accessed January 7, 2009), U.S. Department of Justice, Bureau of Justice Statistics, Census of State and Federal Correctional Facilities 2000, NCJ 198272 (Washington DC: US, Department of Justice 2003), p 3, Table 4.

expectation for system reaction to Hispanic suspects and criminal/juvenile court defendants.

While interesting, such descriptive data offer no information about deservedness of apprehension and punishment. These data may simply be a reflection of the level of criminal offending among the groups, leaving open the possibility of no discrimination against minorities. A critical test of the issue must therefore control for key legal items such as offending levels and criminal history to estimate the level of disproportionate targeting or punishment by the justice system. If sufficient statistical controls are in place, the increased chances of subjects to be arrested for characteristics not inherently legal in nature (e.g., race, ethnicity) is tantamount to differential treatment by police, if not profiling.

The Current Study

With so few and methodologically limited benchmarks for Hispanics, the current study estimates the undue arrest bias experienced by race-ethnic minorities, relative to whites, controlling for a rigorous set of legal and social arrest predictors. Where most early youth surveys did not sample enough Hispanics to generalize to the population, the National Longitudinal Survey of Youth 1997 (NLSY97) administered by the Bureau of Labor Statistics (BLS) oversamples Hispanics, yielding enough cases for sufficient variation on a number of observed outcomes, including arrest. This makes possible one of the first national-level studies on the arrest risk posed by the subject's Hispanic ethnicity status with interaction effects calculated for the midwestern region.

The scant research on arrests of Hispanics suggests that they experience an increased risk for arrest relative to whites, but possibly a decreased risk relative to blacks. In the absence of official national arrest data and prior survey research on arrest for this group, the sentencing research and correctional data help to inform the hypothesis that being Hispanic is a significant risk factor for arrest and that the degree of risk for this group will fall somewhere between that of white and black subjects.

Data and Methods

SAMPLE

In 1997, the NLSY began a random, multistage cluster sample survey of about 9,000 youths 12 to 16 years old as of December 31, 1996, and living in the United States. The initial wave consists of a cross-sectional sample of respondents representative of all youths (n = 6,748) and an oversample of black and Hispanic youths (n = 2,236). These panel data contain a wide range of information collected on respondents each year since, including their delinquency levels, arrests, and other legal and social indicators. Most of the information is obtained through youth self-reports with additional information gathered from the youths' parents and interviewer assessments of the youths' social environments. With the exception of items that are constant over time (race, sex, nativity), each indicator in the study is measured at each wave of analysis.

The subjects in our sample were ages 13 to 17 in 1998, maturing to 20 to 24 years of age by the eighth wave (year 2005). Sample attrition, missing cases, and missing data are observed in the NLSY97, but are rather low compared to prior national youth surveys. Over 80% of subjects in wave 1 are present in each follow-up.[5] For various reasons related to the lack of the youth's knowledge on the matter, parents' unavailability or refusal to answer, unreported sources of income, or nontraditional custodial conditions, one of the largest types of missing data is household income. We kept all cases with information on household income for a standard measure of socioeconomic status (SES), yielding 33,638 records to analyze, or 58% of the available observations across eight waves.

While this may seem like substantial attrition, the main advantage of the person-period data format with such a large number of observations is the ability to retain representativeness despite such omissions (Allison 1994; Western 2002). To account for the possibility that the omission of cases with missing data for SES would bias the results, we repeated the analysis by imputing missing data with the mean household income value, and results were essentially unchanged.[6] On average, each respondent in the sample contributed 6.1 observations to the data set.

MEASURES

DEPENDENT VARIABLE

The dependent variable is the number of new arrests reported by subjects in each of the eight waves.[7] The use of self-reported arrest data has one apparent limitation. While generally considered valid (Farrington et al. 1996; Hindelang, Hirschi, and Weiss 1981; Maxfield, Weiler, and Widom 2000; Thornberry and Krohn 2002), a source of error in self-report arrest data is the ambiguous nature of arrest. This is especially true with juveniles, for whom police have the various disposition options: counsel and release, refer to diversion, write citation, detain for questioning, and take into custody (Bell and Lang 1985; McEachern and Bauzer 1967; Piliavin and Briar 1964).

Many studies match the self-reported arrests of youth with their official arrest records for verification (see Brownfield, Sorenson, and Thomson 2001; Elliott and Voss 1974; Farrington, Loeber, and Stouthamer-Loeber 2003; Hirschfield et al. 2006; Hirschi 1969; Ludwig, Duncan, and Hirschfield 2001; Williams and Gold 1972), but since the NLSY97 does not, the dependent variable defers to a measure of contact with police perceived by subjects as an arrest. Although the vast majority of self-reported arrests show up in official records (Hindelang, Hirschi, and Weiss 1981; Hirschfield et al. 2006; Hirschi 1969), it is possible for some youth to misperceive their contact with the police as an arrest, even if officers use another, less-punitive disposition option.[8]

TEST VARIABLES

Race and ethnicity consist of dummy variables for white, black, and Hispanic respondents, with whites as the omitted race category in all regression analyses.[9] Nativity status is a dummy variable equal to 1 for U.S. born and 0 for foreign born. Dummy variables for region of the country are created, with the northeastern region as the omitted category in regression. The choice to use the Northeast as a baseline from which to gauge the effects of all other regions is informed by prior social science research showing this region is the whitest, wealthiest, and in turn perhaps the most liberal in its political orientation (Eberts 1989; Sahling and Smith 1983; Verdugo 1992).

DEMOGRAPHIC CONTROLS

The group of demographic control items used here explains variance in arrest outcomes in past research. SES is represented by parent-reported household income in each year. Because annual household income typically assumes a log-normal distribution with a positive skew in a large sample, a natural log transformation of income is employed (Sakamoto, Huei-Hwsia, and Tzeng 2000; Wilson 2000). Sex is a dummy variable equal to 1 for males. Age is a continuous variable, from 13 to 24. Geographic place is a dummy variable equal to 1 for urban location.

LEGAL CONTROLS

The NLSY97 contains a battery of self-reported crime and delinquency items, entered into a laptop computer during a self-administered portion of the survey. Subjects report the number of times they have committed any of the listed delinquent acts within the past year, ranging in severity from minor theft to assault with injury.[10] Such measures are well suited to estimating arrest risk since the chances of arrest should increase with the frequency of illegal behavior.

■ *Crime and delinquency.* Substance use items and petty theft comprise minor delinquency. Alcohol use measures the number of occasions in the last 30 days in which respondents consumed five or more alcoholic drinks. Marijuana use measures the number of days respondents used the drug over the past month. The number of times the respondent used cocaine or other hard drugs in the past year is also included. Assault, major theft, handling stolen property, gun carrying, and drug sales comprise serious delinquency. Each is an annual frequency measure, except for gun carrying, which reflects the number of times in the last 30 days in which respondents carried a handgun.

■ *Recode and weighting.* Respondents' exaggeration is certain to be part of any youth survey (see Elliott, Huizinga, and Morse 1987; Maxfield, Weiler, and Widom 2000). Extremely high values may be careless estimates based on respondents' inability or unwillingness to recall the number of incidents. For example, Thornberry and Krohn (2002) have noted "testing effects" as responses given haphazardly to advance to the next question in the event of a lengthy interview. Extremely high counts on delinquency items are outliers with poor face validity, and thus assigned to the highest value in the recode, thereby reducing skewness in their distributions (see Matthews and Agnew 2008).[11]

The weighting procedure developed for the delinquency measures captures the seriousness of each type of delinquency as informed by the literature (see appendix). As some of the most serious forms of delinquency in the study, for example, none of the frequency categories for carrying a gun or committing assault with bodily injury were collapsed, except for the highest categories (beyond six per year). This indicates that either it is a common type of arrest (Snyder 2008) or it is serious enough to warrant an arrest if detected by police. Collapsing more categories for less serious items reflects that they have a low detection ratio (as in the case of drug dealing) or are less likely to warrant an arrest if detected, because of infrequent reporting by citizens and more police discretion, as in the case of minor theft (Black and Reiss 1970; Lundman, Sykes, and Clark 1978).

■ *Criminal history.* Prior record controls for the number of arrests accumulated up to each wave in the analysis. Some researchers emphasize a tendency of patrol officers to become familiar with prior arrestees, perhaps leading to official labeling (Curry 2000; Monahan 1970; Werthman and Piliavin 1967). This, in turn, can lead to further criminal embeddedness as a "secondary" labeling effect (Bernburg, Krohn, and Rivera 2006; Nagin and Paternoster 1991). Having criminal history in the model thus results in a conservative estimate of labeling effects. Any extralegal effects obtained with prior arrests in the model go beyond delinquent propensity and official labeling.

DESCRIPTIVES

Table 2 offers the sample characteristics by race and ethnicity. Beginning with demographic items, the proportion of males in the black sample is slightly less than that of white or Hispanic males. On the whole, blacks are also a bit older than both other race-ethnic groups. The proportion of minorities living in urban settings is significantly higher than for whites. The vast majority of whites and blacks are U.S. born (85 and 83% respectively), while most of the Latino sample is *foreign* born (59%). Both minority groups report significantly less household income than whites, who dominate the northwestern and midwestern regions. The highest concentration of Hispanics is in the West, while the same applies to blacks in the South.

An interesting set of results is obtained for crime and delinquency items by race and ethnicity. Whites report more alcohol consumption, marijuana, hard drug use, and petty theft than either minority group, while minority groups report more assault. Blacks report more frequent gun carrying than whites and Hispanics and slightly more drug dealing than the latter two groups. Latinos report more major theft than both other groups. Both minority groups report more prior arrests and more gang membership. Finally, in this descriptive arena, black arrests are higher than white and Hispanic arrests, but there is no statistical difference between Hispanic and white arrests.

TABLE 2. Sample Characteristics by Race

	Full Sample (n = 8,984)		White (n = 4,665)		Black (n = 2,335)		Hispanic (n = 1,901)	
	Mean	s.d.	Mean	s.d.	Mean	s.d.	Mean	s.d.
RACE-ETHNICITY								
White	.52	.50	—	—	—	—	—	—
Black	.26	.44	—	—	—	—	—	—
Hispanic	.21	.41	—	—	—	—	—	—
DEMOGRAPHIC								
Male	.51	.50	.52	.50	.50†	.50	.51	.49
Age	19.35	2.70	19.32	2.68	19.43†	2.71	19.36	2.70
Urban	.58	.49	.58	.49	.71†	.45	.78†	.41
U.S. Born	.75	.43	.85	.35	.83†	.37	.41†	.49
SES								
Gross Household Income (in thousands)								
	$26.4	49.6	$31.7	56.4	$18.2†	37.2	$23.1†	42.7
REGION								
Northeast	.17	.38	.18	.39	.14†	.34	.14†	.35
Midwest	.23	.42	.29	.45	.17†	.37	.07†	.26
West	.22	.41	.18	.38	.06†	.23	.45†	.50
South	.38	.48	.27	.44	.58†	.49	.26*	.44
LEGAL								
Minor Delinquency								
Alcohol Use	2.84	5.34	3.46	5.70	1.80†	4.46	2.62*	5.23
Marijuana Use	1.68	5.93	1.87	6.15	1.55†	5.87	1.36†	5.36
Hard Drug Use	2.35	25.9	3.20	30.4	.90†	16.7	2.09	23.2
Petty Theft	.08	.40	.09	.43	.06†	.35	.08†	.39
Serious Delinquency								
Assault	.15	.75	.13	.69	.17†	.80	.16†	.80
Gun Carrying	.10	.74	.09	.71	.12†	.83	.09	.70
Drug Sales	1.44	29.2	1.26	26.3	1.79*	34.6	1.46	28.9
Major Theft	.04	.39	.04	.38	.04	.39	.05†	.43
Stolen Property	.04	.39	.043	.40	.037*	.36	.05	.42
Criminal History								
Prior Arrests	.40	1.48	.35	1.34	.51†	1.81	.39†	1.36
Gang Membership	.01	.11	.01	.08	.02†	.14	.02	.14
Arrested	.052	.22	.049	.21	.062†	.24	.049	.21
Arrests	.09	.71	.08	.40	.12†	.96	.09	.57

* Significantly different from white mean at $p < 0.05$. † $p < 0.01$, in a 2 sample t-test with equal variances.

ANALYTIC METHOD

The focus on race and the inclusion of several controls with unchanging values precludes the use of fixed effects, warranting a random effects model (REM) (Johnston and DiNardo 1997; Long and Freese 2003; Wooldridge 2002). The main advantage of REM in a repeated-observation panel design is the error term is uncorrelated across subjects. In addition, unlike fixed effects models, findings from random effects analyses enable inferences about (arrest dynamics in) the larger population from which the sample is drawn, U.S. adolescents and young adults in this case.

Counts with many zero values and with no theoretical upper limit (e.g., number of arrests) are well suited to analysis with Poisson regression (Wooldridge 2002). Although Poisson can yield inefficient estimates when the variance exceeds the mean on the outcome variable,[12] or in the case of serial dependence[13] (Cameron and Trivedi 1986; Cameron and Trivedi 1998; Long 1997; Long and Freese 2003; Wooldridge 2002), it remains the best procedure for this design. Wooldridge (2002, 672) has noted that *random effects* Poisson models, in particular, typically account for overdispersion and serial dependence in the data. Cameron and Trivedi (1998, 279–80) also warn of possible distortion of effects and of potential intercept shift with the alternative, longitudinal negative binomial model for count data.

Multivariate Results

Model 1 in table 3 shows that race-ethnic minority status significantly increases the risk of arrest, net of controls. The lack of a statistically significant difference between the arrest counts of whites and Hispanics in the descriptive arena was suppressed without these other key variables in the model. Consistent with our midrange expectation for Hispanics, the black slope is larger than the Hispanic slope. Black racial status increases the predicted number of arrests by about 0.34 versus 0.15 for Hispanic ethnic status.[14] Some have also found a midrange level of bias against Hispanic youth (Dannefer and Schutt 1982), while others have found equal levels of bias against blacks and Mexican Americans (Bell and Lang 1985). Few prior studies have estimated the effects of Latino ethnic status on arrest with a national sample, however.

Results for control items are mostly as expected, with only a few exceptions. The first is urban location, which yields significant negative effects on arrest, despite past research showing that self-reported juvenile violence (McNulty and Bellair 2003) and official arrest rates for juvenile violence are higher in urban versus nonurban contexts (Osgood and Chambers 2003). Yet Laub (1981) has shown that minor crimes

TABLE 3. Poisson Regression Predicting Arrests

	Model 1		Model 2		Model 3	
	b	SE	*b*	SE	*b*	SE
RACE-ETHNICITY						
Black	.341†	.044	.340†	.044	.268†	.051
Hispanic	.152†	.052	.182†	.055	.120*	.058
DEMOGRAPHIC						
Male	.961†	.044	.960†	.044	.960†	.044
Age	−.028†	.009	−.028†	.009	−.027	.009
Urban	−.259†	.041	−.255†	.041	−.263†	.041
SES						
Gross Household Income	−.148†	.013	−.147†	.013	−.147†	.013
Region						
Midwest	.159†	.055	.149†	.055	.042	.064
West	−.255†	.021	−.227†	.061	−.217†	.061
South	−.083	.038	−.089	.052	−.071	.052
LEGAL						
Minor Delinquency						
Alcohol Use	.011†	.002	.011†	.002	.011†	.002
Marijuana Use	.022†	.001	.022†	.001	.022†	.001
Hard Drug Use	.004†	.000	.004†	.000	.004†	.000
Petty Theft	.186†	.030	.184†	.030	.183†	.030
Serious Delinquency						
Major Theft	.214†	.022	.216†	.021	.218†	.022
Other Property Crime	.005	.019	.003	.019	.004	.019
Assault	.155†	.011	.155†	.011	.154†	.011
Gun Carrying	.030†	.011	.030†	.011	.031†	.011
Drug Sales	.001†	.000	.001†	.000	.001†	.000
Prior Arrests	.053†	.003	.053†	.003	.053†	.003
Gang Membership	.767†	.063	.770†	.063	.776†	.063
U.S. Born	—	—	.085	.050	.079	.050
Black × Midwest	—	—	—	—	.278†	.095
Hispanic × Midwest	—	—	—	—	.351*	.142
Pseudo R^2	.20	.20	.20			

*$p < 0.05$. † $p < 0.01$.

are reported more often in rural versus urban settings. That much of the sample is juvenile, , and that the vast majority of juvenile offenses are not serious or violent in nature (Black and Reiss 1970; Erickson 1971; Ferdinand and Luchterhand 1970; Harris 1986; Lundman, Sykes, and Clark 1978; Piliavin and Briar 1964), provides a possible explanation for our findings.

Much past research also finds that for youthful offenders, arrest increases with age (Butts and Snyder 2006; Elliott, Huizinga, and Morse 1987; McEachern and Bauzer 1967; Shannon 1991; Simcha-Fagan and Schwartz 1986; Werthman and Piliavin 1967; Williams and Gold 1972). Other recent studies find no age effect in youth survey data, however (Hirschfield et al. 2006). Perhaps because we study a longer span of the life course than these prior studies do, our results show that arrest chances decrease with age.

The midwestern region is the only geographic area of the United States yielding a positive, significant effect on arrest frequency. Encouraged by this result, we explore its interactive effects with minority status in a subsequent model. Interestingly, subjects from the western and southern regions experience a reduced risk of arrest, relative to the Midwest and the omitted northeastern category. Model 1 provides the basis for an elaboration that adds nativity status in Model 2 and interaction terms for race and region in Model 3.

With a majority of the Latinos in the sample being foreign born, Model 2 enters nativity status to note any mediating effects it may have on arrest for Latinos primarily. Somewhat consistent with the acculturation effect found in the literature on immigration and crime (Rumbaut et al. 2006; Tonry 1997; Zhou 1997), the U.S.-born coefficient is positive, yet it is not a significant arrest predictor. It does, however, mediate the Latino effect, increasing the size of the Latino coefficient by about 16%. Its entry to the model also somewhat attenuates the midwestern effect by about 6%, suggesting that part of the midwestern effect could be attributed to the growth of the Latino population in the region.

The focus on Latino arrests, coupled with the positive main effect for the Midwest warrants a test for interaction between minority status and the Midwest. The few studies on regional variation in formal social control (Jackson 1989; Kent and Jacobs 2005) do not comment much on trends in the Midwest, but focus on the southern, western, and northeastern regions. The omnibus regression coefficients yield significant, positive effects for both minority × Midwest terms.

PROBING INTERACTIONS

A final analysis section more carefully probes the nature and form of the minority × Midwest interactions for a better depiction of the conditional relationships.

FIGURE 1. Arrests by Region, Moderated by Race

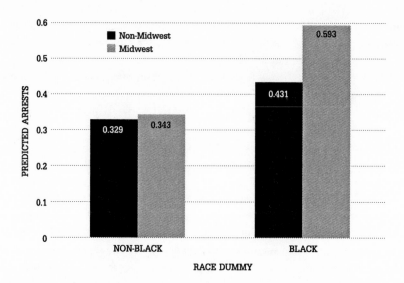

FIGURE 2. Arrests by Race, Moderated by Region

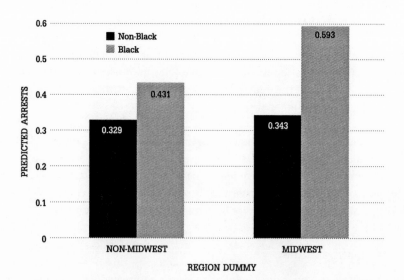

FIGURE 3. Arrests by Region, Moderated by Ethnicity

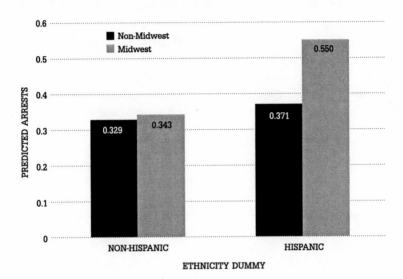

FIGURE 4. Arrests by Ethnicity, Moderated by Region

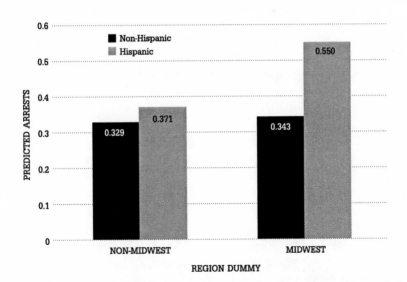

Obtaining the simple slopes by solving for $\hat{Y}$ and plotting values for the focal variables offers a clearer demonstration of effects than those yielded by regression coefficients alone (Aiken and West 1991; Kaufman 2002). It is a way to determine whether conditional effects are truly present,[15] while better illustrating the relational form of the values implied by the interaction.

Results in figure 1 show that race moderates the relationship of the regional dummy variable to the number of arrests. The black category increases the predicted number of arrests by a full 42% for midwestern subjects and by just 23% for non-midwestern subjects, a significant interaction ($t = 3.41, p < 0.01$).

Although the method offers a bit of redundant information, switching the format of the focal variables in figure 2 illustrates that region also moderates the race effect. The midwestern category increases the expected number of arrests for black subjects by 27% and has little effect on nonblack subjects, offering another depiction of the interaction of these two variables ($t = 5.77, p < 0.01$). The black × midwestern interaction was thus symbiotic (i.e., each item significantly moderates the effects of the other).

Using the same format as for blacks, figure 3 plots the first Hispanic × midwestern interaction. Hispanic moderates the relationship of the midwestern region to the number of arrests. It increases the predicted number of arrests by about 38% for midwestern subjects and only by 11% for non-midwesterners, a significant contrast ($t = 2.36, p < 0.05$).

Finally, figure 4 shows that the midwestern region increases the expected number of arrests by 32.5% for Hispanic subjects and by just 4% for non-Hispanics ($t = 2.38, p < 0.05$), a significant interaction. Probing the Hispanic × midwestern interaction has more clearly depicted the nature of the relationship between these variables than with regression coefficients alone, and helps to confirm the results obtained in table 3.

Conclusion

While prior research shows that Latinos are disproportionately convicted and confined in prison, little is known about arrest dynamics for this group. This is one of the first studies to date that estimates Latino effects on arrest versus that of other racial/ethnic groups using a national sample. The findings reveal that writ broadly, race-ethnic minority group status is an arrest risk factor, controlling for key demographic and legal items. Conducting separate tests for the two minority groups, effects for blacks are stronger than for Hispanics in the arrest decision. All other things equal, Hispanics are more likely to be arrested than whites, and blacks are twice as likely as Hispanics to be arrested. This finding supports prior research that suggests that there is a midrange level of arrest bias against Hispanics (Dannefer and Schutt 1982). However, prior research only highlighted these arrest differences in specific jurisdictions or cities.

Respondents from western and southern states experience a decreased risk of arrest, compared to their northeastern and midwestern counterparts. Specifically, the Midwest is the only region with a positive, significant relationship to arrest. As noted, using the Northeast as the omitted category is informed by prior research showing this region is the whitest, wealthiest, and in turn perhaps the most liberal in its political orientation. Recall, however, that in table 1, the northeastern region was the most punitive against Hispanics in terms of incarceration rates and the midwestern region the least. To be sure, having noted the majority of Latinos in the sample were foreign born, we tested a second model that included nativity satus (U.S. born) to reevaluate midwestern and Latino effects. Although it did not achieve statistical significance, the effect for Latinos was strengthened in this model, suggesting that native-born Latinos may be more arrest-prone than their foreign born counterparts. That the value on the Midwestern coefficient slightly decreased suggests this may have regional nuances.

Our specific interest in effects for midwestern Latinos led to a test for interaction effects between minority status and the Midwest. Results show that the Hispanic × Midwest interaction is positive, and significant. The black × Midwest interaction on arrest risk is also both positive and significant. That Hispanic origin moderates the relationship between the midwestern region and the number of arrests tells us that, the risk of arrest for Midwest Latinos is higher compared to Latinos from other regions of the country. It also means that being from the Midwest significantly increases arrest risk for Hispanics compared to whites.

Limitations and Future Research

The current research breaks new ground on Hispanic crime and justice processing in the United States by highlighting the importance of racial/ethnic status and regional variation on the decision to arrest by law enforcement. Yet, more research is needed to paint a full picture of Hispanic arrest risk in the Midwest and throughout the United States. For example, while we now know that even when controlling for current crime levels, criminal history, and other important arrest correlates, Hispanic ethnicity is a risk factor for arrest, there are sure to be important variations within the larger Latino ethnic group by nationality. Studies on Latinos of Cuban, Mexican, or Puerto Rican origin or descent, for example, find important differences between them on crime and justice outcomes (Martinez 2002; Morenoff 2005; Nielsen, Lee, and Martinez 2005; Rumbaut et al. 2006; Urbina 2007). Without being able to distinguish respondents of various Latino ethnic origins in the NLSY, any variation in the arrest risk associated with belonging to a particular Latino subgroup is masked in the current study.

Second, very little is known about the informal processes that take place with law enforcement prior to the arrest encounter. Arrest incidents are defined by a host of legal and extralegal variables that are often complexly related. To date, no single data set or study measures them all, however. Often, a methodological choice must be made between official data, survey data, or observations of police-citizen contacts in the field. Whereas the merits of survey data in evaluating Hispanic arrest risk are demonstrated here, data limitations disallow a full picture of arrest dynamics for all groups. Field observations capture important idiosyncratic elements that are either not measurable with the self-report method or are often not documented or sufficiently detailed in official reports (e.g., complainant demands for arrest, the presence of evidence, and suspect demeanor). Future research should attempt to triangulate the investigation with field data to try to capture some of these elements or, at a minimum, account for unobserved but constant traits such as suspect demeanor with separate equations for race and fixed effects.

Finally, very little is known about the arrest process in later stages in the life course. One of the limitations of this sample is that it only captures self-reported behavior and arrests for adolescents and young adults. The good news is that the U.S. Department of Labor Statistics will continue to collect data on this sample each year. Future research can examine the risk of arrest by race-ethnicity and region for a more mature sample of adults, possibly enabling us to say more about the criminal desistance process that takes place for subjects in their midtwenties to early thirties.

NOTES

1. While NIBRS has the capacity to report data on offenders' ethnicity, only the race indicators remain mandatory data items. The FBI's data collection guidelines do not require recording the arrestee's ethnicity (Data Element 50), noting, "This is an optional data element . . . recorded at the discretion of the reporting agency" (U.S. Department of Justice Federal Bureau of Investigation 2000, 104).

2. Although in census data, over 90% are white (www.census.gov).

3. Dannefur and Schutt (1982) provide an exception with official data.

4. We reference correctional data from this period rather than more current figures since our analysis runs from 1998 to 2005.

5. Overall response rates for the panels used in the current study fell between (N = 8,386) in

1998 and (N = 7,338) in 2005.

6. Imputed results available upon request.

7. Allison (1990) discusses the merits of obtaining repeated measurements of the dependent variable over time for making causal inferences.

8. Claims of arrest in the survey lead to questions about further processing by the justice system. This cannot be used as a validity check, however, because information regarding prosecution and punitive sanctions are also self-reported.

9. Because Asian and Native Americans comprise a small proportion (1% each) of persons arrested in the United States (Snyder 2008), they are not included in the current research.

10. The strongest correlations registered between delinquency items were among the property-related crimes (r = 0.32 to r = 0.45), and for marijuana and alcohol use (r = 0.35). No other correlations were in this range. STATA diagnostics detected no collinearity issues among the set of variables in the study.

11. Delinquent incidence is also likely to experience a decay effect on arrest risk after a certain threshold (Dunford and Elliott 1984).

12. Likelihood ratio tests confirm the presence of overdispersion. Final interaction model: Chi-square = 4514.97, p < 0.0000.

13. Having a prior arrest is a predictor of future arrests (Battin et al. 1998; Curry 2000; Dannefur and Schutt 1982; Piliavin and Briar 1964; Terry 1967), a possible violation of the assumption of independence of observations.

14. Count model coefficients are expressed by the natural logarithm of the outcome as a linear function of a set of predictors (Cameron and Trivedi 1986; 1998; Long and Freese 2003; Wooldridge 2002).

15. For interactions, the significance reading in regression output is considered a global test of significance. In this case, it signals that the interaction slopes are statistically different from zero, when all other variables have a value of zero (Aiken and West 1991; Jaccard and Turrissi 2003). Subsequent t-tests of the interaction simple slopes determine whether relationships of race-ethnicity and region to arrest are truly conditional.

REFERENCES

Aiken, L., and S. West. 1991. *Multiple Regression: Testing and Interpreting Interactions.* Newbury Park, CA: Sage.

Allison, P. D. 1990. "Change Scores as Dependent Variables in Regression Analysis." *Sociological Methodology* 20: 93–114.

———. 1994. "Using Panel Data to Estimate the Effects of Events." *Sociological Methods and Research* 23(2): 174–99.

Battin, S., K. G. Hill, R. Abbott, R. Catalano, and J. D. Hawkins. 1998. "The Contribution of Gang Membership to Delinquency beyond Delinquent Friends. *Criminology* 36(1): 93–116.

Bell, D., and K. Lang. 1985. "The Intake Dispositions of Juvenile Offenders." *Journal of Research in Crime and Delinquency* 22(4): 309–28.

Bernburg, J. G., M. D. Krohn, and C. J. Rivera. 2006. "Official Labeling, Criminal Embeddedness, and Subsequent Delinquency: A Longitudinal Test of Labeling Theory." *Journal of Research in Crime and Delinquency* 43(1): 67–90.

Black, D., and A. Reiss. 1970. "Police Control of Juveniles." *American Sociological Review* 35(1): 63–77.

Brownfield, D., A. M. Sorenson, and K. Thomson. 2001. "Gang Membership, Race, and Social Class: A Test of the Group Hazard and Master Status Hypothesis." *Deviant Behavior* 22: 73–89.

Brownsberger, W. N. 2000. "Race Matters: Disproportionality of Incarceration for Drug Dealing in Massachusetts." *Journal of Drug Issues* 30(2): 345–74.

Butts, J., and H. Snyder. 2006. "Too Soon to Tell: Deciphering Recent Trends in Youth Violence." Issue brief. Chapin Hall, Chicago. Available online: www.chapinhall.org.

California Administrative Office of the Courts Research and Planning Unit. 2001. "Report to the Legislature Pursuant to Penal Code Section 1170.45: The Disposition of Criminal Cases According to the Race and Ethnicity of the Defendant." Available online: www.courtinfo.ca.gov.

Cameron, A. C., and P. K. Trivedi. 1986. "Econometric Models Based on Count Data: Comparisons and Applications of Some Estimators and Tests." *Journal of Applied Econometrics* 1: 29–54.

———. 1998. *Regression Analysis of Count Data.* New York: Cambridge University Press.

Cicourel, A. 1976. *The Social Organization of Juvenile Justice.* New York: Wiley and Sons.

Curry, D. G. 2000. "Self-Reported Gang Involvement and Officially Recorded Delinquency." *Criminology* 38(4): 1253–73.

Dannefer, D., and R. Schutt. 1982. "Race and Juvenile Justice Processing in Court and Police Agencies." *American Journal of Sociology* 87(5): 1113–32.

Dunford F., and D. Elliott. 1984. "Identifying Career Offenders Using Self-Reported Data." *Journal of Research in Crime and Delinquency* 21(1): 57–86.

Eberts, R. W. 1989. "Accounting for Recent Divergence in Regional Wage Differentials." *Economic Review* 25(3): 14–26.

Elliott, D. S., and S. Ageton. 1980. "Reconciling Race and Class Differences in Self-Reported and Official Estimates of Delinquency." *American Sociological Review* 45(1): 95–110.

Elliott, D. S., D. Huizinga, and B. Morse. 1987. "Self-Reported Violent Offending: A Descriptive Analysis of Juvenile Violent Offenders and Their Offending Careers." *Journal of Interpersonal Violence* 1(4): 472–514.

Elliott, D. S., and H. Voss. 1974. *Delinquency and Dropout.* Lexington, MA: DC Heath.

Empey, L. 1982. *American Delinquency: Its Meaning and Construction.* Homewood, IL: Dorsey.

Erickson, M. 1971. "The Group Context of Delinquent Behavior." *Social Problems* 19(1): 114–29.

Farrington, D. P., R. Loeber, and M. Stouthamer-Loeber. 2003. "How Can the Relationship between Race and Violence Be Explained?" In *Violent Crime: Assessing Race and Ethnic Differences,* ed. Darnell F. Hawkins, 213–37. New York: Cambridge University Press.

Farrington D. P., R. Loeber, M. Stouthamer-Loeber, W. B. V. Kammen, and L. Schmidt. 1996. "Self-Reported Delinquency and a Combined Delinquency Seriousness Scale Based on Boys, Others, and Teachers: Concurrent and Predictive Validity for African-Americans and Caucasians." *Criminology* 34(4): 493–518.

Ferdinand, T., and E. Luchterhand. 1970. "Inner City Youth, the Police, the Juvenile Court, and Justice." *Social Problems* 17(4): 510–27.

Glaze, L. E., and T. P. Bonczar. 2008. "Probation and Parole in the U.S., 2006." Bureau of Justice Statistics Report No. NCJ 220218. Available online: www.ojp.usdoj.gov.

Hagan, J., and J. P. Coleman. 2001. "Returning Captives of the American War on Drugs: Issues of Community and Family Reentry." *Crime and Delinquency* 47(3): 352–67.

Hagan, J., and A. Palloni. 1999. "Sociological Criminology and the Mythology of Hispanic

Immigration." *Social Problems* 46(4): 617–32.

Harris, P. M. 1986. "Is the Juvenile Justice System Lenient?" *Criminal Justice Abstracts* 18: 104–18.

Hawkins, D. F., ed. 1995. *Ethnicity, Race, and Crime: Perspectives across Time and Place*. Albany: State University of New York Press.

Hebert, C. 1997. "Sentencing Outcomes of Black, Hispanic, and White Males Convicted under Federal Sentencing Guidelines." *Criminal Justice Review* 22(2): 133–56.

Hindelang, M., T. Hirschi and J. G. Weiss. 1981. *Measuring Delinquency*. Beverly Hills, CA: Sage.

Hirschfield, P., T. Maschi, H. R. White, L. G. Traub, and R. Loeber. 2006. "Mental Health and Juvenile Arrests: Criminality, Criminalization or Compassion?" *Criminology* 44(3): 593–627.

Hirschi, T. 1969. *Causes of Delinquency*. Berkeley: University of California Press.

Huizinga, D., and D. Elliott. 1987. "Juvenile Offenders: Prevalence, Offender Incidence, and Arrest Rates by Race." *Crime and Delinquency* 33(2): 206–23.

Huizinga, D., T. Thornberry, K. Knight, and P. Lovegrove. 2007. "Disproportionate Minority Contact in the Juvenile Justice System: A Study of Differential Minority Arrest/Referral to Court in Three Cities." Unpublished report to the Office of Juvenile Justice and Delinquency Prevention.

Jaccard, J., and R. Turrisi. 2003. *Interaction Effects in Multiple Regression*. 2nd ed. Newbury Park, CA: Sage.

Jackson, P. I. 1989. *Minority Group Threat, Crime, and Policing: Social Context and Social Control*. New York: Praeger.

Johnston, J., and J. DiNardo. 1997. *Econometric Methods*. 4th ed. New York: McGraw-Hill.

Kaufman, J. 2005. "Explaining the Race/Ethnicity–Violence Relationship: Neighborhood Context and Social Psychological Processes." *Justice Quarterly* 22(2): 224–51.

Kaufman, R. 2002. "Interpreting Interactions." Didactic seminar, Annual Meeting of the American Sociological Association.

Kent, S. L., and D. Jacobs. 2005. "Minority Threat and Police Strength from 1980 to 2000: A Fixed Effects Analysis of Non-linear and Interactive Effects in Large U.S. Cities." *Criminology* 43(3): 731–56.

Lattimore, P. K., J. M. McDonald, A. Piquero, R. L. Linster, and C. Visher. 2004. "Studying the Characteristics of Arrest Frequency among Paroled, Youthful Offenders." *Journal of Research in Crime and Delinquency* 41(1): 37–57.

La Free, G. 1985. "Official Reactions to Hispanic Defendants in the Southwest." *Journal of Research in Crime and Delinquency* 22(3): 213–31.

Laub, J. 1981. "Ecological Considerations in Victim Reporting to the Police." *Journal of Criminal Justice* 9(6): 419–30.

Long, J. S. 1997. *Regression Models for Categorical and Limited Dependent Variables*. Washington, DC: Sage.

Long, J. S., and J. Freese. 2003. *Regression Models for Categorical Variables Using Stata*. College Station, TX: Stata Press.

Ludwig, J., G. J. Duncan, and P. Hirschfield. 2001. "Urban Poverty and Juvenile Crime: Evidence from a Randomized Housing Mobility Experiment." *Quarterly Journal of Economics* 116(2): 655–79.

Lundman, R., R. Sykes, and J. P. Clark. 1978. "Police Control of Juveniles: A Replication." *Journal of Research in Crime and Delinquency* 15(1): 74–91.

Lynam, D. R., A. Caspi, T. Moffitt, P. O. Wikstrom, R. Loeber, and S. Novak. 2000. "The Interaction between Impulsivity and Neighborhood Context on Offending: The Effects of Impulsivity are Stronger in Poor Neighborhoods." *Journal of Abnormal Psychology* 109(4): 563–74.

Martinez, R., Jr. 2002. *Latino Homicide: Immigration, Violence, and Community.* New York: Routledge.

———. 2003. "Moving beyond Black and White: African American, Haitian and Latino Homicide in Miami." In *Violent Crime: Assessing Race and Ethnic Differences,* ed. Darnell F. Hawkins, 22–43. New York: Cambridge University Press.

Matthews, S. K., and R. Agnew. 2008. "Extending Deterrence Theory: Do Delinquent Peers Condition the Relationship between Perceptions of Getting Caught and Offending?" *Journal of Research in Crime and Delinquency* 45(2): 91–118.

Maxfield, M. G., B. L. Weiler, and C. S. Widom. 2000. "Comparing Self Reports and Official Records of Arrest." *Journal of Quantitative Criminology* 16(1): 87–110.

McEachern, A. W., and R. Bauzer. 1967. "Factors Related to Disposition in Juvenile Police Contacts." In *Juvenile Gangs in Context: Theory, Research, and Action,* ed. M. Klein and B. G. Myerhoff, 148–60. Englewood Cliffs, NJ: Prentice-Hall.

McNulty, T., and P. Bellair. 2003. "Explaining Racial and Ethnic Differences in Serious Adolescent Violent Behavior." *Criminology* 41(3): 709–48.

Monahan, T. 1970. "Police Dispositions of Juvenile Offenders." *Phylon* 31(2): 129–41.

Morenoff, J. D. 2005. "Racial and Ethnic Disparities in Crime and Delinquency in the US." In *Ethnicity and Causal Mechanisms,* ed. M. Tienda and M. Rutter, 139–73. New York: Cambridge University Press.

Mustard, D. B. 2001. "Racial, Ethnic and Gender Disparities in Sentencing: Evidence from the US Federal Courts." *Journal of Law and Economics* 44(1): 285–314.

Nagin, D., and R. Paternoster. 1991. "On the Relationship of Past to Future Participation in Delinquency." *Criminology* 29(2): 163–89.

National Archive of Criminal Justice Data. National Incident-Based Reporting System Codebook 2000. Available online: www.icpsr.umich.edu.

Nielsen, A., M. T. Lee, and R. Martinez Jr. 2005. "Integrating Race, Place and Motive in Social Disorganization Theory: Lessons from a Comparison of Black and Latino Homicide Types in Two Immigrant Destination Cities." *Criminology* 43(3): 837–72.

Osgood, D. W., and J. Chambers. 2003. "Community Correlates of Rural Youth Violence." *Juvenile Justice Bulletin* May: 1–12.

Petersilia, J. 1985. "Racial Disparities in the Criminal Justice System." *Crime and Delinquency* 31(1): 15–34.

Piliavin, I., and S. Briar. 1964. "Police Encounters with Juveniles." *American Journal of Sociology* 70(2): 206–14.

Royo-Maxwell, S., and J. Davis. 1999. "The Salience of Race and Gender in Pretrial Release Decisions: A Comparison across Multiple Jurisdictions." *Criminal Justice Policy Review* 10(4): 491–502.

Rumbaut, R. G., R. G. Gonzales, G. Komaie, C. V. Morgan, and R. Tafoya-Estrada. 2006. "Immigration and Incarceration: Patterns and Predictors of Imprisonment among First- and Second-Generation Young Adults." In *Immigration and Crime: Ethnicity, Race, and Violence,* ed. R. Martinez and A. Valenzuela, 64–89. New York: New York University Press.

Russell, K. 1998. *The Color of Crime: Racial Hoaxes, White Fear, Black Protectionism, Police Harassment, and Other Macroaggressions.* New York: New York University Press.

Sahling, L., and S. P. Smith. 1983. "Regional Wage Differentials: Has the South Risen Again?" *Review of Economics and Statistics* 65(1): 131–35.

Sakamoto, A., W. Huei-Hwsia, and J. M. Tzeng. 2000. "The Declining Significance of Race among American Men in the Latter Half of the 20th Century." *Demography* 37(1): 41–50.

Sampson, R. J. 1986. "Effects of Socioeconomic Context on Official Reaction to Juvenile Delinquency." *American Sociological Review* 51(6): 876–85.

Sealock, M., and S. S. Simpson. 1998. "Unraveling Bias in Arrest Decisions: The Role of Juvenile Offender Type-scripts." *Justice Quarterly* 15(3): 427–57.

Shannon, L. 1991. *Changing Patterns of Delinquency and Crime.* Boulder, CO: Westview Press.

Simcha-Fagan, O., and J. E. Schwartz. 1986. "Neighborhood and Delinquency: An Assessment of Contextual Effects." *Criminology* 24(4): 667–703.

Sissons, P. 1979. *The Hispanic Experience of Criminal Justice.* Bronx, NY: Hispanic Research Center, Fordham University.

Snyder, H. 2008. "Juvenile Arrest 2006." *OJJDP Bulletin.* NCJ 221338.

Spohn, C., and M. DeLone. 2000. "When Does Race Matter? An Analysis of the Conditions under Which Race Affects Sentence Severity." *Sociology of Crime, Law, and Deviance* 2: 3–37.

Tapia, M. 2010. "Untangling Race and Class Effects in Juvenile Arrest." *Journal of Criminal Justice* 38(3): 255–65.

Tapia, M., and P. M. Harris. 2006. "Race and Revocation: Is There a Penalty for Young, Minority Males?" *Journal of Ethnicity in Criminal Justice* 4(3): 1–24.

Terry, R. 1967. "Discrimination in the Handling of Juvenile Offenders by Social Control Agencies." *Journal of Research in Crime and Delinquency* 4(2): 218–30.

Thornberry T. P., and M. D. Krohn. 2002. "Comparison of Self-Report and Official Data for Measuring Crime." In *Measurement Problems in Criminal Justice Research: Workshop Summary*, ed. J. V. Pepper and C. V. Petrie, 43–94. Washington, DC: National Academies Press.

Tonry, M., ed. 1997. *Ethnicity, Crime, and Immigration: Comparative and Cross-National Perspectives.* Chicago: University of Chicago Press.

Unnever, J. D. 1982. "Direct and Organizational Discrimination in the Sentencing of Drug Offenders." *Social Problems* 30(2): 212–25.

Urbina, M. G. 2007. "Latino/as in the criminal and juvenile justice systems. *Critical Criminology* 15(1): 41–99.

U.S. Census Bureau. 2000. American FactFinder fact sheet. Available online: http://factfinder. census.gov/.

U.S. Department of Justice. Federal Bureau of Investigation, Criminal Justice Information Services Administration. 2000. Uniform Crime Reporting, National Incident-Based Reporting System. NIBRS Data Collection Guidelines. August. Available online: www.fbi.gov.

U.S. Department of Justice. Bureau of Justice Statistics. 2003. Census of State and Federal Correctional Facilities 2000. NCJ 198272. Washington, DC: U.S. Department of Justice.

———. 2008a. "Prison Statistics." Available online: www.ojp.usdoj.gov.

———. 2008b. "Probation and Parole Statistics." Available online: www.ojp.usdoj.gov.

U.S. Department of Justice. Federal Bureau of Investigation, Criminal Justice Information Services Administration. 2000. Uniform Crime Reporting, National Incident-Based Reporting System. NIBRS Data Collection Guidelines. August. Available online: www.fbi.gov.

Verdugo, R. 1992. "Earnings Differentials between Black, Mexican American, and Non-Hispanic White Male Workers: On the Cost of Being a Minority Worker, 1972–1987." *Social Science*

Quarterly 73(3): 663–73.

Walker, S., C. Spohn, and M. DeLone. 2003. *The Color of Justice: Race, Ethnicity, and Crime in America*. 3rd ed. Belmont, CA: Wadsworth.

Walker, N. E., J. M. Senger, F. A. Villarruel, and A. Arboleda. 2004. *Lost Opportunities: The Reality of Latinos in the U.S. Criminal Justice System*. Washington, DC: National Council of La Raza.

Werthman, C., and I. Piliavin. 1967. "Gang Members and the Police." In *The Police: Six Sociological Essays*, ed. D. J. Bordua, 56–98. New York: Wiley and Sons.

Western, B. 2002. "The Impact of Incarceration on Wage Mobility and Inequality." *American Sociological Review* 67(4): 477–98.

Williams, J. R., and M. Gold. 1972. "From Delinquent Behavior to Official Delinquency." *Social Problems* 20(2): 209–29.

Wilson, G. 2000. "Income in Upper-Tier Occupations among Males over the 1st Decade of the Work Career: Is Race Declining in Significance?" *National Journal of Sociology* 12(1): 105–28.

Wikstrom, P., and R. Loeber. 2000. "Do Disadvantaged Neighborhoods Cause Well-Adjusted Children to Become Adolescent Delinquents? A Study of Male Juvenile Serious Offending, Individual Risk and Protective Factors, and Neighborhood Context." *Criminology* 38(4): 1109–43.

Wooldridge, J. 2002. *Econometric Analysis of Cross Section and Panel Data*. Cambridge: MIT Press.

Zatz, M. S. 1984. "Race, Ethnicity, and Determinate Sentencing: A New Dimension to an Old Controversy." *Criminology* 22: 147–71.

Zhou, M. 1997. "Segmented Assimilation: Issues, Controversies, and Recent Research on the New Second Generation." *International Migration Review* 31(4): 825–58.

APPENDIX. GENERAL DELINQUENCY MEASURES, TWELVE-MONTH INCIDENCE

ITEM AND (ORIGINAL SCALE)	RECODE	NEW SCORE
Steal < $50 (0–99)	0	0
	1–2	1
	3–9	2
	11–99	3
Steal > $50 (0–99)	0	0
	1	1
	2	2
	3–4	3
	5–9	4
	10–99	5
Handling stolen property (0–99)	0	0
	1	1
	2	2
	3	3
	4–9	4
	10–99	5
Attack/assault (0–99)	0	0

	1	1
	2	2
	3	3
	4	4
	5	5
	6–10	6
	11–99	7
Sell drugs (0–99)	0	0
	1–3	1
	4–9	2
	10–20	3
	21–98	4
	99	5
Gun carrying (0–30 past month incidence)	0	0
	1–3	1
	4–9	2
	10–20	3
	21–98	4
	99	5

DAVID A. BADILLO

Litigating Bilingual Education: A History of the *Gomez* Decision in Illinois

DURING THE 20TH CENTURY, EDUCATIONAL ISSUES OF SEGREGATION AND LANGUAGE became increasingly interrelated legally. Beginning in 1930 several landmark federal cases in Texas and California addressed unequal treatment in the form of separate "Mexican Schools" with special classes for the Spanish speaking that separated them from Anglo students. During the 1940s, according to education historian Guadalupe San Miguel (1987, 121), most Texas school districts with growing numbers of Mexican students also segregated them "in classrooms, in the teachers' roll books, and especially in extracurricular activities." In 1947 a California appeals court ruled in *Mendez v. Westminster* that segregation of Mexican schoolchildren was illegal and thus unconstitutional, which encouraged Mexican American civil rights advocates to shift their focus back to Texas. There, with the aid of the League of United Latin American Citizens (LULAC), Mexican American parents in 1948 brought a lawsuit against state education officials in Bastrop County. In *Delgado v. Bastrop* a federal district court ruled that school districts could establish segregated facilities for pupils within the same buildings, "in the first grade only and solely for instructional purposes" for those pupils who, according to suitable testing, did not "possess a sufficient familiarity with the English language" (San Miguel 1987, 125; San

Miguel 2001; San Miguel 2004; Olivas 2006; Lopez and Olivas 2008). Following the landmark 1954 United States Supreme Court decision in *Brown v. Board of Education*, under what came to be known as "Texas-style integration," Anglo communities in the Southwest devised strategies to keep their children in neighborhood schools while "integrating" African Americans with Mexican Americans.

Civil rights activism within the Latino community ranges from locally based, grassroots organizing to national organizations that rely on highly trained legal professionals and appeals up to the United States Supreme Court. Before 1970 LULAC and the American GI Forum took the lead in using the courts to fulfill Latino civil rights goals. Since its founding in 1968, however, the Mexican American Legal Defense and Educational Fund (MALDEF) has stood at the forefront of Latino legal activity, linked through its local offices with San Antonio, Los Angeles, and other southwestern barrios. In 1980, it planted itself in Chicago in order to cover the Midwest and more recently in Atlanta for the Southeast. MALDEF has emerged as the primary force for litigation of a wide variety of what might be called "national origin" discrimination cases, including those involving enforcement of the federal 1972 Equal Employment Opportunity Act and the 1974 Equal Educational Opportunity Act. It has also taken the lead in educational litigation cases that have emerged throughout the United States.

This chapter merges history, sociology, and legal studies to explore the workings of MALDEF with respect to language policy in the Midwest. The first section highlights some of the legal issues in federal education cases of the 1970s, particularly those involving aspects of both desegregation and bilingual education, key areas of civil rights litigation. Next the focus shifts to MALDEF's specific response to challenges and circumstances presented in the case of *Gomez v. Illinois State Board of Education*, which culminated in a favorable ruling and settlement in the United States Court of Appeals for the Seventh Circuit in 1987. A concluding section discusses the enhanced effectiveness of bilingual education programs resulting from this litigation, and their increased reach among diverse state and local educational agencies. My sources include contemporary news accounts, court documents, internal memos and reports gleaned from archives, as well as the writings of scholars and other commentators. I have also incorporated an interview with the former Chicago MALDEF staff attorney whose diligence found a willing plaintiff and helped launch the class action lawsuit.

Desegregation as the Legal Route to Bilingual Education

Educational scholar Richard Valencia (2008, 309), who has examined the historic impact of desegregation cases on Mexican Americans, notes that during the late 1960s "the U.S. Department of Justice began a campaign to force state educational agencies into compliance with new federal desegregation rulings." Eliminating segregated school facilities remained the dominant strategy for obtaining educational equality for Latinos until the mid-1970s, when MALDEF and other organizations began to promote bilingual/bicultural education in desegregated settings as the solution to the special needs of Mexican American schoolchildren. MALDEF's full-time staff of trained lawyers established legal precedents through "impact litigation" in the areas of voting rights, employment discrimination, and immigrants' rights, as well as in the educational arena. It also carried out advocacy by lobbying local, state, and federal legislative bodies and promoting positions through negotiation and means other than court challenges. MALDEF frequently represents plaintiffs from LULAC, the American GI Forum and other Latino advocacy groups, though it sets its own legal agenda at the behest of its board of directors (Badillo 2005; Valencia 2005).

Vilma S. Martinez, who served as MALDEF president and general counsel from 1973 to 1982, called attention to a breakthrough in language policy litigation in *Serna v. Portales Municipal Schools* (1974) when the Tenth Circuit Court of Appeals sustained a New Mexico federal district court ruling that specifically mandated bilingual education as a remedy for unequal educational treatment and substandard education. This echoed the reasoning of the pathbreaking Supreme Court decision *Lau v. Nichols*, a class action suit decided that same year in favor of Chinese-speaking children in the San Francisco public schools. The Court declared that equal educational opportunity for students who do not understand English requires not only access to "the same facilities, textbooks, teachers and curriculum" but also to learning the English language (Levin and Moise 1977, 69, 75–77). The High Court also recognized the authority of the Office for Civil Rights (U.S. Department of Education) to establish regulations for school districts receiving federal assistance in order fully to comply with Title VI of the 1964 Civil Rights Act (Martinez 1977; Moran 2007). While not a party to *Lau*, MALDEF lawyers had filed an amicus curiae brief in the Supreme Court appeal noting that Mexican Americans also had much at stake: "Spanish-speaking children are subjected to a dual effect; first, the school's failure to meet their language needs, and second, the psychological damage brought about as a result of the school's failure to meet their language needs" (*Kinney Kinmon Lau v. Nichols* 1972). While *Lau* required school districts to eliminate discriminatory school board policies, even absent statutes indicating intent to segregate, it did not specify bilingual education as the only solution.

Ambiguity also clouded the 1973 Supreme Court decision of *Keyes v. School District No. 1, Denver*, which African Americans originally filed. Here Latino "identifiability" or, more specifically, the question of the legal status of Mexican Americans as a minority for desegregation purposes in schools with a "tri-ethnic"—Anglo–African American–Latino composition—came under examination. MALDEF joined the *Keyes* litigation only after the Supreme Court made its 1973 decision, but thereafter, with the case remanded to district court in order to work out a desegregation remedy, it represented a group of Mexican American parents and teachers. The federal district court ruling in 1974 in Colorado developed into long-running bilingual education litigation, as the Colorado case demonstrated the intricate and often seemingly contradictory relationship between the goals and practices of desegregation and bilingual education. In 1975, the Tenth Circuit approved a partial integration plan but held that bilingual education could not serve as a substitute for desegregation, leaving the specifics of relief to the lower court. Finally, in 1983, a district court judge ordered hiring and training of bilingual teachers and instructional staff, as well as adequate testing and placement of students (San Miguel 1987; Romero 2004; Fernandez and Guskin 1978; Kluger 1976; Bass 1990).

The remedy to language discrimination, as argued in the aforementioned bilingual education cases, was not integration by busing, a strategy African Americans pursued to end the legacies of segregation. Instead, according to MALDEF lawyer Peter Roos and Jane Couch's (1986) correspondence with Michael O'Malley, the remedy was "the increased concentration of teachers and groupings of students on the basis of language and national origin utilizing bilingual education." In other words, "the party most responsible for the existence of segregation," that is, school boards, "will be asked to develop a plan to undo it." Roos saw the major problem facing Latinos as preserving bilingual education programs while undergoing desegregation. The 1975 *Keyes* ruling, he argued, "merely struck down the concept that you can maintain segregated *schools* in the name of bilingual education."

Another case with multiple offshoots was *United States v. Texas*, a federal district court bilingual education case that had become disentangled from the earlier desegregation case of the same name. In a controversial 1981 decision, a sequel to a statewide desegregation ruling a decade earlier that had created turmoil for Texas school officials, Judge William Wayne Justice ordered extensive bilingual instruction across the state after finding pervasive discrimination toward Mexican Americans, equivalent to that practiced against blacks. Judge Justice mandated that all 1,100 Texas public school districts provide Spanish-language instruction to Mexican Americans deficient in English. The following year, however, the U.S. Court of Appeals for the Fifth Circuit reversed his decision, though by then the legislature had already passed bilingual education reforms that broadened earlier mandates to include children in kindergarten and in the higher elementary grades. The appeals court remained unconvinced that permanent damage had accrued from "unintentional" statewide segregation against Mexican American students and mandated that districts retain local control over bilingual and other remedial education programs (Kemerer 1991, 250–52; *United States v. State of Texas* 1982, 53, 63).

In 1982, the Supreme Court decision of *Plyler v. Doe* in a MALDEF case marked a clear legal and constitutional victory. Probably MALDEF's most significant accomplishment, as measured by scope and impact, the case dated back to the Texas legislature's move in 1975 to exclude the children of undocumented immigrants by amending the education code to restrict public schooling to "citizens of the United States or legally admitted aliens." In 1977 MALDEF sought a preliminary injunction challenging the statute and its implementation as a violation of the Equal Protection Clause of the Fourteenth Amendment of the U.S. Constitution ("No state shall make or enforce any law which shall abridge the privileges or immunities of citizens of the United States; nor shall any state deprive any person of life, liberty, or property, without due process of law; nor deny to any person within its jurisdiction the equal protection of the laws"). Further litigation ensued until the U.S. Supreme Court in 1982 upheld the lower court's decision and ruled that the Equal Protection Clause clearly applied to "all persons," including undocumented immigrants (Biegel 1995). The Court also confirmed that immigration and naturalization policy lies within the exclusive powers of federal government. Speaking to its lasting national importance, legal scholar Michael Olivas (2005, 202) notes, "*Plyler* even held out the promise to unite the class interests between immigrant Mexicans and the larger, more established Mexican American community in a way that earlier, important cases litigating jury selection, school finance, and desegregation had not been able to achieve."

Latino Educational Struggles in Illinois

The regional histories of Latinos across the United States differ greatly—in physical environment, urban geography, and cultures, among other indices. However, one astute observer, anthropologist Américo Paredes, argued that Mexican cultural expression, specifically folklore, "knows no borders." In particular, he saw the Texas-Mexico border, above all other regions, as always "contextualized by a deep knowledge of Greater Mexico," which included both inner and outer Mexico: "*México de Adentro*" and "*México de Afuera*" (Paredes 1993a, 8). The latter included "all those other parts of North America where people of Mexican descent have established a presence and have maintained their Mexicanness as a key part of their cultural identity" including, presumably, such relatively far northern reaches as Illinois (Bauman 1993, xi). In Texas, however, as nowhere else, the "border Mexican was *en su tierra* [at home]" even if he had been born in Mexico (Paredes 1993b, 29). This is due to the fact that south Texas Mexican Americans historically came from "immediately across the Rio Grande rather than from distant interior states that have been chief contributors for Mexican immigration to other parts of the U.S." Nonetheless, as geographer Daniel Arreola notes, "South Texas is distinct from other subregions of the larger Hispanic-American borderland." Whereas the persistence of ranching and the expansion of farming in south Texas were major pulls for Mexican labor from the "trans-Rio Grande homeland," Illinois for instance, since the early twentieth century has attracted many migrants from Mexico's central plateau states (Arreola 1993, 61). More recently, chain migration brings migrants from Michoacán and San Luis Potosí directly to suburban and rural settlements, as well as to Chicago, Aurora, and large cities. Thus Chicago and its hinterland, because of the size of its Mexican settlements and their historic interrelationship, developed a version of Mexican American culture unique to the upper Midwest (Valdés 1991; Badillo 2006).

In the civil rights arena, the Midwest has lagged greatly behind the Southwest in Latino legal advocacy. MALDEF finally responded to the region's needs and, in October 1980, opened a Chicago office, supported by a three-year $150,000 grant from the Joyce Foundation. At the start, with several cases already scheduled on its docket, MALDEF began work with local Chicago-area organizations, particularly those interested in voting rights, on preparing a reapportionment plan, designed to encourage the entry of Latinos into the ranks of city council members, state representatives, and congressional members. In its first year, the Chicago office experienced some conflicts while working with personnel from the New York–based Puerto Rican Legal Defense and Education Fund (PRLDEF), which focused primarily on civil rights issues in the Northeast. While successfully collaborating on the *United States v. Chicago Board of Education* desegregation case and on reapportionment, PRLDEF's director of litigation sought to preserve a distinctly Puerto Rican constituency in pleadings and filing. The director maintained that "they could not allow the rights of Puerto Ricans to be lost by treating issues as Latino." MALDEF, meanwhile, favored the approach of joining issues of Chicago's Chicanos and Puerto Ricans, an approach that ultimately won out in the region, according to Virginia Martinez's (1981b) correspondence with Vilma Martinez and others. The first major successful effort, *Del Valle v. State Board of Elections* (October 16, 1981), began over a redistricting challenge and resulted in the creation of two Illinois state representative districts and a senate district deemed to constitute a sufficient majority to elect representatives of their choice. Virginia Martinez's (1981a) report to Vilma Martinez claimed gerrymandering and political cronyism had previously accounted for Latinos having been shut out from virtually all elective offices in Chicago, despite large enclaves in several North Side and South Side wards.

In an effort to reach out to include Chicago's Puerto Rican community and help unify barrio concerns, MALDEF hired Fernando Colón-Navarro as staff attorney in

1983. Colón-Navarro was a Puerto Rican–born lawyer who had recently graduated from the University of Minnesota Law School. He quickly began dealing with the educational problems of Latinos in the greater Chicago area, which included severe overcrowding in urban schools. Colón-Navarro's mentor, Ray Romero, concerned that the dropout rates of Chicago Latinos approached 75%, had implemented several efforts at expanding legal services and advocacy. At first, these educational efforts involved local litigation on overcrowding and desegregation. However, Colón-Navarro soon realized that school officials failed to monitor bilingual education and habitually understated the number of Limited English Proficient students in their districts. These findings prompted him to travel outside of Chicago to contact organizations engaged with Latino families (Colón-Navarro 2008; Zavala 1984).

Onarga, Illinois, in Iroquois County, became an unlikely site in the rural Midwest as a setting for an important bilingual education case among the Mexican immigrant nursery workers who clustered in trailers and overcrowded attics and garages. María Elena Lucas, a onetime nursery worker and later a midwestern organizer for the United Farm Workers and the Farm Labor Organizing Committee, described the duties of workers as taking "cuttings of red dogwood and yellow dogwood and poplars, corkscrew willow, and other trees, [making] piles of them, and then [bringing] them back to the shed for days in cold winter weather." Lucas, a Texas-born Mexican American migrant, recalled of the workers who arrived in the area in the 1970s: "It was mostly illegals who did the [winter work, and] they'd also hire kids real young—fourteen and fifteen years old—as long as they were illegal." After conducting an informal census in mid-1976, Lucas concluded that there "were about fifty-eight families and three hundred or so single guys, about five hundred people." Migrants to Onarga frequently made successive trips across the border, often with their children in tow, and a permanent Latino community formed as former migrants "settled out" from the seasonal midwestern migrant stream that passed through east-central Illinois (Lucas 1993, 183–84; Ruiz 1999).

Beginning in the autumn of 1984, Colón-Navarro (2008) began interviewing "almost everybody in Onarga, even people who lived there for 50 or 60 years, and not one person could name me one Mexican-American kid who had graduated from high school." Onarga, as other isolated localities, simply reported that their district had fewer than 20 Limited English Proficient (LEP) students, which exempted them from a state bilingual education mandate. When he first went to Onarga, however, Colón-Navarro met with about 30 families, each with several children with limited English-speaking ability. After he began sending letters to the district inquiring how they made determinations of which students were proficient in English, it became obvious that no testing had been instituted and therefore the district was in violation of the state act. The principal claimed to have interviewed all of them. When pressed, though, he conceded to Colón-Navarro that such an interview consisted merely of one question: "Do you speak English." An affirmative response, absent any sort of testing, would allow the school to doctor its reports to the state, claiming to have only three of four monolingual Spanish speakers in any given school, and no more than 10 in a district. Such flimsy documentation was all that was necessary for schools to avoid hiring bilingual teachers. After a few discouraging encounters with school officials, Colón-Navarro (2008) concluded that local districts throughout the state "were not using assessment tools."

The poor conditions under which the families lived, along with the high dropout rates, prompted Colón-Navarro to see bilingual education as a civil rights remedy more than merely a controversial pedagogical technique. He observed at the Onarga nurseries, which remained the only source of employment for most Latinos, laborers who engaged in the difficult work of cutting trees by hand with great care to prevent damaging their roots. Some 30-year-old men already suffered from arthritis from working in ice-cold weather without gloves. Colón-Navarro (2008) noticed children 15 years old and without any knowledge of English attending school without being promoted: "They were just waiting until age sixteen, [when] they would quit and go to work in the nursery, and nobody ever questioned that." When confronted with the problem, the state responded that with some 35,000 Illinois students enrolled in bilingual education, they had already done their part in enforcement.

The greatest challenge that MALDEF faced in pursuing litigation was finding a reliable plaintiff, a student with legal standing in the school system. In fact Colón-Navarro spent over a year and a half trying to find the individuals to come forward for a class action suit. He recalls that everyone in town came to know who he was, even the sheriff, who several times followed him to the trailer park where workers and their families lived. After Colón-Navarro returned to his car, the sheriff would follow him out of town. Colón-Navarro used to drive back and forth from downstate Chicago without staying overnight; he remembers one particularly frustrating meeting in Peoria where he spoke for almost two hours but could not find a single client. He almost fell asleep on the return trip to Chicago, having to open the car window to keep himself awake: "It was cold, I was tired, and realized that I had been spending so much time there, driving, driving, driving, and not seeing my children." He began to cry, asking himself what he was doing there with no end to the search in sight (Colón-Navarro 2008).

People were reluctant to get involved, likely because of risks inherent in coming forward as an undocumented worker. Although not technically in jeopardy, they feared their names being divulged to immigration authorities or to employers. Others expressed general hopelessness, or indifference to the importance of English for their children's limited opportunities in the job market. In recounting his signal breakthrough, Colón-Navarro remembers arriving from Chicago one evening in front of 40 or 50 people called by a community organizer. He spoke to them about the difference between English as a second language and bilingual education, and of their rights, noting, "With 20 or more Limited English Proficient kids in your district [schools have] to provide bilingual education." All to no avail until, finally, a very short lady came over to him and said, "You got your client. My kids are being cheated. I want them to be in the lawsuit." Then she added, "My husband doesn't want me to because he doesn't want *el guardia* [the police] to know, or there are going to be problems. But I think this is the right thing to do" (Colón-Navarro 2008).

The willing plaintiff was Margarita Gómez, an undocumented Mexican immigrant. Her son Jorge had begun his education in the Chicago Public Schools, where school officials classified him as Limited English Proficient and placed him in a bilingual class. In 1981, however, the family moved to Onarga. Although he had completed the first grade in Chicago, he was forced to repeat the first grade because school officials believed that the Chicago Public Schools were not good enough. He received no bilingual services and was never evaluated to determine whether he was LEP. At the age of 10 he was beginning fourth grade but was making slow progress. Jorge's younger sister Marisa also began school in Chicago and, like her brother, was forced to repeat kindergarten in Onarga; then she failed the first grade because of her language problems. At the age of nine and attending third grade, her mother realized that she too needed additional assistance. Since Margarita Gómez wanted her children to do more than nursery work, she agreed to cooperate as the case went to trial (Colón-Navarro 1984b).

Later other plaintiffs came forward, including Cristina Isabel Calderón, who was born in Henry, Illinois, two years after her family had moved from Puerto Rico. According to Colón-Navarro's case records, in 1979 the family enrolled Cristina in third grade in Peoria, where she soon developed a learning problem, causing her father to buy books and try to teach her at home. He then decided to transfer Cristina to a Catholic school after Cristina failed third grade. Jaime Escobedo, who was enrolled in the Peoria school system in seventh grade, also exhibited difficulty understanding materials because of his poor English but received no bilingual services. According to his mother, "Teachers did not understand that Jaime speaks 'street' English but cannot function in the classroom" (Colón-Navarro 1984b).

At issue was whether the State of Illinois was responsible for the provision of services to all Limited English Proficient children and whether the state could be held responsible when an "educational agency" (which, MALDEF argued included local districts) failed to fulfill 1703(f) of the 1974 Equal Educational Opportunity Act (EEOA) by taking "appropriate action to overcome language barriers that impede equal participation by its students in its instructional programs." Congress had promulgated the EEOA as an amendment from the floor of the House of Representatives to an omnibus 1974 Education Amendments bill that, according to one legal scholar, "consisted of an assortment of bills dealing with diverse aspects of educational policy, including bills to extend the Bilingual Education Act and the Emergency Secondary Education Act" (Haft 1983, 239).

State regulations required that local districts conduct an annual census, but the State of Illinois offered no guidelines or testing standards, and the decision on how to identify children remained almost exclusively at the discretion of local school officials. Historically, districts such as Onarga routinely misclassified students and neglected to provide programs mandated under the law. For example, the Peoria School District had never sought state or federal funds to provide services to a large LEP group of students, despite a large Latino population, until the influx in 1980 of a large influx of non-English-speaking Vietnamese children. Illinois administered over 20 language proficiency or dominance tests, 11 standardized English tests, and seven standardized reading tests, as well as numerous formal and informal teacher-made tests for dozens of downstate programs, and "in many districts the test is as subjective as a conversation between a teacher and student" (Colón-Navarro 1984a).

Gomez in the Courts

MALDEF had decided from the outset not to sue local districts in state courts. The question then became how to proceed with a bilingual education mandate meeting federal law already on the books. The Illinois General Assembly first passed permissive legislation in 1971 for bilingual education and appropriated funds to support the program. Enabling legislation was passed in 1973, and the mandate required the establishment of transitional bilingual education programs in Illinois public schools effective July 1, 1976. It also provided for state reimbursement of excess costs school districts incurred in providing bilingual education. In 1980 one statute of a statewide Program Evaluation and Summary Report specified that school districts with "twenty or more children of limited English-speaking ability in any such language classification" shall establish "a program in transitional bilingual education for the children therein." A school census required local districts to develop procedures for evaluating all students, including scores on English language proficiency, attendance, and other data that would help determine "if students are transitioning into the regular curriculum." The State Board of Education was to coordinate state and federal programs serving Limited English Proficient students "to assure that resources are effectively combined to meet the transitional needs." In addition, they were delegated the task of preparing and disseminating "rules for the development of local standards," as well as providing "a uniform statewide procedure for collecting and reporting eligibility, program content, and program completion information on an annual basis" (Illinois State Board of Education 1982, 17).

In light of these provisions, the key to proceeding on behalf of the six plaintiffs—Margarita Gómez's two children along with four other Mexican American plaintiffs—hinged on the State Board of Education's lack of enforcement. MALDEF filed a class action lawsuit in federal district court in April 1985 on behalf of Hispanic children in Illinois against the Illinois State Board of Education and the state superintendent of education. It charged that, in the absence of uniform guidelines, many local school districts had avoided their responsibilities for bilingual education. MALDEF sought an injunction requiring the defendants to provide such guidelines and a formal appeals process that would provide remedial programs for properly identified schoolchildren. They stated that lack of uniform testing and "unconstitutional and illegal conduct" produced inconsistent results that "irreparably harmed the plaintiffs" (*Margarita Gomez et al. v. Illinois State Board of Education* 1985, 8).

Nonetheless, after filing the lawsuit, and just as court hearings were to begin, Colón-Navarro lost touch with Margarita Gómez, causing much concern in MALDEF's Chicago office. If the case went to trial, Gómez would need to give a deposition and testify. Without knowing their client's whereabouts, the legal team would not be able to carry the case forward. To their surprise, however, Mrs. Gomez suddenly appeared in Chicago and promptly explained to her surprised attorneys that she and her husband had separated; in the interim she had become involved in organizing Texas farmworkers. Looking back on her transformation, Colón-Navarro (2008) concluded that "she had bloomed." While signing the papers she inquired about the progress of the lawsuit and remained in touch with her team as the trial date approached.

According to Colón-Navarro, who served as cocounsel for the district court case along with Ray Romero, Norma Cantú, and president and general counsel Joaquín Avila, "The state argued that all they had to do was pass the law and not implement or enforce policy at the local level due to lack or time or resources. The judge wanted to dismiss the case without prejudice, which would allow them to file again in state court" (Colón-Navarro 2008). MALDEF declined, arguing instead that it should be dismissed with prejudice. This strategy was a risky tactic, noted Colón-Navarro, since a refusal at the district court level would rule out any sort of refiling on account of the legal doctrine of *res judicata,* which precludes continued litigation between the same parties once the court makes a final judgment. Fortunately for the plaintiffs, in July 1985 the federal district court dismissed the case "with prejudice," thereby paving the way for an appeal to the Seventh Circuit, which encompasses the states of

Illinois, Indiana, and Wisconsin and whose ruling clearly would have broad impact (Colón-Navarro 2008).

Within several weeks MALDEF filed its appeal, contesting the district court judge's ruling that "the only role specified for the State Board of Education [was] drafting regulations," and once a state passed a transitional bilingual education statute, the burden of implementation fell to the local school district. In response to the suit, the Illinois State Board of Education filed a motion to dismiss the case, claiming states are immune from being sued due to an Eleventh Amendment provision. The lower court judge had merely held that Illinois State Board of Education's regulations "must be adhered to by the school districts," and he further decided that the state had met its responsibilities under section 1703(f) of the EEOA, which required "appropriate action" by a state or local school district in remedying language barriers (*Jorge and Marisa Gomez v. Illinois State Board of Education* 1985, 9).

Throughout 1985 the MALDEF legal staff, working out of the San Francisco national headquarters, and with the help of personnel from other regional offices, supervised the writing of briefs and sent pleadings from related cases to assist the Chicago legal staff in the *Gomez* case. Norma Cantú, in charge of the organization's educational litigation, became lead counsel in the proceedings and drew upon her extensive experience in the Texas federal courts. At this time major changes in leadership—nationally and locally—were in the works. MALDEF's board of directors selected Antonia Hernández to replace Avila as president and general counsel in July 1985. Cantú, the director of educational programs who had litigated the *United States v. Texas* and the *Castaneda* cases in the early 1980s, had been involved with most of MALDEF's recent bilingual education cases. Colón-Navarro, who eventually became a law professor and associate dean at Texas Southern University in Houston, left MALDEF before the *Gomez* appeal was decided. Arturo Jauregui became the new Chicago staff attorney. Intensive research followed, including the analysis of recent school census data, dropout rates, administrative codes, legislative activity, and surveys ("MALDEF Annual Report" 1986).

In April 1986 the Seventh Circuit heard oral argument for the appeal; Cantú presented with Jaureguí as cocounsel. Its January 1987 decision reversed the lower court, finding that "as a result of the defendants' failure to prescribe the proper guidelines, LEP children throughout the state have been denied the appropriate educational services they are entitled to under federal and state law. In addition, the defendants have also failed to withhold federal and state funds from the non-complying districts" (*Jorge Gomez, et al. v. Illinois State Board of Education* 1987, 9). The Seventh Circuit also disputed the district court judge's interpretation of the EEOA and asserted the necessity of state oversight of local school districts, citing a 1981 U.S. court of appeals case in Idaho—successfully argued by MALDEF—that state educational agencies have "the power under state law to supervise local districts and, where appropriate, to require minimum standards of instruction" (*Idaho Migrant Council v. Board of Education* 1981, 4–5). The Ninth Circuit also found that "federal law imposes requirements on the State Agency to ensure that plaintiffs' language deficiencies are addressed" and that the term "educational agency" included both state and local school boards (*Jorge Gomez, et al. v. Illinois State Board of Education* 1987, 46). Six years later, the Seventh Circuit concurred and dismissed the claim of state immunity, remanding the case for trial in district court.

Significantly, in support of its ruling on the Equal Educational Opportunity Act, the court of appeals cited its Fifth Circuit counterpart's opinion in *Castaneda v. Pickard* (1981), a spin-off of the *United States v. Texas* case that emerged in Raymondville, an area of particularly concentrated Mexican and Mexican American settlement in the lower Rio Grande Valley. That court had articulated a three-step analysis for assessing compliance of remedies; namely, that the remedies be based on sound educational theory; that they be properly implemented; and that they have favorable results. The remedies, it concluded, need not be bilingual programs: "A court may approve a system that has as its principal goal the rapid development of literacy in English" as long as the district provides "an intensive academic program to assist the student in achieving parity with his or her native English-speaking classmates" (*Castaneda v. Pickard* 1981, 251).

In June 1987, the federal district court heard the plaintiff's motion for class certification for the following identifiable grouping: "All Spanish-speaking children who are or will be enrolled in Illinois public schools, or who are eligible or will be eligible to be enrolled in Illinois public schools, and who should have been, should be, or who have been, assessed as limited English proficient" (*Jorge and Marisa Gomez et al. v. Illinois State Board of Education* 1985, 10). In granting the motion, the court cited census figures gathered by the Illinois State Board of Education indicating that more than 6,000 Spanish-speaking children had not been properly assessed as LEP children. The ruling conceded it possible that there might be hundreds, even thousands, of Spanish-speaking children throughout Illinois who fit, or would in the future fit, into that class and were thus as risk for being deprived of equal educational opportunity. Also included in the decision was acknowledgment of MALDEF's impressive past record and its worthiness as counsel (*Jorge and Marisa Gomez et al. v. Illinois State Board of Education* 1985, 20).

In preparation for that certification, which would pave the way for a successful trial, staff attorney Jauregui assembled affidavits from plaintiffs living in the greater Chicago area. These documents recounted personal experiences of parents testifying to the failure of school officials adequately to monitor student progress in bilingual programs. Among the respondents was Rosa Martínez, mother of three school-age children in suburban Waukegan, who objected to having one of her daughters remain in a bilingual program rather than transitioning out. She believed that while "bilingual education is a good thing for Hispanic children," schools should not children there "for so many years without testing them regularly to determine if they are capable of performing in regular English classes." Another Chicago mother, Margarita Parra, stated that to her knowledge her son was never evaluated when the family moved to a new school to see if he should be tested to determine his English proficiency. She believed that another of her sons who had been in the bilingual program previously, and who "was always enthusiastic in school," quickly developed problems in the new locale after having been placed prematurely in regular English classes. Another parent, Gloria Domínguez, recounted that she was only belatedly informed that the school had transferred her daughter from bilingual education to a regular English class because of "classroom overcrowding" rather than relying on educational considerations, especially regular testing (Jauregui 1987).

To bolster its case for consistent standards, MALDEF also included an affidavit from a former assistant manager of the Illinois State Board of Education, who stated that his superiors opposed an imposition of sanctions against local school districts refusing to comply with the Transitional Bilingual Education Act. He noted, moreover, the widespread failure in several school districts to provide adequate instruction in the students' native language; to institute "clear criteria for the identification of Limited English Proficient students"; to submit applications to provide bilingual education where indicated, and alleged other breaches of required duties due to "the emphasis on the autonomy of local school districts, [which] were left free to do as they pleased," in disregard of the state's Transitional Bilingual Education Act (Jauregui 1987).

After a trial had been scheduled in federal district court, the parties to the *Gomez* case finally settled in July 1988 when the State Board of Education agreed to MALDEF's terms and passed new enforcement regulations. The consent agreement provided that the Illinois State Board of Education monitor regularly the identification and assessment of students in local districts; institute a census of Limited English Proficient students; implement uniform standards for monitoring transitional bilingual education; conduct on-site visits; encourage parent and community participation; and ensure that districts advise parents or legal guardians "of their right to request the district to determine whether such child should be considered for placement in a Transitional Bilingual Education program or a transitional program of instruction, and [make] such determination upon parental request" (Jauregui 1988). Although procedurally distinct from *Castaneda,* which had actually been tried in court, the *Gomez* decision and its settlement—subsequently approved by the district court judge—had the force of federal law.

Beyond Illinois

The long-term educational effects of *Gomez* are hard to judge precisely. Nonetheless, given the influx of Mexican immigrants to Illinois during the 1990s, particularly to the greater Chicago area, its effects must have been significant. Moreover, the "rural rebound" that occurred throughout the state, overcoming the job loss and growing poverty that had disrupted the lives of many residents during the 1980s, boded well for Latinos in areas such as Onarga, where according to the 2000 census, they were just over one-third of the total population of some 1,400 (Walzer and Crump 1996–97, 2). Undocumented migration, primarily from Mexico, rose sharply during the 1970s and 1980s (Crump 1998; Leon 1996). The existence and greater enforcement of transitional bilingual education programs in Illinois school districts with more than 19 students of the same language background led school districts to develop new programs. One rural county in 1994 boasted of a summer migrant education program "focused on providing language development and mathematics in the Spanish language to strengthen native-language skills." It had bilingual teachers, including two from Mexico, who were part of a larger group that that country's Secretaría de Relaciones Exteriores sponsored. Typically, such districts faced shortages of bilingual staff, as well as skepticism about what has been perceived as the controversial nature of bilingual education and general difficulties of migrant students. The program seemed to decrease absentee rates and "increased student enthusiasm, participation, and aspirations for the future" (Montavon and Kinser 1996, 237).

The effects impact of *Gomez* was seen more recently in a July 2008 decision in *United States of America and LULAC-GI Forum v. State of Texas* in the U.S. Court of Appeals for the Fifth Circuit. It involved Texas, a state whose public school population includes over 700,000 Limited English Proficient students. The judge's opinion specifically cited the warning of *Gomez:* "State agencies cannot, in the guise of deferring to local conditions, completely delegate in practice their obligations under the EEOA; otherwise, the term 'educational agency' no longer includes those at the state level." Citing *Gomez*, it further argued that the Texas Education Agency (TEA) "must set guidelines for establishing language remediation programs, and it must ensure those guidelines are implemented" and that "these general measures must constitute 'appropriate action'" in order to withstand judicial review. Therefore, it concluded that under Texas law, the state agency "cannot abdicate its responsibility to rectify the failures of local authorities." MALDEF, the interveners in that case, prevailed by showing that "TEA is failing under the implementation prong or results prong in order for the Court to mandate a remedy." While the Court recognized that it must defer to certain "political solutions" of the legislature, it ordered the State of Texas to begin implementation of a new language program for Limited English Proficient students. The program "could consist of a variation of the current English as a Second Language program with substantially enhanced remedial education," including, of course, some form of bilingual education (*United States of America and LULAC-GI Forum v. State of Texas* 2008, 52–53).

Apart from discussing the legal ramifications of *Gomez*, this chapter seeks insights into legal advocacy strategies of a Latino civil rights organization. The story of predominantly Mexican American tree nursery workers in Onarga, Illinois, highlights an unlikely locale far removed from populous urban barrios, or "gateway cities," such as Chicago, New York, Los Angeles, Miami, and Houston. Recent immigrants to rural and other nonmetropolitan destinations, especially the undocumented, have fewer community networks and institutions, including civil rights organizations, on which to rely. Their children's most obvious educational challenges have much to do with lack of understanding of English. Language difficulties aside, however, even seemingly simple things such as enrolling at the beginning of the school year presents complications for migrant students, who lose time in transferring from one district to another (Trotter 1992, 14–15). Moreover, as sociologist Douglas Massey (2008, 352) notes, small towns and suburbs lack the "well-developed institutions within and outside the immigrant community that facilitate integration and advancement," thereby giving new immigrants in previously homogeneous rural communities much greater visibility. This forces unprecedented cultural, and ultimately legal, interaction with foreign-born, predominantly Spanish-speaking migrants.

Continuing Latin American immigration to the United States suggests that issues in Latino education, including language policy, will increase in importance in the Midwest and across the nation. A persistent shortage of bilingual personnel, for example, has resulted in high teacher/student ratios in Chicago elementary and high schools. Recent trends among in that city indicate that Latinos comprise almost 40% of the public school enrollment, second only to African Americans, who stand at about one-half, while the "Anglo" population has declined to less than 10%. Spanish-speakers represent over 80% of the total number of English Language Learners. Studies have also shown rapid increases among Latinos in suburban Chicago. Civil rights organizations, meanwhile, continue to monitor Chicago Public Schools compliance with court-ordered services on behalf of tens of thousands of children faced with language barriers (Aviles et al. 2006). MALDEF trial attorneys recently introduced testimonies of one parent entitled to receive bilingual education services pursuant to a consent decree in a decades-old desegregation case ("MALDEF Continues to Protect" 2009).

In pressing for bilingual education over the decades, MALDEF has emphasized language and culture as organizing principles for Latinos, an approach that masked deeper differences between what one legal scholar Rachel Moran (1995) has termed their "pluralist" vision of racial and ethnic relations, especially as contained within bilingual education initiatives, as against more "assimilationist" and integrationist aspects of inclusiveness in the legacy of *Brown v. Board of Education.* There are other differences, and of course the two struggles are also complementary in many respects, as the Latino civil rights struggle, including bilingual education, had its roots in overturning isolation and government-imposed segregation—especially on the part of school boards and school districts. It has also sought to broaden available options in schools, employment, housing, and other areas. The *Gomez* case clearly indicates the importance of state and local enforcement of national policies, in combination with effective legal advocacy, in interpreting and upholding the law (Moran 1995).

NOTE

The author acknowledges the assistance of the City University of New York for a 2008–9 PSC-CUNY Research Award and is also grateful to Professor Michael A. Olivas and an anonymous reviewer for helpful comments offered on a draft.

REFERENCES

Arreola, D. D. 1993. "Mexican Origins of South Texas Mexican Americans, 1930." *Journal of Historical Geography* 19 (January): 48–63.

Aviles, A. M., L. Capeheart, E. R. Davila, A. Perez-Miller, and E. Rodriguez-Lucero. 2006. "The Status of Latinos in Chicago Public Schools: Dando un Paso, ¿Pa'lante o Pa'tras?" Chicago: 2nd Legislative District Education Advisory Committee.

Badillo, D. A. 2005. "MALDEF and the Evolution of Latino Civil Rights." University of Notre Dame, Institute for Latino Studies, *Research Reports* 2005.2: 1–18.

———. 2006. *Latinos and the New Immigrant Church.* Baltimore: Johns Hopkins University Press.

Bass, J. 1990. *Unlikely Heroes.* Tuscaloosa: University of Alabama Press.

Bauman, R. 1993. Introduction. In *Folklore and Culture on the Texas-Mexican Border,* by A. Paredes, ix–xxiii. Austin: University of Texas.

Biegel, S. 1995. "The Wisdom of *Plyler v. Doe.*" *Chicano-Latino Law Review* 17 (Fall): 46–63.

Castaneda v. Pickard. 1981. 648 F.2d 989. U.S. Court of Appeals for the Fifth Circuit. June 23.

Colón-Navarro, F. 1984a. Field Notes. Stanford University Libraries, Department of Special Collections, MALDEF Collection , RG9, Box 426, f. 22.

———. 1984b. To Raymond G. Romero. Stanford University Libraries, Department of Special Collections, MALDEF Collection, RG9, Box 426, f.22

———. 2008. Interview by D. A. Badillo. Thurgood Marshall School of Law, Texas Southern University, Houston, November 6.

Crump, J. 1998. "Demographic Trends in Rural Illinois: Growth, Decline, Stabilization, and Diversity."

Rural Research Report (Western Illinois University Institute for Rural Affairs), 9 (Summer): 1–6.

Fernandez, R. R., and J. T. Guskin. 1978. "Bilingual Education Desegregation: A New Dimension in Legal and Educational Decision-Making." In *Bilingual Education,* ed. H. LaFontaine, B. Persky, and L. H. Golubchick, 58–66. Wayne, NJ: Avery.

Jorge Gomez, et al, v. Illinois State Board of Education. 1987. 811 F.2d 1030. U.S. Court of Appeals for the Seventh Circuit. January 30.

Jorge and Marisa Gomez et al. v. Illinois State Board of Education. 1985. 614 F. Supp. 342. U.S. District Court for the Northern District of Illinois. July 24 [Decided August 26, 1987].

Haft, J. D. 1983. "Assuring Equal Educational Opportunity for Language-Minority Students: Bilingual Education and the Equal Educational Opportunity Act of 1974." *Columbia Journal of Law and Social Problems* 18: 209–93.

Idaho Migrant Council v. Board of Education. 1981. 647 F.2d 69. U.S. Court of Appeals for the Ninth Circuit. June 5.

Illinois State Board of Education. 1982. *Bilingual Education Mandate: A Preliminary Report.* Springfield: Illinois State Board of Education.

Jaureguí, A. 1987. Affidavit Files. Stanford University Libraries, Department of Special Collections, MALDEF Collection, RG9, Box 426, f. 29.

————. 1988. To Mary Ellen Coghlan, Illinois Assistant Attorney General (June 24). Stanford University Libraries, Department of Special Collections, MALDEF Collection, RG9, Box 426, f. 30.

Kemerer, F. R. 1991. *William Wayne Justice: A Judicial Biography.* Austin: University of Texas Press.

Kinney Kinmon Lau v. Nichols. 1973. U.S. Supreme Court. Brief of Amici Curiae, Mexican American Legal Defense and Educational Fund, American G.I. Forum, League of United Latin American Citizens, Association of Mexican American Educators submitted July 27. Stanford University Libraries, Department of Special Collections, MALDEF Collection, RG9, Box 121, f. 13.

Kluger, R. 1976. *Simple Justice: The History of Brown v. Board of Education and Black America's Struggle for Equality.* New York: Knopf.

Leon, Edgar. 1996. "Challenges and Solutions for Educating Migrant Students." Working Paper No. 28, Julian Samora Research Institute, Michigan State University.

Levin, B., and P. Moise. 1977. "School Desegregation Litigation in the Seventies and the Use of Social Science Evidence: An Annotated Guide." In *The Courts, Social Science, and School Desegregation,* ed. B. Levin and W. D. Hawley, 50–133. New Brunswick, NJ: Transaction Books.

Lopez, I. H., and M. A. Olivas. 2008. "Jim Crow, Mexican Americans, and the Anti-Subordination Constitution: The Story of *Hernandez v. Texas.*" In *Race Law Stories,* ed. R. F. Moran and D. W. Carbado, 273–310. New York: Foundation Press.

Lucas, María Elena. 1993. *Forged under the Sun / Forjada bajo el sol: The Life of María Elena Lucas.* Ed. F. B. Leeper. Ann Arbor: University of Michigan Press.

"MALDEF Continues to Protect the Rights of 43,000 Children Learning English in Chicago Public Schools." 2009. *MALDEFian.* Available online: MALDEF.org.

"MALDEF Annual Report to the Board of Directors." 1986. April. Stanford University Libraries, Department of Special Collections, MALDEF Collection, RG6, Box 41, f. 1.

Margarita Gomez [et al.] v. Illinois State Board of Education. 1985. Complaint for Declaratory and Injunctive Relief. U.S. District Court for the Northern District of Illinois. April 16.

Martinez, Vilma S. 1977. "Administration of Justice, Speech at the National Hispanic Leadership Conference, Dallas, Texas." Stanford University Libraries, Department of Special Collections,

MALDEF Collection, RG4, Box 93, f. 9.

Martinez, Virginia. 1981a. To Vilma S. Martinez, "Report to Executive Committee for Meeting of February 6, 1981." Stanford University Libraries, Department of Special Collections, MALDEF Collection, RG4, Box 143, f. 1.

———. 1981b. To Vilma S. Martinez, Mike Baller, and Jane Couch, "Puerto Rican Legal Defense and Education Fund" (October 16). Stanford University Libraries, Department of Special Collections, MALDEF Collection, RG2, Box 10, f. 4.

Massey, D. S. 2008. "Assimilation in New Geography." In *New Faces in New Places: The Changing Geography of American Immigration,* ed. D. S. Massey, 343–54. New York: Russell Sage Foundation.

Montavon, M. V., and J. Kinser. 1996. "Programming for Success among Hispanic Migrant Students." In *Children of La Frontera: Binational Efforts to Serve Mexican Migrant and Immigrant Students,* ed. J. L. Flores, 229–38. Charleston, WV: ERIC, Clearinghouse on Rural and Small Schools.

Moran, R. F. 1995. "Foreword—Demography and Distrust: The Latino Challenge to Civil Rights and Immigration Policy in the 1990s and Beyond." *La Raza Law Journal* 8: 1–24.

———. 2007. "The Story of *Lau v Nichols:* Breaking the Silence in Chinatown." In *Education Law Stories,* ed. M. A. Olivas and R. G. Schneider, 111–57. New York: Foundation Press.

Olivas, M. A. 2005. "The Story of *Plyler v. Doe,* the Education of Undocumented Children, and the Polity." In *Immigration Stories,* D. A. Martin and P. H. Schuck, 197–220. New York: Foundation Press.

———, ed. 2006. *"Colored Men" and "Hombres Aquí": Hernandez v. Texas and the Emergence of Mexican-American Lawyering.* Houston: Arte Público Press.

Paredes, A. 1993a. "The Folklore of Groups of Mexican Origin in the United States." In *Folklore and Culture on the Texas-Mexican Border,* by A. Paredes, 3–18. Ed. R. Bauman. Austin: University of Texas.

———. 1993b. "The Problem of Identity in a Changing Culture: Popular Expressions of Culture Conflict along the Lower Rio Grande Border." In *Folklore and Culture on the Texas-Mexican Border,* by A. Paredes, 19–47. Ed. R. Bauman. Austin: University of Texas.

Romero, T. I. 2004. "Our Selma Is Here: The Political and Legal Struggle for Educational Equality in Denver, Colorado, and Multiracial Conundrums in American jurisprudence." *Seattle Journal for Social Justice* 3 (Fall–Winter): 73–142.

Roos, P., and J. Couch. 1976. To J. Michael O'Malley, Acting Chief, Multicultural/Bilingual Division, Department of Health, Education and Welfare, National Institute of Education, Washington, D.C. (July 12). Stanford University Libraries, Department of Special Collections, MALDEF Collection, RG5, Box 109, f. 4.

Ruiz, V. L. 1999. *From Out of the Shadows: Mexican Women in Twentieth-Century America.* New York: Oxford University Press.

San Miguel, Jr., G. 1987. *"Let All of Them Take Heed": Mexican Americans and the Campaign for Educational Equality in Texas, 1910–1981.* Austin: University of Texas Press.

———. 2001. *Brown, Not White: School Integration and the Chicano Movement in Houston.* College Station: Texas A & M University Press.

———. 2004. *Contested Policy: The Rise and Fall of Federal Bilingual Education in the United States, 1960–2001.* Denton: University of North Texas Press.

Trotter, A. 1992. "Harvest of Dreams." *American School Board Journal* 179 (August): 14–19.

United States of America and LULAC-GI Forum v. State of Texas. 2008. 6:71-CV-5281 WWJ. U.S. District Court for the Eastern District of Texas. July 24.

United States v. State of Texas. 1982. 680 F.2d 356. U.S. Court of Appeals for the Fifth Circuit. July 12.

Valdés, D. N. 1991. *Al Norte: Agricultural Workers in the Great Lakes Region, 1917–1970.* Austin: University of Texas Press.

Valencia, R. R. 2005. "The Mexican Struggle for Equal Educational Opportunity in *Mendez v. Westminster:* Helping to Pave the Way for *Brown v. Board of Education.*" *Teachers College Record* 107: 389–423.

———. 2008. *Chicano Students and the Courts: The Mexican American Legal Struggle for Educational Equality.* New York: New York University Press.

Walzer, N., and J. Crump. 1996–97. "Economic Trends in Rural Illinois." *Rural Research Report* (Western Illinois University Institute for Rural Affairs), 8 (Winter): 1–8.

Zavala, A. 1984. "Maldef pide construcción de mas escuelas." *El Mañana: Chicago,* July 4.

JENNIFER TELLO BUNTIN

Reaching across Borders: The Transnationalizing Effect of Mexican Migration on Public Schools on the Outskirts of Chicago

IN 2002 A LOCAL NEWSPAPER REPORTED ON THE START OF A DISTANCE LEARNING program at an Aurora, Illinois, high school that would link adult students in Aurora with teachers in Mexico via satellite (Moore 2002).

[DISTRICT ONE] READY TO LAUNCH PARTNERSHIP WITH MEXICO
Distance learning: Satellite link will allow immigrants to complete education

AURORA—People walking or driving past [District One] High School might notice for the first time a large object on the roof of the building. A satellite dish that will link the school to Mexico for a distance-learning program was installed this week. It should be tested and fully functional by Monday, when administrators meet with local educators and officials from the Mexican Consulate to kick off the adult education program, the district's technology coordinator said. The satellite link facilitates real-time communication between the school and educators in Mexico . . .

The district has partnered with the Mexican Consulate and a local community organization to help Aurora's Mexican immigrants complete the education they might have left behind when they came to the United States. . . . Participants who complete the program will earn a certificate from the Mexican Minister of Education. (Moore 2002; organization and individual names obscured).

This program, called Plazas Comunitarias, was a partnership between the local school district, the Mexican government, and a local community organization. Teachers in Mexico were to instruct participants via satellite and, upon completion of the program, each student would receive a degree from the Mexican minister of education.

The program is intriguing. Since the early 20th century, public education has been a primary vehicle for national assimilation and Americanization projects, a goal at odds with the introduction of transnational elements to the institution. Yet here was a story of a local school district working directly with the Mexican government to provide community residents with Mexican educational certifications. The transnationalism literature suggests that at least some immigrant communities in the United States develop and maintain strong ties with their home communities and nations. Recent research by Alejandro Portes, Luis Guarnizo and colleagues (Portes, Escobar, and Radford 2005; Guarnizo, Portes, and Haller 2003) provides insight into transnational organizations that serve the political, social, and economic needs of immigrants. However, Aurora's distance learning partnership with Mexico differs from these types of organizations in a crucial way. The transnational organizations these scholars describe are *immigrant-based* organizations, whereas the school district in Aurora is part of a broader community institution.

The distance learning program, as well as subsequent observations of Aurora, led to the central questions of this chapter: How do receiving community institutions, like public schools, respond to the arrival and development of a transnational migrant population? Furthermore, what are the implications of those responses for both the immigrants and the community at large? This chapter argues that current approaches to studying migration processes are unable to address these questions because the study of migrants and their families has been removed from the study of the communities in which they are embedded. Immigrants and their families are often portrayed as isolated and socially disconnected from the rest of the receiving community. Observations in Aurora, however, suggest that migrants and their families interact with nonmigrants of various ethnic origins in a multitude of social and institutional contexts, such as schools, churches, workplaces, and stores.[1] Furthermore, these receiving communities are not static venues, but dynamic communities that respond to and are changed by the presence of a transnational immigrant population. In other words, migration is a social process that transforms not only the lives of the migrants, but also the communities they travel between. These transformations have consequences for both immigrant and nonimmigrant residents. Current approaches that focus on the immigrants in isolation obscure these transformations and their implications.

Public education is a key research site for uncovering the ways that the presence of immigrants transforms a community. First, schools are the frontier of any dramatic population change. They often deal with the impact of changing demographics long before other parts of the community even perceive the change. Second, schools play an important role in the local community beyond the obvious function of educating children. They are cornerstones of community life, bringing together neighboring families in a multitude of social activities. They also interact frequently and intimately with local political, social, and cultural organizations. Thus, public education is an important element within an intertwined set of institutional and social relationships that shape the community as a whole. Finally, as mentioned above, the role of public schools in the United States has historically included facilitating the assimilation of new immigrants into American society and culture. This institutional goal is seemingly at odds with programs like Plazas Comunitarias that enhance immigrants' connection to their homeland rather than sever it.

In Aurora, the challenges of a rapidly increasing Spanish-speaking, primarily Mexican-origin population motivated school administrators to reach across national borders in search of new ways to bridge a gap of language and culture between the services schools provide and the changing needs of their student body. Specifically, one Aurora school district enacted programs designed to create transnational links with Mexico, the primary sending country of its immigrant population. Plazas Comunitarias demonstrates the ability of a local community to interact directly with a foreign government in order to obtain services for adults in the community. In addition, teacher recruitment trips to Mexico show the desire, as well as the challenges, of finding teachers who can connect with immigrant students in both language and culture.

However, the programs discussed here also elucidate the fact that transnational processes at the local level do not exist outside of the broader institutional and political context of the receiving nation. Rather, this case study demonstrates the tension between transnational endeavors at the local level and the continued power of the national government to shape and control these cross-border relationships and interactions. For example, immigration and educational policies imposed upon teacher recruitment trips to Mexico from the national level significantly affected school administrators' transnational endeavors. Despite the desire at the local level to forge a transnational connection with the sending nation within the classroom, embodied by teachers recruited directly from Mexico, national and state-level policies made this connection difficult to maintain. International recruiting continued, but not in Mexico, primarily as a result of post-9/11 immigration policies and the No Child Left Behind Act of 2001.

Despite these challenges, the very existence of these programs suggests that this local community institution is reorienting itself, albeit subtly, into a broader social, economic, and political network that is not fully contained by the nation-state. Not only are migrants maintaining transnational connections with their communities and nations abroad, but the receiving community itself is experimenting with these connections. By reaching across borders and engaging in independent relations with foreign governments and institutions, the programs District One developed represent a transnationalizing effect of migration on the receiving community. The long-term impact of these transnational connections may as yet be unknown, but their presence suggests that there are changes afoot that have implications not only for the immigrants, but for the communities they settle in as well.

The following pages present a review and critique of the assimilationist and transnational perspectives on migration. The primary limitation of both literatures is the same: the migrant or migrant group is the fundamental object of analysis. This focus ignores their embeddedness within the broader community and obscures their social engagement with nonmigrants of diverse ethnic backgrounds. Such an analysis is therefore unable to address the ways that the community is changing or how these changes may, in turn, alter the experiences of the migrants within it. The next section introduces the research site, Aurora, Illinois, and its public school districts. The rest of the chapter is dedicated to a description and analysis of District One's[2] interactions with Mexico. The chapter concludes with a discussion of the empirical and theoretical implications of these "transnationalizing" programs.

Assimilation and Transnationalism

Since the early 20th century and the birth of American sociology, immigration has been a primary object of sociological analysis. From the outset Chicago School scholars, such as W. I. Thomas, Robert Park, and Ernest Burgess, analyzed immigration as a key element of the urban landscape. Since those early days, and particularly in the last several decades, the literature on international migration (to the United States and elsewhere) has grown immensely, spanning multiple disciplines and including both quantitative and qualitative analysis.

Throughout the literature on migration two approaches permeate: the assimilationist perspective[3] and the transnationalist perspective. Both perspectives take the migrant or migrant group as the object of analysis. However, assimilationists focus on immigrants' experiences in the new society, while transnationalists focus on their continued connections to the homeland. In both literatures, the study of migration has been largely removed from the study of the communities in which it is embedded.

ASSIMILATION

The traditional approach to studying immigrants originates in the early 20th century Chicago School work of Park, Burgess, and Thomas. These studies of immigrant assimilation look at the social, cultural, and economic processes of leaving behind the home country and embracing the new. The Chicago School is the root of assimilation as a sociological concept. However, the mid-20th century saw the development of assimilation theory as it is commonly understood today. In their excellent review of the literature, Richard Alba and Victor Nee (2003, 18–35) identify Milton Gordon's *Assimilation in American Life* (1964) as the source of the major elements of assimilation that are associated with the traditional theory: "It is with his book that a canonical account takes on a sharply etched conceptual profile" (Alba and Nee 2003, 23). From Gordon we gain the conceptualization of assimilation as a primarily unidirectional process in which the immigrant group adopts the cultural patterns of the host society, which, in the American case, refers to a white, Protestant, middle-class culture. To this foundation, Herbert Gans (1973) and Neil Sandberg (1973) contribute the concept of "straight-line assimilation," or assimilation that occurs over several generations, each one taking another step closer to absorbing the host culture and another step away from the ethnic culture and community.

Further developing the traditional perspective, Peter Blau and Otis Dudley Duncan's (1967) work on status attainment shifts attention from cultural and structural assimilation to an examination of social mobility, "reinforce[ing] the view that assimilation and social mobility are inextricably linked (and, conversely, that there is no assimilation if social mobility has not also occurred)" (Alba and Nee 2003, 28). In later work, residential mobility was also added to the model, formalized by Douglas Massey's (1985) "spatial assimilation," which refers to a socioeconomic process that can be observed through the residential distribution of immigrant or ethnic groups across the city. In these works through the mid-1980s the fundamental sociological approach to assimilation describes a unidirectional process in which immigrants take on the culture of the host society. In addition, assimilation theory emphasizes socioeconomic status, conflating assimilation with upward social and economic mobility.[4] This perspective describes a host society and culture that remains relatively unchanged by the presence of the immigrants. In other words, migration is presented as a process in which all change occurs within the immigrants as they shed their "old country" ways and connections in return for socioeconomic success and acceptance in the new country.

TRANSNATIONALISM

An alternative approach to the study of immigrants was born in large part out of the dissatisfaction of some scholars with the traditional assimilationist perspective. The transnational perspective "explicitly challenges the bipolar model of 'old country' and 'new country,' of 'back home' and 'new home'" (Straughan and Hondagneu-Sotelo 2002, 199–200). Jeremy Straughan and Pierrette Hondagneu-Sotelo (2002) argue that immigrant communities create and maintain economic, political, and cultural links to their homelands that do not appear to break down over time in the traditional process of assimilation into the American mainstream. Thus, while assimilation theory focuses on the migrants' experiences in the new society, transnational scholars examine their continued connection to their homelands.

The term *transnationalism* arose to refer to these connections, initially in a fairly unspecified manner. Soon, however, scholars began to attempt a more theoretically precise understanding of these relations. Frederic Wakeman (1988), for example, cites advances in technology as the key to understanding the strong connections current immigrants maintain with their home communities. Roger Rouse develops the concept even further. He argues that

> through the continuous circulation of people, money, goods, and information, the various settlements have become so closely woven together that, in an important sense, they have come to *constitute a single community spread across a variety of sites,* something I refer to as a "transnational migrant circuit." (Rouse 1991, 14; emphasis added)

From Rouse's perspective a transnational migrant circuit is not simply movement back and forth between multiple communities or social contact with the community of origin. Rather, it is the creation of a new kind of community that is not dependent upon physical proximity. The concept of community is delinked from geographic territory, to include both the migrants and those left behind in the sending communities.

Further developing the concept and specifying the ways these transnational connections are maintained, Linda Basch, Nina Glick Schiller, and Cristine Szanton Blanc (1994) introduced a definition of transnationalism that is now widely used:

> We define "transnationalism" as the processes by which immigrants forge and sustain multi-stranded social relations that link together their societies of origin and settlement. We call these processes transnationalism to emphasize that many immigrants today build social fields that cross geographic, cultural, and political borders. (Basch, Schiller, and Blanc 1994, 7)

Beginning with this concept, the authors build a theoretical framework for the study of transnational communities that seeks to uncover these multilevel transnational connections. Their conceptualization does not require that one limit the analysis to migrants. However, most transnational migration studies do focus primarily on migrants, with some inclusion of nonmigrants in the sending community.

The transnationalists have added an important element to our understanding of the migrant experience by acknowledging and investigating their continued connections to their homelands. However, this literature has not seriously challenged the assimilationist perspective. In focusing their attention on the relations between migrants and their sending communities and nations, transnationalists address important relationships that are left out of the assimilation studies. Yet they leave the analysis of the migrants' connections to the receiving community relatively untouched. Rather than challenging the assimilationist perspective, the transnational migration scholarship has grown parallel to the assimilation literature.

Consequently, two relatively discrete lines of inquiry have developed. Both take the migrant or migrant group as the primary object of analysis, but consider separate aspects of their social relationships. Transnationalists focus on migrants' continued connection with their home communities or nations, while assimilationists focus on their growing involvement in the new society. However, neither perspective really addresses the immigrants' embeddedness within dynamic receiving communities that respond to and are changed by their presence. Building on key insights from both perspectives, the approach demonstrated here looks beyond the immigrant community, recognizing that immigrants are also part of a larger receiving community that is shaped by their presence. By broadening our gaze, we are able to examine the responses of these communities and consider their implications for both immigrant and nonimmigrant residents.

Beyond the Immigrant Community

Basch, Schiller, and Blanc's definition of transnationalism, like Rouse's transnational migration circuit, does allow for an analysis of community within the context of migration. However, it is the sending community that has received more attention in this regard. Recent studies of transnational migration have begun to analyze transformations within the sending communities as a result of migration. Peggy Levitt's research (1999; 2001), for instance, demonstrates that the flow of people, money, and "social remittances" (ideas, norms, practices, identities) within these transnational spaces may have a transformative effect on nonmigrants in the home communities. For example, nonmigrants in the sending communities may

234 ■ Jennifer Tello Buntin

experiment with new gender roles, new ideas about politics, or new organizing strategies (Levitt 2001).

Research on hometown associations also develops our understanding of the connections between migrants and their home communities (Çağlar 2006; Orozco 2004; Orozco 2002). Hometown associations (HTAs) are organized groups of migrants who hail from the same community in the sending nation. Like the mutual aid societies of the early 20th century, HTAs organize resources in the receiving community and provide social connections for migrants coming from the same sending community. In recent years, their organizational complexity, as well as the political and economic relevance they have for the sending nation, has increased. These organizations sometimes deal directly with the state and national governments of their countries of origin and are recognized as important agents of development in Latin America (Orozco 2002) and elsewhere (Çağlar 2006). In response, many sending countries have become economically dependent on the remittances migrants send home and have developed policies to support their continuation (Levitt and Jaworsky 2007).

It is now clear that transnational migration has implications not just for the migrants but also for the individuals, communities, and nations they left behind. However, there is an assumption in the migration literature that precludes a similar analysis of the impact of transnational migration on the broader receiving community. While migrants are often perceived to be deeply connected to their home communities and nations, their relations within the receiving community are assumed to be confined within the immigrant or ethnic community. Nina Glick Schiller, Ayse Çağlar, and Thaddeus C. Gulbrandsen critique "the prevailing assumption that immigrants live and worship within distinct 'ethnic communities'" (2006, 612). This assumption underlies much of the migration literature and limits its analytic capabilities. As Schiller and her colleagues argue, this assumption "shapes—and in our opinion, obscures—the diversity of migrants' relationships" (613).

One of the most provocative aspects of Basch, Schiller, and Blanc's (1994) definition of transnationalism is the idea that transnational migrations not only tie transmigrants to multiple societies, but also link these places together. Migration scholars have not yet fully capitalized on this theoretical insight. As noted above, migration studies tend to focus exclusively on the experiences of the migrants themselves. Yet Basch, Schiller, and Blanc's framework allows for a broader conceptualization of the migration process as a social phenomenon that provides a link between geographically distant places. "We define 'transnationalism' as the processes by which immigrants forge and sustain multi-stranded social relations that *link together* their societies of origin and settlement." (Basch, Schiller and Blanc 1994, 7; emphasis added). In other words, migration has implications not just for the migrants, but also for the societies and communities they travel between. In addition, the responses of these communities, in turn, have implications for the experiences of the migrants traveling between them.

In their revised version of assimilation theory, Alba and Nee (2003) also consider the possibility that the presence of immigrants transforms the receiving society. They argue for a return to the original concept of assimilation presented by Robert Park in the *Introduction to the Science of Sociology* (Park and Burgess 1921). In this classic text, Park defines assimilation as "a process of *interpenetration and fusion* in which persons and groups acquire the memories, sentiments, and attitudes of other persons and groups and, by sharing their experience and history, are incorporated with them in a common cultural life" (1921, 735; emphasis added). From this definition, Alba and Nee develop an alternative formulation that avoids many of the pitfalls of the traditional concept. This "new assimilation theory" does not assume a static mainstream culture. Rather, it allows for the possibility that the assimilation process engenders change within the mainstream as well as within the immigrant or ethnic group. The emphasis is on cultural solidarity, which does not imply a replacement of one culture for another. Alba and Nee point out Park's use of the terms *interpenetration* and *fusion* in his discussion of this social process, arguing that this definition "expresses an understanding of assimilation with contemporary appeal, leaving ample room for the persistence of ethnic elements set within a common national frame" (Alba and Nee 2003, 20).

Taken together, these theoretical insights allow an understanding of migration as a dynamic process that transforms not just the lives of the immigrants, but the communities they live in as well. International migration flows are transforming communities across the United States and elsewhere. In its current state, however, migration theory does not address these transformations because of its focus on the migrant as the object of analysis and the assumption that migrants are socially isolated from the rest of the community. Consequently, it is also unable to examine the ways that these community transformations affect the experience of the migrants themselves. By recognizing that immigrants are also part of the broader receiving community, we gain empirical and theoretical insights into the process and consequences of migration that have been heretofore obscured. The transnationalizing effect on public schools, as described in the rest of this chapter, is but one example of these possibilities.

Case Study: Aurora, Illinois

As the 20th century came to a close, 2000 U.S. Census data held surprising results for demographers and migration scholars. Rather than the expected pattern of continued concentration in a handful of large U.S. central cities, immigrant settlement in the 1990s exhibited a striking pattern of geographic dispersion. One can now find significant numbers of immigrants in the suburbs of traditional immigrant urban destinations (like Chicago) as well as in smaller metropolitan and rural communities across the country, particularly in the Midwest and South. Contrary to the traditional expectations rooted in the Chicago School's ecological approach (Park and Burgess 1984 [1925]), new immigrants are no longer limiting themselves to the traditional arrival ports of the central city and are moving directly to these new suburban and small-town destinations.

A key element of this process of dispersion during the 1990s was the movement of Mexican immigrants and Latinos more broadly to suburban communities across the United States. For example, 54% of Latinos in the United States resided in the suburbs in 2000, an increase of 71% since 1990 (Suro and Singer 2002). Even in the "established Latino metros" like Chicago, much of the Latino population growth is occurring in the suburbs rather than the central city. In the Chicago metropolitan area, 63% of the Latino population growth during the 1990s occurred in the suburbs (Suro and Singer 2002). Between 1990 and 2006, the number of Latinos residing in the Chicago suburbs more than tripled. By 2006, more Latinos lived in the suburbs of the Chicago metro than in the central city (Institute for Latino Studies 2008).[5] These suburban Latinos are both immigrant and native-born persons, and in 2000 approximately half were of Mexican origin (Paral et al. 2004). Furthermore, by 2000, 49% of Mexican immigrants in the Chicago metropolitan area resided in the suburbs, and that number continued to increase during the first decade of the 21st century.

The data for this chapter are drawn from a case study of Aurora, Illinois, located on the western edge of the Chicago metropolitan area, approximately 40 miles from the central city. Based on common perceptions of the suburbs, one would expect this area to exemplify typical suburban sprawl—white, middle-class suburban subdivisions and retail corridors—and it does hold those elements. However, a closer look at the community also uncovers a number of streets and neighborhoods Mexican residents clearly dominate. Passing vehicles sport Mexican flags and the names of Mexican states on the back windows. Street vendors offer churros and *helado* (ice cream) to passersby. Signs in Spanish are dominant in some areas, identifying *panaderías* (bakeries) and *carnicerías* (markets). *Agencias de viajes* (travel agencies) advertise special travel rates to Mexico. Local schools as well as banks, churches, and other service providers maintain announcement signs in Spanish. Often these signs are not translated into English. In the shopping malls and "big box" stores, it is not uncommon to hear both customers and employees speaking Spanish. In fact, aside from the city of Chicago and adjacent Cicero, Aurora holds the largest concentration of Mexican immigrants in the Chicago metropolitan area (Paral and

TABLE 1. Latino Population Growth in Aurora, Illinois, 1990–2007

	1990	2000	2007
Total	99,581	142,990	176,413
Latino	22,864	46,557	66,769
Percentage	23.0	32.6	37.8
Mexican	19,169	39,351	59,645
Percentage	19.2	27.5	33.8

Sources: U.S. Census Bureau, 2008a, 2008b, and 2008c.

Norkewicz 2003). As the next section shows, the majority of these immigrants have arrived in Aurora since the 1990s. These demographic shifts make Aurora an ideal research site in which to examine the ways that a growing transnational immigrant population transforms the receiving community.

The bulk of the data for this project comes from in-depth interviews with school administrators and teachers. Quantitative data on the city and its Latino and Mexican population is drawn from the 1990 and 2000 U.S. census surveys and the 2005–7 American Community Survey Three Year Estimates. Also examined are relevant archival and public records, primarily newspaper coverage of school-related events and activities involving Latino community members in Aurora. Finally, the interviews are supplemented by qualitative observations of activities and events within the school district, such as school board meetings, which provide additional insight into the transformations occurring in this local community institution.

DEMOGRAPHIC AND HISTORICAL BACKGROUND

Since 1990, Aurora has experienced a huge population growth, from 99,581 residents to an estimated 176,413 in 2007. A significant portion of this growth was due to the entrance of Latinos, particularly of Mexican origin, migrating directly to this city at the edge of the Chicago metropolitan area. According to 2000 census data, 39,351 persons of Mexican origin resided in Aurora, 57.6% of whom were foreign born. By 2007, the Census Bureau estimates that the number of Mexican-origin residents had grown to 59,645. Overall, nearly 40% of Aurora's population was Latino in 2007. Approximately 89% of them were of Mexican origin. Table 1 presents this population growth.

Aurora is a fast-growing area with significantly increasing racial/ethnic diversity,[6] as well as socioeconomic diversity. A rapidly increasing Latino and immigrant population is only one of the dramatic changes that this area is currently undergoing.

Several additional processes are relevant as a context for the changes in the Latino population. First, the dramatic population growth brings challenges that must be considered. New housing is being rapidly constructed; there is a greater demand for grocery stores, schools, community services, commuting options, and more. In addition, outer suburban areas like Aurora are being incorporated into the metropolis.

In times past, Aurora, which is over 40 miles away from downtown Chicago, was an independent city and would not have been considered a suburb.[7] The original source of its population and economic growth in the 1850s can be attributed to the railroad. Aurora served as a headquarters for the Chicago, Burlington and Quincy Railroad (CB & Q). In 1856, the CB & Q established maintenance yards in Aurora, making the railroad the city's primary industry for decades to come. These repair yards, in fact, were the employment draw for a small number of Mexican immigrants that came to Aurora in the early 20th century. Aurora historian Susan Palmer (1986) cites the railroad's better pay and housing provisions as the initial pull for Mexican migrants who were drawn out of midwestern farm labor. With year-round work available at the repair yards, some migrant families settled more permanently in the city and surrounding area. The growth of more manufacturing plants along the rail lines provided additional job opportunities through the 1920s. By 1920, eight factories manufactured machinery in Aurora, and another five companies produced steel office furniture and factory equipment (Peterson 1990). In addition, five railroads ran through Aurora.

George L. Edson (1925), a census taker for the U.S. Department of Labor, counted 700 Mexican residents (men, women, and children) in Aurora in 1925.[8] According to U.S. census data, the total population of Aurora grew from 36,397 in 1920 to 46,589 in 1930 (U.S. Census Bureau 1930). Based on Edson's count, then, the Mexican population of Aurora in this period was less than 2% of the total. He found that the railroads employed the majority of the male Mexican residents in 1925, and he counted approximately four times as many men as women. He also observed very little business or institutional development among the Mexican population. "In a business way the Aurora Mexicans have nothing. The nearest they come to it is a barber shop at 362 Broadway run by a chap who was born in Mexico but his father was a Spaniard and his mother was Greek and he claims to be an American" (Edson 1925, 7). Edson's observations provide a useful historical comparison for the dramatic increase in the number of Mexican-origin residents in recent decades, as well as for their increased organizational and economic development.

The Great Depression interrupted Aurora's industrial growth, and economic and population increases did not build momentum again until the 1950s, when the city again attracted new industry. In the past several decades the city has been trying to reinvent itself, with mixed results, from an industrial center into what we might term an "edge city" with a more high-tech, professional character. Since the 1980s, "Aurora has developed from an industrial city in decline to a growing high-tech hub" (Peterson 1990, 221). The early 1980s were a period of revitalization for the city, including the restoration of downtown buildings, the addition and development of entertainment and shopping centers, and the quick growth of the housing and commercial real estate industry (Peterson 1990).

Driving through Aurora today, one sees both its industrial heritage and older working-class, and increasingly Latino, neighborhoods, as well as the prototypical suburban middle-class housing subdivisions and shopping centers. As the Chicago metropolitan area expands to incorporate it more fully, Aurora demonstrates the complexity of the attendant social, economic, and physical transformations. A related process is the loss of farming and the rural character of the surrounding area, which is also happening throughout the outer suburbs. Open spaces are being closed; farmland has mostly disappeared to make way for shopping malls and housing subdivisions. The landscape itself expresses the social processes involved as older, working-class neighborhoods become adjacent to middle-class subdivisions, and cornfields still occasionally lurk in the shadows of strip malls and newly constructed office complexes.

Thus, the last 25 years have been a time of major change to the city of Aurora. In the midst of these structural changes, and no doubt in response to them, the Latino population has boomed. Not only doubling in size, it has also increased as a proportion of the city's population significantly between 1990 and 2000. While the Mexican community in Aurora may be fairly old, it is the recent increase in size and proportion that maps onto other socio-spatial changes in the metropolitan area. At the forefront of this fast-paced population shift are Aurora's public schools.

AURORA PUBLIC SCHOOLS

The programs discussed in this chapter were developed by school administrators in District One, the school district most affected by the growth of the Mexican population in Aurora. A comparison of Aurora's three public school districts demonstrates not only the speed with which District One's student body shifted to primarily Latino and Mexican-origin, but also the concentration of Latinos within this district. It also illustrates the degree of social and economic inequality that accompanies this concentration. For District One, the last two decades have led to a near crisis: a fast-growing student population with greater needs for bilingual resources combined with comparatively low local funding.

Table 2 shows that the increase in Latino students in District One clearly maps onto the overall demographic change in Aurora described in the previous section. Between 1996 and 2006, the number of total students increased from 8,559 to 12,316.

TABLE 2. Latino Students in District One, 1996–2006

	1996	2002	2006
Total students	8,559	11,238	12,316
Latino students	5,069	8,417	9,951
Percentage	59.2	74.9	80.8

Source: 1996 data provided by District One; Illinois State Board of Education 2002, 2006.

TABLE 3. Comparison of Aurora School Districts, 2006

	District 1	District 2	District 3
Total number of students	12,316	12,301	27,813
% Latino	80.8	40.6	6.1
% LEP	36.8	8.2	3.0
State test performance*	59.5	69.6	88.0
Total annual budget	$91 million	$104 million	$248 million
% Local Funding	34.0	55.3	83.1

Source: Illinois State Board of Education 2006.
*Percentage meeting or exceeding Illinois Learning Standards on all state tests, 2005–06.

In that same period, the number of Latino students nearly doubled, from 5,069 to 9,951. In 1996, Latinos accounted for 59.2% of the District One student body. By 2006, that percentage had increased to 80.8.

A pattern of ethnic concentration is apparent when District One is compared to other school districts in Aurora (table 3). There are three school districts in Aurora: District One, District Two, and District Three (which also includes portions of neighboring towns). District One provides education for 12,316 children, not to mention the adults it reaches through its adult education programs. For comparison, District Two serves 12,301 children. District Three, by far the largest and wealthiest district, serves 27,813 students. District One is 80.8% Latino, while District Two and District Three are 40.6% and 6.1%, respectively. Since public school assignment is determined by where one lives, it is clear that Latino families reside predominantly within District One. In fact, Latinos account for more than half of the students in all 12 of its elementary schools. Two-thirds of the elementary schools are at least 75% Latino. One elementary school is 95.7% Latino.

Table 3 shows that this ethnic concentration is accompanied by educational inequality. In District Three, which is over 80% white, 88% of students met or exceeded Illinois Learning Standards on standardized tests. In District Two, 69.6% of students met these standards. And in District One, only 59.5% of students met the state educational standards. An additional factor to consider is the percentage of students categorized as Limited English Proficient (LEP), requiring additional resources. In District One, 36.8% of students in 2006 were defined as LEP. In District Two and District Three, this percentage was 8.2 and 3.0, respectively (Illinois State Board of Education 2006).

Finally, while the academic performance of District One students suffers and many of its students require additional resources in the form of bilingual services, this district is also the poorest of the three. It is also the most dependent on state and federal funding, as a result of low property values within the district. For the 2004–5 academic year, District One's total budget was just over $91 million. District Two had a budget of almost $104 million. District Three had a budget of just over $248 million. Even taking into consideration its significantly larger size, it is clear that District Three is much better funded than either of the other two districts (Illinois State Board of Education 2006). This economic status is a result of the higher property values within District Three.

District Three derives 80% of its annual funding from local property taxes. In contrast, District One receives only 28.6% of its funding locally. District Two receives half of its support locally and half from state and federal sources.[9] District One's greater dependence on state and federal monies reflects the lower economic position of the community it serves, since local school funding is primarily produced via property taxes and is thus dependent on the property values within the district's boundaries. In addition, District One's greater dependency on the state and federal government may leave it more vulnerable to the whims of actors and agencies outside of the local community. For example, state or federal decisions to cut education spending would have a disastrous effect on District One, while neighboring District Three might notice little difference.

In an attempt to respond to this socioeconomic crisis, District One reached across national borders to fulfill the changing needs of its students and their families. Programs like the distance learning partnership with Mexico and the teacher recruitment trips reveal a subtle transnationalizing process in the schools and community that has important implications for both immigrant and nonimmigrant residents.

Transnational Programs in Aurora Schools

As mentioned earlier, the purpose of Plazas Comunitarias, the distance learning partnership with Mexico, was to reconnect adult Mexican immigrants with the

Mexican school system they left behind. The program was cosponsored by District One, by a local community organization with ties to Aurora's Mexican immigrant community, and by the Mexican government via the consul office in Chicago. A satellite dish on the roof of District One's high school brought Mexican classroom courses into a computer lab. Students who completed the program received a degree from the Mexican minister of education that is equivalent to a ninth grade education in the United States. According to Margaret,[10] the director of bilingual programs at the time, "A GED in the States is much different from finishing your *secondaria* in Mexico, and a lot of parents had not gone through the high school, even the middle school grades. . . . We were providing them with a way to finish a degree in a native language via Mexico."

This degree is recognized by the United States, and the courses provided can also be used to prepare for the GED exam. The Mexican government contributed the satellite dish, antenna, teacher training, textbooks, exams, and guidance on the Internet. District One provided a classroom and facilitators (Moore 2002). The program was part of an initiative by the Mexican government that seeks to expand and reinforce connections between Mexico and its citizens abroad, particularly in the United States. In 1990, Mexico created the Program for Mexican Communities Abroad (PCME) and, in 2003, the Institute of Mexicans Abroad (IME). Gustavo Cano and Alexandra Delano (2007) observe a deepening in recent years in the relationship between the Mexican government and Mexican emigrant communities.

> With the formation of the IME and the CCIME [the Advisory Council of the IME], the institutionalisation of this transnational relationship goes beyond any precedent in the history of the Mexican government's efforts to address the needs of the Mexican immigrant community from both sides of the border. The IME is the first transnational institution emanated from the official structure of the Mexican government, with specific programs and activities oriented to address the needs of the Mexican community in the US from a federal perspective . . . (Cano and Delano 2007, 42).

As one element of this larger national project, Plazas Comunitarias was also instituted in several other locations throughout the Chicago metropolitan area and in other U.S. cities.[11] According to Carlos M. Sada, former consul general of Mexico in Chicago,

> Plazas Comunitarias educational services through distance and open learning is a national project that has been working in Mexico for many decades. Today, the Mexican government through its Ministry of Foreign Affairs, of Public Education and its Consulates, target the Mexican communities all over the United States . . . Plazas Comunitarias

E-Mexico in the United States is a commitment of the Mexican government and the local authorities to offer alternative education to Mexicans and Latinos using the most advanced technology and learning methodologies.[12]

This distance learning program demonstrated a remarkable coalition of city education officials, the local Mexican community, and the Mexican government, which clearly recognized a significant Mexican immigrant population in Aurora. The program's very existence in this city that is almost 40 miles from central Chicago is an example of how this quickly growing Mexican immigrant community is creating change in its suburban home. Even more interestingly, it demonstrates an response by the school district and the receiving community to the influx of Mexican immigrants in a way that *strengthens,* rather than weakens, their connections to Mexico. It is also an example of a local institution interacting directly with a foreign government without the intervention of its own national government. This relationship challenges the traditional state-centric view of international relations, which assumes that all cross-border political and economic interactions are mediated by the nation-state.

A second program within the school district with even greater potential for transforming Aurora schools is the district's teacher recruitment trips to Mexico. Starting in the late 1990s, District One administrators began trips to Mexico and Puerto Rico to fill its increasing need for bilingual education teachers. They later added trips to Spain as well. To recruit in Mexico, administrators worked with universities in Mexico City, Guadalajara, and Monterey, holding recruitment events that drew applicants from all over Mexico. Teachers who participated in this program responded to an advertisement in the newspaper and came for a daylong process of test-taking and interviews. Applicants who were offered positions in the school district then had to apply for H-1B temporary visas, working with an immigration attorney recommended by the district (although all costs were paid by the applicant). The recruitment trips were held in October for the following school year, so that all of the visa and teaching certification paperwork could be completed in time.

In addition to the work visa, applicants from Mexico generally had to complete additional training in the United States in order to be properly certified to teach in U.S. schools. Since the Mexican educational system is not easily comparable to the U.S. system, most came with a Type 29 teaching certificate, an emergency certificate that allows anyone with a bachelor's degree to be hired as a teacher while obtaining a teaching certification. The recruits were given eight years to complete the additional courses and requirements.

Three elementary teachers from Mexico who still live and teach in Aurora were interviewed for this research project. They described their students as feeling closely connected to Mexico as "home," whether they had been there or not. Some were born in the United States, some came directly from Mexico, but the children felt an intimate cultural connection to Mexico. One teacher, Anna, described this connection best:

> I think it's kind of difficult to work with bilingual students when sometimes you don't understand their culture. And this is—maybe, one of the things I had in common with the students is that we came from the main social cultural background. I understand most of the problems they have, the custom; the culture part is very easy to understand for me.

She also describes a stronger connection with her students' parents, who may feel uncomfortable at the school because of their language ability or immigrant status.

> I think they can find in my person somebody who they can trust. I know they are not afraid to come to the school and talk to me, because first of all we are going to talk in the same language, we are going to share something we know is from our culture. That's what I have.

The teachers, as well as Margaret, the bilingual education director at the time, perceived an advantage for their students to have not only a Spanish-speaking instructor, but one who can connect with them culturally as well. Even though they may not be from exactly the same parts of Mexico or from the same socioeconomic background, there is recognition of a shared cultural heritage that cannot be re-created by teachers from Puerto Rico, Spain, or the United States. Maria, another teacher from Mexico said,

> The difference that I see is when they have a Spanish teacher from Spain, it's because Spain is in Europe! So that is totally, you know, a great difference; the mentality, the culture is different because they are Europeans. . . . Most of the Europeans, their status, I mean their social status, is higher. And even though I have—my social status was different from [my students]—I am from México . . . just the feeling that they are Mexicans, my *paisanos* I would say, you know? They're Mexicans and you love them. It's like they are my people. Even when they are different in social status, . . . they are my people. And the Spanish people from Spain, I don't think they feel this.

Thus, the teacher recruitment program created a transnational connection within the classroom, embodied by teachers recruited directly from the immigrants' sending nation.

As discussed below, this connection was difficult to maintain over the long term. However, it demonstrates one way in which the response of a community institution can change the context of reception for incoming Mexican immigrant families. The presence of these Mexican teachers, many of whom continue to teach in District One today, provides a school experience that recognizes and participates in the social and cultural connection that many of its students and their families maintain with Mexico.

The Continued Influence of the Nation-State

While the stories of these programs demonstrate a creative response by local school administrators to the growth of a transnational migrant population in their community, the stories also support the argument of many globalization scholars regarding the continued power of the nation-state. The administrators responded to the changing needs of their students by developing direct relationships with foreign nations, institutions, and organizations without the intervention of the U.S. government. However, immigration and educational policies at the national level still placed limitations on the ability of the local school district to maintain these relationships. The result is a process of transnationalization within the schools that is partial and unstable. However, the very existence of programs like these within a receiving community suggests that these communities are beginning to connect to a broader social, economic, and political network that is not fully contained by the nation-state.

So, despite newspaper coverage and an elaborate opening ceremony, the distance learning partnership with Mexico was short-lived. According to Margaret, the program only lasted one year, served about 25 to 30 adult students, and was disbanded. A new superintendent entered the scene the next year who, according to Margaret, was much less supportive of the bilingual program in general. Margaret was moved to a different position, and the bilingual program was scaled back. In addition, the two teachers who facilitated the distance learning program returned to Mexico and were not replaced. The school district decided to no longer fund the program.

So, despite the program's promise for creating a transnational link with Mexico within the schools, the school district was ultimately unable to maintain the connection because of changes in the motivations and priorities of the administration. These motivations and priorities are shaped by the institutional structure of the public school system. The new superintendent acted within a set of expectations for which creating transnational connections is not a priority and is, at some level, at odds with it.

Since the early 20th century, public schools have been a primary setting for national assimilation and Americanization projects, sometimes explicitly, sometimes more subtly. Various approaches to these goals have dominated over the years, but the important role of schools in these processes remains unchanged. In 1926, one scholar argued in the *American Journal of Sociology*, "There is left only one Americanization force . . . an efficient American public schools system" (Speek 1926, 249).

In 2002, education researcher Margaret Gibson argued that Latino youth today face similar assimilationist pressures that immigrant children faced a century ago. In the early 1900s,

> Few educators saw need for reform in the way schools were structured or in the concept
> of Americanization that they embodied. Too little has changed. Although schools today
> may explicitly advocate respect for cultural differences and provide immigrant students
> far more specialized instructional assistance than was the case a century ago, the goal
> in the minds of many educators and policy makers remains one of cultural replacement
> and eventual assimilation. (Gibson 2002, 245).

In other words, the distance learning program, which sought to strengthen rather than weaken the connection between immigrants and their sending nation, failed at least partly as a result of its conflict with the assimilationist orientation of the institution.

In addition, the U.S. Congress enacted the No Child Left Behind Act in 2001, which created more stringent requirements for who can teach in a public school classroom. The policy requires "highly qualified teachers" in every classroom. A "highly qualified teacher" has a bachelor's degree; full state certification and licensure; and demonstrated competency, as defined by the state, in every subject he or she teaches (U.S. Department of Education 2001).[13] In District One, this means that every teacher must pass a basic skills test in English and the emergency certificates are no longer an option. Commented Margaret, "No Child Left Behind has impacted greatly all of our efforts [in recruiting teachers from Mexico]. We've lost some great teachers because they couldn't pass the Basic Skill Test in English)."

The students' need for Spanish-speaking teachers was hindered by the federal and state requirements for teachers who are fluent in English. For Spanish-speaking students in District One, a "highly qualified teacher" may have a very different meaning than the federal mandate requires, but these needs were not recognized by the federal policy. For example, the current school board president, a longtime Anglo resident of Aurora, described bilingual education primarily as a pathway to English fluency. In contrast, Jorge, a Mexican immigrant who worked closely with the schools as the director of a local nonprofit organization, portrayed bilingual education as a way to preserve Spanish fluency among immigrant and second-generation children. He wanted the schools to recognize that "it was okay for our children to speak Spanish. . . . Our kids are going to learn English, that's not the problem. The thing is, if they speak Spanish that's already an asset that they can utilize later in life." In other words, what constitutes a "highly qualified" bilingual education teacher may be different depending on which perspective is taken regarding the purpose of bilingual education.

Ultimately, according to Margaret, the recruitment trips to Mexico were discontinued as a consequence of three factors: the paperwork and effort involved in obtaining visas for the teachers, particularly after 9/11; the certification difficulties that arose as a result of No Child Left Behind; and the lack of support by the superintendent at the time. So the local efforts to create a transnational link to the sending nation of the immigrant families in their district were thwarted primarily by obstacles created by national and state-level policies regarding immigration and public education, in conjunction with the assimilationist orientation of the institution. Perhaps alone, the visa issues would have been manageable, but in combination with No Child Left Behind, a policy not specifically intended to prevent cross-border connections, recruitment in Mexico was no longer tenable.

However, the school district continued to recruit in Puerto Rico, where immigration policy was not relevant and where the educational system was compatible and intertwined with the U.S. system. Thus, the school district could recruit at Puerto Rican universities and obtain teachers already holding teaching certificates recognized in the United States who could travel freely in the United States without a visa.

In addition to Puerto Rico, District One also began a recruitment program in Spain, with very different experiences than it had in Mexico. First of all, the perceived motivation of teachers coming from Spain was different. While teachers from Mexico were perceived as coming to the United States with the goal of staying long term, Spanish teachers were viewed as desiring a temporary cultural experience with plans to return home after a relatively short time.[14] As a result, the two groups of teachers, recruited for the *same* set of jobs, were defined quite differently by U.S. immigration law. The teachers from Mexico were categorized as temporary workers in highly skilled positions, requiring the H-1B visa. Alternatively, the Spanish teachers obtained J-1 visas, included under the Exchange Visitor Program, which is

carried out under the provisions of the Mutual Educational and Cultural Exchange Act of 1961, as amended. The purpose of the Act is to increase mutual understanding between the people of the United States and the people of other countries by means of educational and cultural exchanges. International educational and cultural exchanges are one of the most effective means of developing *lasting and meaningful relationships*. They provide *an extremely valuable opportunity* to experience the United States and our way of life. Foreign nationals come to the United States to participate in a wide variety of educational and cultural exchange programs. (U.S. Department of State 2008; emphasis added)

Hence the relationships and perceptions at the national level greatly influenced the school district's ability to recruit teachers internationally. Teachers from Mexico were perceived as temporary workers, while the Spanish teachers were perceived as cultural travelers. The language used by the U.S. State Department also denotes a sense of social and cultural value in the J-1 visa not present in the H-1B visa, which describes a solely economic need for individuals with certain job skills.

In addition, because holders of J-1 visas were perceived as exchange teachers, the No Child Left Behind requirements were less problematic for them. Finally, District One's recruitment trips to Spain were well facilitated by the Spanish consulate, a factor that made a significant difference for the school district. According to Margaret, the Spanish consulate took care of all of the visa arrangements and some of the initial teaching certification testing. The consulate set up the interviews and even organized the school administrators' travel arrangements. This government support was in stark contrast with the experiences in Mexico, where the Mexican government, according to Margaret, was an additional barrier to gaining access to the applicants.

> The way the recruiting is set up with Spain is wonderfully organized. Spain takes care of a lot of the testing, a lot of those initial pieces that are required for certification. The embassy does all that, we didn't have that in Mexico. We took all of that on ourselves and it was a lot more work for us. So we've continued to recruit in Spain and in Puerto Rico, but we've had to give up the recruitment in Mexico, just because it was too difficult. And that's unfortunate because those are the teachers that understand our kids.

And so today in District One schools Spanish-speaking students are taught primarily by teachers from Spain and Puerto Rico (as well as the United States), although some from the Mexico recruitment program remain. Like Margaret, other teachers from Mexico perceived an advantage for their students in having an instructor who could connect with them culturally. Even though they may not be from the same part of Mexico, students and teachers shared a cultural heritage that cannot be re-created by teachers from Puerto Rico, Spain, or the United States. Thus, the teacher recruitment program had the potential for creating and maintaining a transnational connection within the classroom, embodied by teachers recruited directly from Mexico. However, as a result of obstacles created by national and state-level policies, this connection could not be sustained. Instead, connections to other countries were substituted based solely on a language, rather than a "multi-stranded" (Basch, Schiller, and Blanc 1994, 7) linkage rooted in the social and cultural realities of the transnational Mexican immigrant community in Aurora.

Discussion

The programs described in this chapter support the argument that migration needs to be reconceptualized as a dynamic process that transforms not just the immigrants, but the communities they live in as well. Communities across the globe are being transformed by migration. In its current state, however, scholarship does not address these transformations, for two reasons. First, the migration literature focuses too exclusively on the migrant or migrant group as the object of analysis. Second, there is a prevailing assumption that the social lives of migrants within the receiving community are confined to the immigrant or ethnic community. By including communities, both sending and receiving, as legitimate objects of analysis, we are able to overcome these limitations and perceive migration as social process that is deeply embedded within communities that shape and are shaped by its presence.

This approach uncovers an intriguing community response to migration: institutional transnationalization. Through the creation of the distance learning program and teacher recruitment in Mexico, District One built cross-border connections with the Mexican government and education institutions that do not make sense outside of the context of the migration flows between Aurora and Mexico. This is particularly surprising given the powerful national focus of U.S. public education. Since the early 20th century, public education has been a primary vehicle for national assimilation and Americanization projects, a goal seemingly at odds with the introduction of transnational elements to the institution. Yet in Aurora and elsewhere we can observe the development of transnational programs within local school districts, despite this nationally oriented institutional context. For example, in response to a similar influx of Mexican immigrants, school and community leaders in Conasauga, Georgia, partnered with a Mexican university for the development of their bilingual education program (Hamann 2002; Zúñiga et al. 2002).

The growth of a substantial Mexican immigrant population in Aurora within a relatively short period created a need for additional resources within District One, particularly for bilingual teachers and Spanish-language programs that could connect the schools to immigrant families. These new challenges for the school district came with little precedent and no operating manuals. School administrators had to come up with new ways of responding to the changing student population. One of these responses was to reach across national borders and create partnerships with the Mexican government and universities.

The growth of the Mexican immigrant population in Aurora since the 1990s is due in large part to the changes in the economic geography of the Chicago metropolitan area as a consequence of globalization. At the same time, current processes of globalization have destabilized the traditional state-centric perception of political and economic activity (Sassen 2002), creating opportunities for local institutions and actors to engage independently in transnational relationships with communities, organizations, and institutions beyond their national borders. The mediation of the nation-state is no longer a requirement for cross-border interactions. Socially and politically active immigrants, like Jorge in Aurora, may provide the needed social link for these transnational relationships instead. As mentioned above, Jorge was the director of the community organization that participated in the distance learning partnership with Mexico. In addition to this role in the local community, Jorge was also the first Latino member of District One's school board in the 1990s and the first president of the Federation of Clubs of Michoacán in the Chicago area, an organization that unites the many hometown associations from sending communities in the Mexican state of Michoacán. The combination of his and other migrants' local and transnational social and political endeavors created new opportunities for receiving communities like Aurora to engage in cross-border interactions in order to meet the needs and desires of their residents.

Recent research by Luis Guarnizo, Roger Waldinger, and others (Guarnizo, Portes, and Haller 2003; Waldinger 2008) suggests that very few immigrants actually participate in transnational political or economic activities. However, not much is known about the potential of these few transnational actors as links between diverse and geographically distant social networks.[15] My research suggests that such individuals may be a key factor in the transnationalizing processes described in this chapter. Furthermore, these links may not necessarily come only from the immigrant community. In Conasauga, for example, a local Anglo businessman used his international business network as a way to reach out to the Mexican university that participated in the school district's construction of a new bilingual education program (Hamann 2002). Similarly, in Marshalltown, Iowa, applied anthropologists Mark Grey and Anne Woodrick (2005) facilitated a relationship between that receiving community and the sending community of the majority of its new immigrant residents, Villachuato in Michoacán. Thus, there are multiple possibilities for facilitating these new opportunities for transnational activities within the receiving community. District One's engagement with Mexico is but one example of these new possibilities. More research is needed on this subject, hitherto obscured by the study of migrants in isolation from the communities they are embedded within.

Conclusion

The programs developed by District One demonstrate one way that a local institution, public education, has responded to the growth of a transnational migrant population in the community. By reaching across borders and engaging in independent relations with government and universities in Mexico, they represent a transnationalizing effect of migration on the receiving community. These transnational activities suggest a new understanding within the community regarding its interconnection with people and places beyond its national borders. Despite the national orientation of public education and its historic role of promoting immigrant assimilation, the school district responded to the needs and interests of the community by creating relationships with Mexico that would strengthen, rather than weaken, the ties of immigrant residents to their home country.

This response suggests that the community institution is reorienting itself, however subtly, into a broader social, economic, and political network that is not fully contained by the nation-state. As globalization scholar Saskia Sassen observes, "The national container of social process and power is cracked" (2002, 18). Within this context, cross-border interactions and relationships are not the exclusive territory of nation-states. Not only are migrants able to maintain transnational connections with their communities and nations abroad, but the receiving community itself is experimenting with these connections. The long-term impact of these connections may yet be unknown, but the mere fact of their existence suggests that there are changes afoot that have implications for both migrants and nonmigrants in the community.

For the community, these programs suggest that one consequence of migration is the potential for creating cross-border relationships without the mediation of the nation-state. These transnational relationships may alter the perspective of (at least some of) its residents regarding the community's interconnection with people and places outside of its national borders. These relationships may also offer new social and economic resources for communities struggling to redefine themselves in the global era.

For the migrants, these programs suggest a context of reception that cannot be simplified to an analysis of national-level factors like immigration policy. In other words, the ways in which local communities interpret and negotiate these national policies also shape the context of reception for the immigrants. In addition, this context of reception is influenced by the presence of the migrants at the local level as community institutions respond to the immediate needs and interests of the receiving community. Migration is a social process embedded within dynamic communities that change and are changed by the immigrants. More research is needed to understand these interactions and place them within the context of the migration process.

Therefore, what these programs illustrate are new opportunities for social, political, and economic engagement under conditions of globalization, as well as the tension between local and national interests. The stories of these programs reveal the contested and partial nature of these transnational processes at the local level. They present a sort of "two steps forward, three steps back" experience, with the ultimate result still to be revealed. Yet, even at this point, we can observe important transformations occurring in a heretofore locally and nationally oriented institution—public education.

NOTES

1. Schiller, Çağlar, and Gulbrandsen (2006) make a similar observation in their fieldwork in Manchester, New Hampshire.

2. Pseudonyms are used for names of all school districts.

3. Other terms may be used in place of *assimilation*, such as *incorporation* or *acculturation*. The focus, though, is generally the same: an examination of the ways that the migrants change to become more like the receiving group.

4. Alejandro Portes and his colleagues challenge the uniformity of these socioeconomic outcomes, arguing for the concept of "segmented assimilation," which recognizes the importance of color, location, and labor market structure in determining the socioeconomic outcomes of immigrant families across generations (Portes and Zhou 1993; Portes and Rumbaut 1996).

5. According to U.S. census data, 291,053 Latinos resided in the Chicago suburbs in 1990. By 2006, that number had more than tripled to 939,296. In comparison, growth within the city was much less dramatic. In 1990, 545,852 Latinos resided in the city of Chicago. By 2006, the city's Latino population had grown to 768,514 (Institute for Latino Studies 2008).

6. In addition to the growing Latino population, African Americans comprise approximately 11% of the city's population (U.S. Census Bureau 2008c).

7. One might argue that the size of this city might preclude its categorization as a "suburb." The idea that suburbs are small bedroom communities whose residents commute to the city for work clearly does not fit this area. However, within the current context of shifting urban spatial organization and the emergence of economically relevant edge cities, as described in an earlier section, it is clear that the relationship between Chicago and Aurora is also shifting. Accordingly, the term *suburb* is used to note Aurora's incorporation and spatial location within the metropolis.

8. Palmer (1986) estimates there were 355 adult Mexicans in Aurora between 1915 and 1931. Palmer did not find census data for this period to be trustworthy, so she instead depended on city directories for her count, although inaccuracy remains. Her estimation is very similar to Edson's (1925) count of employed males (361), though, suggesting that her method may have missed a significant number of women, children, and unemployed men. In addition, she uses a much longer time frame for her count.

9. These numbers are based on the 2004–5 academic year (Illinois State Board of Education 2006).

10. Pseudonyms are provided for all individuals interviewed.

11. Plazas Comunitarias is also available within Mexico.

12. Invitation to the program's opening ceremony, dated March 7, 2002; letter provided by an informant.

13. See www.ed.gov/nclb for full details.

14. According to Margaret, quite a few of the Spanish teachers do stay long term. However, it is the perception that they will stay temporarily that facilitates the recruitment process, not the reality.

15. In their research with leaders of transnational immigrant organizations, Portes, Escobar, and Arana (2008) do note that these actors often perceive little contradiction between engaging in transnational and host country politics simultaneously. However, the implications of these simultaneous activities, for both immigrants and nonimmigrants, have yet to be investigated.

REFERENCES

Alba, R., and V. Nee. 2003. *Remaking the American Mainstream: Assimilation and Contemporary Immigration.* Cambridge: Harvard University Press.

Basch, L. G., N. G. Schiller, and C. S. Blanc. 1994. *Nations Unbound: Transnational Projects, Post-Colonial Predicaments and Deterritorialized Nation-States.* Amsterdam: Gordon & Breach Science Publishers.

Blau, P., and O. D. Duncan. 1967. *The American Occupational Structure.* New York: Wiley.

Çağlar, A. 2006. "Hometown Associations, the Rescaling of State Spatiality and Migrant Grassroots Transnationalism." *Global Networks* 6: 1–22.

Cano, G., and A. Delano. 2007. "The Mexican Government and Organised Mexican Immigrants in the United States: A Historical Analysis of Political Transnationalism, 1848–2005." Working Paper No. 148, Center for Comparative Immigration Studies, University of California, San Diego.

Edson, G. L. 1925. *Mexicans in Aurora, Illinois.* Washington, DC: U.S. Department of Labor, Department of Labor Statistics.

Gans, H. 1973. "Introduction." In *Ethnic Identity and Assimilation: The Polish Community*, ed. N. Sandberg, ii–iv. New York: Praeger.

Gibson, M. A. 2002. "The New Latino Diaspora and Educational Policy." In *Education in the New Latino Diaspora: Policy and the Politics of Identity*, ed. S. Wortham, E. G. Murillo Jr., and E. T. Hamann, 241–52. Westport, CT: Ablex.

Gordon, M. 1964. *Assimilation in American Life: The Role of Race, Religion, and National Origins.* New York: Oxford University Press.

Grey, M. A., and A. C. Woodrick. 2005. "'Latinos Have Revitalized Our Community': Mexican Migration and Anglo Responses in Marshalltown, Iowa." In *New Destinations: Mexican Immigration in the United States*, ed. V. Zúñiga and R. Hernández-León, 133–54. New York: Russell Sage Foundation.

Guarnizo, L. E., A. Portes, and W. Haller. 2003. "Assimilation and Transnationalism: Determinants of Transnational Political Action among Contemporary Migrants." *American Journal of Sociology* 108: 1211–48.

Hamann, E. T. 2002. "¿*Un Paso Adelante?* The Politics of Bilingual Education, Latino Student Accommodation, and School District Management in Southern Appalachia." In *Education in the New Latino Diaspora: Policy and the Politics of Identity*, ed. S. Wortham, E. G. Murillo Jr., and E. T. Hamann, 67–97.Westport, CT: Ablex.

Illinois State Board of Education. 2002. Illinois School District Report Cards. http://iirc.niu.edu.

———. 2006. Illinois School District Report Cards. http://iirc.niu.edu.

Institute for Latino Studies. 2008. Data for CMAP Snapshot. University of Notre Dame.

Levitt, P. 1999. "Social Remittances: A Local-Level, Migration-Driven Form of Cultural Diffusion." *International Migration Review* 32: 926–49.

———. 2001. *The Transnational Villagers.* Berkeley: University of California Press.

Levitt, P., and B. N. Jaworsky. 2007. "Transnational Migration Studies: Past Developments and Future Trends." *Annual Review of Sociology* 33: 129–56.

Massey, D. 1985. "Ethnic Residential Segregation: A Theoretical Synthesis and Empirical Review." *Sociology and Social Research* 69: 315–50.

Moore, M. E. 2002. "East Ready to Launch Partnership with Mexico." *Aurora Beacon-News*, March 16.

Orozco, M. 2002. "Latino Hometown Associations as Agents of Development in Latin America." June. Inter-American Dialogue, Washington, DC.

Orozco, M., with M. LaPointe. 2004. "Mexican Hometown Associations and Development Opportunities." *Journal of International Affairs* 57: 1–21.

Palmer, S. 1986. "Building Ethnic Communities in a Small City: Romanians and Mexicans in Aurora, Illinois, 1900–1940." Ph.D. diss., Northern Illinois University.

Paral, R., T. Ready, S. Chun, and W. Sun. 2004. *Latino Demographic Growth in Metropolitan Chicago.* Notre Dame, IN: Institute for Latino Studies, University of Notre Dame.

Paral, R., and M. Norkewicz. 2003. *The Metro-Chicago Immigration Fact Book.* Chicago: Institute for Metropolitan Affairs, Roosevelt University.

Park, R. E., and E. W. Burgess. 1921. *Introduction to the Science of Sociology.* Chicago: University of Chicago Press.

———. 1984 [1925]. *The City: Suggestions for the Investigation of Human Behavior in the Urban Environment.* Chicago: University of Chicago Press.

Peterson, N. 1990. "Aurora." In *Local Community Fact Book: Chicago Metropolitan Area, 1990*, ed. Chicago Fact Book Consortium, 221. Chicago: Academy Chicago.

Portes, A., C. Escobar, and A. W. Radford. 2005. "Immigrant Transnational Organizations and Development: A Comparative Study." Working Paper 05<hy>07, Center for Migration and Development, Princeton University.

Portes, A., C. Escobar, and R. Arana. 2008. "Bridging the Gap: Transnational and Ethnic Organizations in the Political Incorporation of Immigrants in the United States." *Ethnic and Racial Studies* 31: 1056–90.

Portes, A. and R. G. Rumbaut. 1996. *Immigrant America: A Portrait.* 2nd ed. Berkeley: University of California Press.

Portes, A., and M. Zhou. 1993. "The New Second Generation: Segmented Assimilation and Its Variants." *Annals of the American Academy of Political and Social Science* 530: 74–96.

Rouse, R. 1991. "Mexican Migration and the Social space of Postmodernism." *Diaspora* 1: 8–23.

Sandberg, N. 1973. *Ethnic Identity and Assimilation: The Polish Community*. New York: Praeger.

Sassen, S. 2002. "The Repositioning of Citizenship: Emergent Subjects and Spaces for Politics." *Berkeley Journal of Sociology* 46: 41–66.

Schiller, N. G., A. Çağlar, and T. C. Gulbrandsen. 2006. "Beyond the Ethnic Lens: Locality, Globality, and Born-Again Incorporation." *American Ethnologist* 33: 612–33.

Speek, P. A. 1926. "The Meaning of Nationality and Americanization." *American Journal of Sociology* 32: 237–49.

Straughan, J., and P. Hondagneu-Sotelo. 2002. "From Immigrants in the City, to Immigrant City." In *From Chicago to LA: Making Sense of Urban Theory*, ed. M. Dear, 183–211. Thousand Oaks, CA: Sage.

Suro, R., and A. Singer. 2002. *Latino Growth in Metropolitan America: Changing Patterns, New Locations*. Washington, DC: Brookings Institution, Center on Urban & Metropolitan Policy and the Pew Hispanic Center.

U.S. Census Bureau. 1930. *1930 Census of Population and Housing*, vol. 3, part 1. Washington, DC: U.S. Census Bureau.

———. 2008a. "Profile of General Demographic Characteristics for Aurora, Illinois, 1990." Available online: http://factfinder.census.gov.

———. 2008b. "Profile of General Demographic Characteristics for Aurora, Illinois, 2000." Available online: http://factfinder.census.gov.

———. 2008c. "American Community Survey, 2005–2007 Three Year Estimates for Aurora, Illinois." Available online: http://factfinder.census.gov.

U.S. Department of Education. 2001. No Child Left Behind Act of 2001. Available online: http://www.nclb.gov.

U.S. Department of State. 2008. "Overview: About the Exchange Visitors Program." Available online: http://www.state.gov.

Wakeman, F. 1988. "Transnational and Comparative Research." *Items* 42: 85–89.

Waldinger, R. 2008. "Between 'Here' and 'There': Immigrant Cross-Border Activities and Loyalties." *International Migration Review* 42: 3–29.

Zúñiga, V., R. Hernández-León, J. L. Shadduck- Hernández, and M. Olivia Villareal. 2002. "The New Paths of Mexican Immigrants in the United States: Challenges for Education and the Role of Mexican universities." In *Education in the New Latino Diaspora: Policy and the Politics of Identity*, ed. S. Wortham, E. G. Murillo Jr., and E. T. Hamann, 99–116. Westport, CT: Ablex.

MARIA JOSEFA SANTOS and ANTONIO CASTRO-ESCOBAR

Increasing Knowledge and Networking Opportunities for Small-Scale Mexican Growers in Southwest Michigan

IN AGRICULTURE, MICHIGAN'S SECOND LARGEST INDUSTRY, HISPANICS ARE becoming increasingly important. In 2006, Hispanics made up only 3.9% (393,281) of Michigan's total population; however, this figure represents a 20.3% increase over the previous six years. Furthermore, Michigan ranks fourth in the nation in the number of seasonal agricultural migrant workers, with approximately 45,000 annually, most of whom are Hispanics. The majority of these workers come from Mexico, following the southern migrant stream and harvesting crops in Texas, Florida, North Carolina, and South Carolina before reaching Michigan. Texas, followed by California, New Mexico, Colorado, Oklahoma, Washington, Idaho, and Michigan, had the largest number of Hispanic farm owners and the largest acreage in farm holdings in 2002 (A. López 2007).

Moreover, it is well known that the grower population in Michigan and throughout the United States is aging; the average age of Michigan growers is about 60 years, and their progeny are not likely to continue farming. Alternatively, the average age among Mexican growers is 35–40 years, and it is more likely that their descendants will continue the farming tradition (A. López 2007). For this reason, it is important to pay attention to Hispanic farmers and their business needs. Another important reason to pay attention to these growers is that ethnic groups often introduce new crop varieties that are native to their country of origin and, as a consequence, help to open new niche markets and new business opportunities. Growing crops native to their country of origin helps immigrant groups satisfy the need for products that bring back memories from their country of origin, and helps the community to form cultural bonds.

In short, the number of Mexican growers has increased considerably and is beginning to form an important entrepreneurial group in southwest Michigan. For this reason, programs, projects, courses, businesses, educational, and governmental institutions need to make adjustments to meet the needs of this important new group of grower-entrepreneurs. To date, the main sources of knowledge for these growers have been a few individuals that belong to the same ethnic group. Lacking experience, Mexican growers have a great need for information and training in basic agricultural practices; moreover, they also struggle to become integrated into their new communities and Michigan's agricultural system.

The objective of this chapter is to show the needs experienced by a group of Mexican growers who acquired farmland in southwest Michigan, the different strategies these growers follow to meet such needs, and how educational, state, federal, and nonprofit agencies, by working together, try to meet the needs of this group of Mexican growers. The chapter describes key obstacles to fulfilling these needs, as well as offering several practical recommendations for improving the relationship between these agencies and the Mexican growers. To accomplish these objectives, 22 Mexican agricultural entrepreneurs in southwest Michigan were interviewed, as well as two Extension staff members from Michigan State University, and one staff member from an agency that supports agriculture in Michigan. This study was conducted in the 2007–8 academic year.

Background

Michigan's agricultural sector is the second most important industry in the state, following only the automobile industry (at least until recently). The state's agribusiness segment generates nearly $64 billion in economic activity and employs one million people. Michigan's agri-food sector would rank 62nd if it appeared on the Fortune 500 list. It is estimated that from 2006 through 2011, the state could see an additional $1 billion economic boost from the agri-food sector; this could create up to an additional 23,000 new jobs annually, according to a study by Michigan State University's Product Center. Michigan ranks fifth and eighth nationally in exports of fruits and vegetables, respectively. According to the same study, Michigan exports

TABLE 1. Michigan Commodities Ranked First in U.S. Agriculture, 2007

	Unit	Quantity (1,000)	% of U.S. Production
Beans, dry, black	Cwt	1,540	55.5
Beans, dry, cranberry	Cwt	88	71.0
Beans, dry, small red	Cwt	253	47.3
Blueberries	Pound	93,000	32.8
Cherries, tart	Pound	196,000	77.4
Cucumbers (for pickles)	Ton	156.4	30.8
Flowering hanging baskets	Number	6,070	20.7
Geraniums (seed and cuttings)	Pots	22,591	36.1
Impatiens	Flats	2,156	24.1
Petunias	Flats	1,515	22.1

Sources: Keweno, 2009; Michigan 2008–9 Highlights, National Agricultural Statistics Service, Michigan Field Office, Michigan Department of Agriculture.

about one-third of its agricultural commodities each year, generating more than $1 billion and supporting nearly 13,000 jobs (Michigan Department of Agriculture 2008). Thus, agriculture is immensely important to Michigan's economic health.

Michigan's agriculture is also the second most diverse in the nation in the number of crops grown; only California surpasses it. Michigan produces over 200 commodities on a commercial basis. In 2008, the state ranked ninth in the United States in milk production, producing 7.8 billion pounds of milk with farm sales of $1.5 billion. Michigan's nursery and perennial production is ranked fifth nationally, while its floriculture industry and Christmas tree production rank first and fourth in the nation, respectively. Combined, these industries represent over $790 million in wholesale value. Table 1 provides some of Michigan's agricultural commodities that ranked first in 2007 according to the United States Department of Agriculture (Kleweno 2008–9).

Southwest Michigan, in particular, has a number of features that lure Mexican growers. First, it is rich in agricultural production. In addition, most crops grown in the area are labor intensive, providing additional employment opportunities for these business owners, many of whom are both growers and workers. Mexican growers indicate that small-town life and the region's proximity to Chicago are additional reasons for moving to southwest Michigan. The proximity to Chicago has several advantages for Mexican growers; it provides an avenue for commercial exchange between Michigan and Illinois, and allows growers to maintain familial

FIGURE 1. Farms with Hispanic Operators

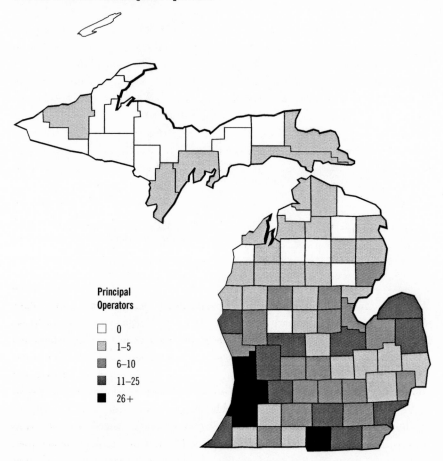

Principal
Operators

☐ 0

1–5

6–10

11–25

■ 26+

Note: Numbers indicate operators in specific counties.
Source: 2007 Census of Agriculture, state profile. Michigan Spanish, Hispanic, and Latinos in Agriculture.

connections. In addition, some Mexican growers are weekend farmers and work in Chicago during the week.

The 2007 Census of Agriculture (USDA 2009) reports that Hispanics operate more than 615 farms in Michigan. Figure 1 shows the number and location of these farms. Marinez and García (2004) argue that there are likely more than 615 Hispanic farms in Michigan. They explain that names of several Hispanic farmers do not appear on the title of ownership of their land; thus they are not registered in the census. Furthermore, others bought their farms recently (less than two years) and do not appear in registries yet.

The agriculture census (USDA 2009) reports that the average size of farms operated by Latinos in Michigan in 2007 was 89 acres. However, only 27 Latino farmers earned 100% of their income from agricultural activity (USDA 2009). A. López (2007), who wrote a doctoral dissertation on Hispanic blueberry farmers in southwest Michigan, found that on average in Michigan's southwest counties (Allegan, Kalamazoo, Van Buren, Berrien, and Cass) Hispanic-owned farms are about 26.4 acres. The smallest farm was 2 acres and the largest 480 acres. He also reports that only 20% of these entrepreneurs have some previous agricultural experience, and the financial and social capital they used to purchase and operate a farm most often comes from a non-agricultural-related activity.

These Mexican businesses fit what the Inter-American Bank for Development (1997) classifies as a microfirm: a subsistence production entity that is in many cases outside the margins of the regulatory system. In a microfirm, the owner carries out the majority of the business activities, the employees are often family members, and there is usually no separation between family and business. These business units often become employment options for millions of families that remain at the verge of poverty. They help families to mitigate the impacts of economic cycles, allow better income distribution, and create conditions for growth and development. These businesses share other characteristics: they open with small start-up capital and use simple production, commercialization, and distribution processes (J. N. López 2007). Similarly, they commonly lack several features: resources for employee and owner training, permanent market monitoring, and long-term investment strategies designed to access markets in a competitive manner (J. N. López 2007).

For such entrepreneurs purchasing land in southwest Michigan, blueberries were a natural choice. The farmlands Mexican growers acquired were, in many cases, already in blueberry production. Mexican growers did not get into the blueberry business because they knew how to grow blueberries or because it made economic sense to them. Rather, they began farming the crop because blueberries are the main crop grown in the area. In addition, the availability of these farmlands made it easier to generate an income for supporting a family. Some Mexican growers are already beginning to grow tomatillos, tomatoes, hot peppers, zucchinis, melons, and watermelons. However, the motivation to experiment with crops that do not rank high in the state probably has to do with the farmers' cultural upbringing or the growing demand for such crops by the state's Hispanic population. In short, blueberries are the crop of choice for Mexican growers by default. Despite the flirtation with increasing crop diversity, Mexican growers are mainly involved in blueberry production.

These entrepreneurs share many other characteristics. One could classify the growers in southwest Michigan according to Moctezuma's (2002) definition of migrant entrepreneurs. These are migrants who have moved from saving to investment and are now owners of businesses. The difference between the migrant entrepreneurs Moctezuma mentions and the Mexican growers in southwest Michigan is that some of these migrants already had invested in their country of origin. In most cases, however, their legal status and migratory lifestyle restricts the amount of money invested in their community of origin. In addition, many of these migrants have brought their relatives to the United States, making the relationship with their country of origin more distant and continued investing more tenuous. One can also view these farmers from the perspective traditionally known in the literature as ethnic entrepreneurship (Menzies et al. 2007); although these enterprises are nontraditional Mexican businesses, more and more Mexicans are becoming farming entrepreneurs.

The majority of Hispanic growers come from small agricultural communities in Mexico. This is probably one of the main reasons why they adapt easily to the culture and life of a small town. However, while adapting, they also form communities, groups, and networks that represent the Mexican way of life. For example, in the southwest Michigan counties one can find Mexican stores and restaurants, and signs in the homes depicting the ethnic origin of the inhabitants. These signs vary from an image of the Virgin of Guadalupe to a Mexican soccer team flag. In the counties one might also find fiestas and gatherings attended by *paisanos* from across the region or state.

All of these growers had work experience in the formal sector, mostly in manufacturing. These experiences seem to have helped them integrate into the U.S. work environment. A. López (2007) reports that Hispanic farm owners had diverse labor backgrounds: 32.8% had worked in services, 13.8% had worked in manufacturing, 6.9% had owned small businesses, 5% had worked in construction, 8.6% had retired, 3.4% had worked in the food packing industry, and 3.4% had worked in education. Less than 2% had previously worked in seasonal agriculture.

Finally, in part because of their lack of agricultural experience, these Mexican growers tend to have little knowledge of the sector in which they are investing, U.S. farmland, or the commercial crops they grow. Furthermore, most of the farmers do not understand English, and, unlike U.S. agricultural producers who have sound educational traditions, they tend to have limited formal education. They do not attend seminars and they do not assimilate knowledge found in books, articles, or the Internet. In short, they have a limited understanding of the context of the U.S. agricultural system. What they do know, they have learned from the experience. They use experiences from their own properties or those of their neighbors, relatives and countrymen:

"Yo no sabía cómo plantar la bluberry y después de desmontar mi terreno, fui al terreno de mi vecino y medí la distancia entre surcos y la distancia entre plantas y así plante mi bluberry." I did not know how to plant blueberries so, after clearing my forest land, I went to my neighbor's blueberry plantation and measured the distance between rows and blueberry plants, and I planted my blueberries the same way. (Castro 2008)

What is becoming clear is that these growers have particular knowledge needs regarding production, but those needs may extend to the market as well. Furthermore, their needs are not currently being fulfilled by state, federal, or nonprofit service providers. After reviewing the data and methodology used in this study, this chapter describes these needs as well as the institutional obstacles to their fulfillment. In addition, recommendations are made for improving the relationship and communication flow between these organizations and Michigan's growing number of Latino farmers.

Data and Methodology

We used several strategies to collect information on these growers and their needs: close analysis of courses and trainings offered to Mexican producers by one of the authors of this work; interviews and personal conversations with Mexican producers and their close relatives who are also farm owners and regular training attendees; and participation by the authors in Mexican growers' meetings where we documented their specific knowledge and training needs. Regarding the service delivery agencies (state, federal, and nonprofit agencies and Michigan State University Extension), we talked with individuals who are heavily involved in providing training to Mexican growers.

The strategy used to study Mexican growers was the classic anthropological method, and began by making an ethnographic assessment of the training courses agencies offered to these growers. Open interviews with 22 producers, farm visits, and a genealogy of two of the most important families in the community complemented the assessment of courses. Agricultural agents, Extension officers, and educational volunteers who have provided courses and instruction to these entrepreneurs provided further information. Qualitative in-depth interviews lasting approximately one hour were performed. In the interviews, the informants told the story of their farms' start-up and development, focusing on the roles their relatives and *paisanos* played in providing necessary monetary capital and knowledge. The genealogies illuminated the role that family networks play in the marketing strategies the families follow. Analysis was conducted on a case-by-case basis, focusing on the following elements: the farm's regional profile; consideration of how cultural, productive, organizational, and commercial resources were used in the farm's development; and analysis of the network mechanisms.

In the analysis of the educational courses, we examined the questions producers had for instructors and paid particular attention to recording growers' comments, as well as the communication exchange between growers during and after educational courses. The purpose of this exercise was to document the way the social strategies are utilized to solve farm operation problems, as well as the growers' knowledge of agencies, programs, laws, and rules. This chapter also draws information from published case stories of southwestern Michigan farmers, particularly A. López's dissertation (2007) and Marinez and García's research report (2004). A. López's dissertation is a mixed-methods study of Hispanic farmers from four southwestern Michigan counties (Allegan, Berrien, Cass, and Van Buren). The quantitative part of the A. López study is based on 82 interviews with farmers in the four counties. The qualitative study is based on 12 in-depth interviews. In the two groups of farmers, 60 were born in Mexico, and 22 were born in the United States. Percentages cited here are from the quantitative study. The Marinez and García study was conducted over a two-year period from 1999 to 2001; data were gathered through both formal and informal interviews with Latino farmers in Van Buren County, Michigan. Given these farmers' concentration in blueberry growing, their study focused on Latino blueberry farmers.

Findings

Based on the data described above, this chapter presents two sets of findings regarding the experiences of Latino growers in southwest Michigan with state, federal, and nonprofit agricultural organizations. The needs and experiences of the growers are described in the following section. These findings are followed by an analysis of the agencies and programs designed to meet the needs of growers in general, and the programs created to target Latino and minority growers specifically. Taken together, these findings reveal the disconnect between the programs offered and the particular needs of Latino growers in Michigan.

LATINO GROWERS' NEEDS

Compared to mainstream American growers, Mexican farmers lack or have limited access to credit and educational programs. Instead, they use other strategies to obtain information to operate their farms, such as social, cultural, and family networks along with observations of the local landscape. Nonetheless, as A. López (2007) demonstrates, the main problem these growers face is the lack of information on agricultural agencies and their programs. Information is turned into knowledge when it has cognitive and technical components. The cognitive component refers to mental models individuals hold, such as maps, beliefs, paradigms, and points of view. The technical component refers to technical knowledge and abilities that can be applied in a specific context (Nonaka and Takeushi 1995). The problem for Mexican farmers lies in accessing technical knowledge. Mexican entrepreneurs, including the first ones who started businesses in southwest Michigan, have not been able to immerse themselves in the local technical-based knowledge network, thus putting themselves at a disadvantage compared to their local and national counterparts. In addition, nearly 70% lack access to credit and do not have the ability to speak or understand English. The lack of information on agricultural agencies and their programs and the inability to speak and understand English makes the interaction between agencies and Mexican growers even more challenging.

As Mexican growers learn to grow crops, it is also necessary that they learn the commercialization process. There are several packaging companies that purchase fruit from local growers, some the same day it is harvested. Packaging companies pay a better price for hand-harvested blueberries destined for fresh markets; they pay a lower price for machine-harvested blueberries destined for processing markets. The payment strategy varies; growers can be paid at the current market price or they can enter into a set payment agreement. In a set pay agreement, growers are paid at an agreed price regardless of the market's state.

In addition, knowledge of pest management is a key strategy for Mexican growers' successful commercialization. Mexican growers need to know which pesticides to purchase and how to apply them. The main obstacle Mexican growers face in purchasing and applying certain pesticides is the required pesticide applicator certification. Pesticide dealers cannot sell restricted pesticides to growers unless they hold a valid pesticide applicator certification card. To obtain the certification, Mexican growers need training to acquire the technical knowledge to pass the certification exam.

With pesticide applicator certification, Mexican growers can purchase the pesticides they need and can also apply them as needed. Before obtaining certification, Mexican growers had to hire firms to make pesticide applications. Often these firms applied pesticides that were not ideal for the crop.

"Las avionetas aplican los químicos que quieren, nunca se detienen a ver si son los que realmente necesitan nuestros campos. Nos acomodan de acuerdo al rol de turnos que ellos hacen y cada rociada nos cuesta alrededor de 500 dólares." The airplanes apply the chemicals they want to; they do not stop to see if those are the chemicals needed by our

crops. They arrange us according to their own spraying schedule and every spray costs us about $500 dollars. (Santos 2007–8)

Relying only on aerial pesticide applicators puts Mexican growers at a disadvantage because often the aerial applicators take care of the largest growers first. Economically, it makes sense for aerial applicators to serve the largest farms first and small Mexican farms last. Mexican growers have also realized that firms would apply the pesticide with little consideration given to the type of crop or pest. In some cases, according to several Mexican growers interviewed, they made applications to the wrong farm. These conditions leave crops vulnerable to pest pressure and result in economic losses. Another challenge for Mexican growers was the request by packaging plants for records of pesticide applications, as those records were held by the pesticide application firms. Thus, it was not always convenient for Mexican growers to obtain pesticide records when they were needed.

Mexican growers might receive a pesticide label from the commercial pesticide applicator or from the chemical store. However, reading the pesticide label was another challenge. In addition to label information, there is application information growers must follow because some pesticide laws require it. This information includes total amount applied, date and time of the application, and location of the application. Therefore, information about pesticide applications and pest management is vital for the proper management of growers' farms. It is also very important for Mexican growers selling their products to the packaging plants; packaging plants may require such information before they accept produce.

In addition to understanding the specific knowledge these growers need, it is important to recognize the role that family and community play in providing information and support for agricultural ventures. These networks allow farmers to obtain necessary information and provide valuable support that enables family members to migrate to a new job or to start up a new business. The first family members to make a move and who succeed in a new job become the source for monetary capital, social capital, and information for those who follow them. Those first family groups are usually part of larger networks that include more distant relatives, friends, and *paisanos* who, in most cases, come from the same rural locality. This is the type of network found in southwest Michigan. It is important to emphasize that only these types of rural localities are capable of generating strong networks by which migrants develop personal, social, cultural, and economic ties with receptive communities (Alarcón 2003).

Through their *paisano* and family networks, Mexican growers have managed to take advantage of local opportunities and local training programs to succeed in their business journey. This approach requires growers to be part of social networks, and these social networks have a dual role in the transmission of knowledge among small rural businesses: first, as a source of new business ideas, and second, as a new way to organize business operations to gain cost savings and competitive advantage and to enter the customer-supplier chain.

Farm operation also depends on individual and collective resources, in other words, cultural capital available to farm owners. Cultural capital can be transformed into monetary capital with a business model for family or individual production, and into social capital by collective and reciprocal collaboration of the farming community.

In addition to the networks described, Mexican growers gain the knowledge needed to cultivate the land by observing the local landscape. They then adapt practices and strategies to meet their own needs.

This chapter also considers the flow of information in knowledge spaces, or knowledge as a result of the interactions between governmental, educational, and nonprofit institutions; business enterprises; and Mexican growers. The concept of knowledge spaces is used to designate networking and learning processes among several actors. Knowledge spaces are lateral, bilateral, or trilateral relationships that are constituted by learning processes among actors from farms, governmental agencies, universities, and technical schools. This concept includes the flow of knowledge among actors in the knowledge space that can be used by individuals or family groups to achieve specific social and economic goals. The knowledge space for Mexican growers in southwest Michigan includes state and federal agencies, business groups, norms, rules, laws, and values.

The development and use of networks and knowledge accumulated in this knowledge space is very important in the initial phase of farms and business in southwest Michigan. Networks and knowledge spaces contribute to finding ways to decode the knowledge Mexican producers need to operate their farms. These networks act as long-term supports and exchanges of knowledge among Mexican growers. New Mexican entrepreneurs, however, also need to be immersed in existing local and national networks that can provide knowledge required to access domestic markets and guide interactions with domestic producers, local and external trading companies, and buyers. Immersion in local and national networks will require that Mexican growers develop a reputation for delivering produce on time, which entails coordination among producer, transporter, and purchasers for delivery of goods that conform to the price and quality U.S. markets desire. A generalized confidence in new entrepreneurs is essential for all these transactional processes to work (Storper, Laninas, and Mercado 2006). A regional perspective is also necessary to identify existing knowledge opportunities present in a specific region or social or economic sector; and since knowledge opportunities are sustained by relationships, they can have a major impact on regional, social, and economic development (Casas, De Gortari, and Santos 2000). Hence, the importance of knowledge spaces in Mexican grower's networks.

Knowledge opportunities among Mexican growers are a challenge to sustain because these growers do not have enough farming experience, and thus lack skills in technical crop management (such as expertise in use of fertilizers and pesticides), human resource management, and marketing strategies that would allow them to interact confidently with American growers or governmental and educational agencies. This is one reason why Mexican growers do not feel comfortable participating in training together with their non-Mexican counterparts. Thus, like many ethnic entrepreneurs, Mexican growers face many barriers they must overcome to enter and compete in the agricultural and service markets.

AGENCIES AND THEIR PROGRAMS

There are several governmental agencies, programs, and offices at the federal, state, and local level that support, finance, and regulate the agricultural sector in the state. In addition, Michigan State University Extension and the Michigan Food and Farming Systems (MIFFS), a nongovernmental organization (NGO), also work with agricultural growers in Michigan. This section provides an overview of some of the activities of these institutions, and analyzes their success and failure at meeting the needs of Mexican growers in southwest Michigan.

The United States Department of Agriculture (USDA) administers several loan and conservation programs directed to help socially disadvantaged farmers through the Farm Service Agency (FSA) and the Natural Resource and Conservation Service (NRCS). The FSA oversees farm commodity, credit, and disaster loan and conservation programs to improve the economic stability of the agricultural industry. The FSA also makes and guarantees loans to approved socially disadvantaged applicants to buy and operate family-size farms and ranches. The Natural Resource and Conservation Service provides technical and financial assistance for conservation activities. Its goal is to help with soil, water, and other natural resource conservation through programs available to growers, including underserved and socially disadvantaged farmers and ranchers; participation in NRCS programs is voluntary.

At the state level, the Michigan Department of Agriculture (MDA) promotes agriculture production and implements laws and regulations that protect the environment, animal and human health, and food supply. The MDA is divided into several divisions; however, this study focuses on the Pesticide and Plant Pest Management Division. This division is important for current purposes because it works closely with Mexican growers. It implements several pesticide programs that directly affect these growers. These programs include the federal worker protection standard for agricultural pesticides, the restricted-use pesticide record-keeping and the pesticide certification program. For the purpose of this study, we focus on the pesticide certification program, which is offered in Spanish and provides a way for Mexican growers to access programs and training opportunities other agencies or institutions offer. The pesticide certification program not only allows these growers to purchase restricted-use pesticides, but also teaches them the proper and safe use of pesticides. Another benefit of the pesticide certification program is that some food processors may require growers to be certified before they purchase the grower's produce. In addition, certain cost-share federal programs often require growers to have pesticide certification to participate. Finally, another very important function of the pesticide certification program is that it enables other agencies like the USDA and Michigan State University (MSU) Extension to have an audience for promoting their programs. Without this venue, it would be more difficult for these agencies to reach Mexican growers.

MSU Extension provides knowledge-based educational programs to growers and citizens of the state to improve their lives and communities. Michigan counties, in cooperation with on-campus faculty members, implement programs directed to agriculture and natural resources, children, youth, and families, and to foster community and economic development. MSU Extension seeks to ensure that outreach programs reach Michigan citizens through a variety of educational strategies, technologies, and collaborative arrangements.

MIFFS promotes programs vital to advancing and sustaining food and farming in which agricultural productivity, environmental stewardship, and profitability reinforce each other for the benefit of Michigan's communities. One of these programs is the Multicultural Farmers Program, which connects limited-resource and family farmers to available resources, production information, technical assistance, and marketing opportunities. This program tries to reach and integrate African American and Hispanic growers into the agricultural and knowledge-based system.

These agencies have a vested interest in reaching Mexican growers and attracting them to participate in their programs and have made valiant efforts to reach and attract these growers. However, Mexican growers generally do not participate in, or are excluded from, these programs because of institutional barriers. Agencies are now making extra efforts to reach Mexican growers by implementing new and innovative outreach and educational methods that are culturally and technically friendly to this audience. These efforts originated from two fronts. First, the USDA had a mandate to make extra efforts to reach African American and small limited-resource growers, including Hispanic and Mexican growers; the goal was to make limited-resource growers aware of USDA farm programs. Second, the Michigan

Department of Agriculture was interested in finding out why African American and Hispanic and Mexican growers were not participating in pesticide certification and other pesticide safety programs.

The MDA was aware that Mexican growers were farming and using pesticides. Given the requirements for purchasing and using certain pesticides, MDA wondered how these growers were obtaining pesticides and if they were using them correctly. To answer these questions, the MDA joined forces with the USDA-NRCS to reach Mexican growers. In the first attempt, MDA staff members[1] began collecting Spanish-origin surnames from address books, visited Mexican restaurants, stores, and Catholic churches in Grand Rapids, Holland, Lawrence, Paw Paw, Cassopolis, and any other communities in which they had leads for possible Mexican residents. Once the contact was made, the residents were asked if they were involved in farming or if they knew anyone involved in farming.

After the list of Mexican growers was developed, MDA staff invited Mexican growers to attend pesticide certification courses offered in Spanish. It also translated into Spanish the study manual used to prepare Michigan growers for the pesticide applicator certification test. It soon became apparent, however, that translating the study manual was not enough to attract Mexican growers to training sessions.

Other techniques were needed to motivate Mexican growers to attend training sessions and to take the pesticide applicator certification exam. MDA staff turned to experiential teaching/learning approaches, such as that by Roberts (2000), who suggests that "show how," or face-to-face demonstrations and social interactions, are critical for the efficient translation and transfer of knowledge. Translation is critical for the efficient transfer of knowledge, especially relative to knowledge-based technologies. In addition, translation mechanisms require that *translators* have the proper technical background and sociocultural insights to translate and decode technical agricultural knowledge so growers can understand it. A translator needs several key abilities and functions to effectively train producers who are not familiar with agricultural production systems, and to turn producer problems (plant nutrition, pest management, environmental management) into demonstration practices that promote learning. They need to exchange and share experiences with producers; find solutions to problems in a sociocultural context; and constantly interact with Mexican growers to develop the capacity to interpret and anticipate the needs of this community. For example, Mexican growers frequently do not specifically acknowledge a problem or need for assistance, but rather tell a story about it. Therefore, translators need to have the ability to interpret the needs of these growers in a sociocultural context. To fully understand the role of a translator, Choo's (1998) definition of a third type of knowledge, cultural knowledge, is useful. It refers to "suppositions" and beliefs used to describe and explain a reality in commonly accepted terms that add value and meaning to new information. Cultural knowledge is not codified; it is defined through group relationships.

In addition, Mexican growers frequently need the sociocultural reference that can help them translate learning into useful instant knowledge they can put into practice to operate their farms. With this in mind, a new strategy of training Mexican growers in integrated pest management was put into place by the MDA. Integrated pest management, going beyond simple pesticide use, is an important crop management tool that is gaining popularity among growers in the United States and around the world. This training strategy includes basic information needed to pass the pesticide applicator certification exam but presented in terminology that is easy for Mexican growers to understand and assimilate.

Mexican growers seemed to understand and like this approach; the training was relatively successful. However, the most important part in the success of the training was gaining the trust of Mexican growers. Trust was important for attracting them to training courses, encouraging them to take the pesticide applicator certification exam, and, finally, convincing growers to infuse what they had learned into their farming practices. Gaining the trust of Mexican growers was not easy. The usefulness of the trainings, the benefits of obtaining the pesticide applicator certification, and the fact that the trainer administering the exam was a *paisano* were not enough to ensure that Mexican growers would attend the trainings or cooperate with a system that had ignored them for so long.

To develop trust with Mexican producers, MDA educators first began working with a small group of growers; these growers were the most willing and open to learning. Slowly, other Mexican growers followed. As Dyer and Ross (2007) show, ethnic business owners receive information and advice about business activities from their ethnic business fellows. Similarly, Mexican growers share business experiences with their family members and their *paisanos.* One of these experiences was the benefits of obtaining the pesticide applicator certification; as Mexican growers began sharing these experiences, more growers were willing to participate in pesticide applicator and other training courses. Training courses became fairly popular with Mexican growers, with training sessions having approximately 40 new growers in attendance; of these 40, approximately 25 continue with the training and obtain their pesticide applicator certification.

Given the importance of and growing interest in the integrated pest management (IPM) concept in the U.S. agricultural system, Michigan State University Extension designed an integrated pest management curriculum several years ago. This program is offered at Michigan State University's Trevor Nichols experimental station located in Fennville and is available to Hispanic growers. One of the limitations of this program is that it has been targeted mainly to agricultural workers who want to start a scouting business or to Hispanic farmworkers sent to IPM programs by employers. Even though the instructor is of Mexican origin and the handout in the IPM course is in Spanish, the program has had limited success in attracting Mexican growers.

Besides the IPM curriculum offered in Fennville, another group from MSU targeted Mexican producers in 2008 with a workshop entitled IPM and Nutrient Management Planning: Addressing Farm Production and Resource Conservation. The workshop had two main objectives. One was to introduce federal and state support programs available to Hispanic and Mexican producers. The second was to promote agricultural practices to help Mexican farmers increase production and profits in a manner that also conserves natural resources. The main challenge of the workshop was to translate the content into useful knowledge that Mexican farmers could assimilate. The subjects covered in the program included IPM basics, with an emphasis on fruits, pesticide education training, conservation plan concepts, basics of nutrient management with an emphasis on fruits, conservation practices, and resources state and federal agencies offer to Mexican growers.

To accomplish these objectives, the organizers (planners, coordinators, speakers, and translators) followed several strategies. First, they carefully translated sessions into Spanish, adding personal experiences to improve presentations. Beyond simple translation, the organizers also explained technical skills, including technical knowledge, institutional frameworks, institutional workings, and trust. The final workshop was a farm walk, held *in situ* on a trusted Mexican grower's farm. The objective of this session was to show growers different situations, conditions, and potential problems. These included pesticide poisoning, dangers due to pesticide spillage, and natural resources conservation that could be added for better crop management. In addition to helping Mexican growers learn crop management practices, this session also helped connect agency specialists with Mexican growers through face-to-face interactions, which facilitated addressing doubts and complaints.

The IPM workshop was viewed as useful by Mexican growers, as reflected in the results of the assessment of the workshop; 88% indicated that they were "likely" and "very likely" to adopt IPM practices. Mexican farmers were asked as part of the assessment several important questions that had to do with crop management, such as, What is the pH of the soil and why is it useful to measure? and How could one increase or decrease soil acidity? Additionally, they were able to learn how to take soil samples for soil analysis, and how to access available federal programs. Finally, Mexican growers learned the importance of foliage analysis for plant nutrition, and the importance of implementing a plant nutrition program beyond the annual agricultural cycle.

To capture the attention of Mexican growers, the specialist followed a strategy of establishing a relationship between plant nutrition and healthy blueberry plants that could result in increased production. The translator used this situation to encourage the producers to carry out different crop strategies for the next crop year. The workshop also helped small Mexican growers to gain firsthand understanding of the U.S. agricultural system and how it relates to crop management.

The pesticide applicator certification and the IPM and Nutrient Management Planning: Addressing Farm Production and Resource Conservation workshops are two good examples of how educational programs targeted to Mexican growers can work if they are designed to meet their needs (language, time constraints, and decoding technical terminology). Granted, these courses should not be an isolated effort if agencies want to maintain the trust of Mexican growers; there must be follow-up sessions with growers interested in implementing IPM practices programs and enrollment in federal and state programs. Mexican farmers learn foremost from shared experiences among their ethnic counterparts and *paisano* networks. Educators also need to keep in mind the sociocultural and educational needs of Mexican growers when designing training courses and strategies to increase growers' participation in training programs. The pesticide applicator certification and the IPM program are examples of how Mexican growers begin to immerse themselves in the knowledge space available in southwest Michigan and how agricultural agencies can more effectively facilitate this immersion.

Discussion

On the surface, it looks like agencies have long made attempts to reach and work with Mexican growers. Yet state and federal agencies have not been able to develop sustained training and educational programs for them. This section outlines some of the main obstacles to these relationships and makes several recommendations for changes both within the agencies and among the growers that would significantly improve the relationship between growers and agencies, as well as increase the overall success of Mexican farms.

First, the authors' view is that a lack of coordinated efforts among state and federal agencies in part prevents the development of long-term and sustained training and educational programs for Mexican growers. To date, such agencies have not been set up to dedicate a full-time person to work in the long term with Mexican growers. Rather, they have employees assigned to oversee agricultural programs that apply across the agricultural industry, including Mexican growers. Often these employees cannot devote the needed time and accommodations to help small and socially disadvantaged Mexican growers.

In addition, there is need for steady funding allocated to state and federal agencies so they can have a sustained presence in assisting Mexican growers. As of now, funding to develop training and educational programs comes in the form of federal grants, leaving agencies to compete for these funds. Funding based on competitive grants does not provide the right mechanism for properly addressing the needs of Mexican growers. It creates a culture of unnecessary competition among agencies, rather than fostering a culture of cooperation. This competitive culture percolates down to individual Mexican growers, forcing them to take sides and decide which group of grantees to belong to and work with. This is not healthy for agencies or growers because it prevents the formation of self-sustained, long-term, trusting relationships. The competitive culture also negatively affects agencies because it forces them to compete not only for money but also for audiences. In the end, this approach results in compartmentalized and broken relationships among service agencies and growers rather than long-term relationships and cooperation. Moreover, funding usually comes in a short cycle, at the most for two years; this is not enough to develop long-term grower-agency relationships.

While some programs, projects, plans, and educational courses cannot be easily modified to meet the specific needs of Mexican growers, these programs can be made more accessible and culturally sensitive to their training needs. Doing so could help Mexican growers to become part of the agricultural system. There are simple, immediate steps that agencies and trainers can take to help in this endeavor. First, training courses should be made available at times when Mexican producers are able to attend. Agencies could not only translate educational materials into Spanish, but use terminology that is meaningful and easy to understand by Mexican growers, decoding program brochures and manuals so these growers can understand them. Most importantly, agencies and trainers need to recognize that Mexican growers have unique environmental, commercial, and knowledge needs that differ from those of mainstream growers.

Furthermore, it is important to consider that the programs designed for the traditional American farmer may not meet the needs of Mexican growers. Mexican growers have varied educational levels and cultural backgrounds, and limited knowledge of the governmental and Extension agricultural system. Trust and positive learning experiences with programs offered by governmental and Extension agencies are critical for Mexican growers to adopt to and integrate into the United States agricultural system. A majority of Mexican growers are newcomers to the agricultural sector and to the region, and are usually immersed in *paisano* family networks. This position can be beneficial, but in some cases it makes farming difficult because of the number of individuals involved in the decision-making process. This collective process of decision making needs to be taken into account by training programs that presuppose individual decision-making. Finally, it is very important to document stories and educational methods that have worked well with Mexican growers so they can be shared with other trainers and growers.

As for the Mexican growers, there is a need for better organization among them. For example, it would be a lot easier for agencies to communicate and promote programs available to Mexican growers if they were organized in the form of a Hispanic growers association. The association could help Mexican growers foster relationships among themselves. Working together would promote group roles and responsibilities, which would prepare farmers to take on the responsibility of running a co-op. Furthermore, communication between agencies and growers would be easier because agencies would communicate with the association rather than individuals. An association would also give Mexican growers an organized voice to request more effective programs and projects that could assist them with their farming.

Mexican growers also need an integrated pest management or pest scout who could assist in identification and monitoring of pests, and provide timely and accurate pesticide recommendations. A Mexican grower or a Spanish-speaking graduate of the IPM program could fill this role. Similarly, there is a need for a commercial licensed pesticide applicator among Mexican growers to provide pesticide application services when needed by Mexican growers. At this point, Mexican growers rely mainly on the services provided by aerial commercial pesticide applicators. A number of Mexican growers have their pesticide applicator certification credential, but they do not yet feel confident in making their own pesticide applications, or making pesticide applications for others as a business because to do so they would need a commercial pesticide applicator license, which has additional requirements.

Beyond specific needs, however, these growers also face great opportunities. In many cases, it is the service business system that brings Mexican growers into direct contact with the requirements of the American agricultural marketing system. For example, packaging facilities and fruit and vegetable dealers may ask for information about sanitation practices, pesticide use records, and environmental protection practices. Information about production practices is more essential than ever in agricultural products because of recent outbreaks of food-related illnesses. It is essential for Mexican growers to be aware of these requirements so they can sell their agricultural products.

There are different providers of agricultural inputs (seeds, agricultural tools, plants, and fertilizers) where Mexican growers purchase what they need for farm production. There are about 18 agricultural dealer stores in the area where Mexican growers farm. Five of them are located in Allegan County; three are located in Van Buren County, and about 10 in nearby Berrien County. At this point, there are no Hispanic growers involved in this business.

There are also several nurseries in the area where Mexican growers can purchase nursery stock and tomato and pepper seedlings. This sector seems to interest Mexican growers. A few Mexican growers are now selling blueberry stock to other Mexican growers. A few others have started a small greenhouse business to produce tomatillo and tomato seedlings, and herbs that they plan to sell to Mexican producers. Even though Mexican growers are beginning to move into this area, more are needed to cover the demand for these crops.

Regarding pesticides, a good number of Mexican growers have obtained their pesticide applicator certification. There are about 70 Mexican growers with pesticide applicator certification in southwest Michigan, with approximately half of these growers having obtained their certification in 2008. Even though Mexican growers can now apply their own pesticides, many of them still use the services of aerial pesticide application firms. There are about 22 licensed aerial pesticide application firms in Michigan. At least five are located in the area close to where Mexican growers farm. The few Mexican growers who do not use the services of aerial pesticide applications firms apply their own pesticides with tractor- or truck-pulled sprayers. This is another service area where few Mexican growers are involved. This study found only two Mexican growers who have started a terrestrial pesticide application business.

There are about seven packaging facilities in southwest Michigan where Mexican growers sell their produce. The majority of these facilities are for fruit crops, including blueberries, apples, peaches, pears, and grapes. Most Mexican growers sell their products locally at these packaging plants; a few others take their products by truck to Chicago. Mexican growers who produce tomatoes, peppers, or other vegetables sell their product at local Mexican stores in the area, or they may take their product to Chicago. There are very few Mexican growers involved in this service area. Indeed, the researchers became aware of only one Mexican grower who started a blueberry packaging enterprise.

In short, while state, federal, and nonprofit agricultural agencies have made some effort to reach out to Latino growers in Michigan, thus far these attempts have had limited success. With a clearer sense of the specific needs and interests of this group, agencies can more effectively design programs and courses that meet their needs. Furthermore, with improved relationships with these agencies, Latino growers can improve and expand their role in the state's agricultural market.

Conclusion

Mexican growers are forming an important group of entrepreneurs in southwest Michigan. They are purchasing farmland, stores, and restaurants. They rely on family or friendship connections to find out about investing opportunities. Most Mexican growers in this area are in blueberry production. Many lack knowledge in crop management, and they have limited or no knowledge of agencies and training opportunities available to them. For the most part, Mexican growers rely on *paisano* family networks to obtain knowledge and information to manage their businesses.

Given the importance of agriculture in Michigan, and the importance of Hispanics in the agricultural sector, it is essential that agencies and educational institutions pay attention to the needs of Mexican growers because they will become the growers of the future. Governmental and educational agencies have made some attempts to reach and attract Mexican growers to their training programs, but with limited success. However, two educational programs described here, the pesticide application certification training and the IPM and Nutrient Management Planning course, are popular among Mexican growers and provide interactions and relationships that improve the trust between agencies and growers. These programs can be used by agencies as models for creating additional programs that will attract and assist Mexican growers in taking an active role in the state's agricultural system.

This chapter also identified needs and opportunities that can be used by agencies to design educational and training programs that conform with the cultural and literacy needs of Mexican growers. For example, there is a need to develop a series of *translation* mechanisms that will make it easier for Mexican growers to become part of the U.S. agricultural system. More importantly, they could become role models for other new growers that arrive to southwest Michigan. These mechanisms include not only translating courses and programs into Spanish, but also using teaching techniques that respond to the educational and sociocultural background of the audience. In particular, recognizing the importance of family and *paisano* relationships in the decision-making process of Mexican growers is crucial. Programs assuming individual decision-making processes cannot address some of the issues faced by this group of growers. Overall, gaining the trust of these new Latino growers is one of the greatest challenges for agricultural agencies. To meet this challenge, new educational and recruitment approaches are needed.

Additionally, the findings presented here suggest ways that the growers themselves can improve their position within Michigan's agricultural industry. First and foremost, the creation of a Hispanic growers association would improve the flow of communication between growers and agencies, as well as develop professional relationships among the growers. Such an association would also provide support for individuals seeking to expand their role in the industry, as licensed pesticide applicators, suppliers, and so forth. It would also give Latino growers a more organized voice to request more effective programs and training from agricultural agencies.

Census data suggest that Latinos will become increasingly important to

Michigan's agricultural industry in the years to come. In response, state, federal and nonprofit agricultural agencies need to meet more effectively the needs of this important new entrepreneurial group. Helping these new growers to integrate successfully into the industry will be beneficial not only for the growers but for the agricultural industry and the state economy.

NOTE

1. Antonio Castro-Escobar participated in these sessions as part of the Michigan Department of Agriculture.

REFERENCES

Alarcón, R. 2003. "La formación de una diáspora: Migrantes de Cabinda, Michoacán en California." In *Diáspora Michoacana,* ed. G. López Castro, 289–306. El Colegio de Michoacán y Gobierno del Estado de Michoacán.

Adler, P. S., and S. W. Kwon. 2002. "Social Capital: Prospects for a New Concept." *Academy of Management Review* 27(1): 17–40.

Casas, R., R. De Gortari, and M. J. Santos. 2000. "The Building of Knowledge Spaces in Mexico: A Regional Approach to Networking." *Research Policy* 29: 225–41.

Castro-Escobar, A. 2008. "Manejo Integrado de Plagas." Available online: www.miffs.org/mffc/2008/IPM - Castro-Escobar 011908.pdf.

Choo, C. W. 1998. *The Knowing Organization: How Organizations Use Information to Construct Meaning, Create Knowledge, and Make Decisions.* New York: Oxford University Press.

Dyer, L. M., and C. A. Ross. 2007. "Ethnic Business Owners and Their Advisors: The Effects of Common Ethnicity." In *Handbook of Research and Ethic Minority Entrepreneurship,* ed. L. P. Dana, 117–31. Cheltenham, UK: Edward Elgar.

Inter-American Bank for Development. 1997. "Microenterprise Development Strategy." Available online: http://idbdocs.iadb.org/wsdocs/getdocument.aspx?docnum=1481386.

Kleweno, D. 2009. "Michigan 2008–2009 Highlights." National Agricultural Statistics Service, Michigan Field Office, Michigan Department of Agriculture. Available online: http://www.nass.usda.gov.

López, A. B. 2007. "A Case Study of Hispanic Farmers in Four Southwestern Michigan Counties." Ph.D. diss., Department of Agriculture and Natural Resources Education and Communication Systems, Michigan State University.

López, J. N. 2007. "Elementos de integración de microempresas rurales en el oriente del estado de México en los primeros años del siglo XXI." *Contaduría y Adminsitración* 221 (January–April).

Marinez, J., and V. García. 2004. "New Latino Farmers in the Midwest: The Case of Southwest Michigan." Cambio de Colores conference, "Latinos in Missouri: Gateway in New Community." Available online: www.cambiodecolores.org.

Menzies, V. T., L. J. Filion, G. A. Brenner, and S. Elgie. 2007. "Measuring Ethnic Community

Involvement: Development and Initial Testing of an Index." *Journal of Small Business Management* 45(2): 267–82.

Michigan Department of Agriculture. 2008. "Governor Praises 2007 Achievements and Growth in Michigan's Food and Agriculture Industry." Available online: www.michigan.gov.

Mitchell, J. C. 1969. *Social Networks in Urban Situations*. Manchester: Manchester University Press.

Moctezuma, M. 2002. "Los migrantes mexicanos en estados unidos y la inversion productiva en México." *Migraciones Internacionales* 1(3):149–62.

Nonaka, I., and H. Takeuchi. 1995. *The Knowledge-Creating Company: How Japanese Companies Create the Dynamics of Innovation*. New York: Oxford University Press.

Rivera-Sánchez, L. 2003. "Transformaciones comunitarias y remesas socio-culturales de los migrantes mixtecos poblanos." Prepared for the First International Colloquium on Migration and Development, "Transnationalism and New Perspectives on Integration," October.

Roberts, J. 2000. "From Know-How to Show-How? Questioning the Role of Information and Communication Technologies in Knowledge Transfer." *Technology Analysis & Strategic Management* 12(4): 429–43.

Santos, M. J. 2007–8. "Fieldwork in Southwest Michigan Counties." Interviews and field work diaries.

Storper, M., L. Laninas, and A. Mercado. 2006. "Society, Community and Development: A Tale of Two Regions." In *The Economic Geography of Innovation*, ed. Karen R. Polenske, 310–39. Cambridge: Cambridge University Press.

Tunal, S. G. 2003. "El problema de la clasificación de las microempresas." *Actualidad Contable FACES* (Venzuela) 6 (7): 78–91.

Torres, L. P., and L. Rodriguez. 2007. "Desarrollo local y microempresas agropecuarias en la ciudad de México." *Comercio Exterior* 57(1): 40–54.

U.S. Department of Agriculture (USDA). 2009. 2007 Census of Agriculture: State Profile: Michigan Spanish, Hispanic, and Latinos in Agriculture. Available online: www.agcensus.usda.gov.

GEORGE VARGAS

CitySpirit: A People's Mural in Detroit's Mexicantown

FOR MORE THAN 30 YEARS, THOUSANDS OF VIEWERS, BOTH RESIDENTS AND VISI-
tors, have enjoyed Detroit's oldest standing outdoor Mexican American / Chicano
mural, commonly known as *CitySpirit.* An example of public art well integrated
with a living space, the mural is prominently located on a busy street corner in
Mexicantown, a vibrant Detroit community possessing the largest concentration
of Latinos/Chicanos in Michigan. Painted in 1979 by Michigan muralists Martin
Moreno (who now lives in Arizona) and me (I now teach in Texas), the mural has
been cherished and protected by the neighborhood since its birth, surviving urban
construction and the ravages of time.

Today, *CitySpirit* remains a major monument that is an integral part of the city's
growing public art scene. Moreover, *CitySpirit* is a visual metaphor that symbolizes
the unfolding history and cultural identity of Mexicantown and its inhabitants. At
another level, it represents a multicultural or world view, reflecting the racial/ethnic
mixed culture of Detroit's metropolitan population and the world at large.

In this essay I offer a brief history and iconographic analysis of the mural to
help readers better understand, and, I hope, better appreciate the significance of

FIGURE 1. *CitySpirit* Mural. Martin Moreno and George Vargas, 1979. Hubbard Richard Building, Detroit, Mexicantown. Reproduced with the permission of the artists. Photo by George Vargas, 2005.

CitySpirit—a living example of contemporary American public art situated in a multicultural city.

History

In the summer of 1979, the Hubbard Richard Agency in Detroit commissioned Michigan artists Martin Moreno and me to create an outdoor mural on their building located at the corner of Saint Anne (Ste. Anne) and Bagley Streets, in an effort to decorate the heavily trafficked corner.

I was familiar with this area in southwest Detroit, having previously directed various art and educational programs in Mexicantown. Upon receiving the mural commission, I immediately pictured a public mural beautifying this popular street corner.[1]

Located in *el corazon del barrio*, the heart of the Latino community, the mural site is surrounded by a growing, diverse racial/ethnic population, all living in the shadow of the great Ambassador Bridge, the border crossing that links the United

States and Canada. More than mere wall decoration, the mural paints a portrait of one of Detroit's culturally rich neighborhoods, which also is the home base for many of the city's immigrants.

From the start the mural project generated lots of excitement and support in the neighborhood with both residents and community organizations contributing to its progress. Neighborhood activist Carolina Ramon directed the mural project and recruited community members to help Martin and me with the general design.

I had more time to start up the Detroit mural project than Moreno, who was busy painting murals in Adrian, Michigan, so I worked with Carolina to seek resources and funding. I also met with community residents to request their support and input before we started the scaled drawing for the mural.

Carolina soon secured funds from the National Endowment for the Arts City Spirit Program, coordinated by Detroit's Cultural Arts Department. Ste. Anne's Catholic Church donated the use of its scaffolding in an effort to help the community that the church has long served.

The mural as a work in progress acted as a magnet, attracting positive energy. Throughout its creation, neighbors brought gifts of food and drink as we worked on the scaffolding in the heat of summer's sun. Curious youngsters asked questions; many had never seen a mural in progress. Local artists frequently stopped by to note progress and make suggestions. Others familiar with the murals of Los Tres Grandes ("The Big Three"—Mexican modern artists Orozco, Rivera, and Siqueiros) visited the mural site to share their observations about art and politics.

To our delight, residents and visitors alike praised our work, as we painted through the summer months. When observers asked questions, we took the time to describe the mural and its meaning; the scaffold became our lectern. As the painting neared completion, many residents perceived the mural as pure art. Others proudly pointed to the painted wall and called it a "pretty picture" that represented their unique neighborhood.

Finished in late fall of the same year, the mural was soon dedicated at a lively celebration and was well received by the broader community.

We finished painting in October before the frost set in, but kept the scaffolding up. We needed to apply a protective sealant to the mural. The ceremony was staged on the sidewalk in front of the mural, with people spilling out into the streets. City Hall officials, clergy from Ste. Anne's Church, community activists, and residents of Mexicantown dedicated the mural to the people of the city of Detroit.

Shortly after its dedication, Hubbard Richard erected security lights, both to protect and to illuminate the mural so it could be viewed at night. Because of the community's sense of pride and constant vigilance, the mural suffered little if any graffiti or vandalism. Interestingly, teachers, community artists, parents, and elders

FIGURE 2. *CitySpirit* Mural. Martin Moreno and George Vargas, 1979. Restoration of Hubbard Richard Building, Detroit, Mexicantown. Reproduced with the permission of the artists. Photo by George Vargas, 1983.

in the neighborhood spoke earnestly to youth about the mural's importance, both to encourage young artists to pursue careers in the visual arts and to instill a sense of community pride.

As public artists we were committed to our vision of beautifying Mexicantown through art, but our presence represented much more. The community embraced us as two professional artists who came from similar working-class roots. We shared past experiences as migrant laborers and factory workers; and we both escaped a lifetime of manual labor by earning college degrees in the arts and education. Our presence in Mexicantown sent a powerful message to its young people—you can aspire to more. Working together on this project, Martin and I were kept mindful of our humble roots. Our shared experience contributed to the direction of our lives—we both have focused much of our time and energy to the cultural development of the broader Latino pueblo. I like to think that our presence contributed to a better future for one or two of those curious children who experienced the creation of the *CitySpirit* mural so long ago, in 1979.

In 1983 the old Hubbard Richard building underwent a massive renovation. The architects and contractors performed a virtual miracle: they demolished and rebuilt nearly the entire building but managed to keep the community's beloved mural intact, making sure not to damage the integrity of the wall or destroy the painting. Upon completion of the new architecture, the builders joined the old mural wall with the new building, creating an exciting expression in architecture that testifies to the power of public art. The facade of the newly constructed building reflects a recognizable architectural style that was influenced by ancient Mexican pyramids and temples. Hubbard Richard now shared the new building with the Roberto Clemente Recreation Center (named after the Puerto Rican baseball star).

Indeed, it was a pleasant surprise to see architects design the new building to complement the ancient Mexican architecture featured in our mural. More so, I was awed by the builder's engineering feat, literally constructing an entire building around the old wall that contained the mural.

By 1997, after nearly two decades of severe Michigan winters and intense summers, the mural's painted surface was suffering from extensive peeling and faded colors. *CitySpirit* desperately needed restoration. Bagley Housing, a housing development agency located across the street from the mural site, commissioned Detroit artists Vito Valdez and Kelly Callahan to restore the mural. After consulting with Moreno and me, the duo used old photographs of the mural to complete the restoration, bringing it back to its original magnificence. In spring 2000, I reinaugurated the mural and gave a lecture on its history and meaning before an appreciative group of art lovers. To commemorate its restoration, Bagley Housing printed a colorful poster of *CitySpirit.*

In the new century, *CitySpirit* prevails as a recognized symbol of Mexicantown. It is the only outdoor public mural from the Latino mural renaissance of the 1970s that has survived in the Motor City. While Mexicantown slowly changes, and new housing developments pop up, along with new retail businesses and restaurants, *CitySpirit* remains a prominent public expression on a crowded street corner, symbolizing the indomitable spirit of Mexicantown and the city.

Design and Techniques

After consulting with community members, Moreno and I first studied the architectural integrity of the wall and designed the mural according to the theory of architectonics: architectural decoration that complements the built and cultural environment. One of the most recognized models that we considered was Diego Rivera's *Detroit Industry* fresco cycle executed in 1932 and 1933 at the Detroit Institute of Arts. The *CitySpirit* design presents a historical and cultural picture of the city of Detroit and the state of Michigan, from ancient to modern times. Inspired by Rivera's complex but accurate narrative of the agricultural, industrial, and scientific technology of a modern era in Michigan, we first organized the design elements within a symmetrical framework as determined by the ages-old method of tripartite division. Moreno and I divided the mural design into three general parts: a simple tree placed in the center of the wall unified the ancient (right side) and contemporary (left side) worlds. Next, Moreno and I incorporated traditional techniques of Gothic and Renaissance painters in our composition. For instance, we used overlapping perspective and linear perspective to achieve spatial depth and illusionism.

Most important, we wanted viewers to be able to read our mural easily as they walked or drove by; therefore we deliberately used a representational style on a large scale. Before painting began, we first needed to fill in cracks and holes in the brickwork, then sand and prime the wall. The brick surface proved to be a major challenge to us while prepping the wall, because the masonry was old and discolored, as well as uneven and cracked in many spots. After repairing the surface, we primed the wall several times to give us a suitable painting surface.

Next, with charcoal sticks in hand we transferred the design from a pencil drawing to the large blank wall, using the Renaissance grid method. Then Martin and I roughly painted in the images on the surface, applying a wash of diluted sepia color on which we could easily make any corrections. We took our time roughing out the design in sepia washes, adjusting visual elements for proportion and scale to fit the size of the wall peculiar to that building. We could not apply any color until we both agreed to the general design as we had outlined it on the wall.

Next, we brushed thin layers of color to the wall, followed by successive layers of paint, building a thicker consistency of color; at the same time we were carefully modeling the forms toward three-dimensionality. Martin and I used quality acrylic paints to paint the mural; the medium worked well in covering the hard surface and providing a sense of depth to the modeled images. Because we had to cover a big brick wall with multiple layers of color, we destroyed many brushes in the process. Layer after layer, we used strong, bright colors to draw visual attention to the overall design and added just enough highlights and details to the images to give visual accent to the mural. We were careful not to add too many images or too much detail in the design for fear of distracting passersby from the overall visual effect. When finished, the mural incorporated several levels of meaning because of its symbolic content.

Iconographic Analysis

Upon analysis of its iconography, the mural reveals multiple meanings in theme and content as expressed through signs and symbols. My interpretation of *CitySpirit* specifically describes the mural painting and also refers to a broader, more universal meaning.

TREE

First and foremost, the giant, ancient tree at the center of the mural is a universal symbol of life, the trunk of humanity. It also stands for the indigenous peoples who built advanced civilizations in the New World, or *Nuevo Mundo*. The venerable tree appears to be growing up through the ground, eventually breaking through the foundation of human civilization itself. With its roots deeply attached to the primordial earth, the tree symbolizes the unique wellspring of Michigan agriculture, as well as Michigan's natural resources. Generally, the tree reminds us of Michigan's vital lumber and Christmas tree industries, which have contributed to the state's economy.

We painted our tree in muted brown colors, with its top branches and deep green leaves painted in a dappled light. Our tree represents all the trees in Michigan that beautifully decorate the natural landscape and have provided resources for people from prehistory to the present.

In a broader interpretation, Moreno and I showcased the tree in *CitySpirit* to symbolize how trees have been depicted and employed in art and religion throughout history. Our cosmic tree represents diverse religions that can be found in Detroit, such as Christianity, Judaism, Buddhism, and Islam, and the tree symbol has different meanings in each one. For instance, the Jewish menorah is made in the form of a tree whose branches hold candles that shine divine light into the darkness. Buddha is sometimes pictured sitting blissfully under the Tree of Great Awakening and Wisdom.

Renowned historian James Hall (1974, 307) explains that early religions revered the tree as a "sacred object inhabited by a god." Led by druid priests, Celtic folk worshiped the Sacred Oak, which was inhabited by the feminine divine. This tree cult became powerful and widespread; the Irish continued the practice of druidism even after they were introduced to early Christianity. To buttress the church's conversion of tree cultists, monks informed the Irish that St. Patrick had been educated by a druid (Walker 1983, 256–57). Throughout the world, many premodern and advanced peoples have worshipped the great Mother Goddess in the form of a tree. In Mesopotamia and the Near East, the tree traditionally depicted fertility and regeneration; it was "associated with the cult of the earth goddess," who was worshiped to encourage a bountiful harvest (Hall 1974, 307). The tree is repeatedly featured in Egyptian, pre-Columbian, and Christian sacred art, standing as a source of life and cosmic energy. The Egyptian sun god Re came from the "Lady Sycamore" tree, from whose fruit yields a milky substance associated with the Mother Goddess (Lurker 1974, 119; Cooper 1978, 168). In Mayan cosmology the World Tree is a supernatural source from which "human forms flow" (Miller 1986, 64). The World Tree as pictured in a Mayan relief stela at the Izapa site is one such example.

Artists have used the tree in frescoes, relief carvings, and illuminated manuscripts to promote Christian teachings. As represented in sacred art, the Tree of Knowledge in Eden prefigures the crucifixion of Jesus Christ on the hill of Golgotha. The wooden crucifix in turn leads to his deposition, entombment, and resurrection. For Christians the wooden cross signifies death, resurrection, and redemption.[2]

In modern times the tree plays a distinct role in human politics, its historical image decorating numerous city seals and state flags. Various towns in Europe and America protect and celebrate trees where charters and treaties have been signed. In Austin, Texas, the Treaty Oak is more that 500 years old, the only remaining tree of the original 14 Council of Oak Trees, where, according to folklore, Texas Indian tribes met peaceably to settle their disagreements.

Most of all, the tree represents the whole, the synthesis of earth, water, and heaven (Cooper 1978, 176). It joins the three worlds, making communication between them possible. The tree stands for feminine power and fecundity.

In our mural painting, Martin and I show the tree as the Great Mother, who loves, nourishes, protects, and shelters humanity.

While making preliminary sketches at the mural site, I noticed maples, oaks, and elms surrounding the Hubbard Richard Agency and nearby houses. The old tree in *CitySpirit* is a composite of these trees. Many of these neighborhood trees have disappeared over time because of disease and urbanization. Despite this tree's great age, its thick roots are firmly planted in the earth. The Great Mother Goddess who gives us the air that we breathe lives in the earth and manifests herself as the tree.

GEOLOGY OF MICHIGAN

Below the *CitySpirit* tree, the remarkable geology of Michigan is shown, a source of valuable minerals and fuels in the Great Lakes region. Coal and iron ore are used in the production of steel, which in turn is used in the manufacture of automobiles, the state's leading industry. The strata also contain ancient fossils, referring to the land's primal life forms. Earth nourishes humanity. We humans are obliged, in turn, to protect and respect this important source of nonreplaceable wealth that has sustained many peoples throughout our history, from the oldest to the newest of generations.

Using the painted wall, Martin and I were keen on educating viewers about the earth's ecology. We were promoting a "green footprint" long before it was a trend. Our simple message in *CitySpirit:* preserve our planet Earth or humanity perishes.

The Hands of God support and protect the tree. On the right, a masculine-looking hand juts out from Mother Earth, symbolizing male and female elements—the duality principle. On the left, the Hand of God is made of steel, representing our dependence on the precious metals found in the soil of Michigan. Many workers labored to process elements in making steel, used to manufacture airplanes, tanks, and cars, all products associated with Michigan.

We presented the state's geology in the painting to reference both natural resources that drive the steel industry and River Rouge, the giant foundry located near Mexicantown. This foundry produces the steel used in industrial factories in Detroit and throughout Michigan. Both Moreno and I worked in factories, as did our fathers, family members, and friends, and we wanted to pay homage to the working class in Michigan. Together, the two hands represent the enduring spirit of the American worker.

AFRICAN PRESENCE IN MICHIGAN

Directly in the center (womb) of the tree trunk, one sees two monumental figures. The dark-colored African statue on the right, carved in the tree trunk itself, refers to the genius of great African civilizations, as well as African Americans' contributions to the economic prosperity of the state and nation. Its right hand is extended in a gesture of peace and goodwill. The statue also pays tribute to Detroit African Americans' unique achievements in the visual, performing, and literary arts.

The African American community in Detroit is one of the biggest in the United States, but often it is ignored or slighted in American history. By positioning the African statue in the center of our mural, we wanted to emphasize that black people, like Latinos, helped to build Michigan by contributing their creative, physical, and intellectual skills to the prosperity of the state. Numerous historical figures and celebrities are associated with Michigan. Civil rights leaders Sojourner Truth, Rosa Parks, and Malcolm X lived and worked in Michigan. Born in Detroit, Dr. Ralph Bunche attended Harvard, won the Nobel Peace Prize, and became undersecretary general to the United Nations. Inventor Elijah McCoy ("the real McCoy") and basketball legend Earvin "Magic" Johnson also came from Michigan. Singers Aretha Franklin and Stevie Wonder contributed to Detroit's "soul" music scene. Boxing champion Joe "The Brown Bomber" Louis grew up in Detroit, quitting his Ford factory job to train for the square ring. Poet and publisher Dudley Randall also worked at Ford before he became an internationally recognized writer. Many great musicians, like world-famous McKinney's Cotton Pickers, played in jazz clubs located in the black neighborhood of Paradise Valley; Motown was born here in the Motor City!

MICHIGAN INDIANS AND THE MEXICAN CONNECTION

The colorful kachina figure on the left, in the tree's "womb," represents the Native American presence in Detroit. The symbols on the kachina reflect the widespread cultural influence of the ancient Mexican rain/water god (Tlaloc or Chac) found in numerous Indian cultures. By featuring the presence of ancient Mexico in Michigan, Moreno and I wanted to underscore the ongoing relationship that has existed between Mexico and North America since prehistory while calling attention to the loss of Native cultures.

Inspired by Mexican cosmology, the kachina figure is carved from the trunk of the tree and painted in sacred colors, red, yellow, blue, and black; it stands in the niche of the trunk watching the passersby, neither judging nor threatening. Its power is its silence. Native peoples of Michigan include 12 tribes representing the Chippewa, Ottawa, and Potawatomi. Since the European invasion and Anglo settlement of Michigan, they have lost precious land and have suffered the loss of many of their traditions and language. Michigan's Native Americans are truly a minority population, as their numbers have dwindled to a fraction of 1% in the state population. Mexicans and Mexican Americans or Chicanos possess a mixed culture, which includes indigenous roots. Exploited as territorial minorities, Chicanos and other Latinos must help our Native American neighbors because we share the similar experience of oppression. Moreno and I placed the Indian figure in the center of the mural to honor the glorious Indian past and to stress the long history between Indians of Mexico and Michigan.

In 1890, Michigan historian Silas Farmer presented the famous explorer Alexander von Humboldt's theory that Michigan was the original home of ancient Mexican Indians, perhaps the Mexica-Azteca legendary birthplace known as Aztlán. Dennis N. Valdes, a more contemporary Michigan historian, notes that Michigan and Mexico are linguistically related. *Michoacán*, the ancient word for the state of Mexico, means "place of fish." It may be related to the Algonquian Indian word *Michigan*, which means "land of great waters" (Valdes 1982, 96).

Through my comparative studies of ancient Mexican art and early Michigan art and their shared iconography, I have proposed that "the Pre-Columbian/Mexican connection found in Michigan links the Mexican cultural influence to the development of Indian cultures in the Great Lakes region as well as to the other Indian cultures of ancient America" (Vargas 1988, 21–43). The ancient Indian civilizations of the Great Lakes were economically linked to the vast trade network of the Mexicans to the south. Precious goods were constantly exchanged between Indians of the Great Lakes and Mexican Indians. Migration transmitted new knowledge between south and north. Mexican Indians also introduced their "holy trinity" of corn, squash, and beans to Michigan Indians, which dramatically transformed the diet and primitive farm economy in the north.

The Mexican influence is further reflected in the achievements of the famous Hopewell mound builders of southern Michigan, who affected other Michigan tribes. The Great Mound of River Rouge at neighboring Delray is but one of many earthworks depicting the influence of these Hopewell mound builders and their special culture, while reflecting Mexican-inspired cosmology and Mexican-style sacred architecture.

This Mexican connection strongly affected the society, medicine, and religion of Michigan Indians. Because of their historical presence in Michigan, it is no wonder that today some Mexicans and Chicanos fondly call Detroit the "Aztlán of the north" or *Aztlán del norte.*

Many residents of Mexicantown express their Mexican heritage by decorating the barrio like their neighborhoods back home in Mexico. Traveling through Mexicantown, one gets the feel of being in a lively "Mexican town"—brightly painted homes line busy streets, most landscaped with bright flowers and garden shrines to saints. Occasional clusters of assorted businesses—tortilla factories, barber shops, gift shops, restaurants, and bars—add variety and convenience to the neighborhood's ethnic landscape. Popular Mexican music blasts through speakers from cars and trucks adorned with images of the beloved *Virgen de Guadalupe,* Mexican revolutionaries, Aztecs, and feathered serpents. Some residents rarely leave this modern-day Aztlán as it provides what they need to survive away from their spiritual home, Mexico.

QUETZALCOATL

The ancient Amerindian world is pictured on the right side of the mural. The influences of Mesoamerican civilizations still reverberate in our contemporary world in the realms of architecture, medicine, science, mathematics, religion, and the arts. In the center of the right panel, the Mexican god Quetzalcoatl (meaning "plumed" or "feathered serpent") stands protecting his creation—the American continent, indeed the entire planet Earth. With arms and legs spread, he assumes the recognized stance of Leonardo da Vinci's geometrically rendered drawing of *Vitruvian Man.*[3] Da Vinci's Renaissance man has morphed into a Prometheus-like god. The dusky colored god wears only a ceremonial loincloth and a fanlike headdress of red and yellow feathers.

God of life and wind, Quetzalcoatl appears as the great benefactor of mankind, full of divine love and practical wisdom. He is credited with the discovery of corn, the keystone in the Mexican/Amerindian diet. He cultivated the arts (for example, mosaics and feather work) and industry (for example, dyeing cotton different colors when weaving fabric). Moreover, he introduced the concept of time and the calendar—a tool used in planting and harvesting crops, as well as in cosmic prophecy.[4] An ever-popular icon in Mexican and Chicano culture, this benevolent creator god is a bridge to earth, water, and the heavens. His presence in the mural also reminds us of his self-sacrifice and his promise to return in the future to liberate his people. Quetzalcoatl will deliver them from the Fifth Sun into the new Sixth Sun/ World of consciousness, which, according to ancient Mexican prophecy, will occur in our twenty-first century.

In 1979, I was building my career as an art historian while continuing my profession as an artist. When teaching students about Aztec mythology, I noticed that they favored Quetzalcoatl over other Mexican gods in the pantheon. In portraying their cultural heroes, Latino students in particular repeatedly pictured Quetzalcoatl accompanied by the Virgin of Guadalupe and, sometimes, Jesus Christ. To Mexican/ Mexican American artists, performers, and poets, Quetzalcoatl is a living god, as inspirational as the Virgin of Guadalupe, revolutionary fighter Zapata, United Farm Workers leader César Chávez, or modern painter Frida Kahlo. In *CitySpirit*, Quetzalcoatl symbolizes divine love, creative freedom, and imagination, a spiritual figure unencumbered by the political strife of mankind.

MOON

Behind Quetzalcoatl, a huge full moon arises, a symbol of superfecundity, intense passion, eternal renewal, and the feminine principle. (In some societies, the moon is masculine, but no matter, since it still exerts awesome regenerative powers.) From prehistoric times to the present era, the moon has been a constant influence on humanity. Our Stone Age descendents observed the moon moving through its phases, symbolizing cyclical time. Eventually, lunar movement was recorded to construct the earliest of calendars. The moon represents the mysterious and dark self in world cultures and is believed to have control over matters of romance. In contemporary times, Luna, the Roman moon goddess, is blamed for foolish acts, criminal activity, and even lunacy. In the mural, the moon represents the awesome feminine divine.

Indeed, the moon ruled over creation of the mural itself. At the end of a long day of painting the wall, I was breaking down the scaffolding when I noticed the moon rising over the city. I watched, entranced, as she broke through the layers of pollution, emerging finally, clean and strong, poised to shine down upon the gritty city of Detroit all night long. I took this event as a good omen. The moon and the sun were part of the original mural design, but after my experience, we redesigned the proportion and color of the moon, enlarging the moon's image and brightening the color, predominately with yellow ochre to give it a warm feeling.

TLALOC/CHAC

The reclining Chac Mool sculptural figure located on the lower right side of the mural refers to the primeval Mexican rain god Tlaloc, who typically holds a bowl-like receptacle in its hands, meant to contain offerings. Placed in front of the most important temples in Mexican ceremonial centers, the Chac sometimes held a simple compass indicating both the axis and the Four Corners of the earth. In late Mayan times, the statue likely represented a fallen warrior or warrior-king. In modern times, celebrated British sculptor Henry Moore created a distinct abstract reclining figure, inspired in part by ancient and primitive art expressions, such as the Mayan Chac.

The Chac Mool in *CitySpirit* signifies both the precious rain god and the fallen warrior, the fighter who fought against the European invaders of the New World; the man and woman soldier of the Mexican Revolution; the veteran of the great world war against fascism. Latino soldiers have defended our country in Vietnam, Panama, the Persian Gulf, and Middle East. In all these wars, Mexican American warriors have earned their fair share of medals; still their accomplishments are minimized in textbooks and documentaries.

ANCIENT MEXICAN ARCHITECTURE

In the mural, advanced Mexican civilizations (most notably the Olmec, Teotihuacan, Toltec, Aztec, and Mayan cultures) are symbolized by their supreme achievement: sacred architecture and monumental architectural decoration. The actual construction and decoration of pyramidal temples, tombs, and other structures were unified by a shared Mexican cosmology, mediated for worshippers by various priestly orders, much as priests in Egypt controlled the pyramid-temples in Egypt. The most significant temples were dedicated to respective cult gods or favored city-gods, and the architectural style in each urban center identified a certain Mexican Indian culture. Many temples could actually be "read" as prayers; some acted as giant timepieces or sundials, allowing the viewer to tell the time of day or note the season according to the Mexican calendar system.

Ceremonial centers were carefully laid out corresponding to a cosmic orientation and painted in brilliant colors, decorated with hieroglyphic writings and monumental sculptures. The pyramid-temple was a "man-made mountain," which symbolized the sacred home of ancestors and gods, as well as a source of precious water.

Near the tree, Martin and I painted a Mayan temple, which synthesizes two famous Mayan temples found in Chichen Itza: El Castillo and El Caracol ("The Castle" and "The Snail," so-called by modern-day discoverers). Both temples were dedicated to Quetzalcoatl. The former was constructed to follow the movements in the heavens. During the solar equinoxes, the pyramid cast a shadow that depicts a moving serpent. The Caracol was used as a scientific observatory to study and record cosmic movements. In ancient Mexico round buildings were usually dedicated to Quetzalcoatl (astronomically associated with the planet Venus). Thus, the temple purposely resembles a conch shell, part of the wind god's headdress. Near the Chac Mool statue in the mural, a column decorated with the ever-popular motif, a feathered serpent, visually represents the special role that this fertility god played in Mexican cosmology and religious architecture.

The pyramid is a familiar image in Mexicantown, replicated in popular culture. Many gift stores and restaurants, for example, reproduce the pyramid in their goods and marketing. Therefore, our mural with its ancient Mexican pyramid-temple only reflected back what already existed in the community. The pyramid and Chac were done in warm ochre and brown; by contrast, and for visual balance, we used cool blue to paint the relief column with the serpent.

MEXICANTOWN

In the left panel, modern Mexicantown emerges as a major junction in the Latino community, underscoring the distinct history of Mexicans and Chicanos living in Detroit. They share the mestizo ("mixed blood"—a New World genetic mixture of Indian, European/Spanish, and African characteristics) experience with other Latinos in the United States. Detroit's growing Latino population includes immigrants from Mexico and Latin America. Because of their steady demographic increase, Latinos continuously revitalize industry, urban culture, and the arts. In modern times Michigan Latinos have worked in forests, agricultural fields, and mines. They build railroads and highways, and make our world-famous cars. Today, Latinos are gradually entering all sectors of public and private work, blue collar, pink collar, and white collar alike. Additionally, Latino consumers represent a new economic market, as well as an increasingly major voting bloc in national politics. Soon the Latino peoples will become a majority population throughout the United States.

Near the steel hand, viewers can see the old Hubbard Richard building, and Ste. Anne's Church, the city's oldest Catholic Church, which was founded by French fur trader Antoine de la Mothe Cadillac, who earlier established Detroit in 1701. Ste. Anne's is a fine example of French-Gothic architecture, with its circular stained-glass window resting between its twin towers. Moreno and I featured Ste. Anne's in their mural because of the key role it has played in the community as an organizing social force and a staunch arts patron in the Latino *colonia*.

In the mural the Ambassador Bridge, built in the 1950s and presently the busiest international bridge in the United States, is seen directly behind Ste. Anne's Church. Actually, the Ambassador and Ste. Anne's are in close proximity to each other, with industries, warehouses, homes, and businesses sandwiched between the two structures that dominate the cityscape for miles.

Note the crack in the sidewalk in front of Hubbard Richard, indicating the spot from which the mural was born, sprouting from hard concrete and asphalt. Aware that major urban renewal was being planned for the future, Moreno and I also painted into the mural a new plaza with trees (below the church) as a symbol of rejuvenation. Across the street (Bagley), a tortilla factory, a Mexican restaurant, and other local businesses stand along the busy thoroughfare. The street directs our vision diagonally to the hub of downtown Detroit, characterized by the towering Renaissance Center and other distinct urban landmarks.

We painted the street scene to mirror the real environment of Mexicantown. We even included the Hubbard Richard building with the very wall that features the mural. The buildings are mostly rendered in white or light colors so that they visually balance against the blue sky. The redbrick Ste. Anne's church is portrayed larger than other buildings to emphasize its role as a source of spiritual inspiration that goes beyond Christianity.

SUN

The moon's counterpart, a rising sun (left side) symbolizes ancient history giving way to contemporary times. In Mexican mythology, the present sun is known as the Fifth Sun or *Quinto Sol,* and the Aztecs who worshipped it called themselves "People of the Sun." Many present-day Mexicans and Chicanos believe that they are directly descended from Aztecs, ready to fulfill prophecy with the birth of the new cosmic order.

We wanted to picture the sun as a big ball of solar energy, with yellow and red flames bursting from its fiery surface, instead of a simply painted orb. Perhaps during winter months of cloudy days, the sun in our mural would provide to viewers a sense of warmth and hope that anticipates spring.

LATINO LABOR HISTORY

Above the sun, a man and woman toil in an unnamed auto factory. The pair represents Latinos and other noble workers who contribute to the overall cultural and financial growth of the city, and as well to the economic progress of the state of Michigan and the country—Latino achievements that have been largely under-reported in Michigan history. Thus, the mural gains greater meaning in terms of U.S. labor history; *CitySpirit* is a monument that pays homage to scores of Latino workers who have sweated and bled in Michigan's fields, railroads, foundries, factories, kitchens, and highways, struggling without historical recognition and social equality.

Recent Developments

For several years now, Mexicantown has been undergoing massive reconstruction. The Michigan Department of Transportation (MDOT) Ambassador Bridge Gateway Project has tremendously altered Mexicantown, including the *CitySpirit* mural site. Ste. Anne Street, along with many other streets in Mexicantown, was shut down for months. The Gateway Project was originally scheduled for completion in 2009, but it is not finished at the time I am writing. It is the single biggest road construction project in state history, with an estimated price tag of $232 million (Campbell 2007, 1). The project aims to improve highway connections to the Ambassador Bridge from Windsor, Canada, to Detroit, and, eventually, to give better access to Mexicantown as well. According to MDOT leadership, the project plans include

- Reconstruction of parts of interstate highways I-75 and I-96
- An expanded International Welcome Center and Mercado (Mexican Market)
- A new pedestrian bridge that will span busy I-75, linking east and west Mexicantown
- New light fixtures, landscaping, and perhaps public art (Michigan Department of Transportation 2007, 1)

Numerous civic leaders and MDOT administrators concede that the project might exceed the original budget and that the physical construction has already caused considerable disruption to residents and businesses alike. MDOT has joined forces with the City of Detroit and the Mexicantown Community Development Corporation (MCDC) in a partnership to direct the large-scale urban renewal and economic development of the area surrounding the bridge, including Mexicantown. Yet the neighborhood is paralyzed by ongoing construction. Trucks and construction equipment loudly rumble down narrow residential streets, while regular visitors and tourists are detoured away from Mexicantown.

Economically speaking, the entire southwest Detroit area where Mexicantown is located is affected by Gateway construction. One MDOT planner admits, "[The]

FIGURE 3. *CitySpirit* Mural. Martin Moreno and George Vargas, 1979. Hubbard Richard Building, Detroit, Mexicantown. Construction by Michigan Department of Transportation (MDOT) for Ambassador Bridge Gateway Project. Reproduced with the permission of the artists. Photo by George Vargas, 2007.

MDOT Gateway Project will be challenging. . . . Historically, Mexican Town has seen challenges." The planner refers to the original construction of the Chrysler I-75 freeway in 1964, which "cut through the community. . . . Many residents began closing shop and relocating" (Michigan Department of Transportation 2007, 2). The freeway literally split Mexicantown in two, as well as affecting Detroit's so-called Black Bottom community, a vital African American community. The highway brought severe economic and cultural decline for both Latino and African American communities.

Because Detroit is notorious for corruption and graft, many citizens are skeptical of the long-range benefits of the Gateway Project, regardless of expensive public relations promotions, whose theme is ironically named "Connecting Neighbors." Eric T. Campbell (2007, 1) reports that "southwest Detroit residents are confused about what's happening in their community and have suspicions that the project is just the beginning of a second span [on the Ambassador Bridge]. . . . [They] ultimately fear the project will exclude them." Campbell contends that the Gateway Project is financed in part by the Detroit International Bridge Company (DIBC) which is also "pushing to build a second span of the Ambassador Bridge." Apparently the privately owned DIBC is controlled by Manuel Maroun, who also owns the Ambassador Bridge and is quietly negotiating with certain Detroit city officials and state legislators to build a second bridge span west of the first. Campbell (2007, 3) further states that Canadian newspaper *The Windsor Star* has reported that some construction has already begun in Windsor.

For the City of Detroit, the Gateway Project may be built on good intentions, but for Mexicantown the project has brought hostility between residents and MCDC and DIBC. Private investors, Latino and non-Latino alike, have made critical decisions without considering the public's welfare and health. Main arteries in and out of Mexicantown are shut down; construction has thwarted residents attempting to work and shop in their own neighborhood. People are suffering from extreme levels of noise, dust, and pollution, not to mention lack of sleep. *CitySpirit* is blocked by construction, with crews tearing up the street directly in front of the mural.

Public artist and neighborhood resident Vito Valdez is gravely concerned that the mural's relentless exposure to layer upon layer of heavy dust will ultimately damage the wall's surface. Additionally, the vibrations from heavy construction might possibly crack the foundation of the Hubbard Richard building. Valdez is busy writing a proposal to solicit funds to re-restore the mural once again after the construction is completed!

Hopefully, when the Gateway Project is finished, many more people will get a chance to see the mural that refuses to die.

Artists' Comments

Three leading Detroit-area artists offer comments and opinions on *CitySpirit*, expanding upon the meaning of the mural for the reader.

MARY LAREDO HERBECK
MIXED-MEDIA SCULPTOR, COMMUNITY ARTS ORGANIZER, ART GALLERY DIRECTOR

The *CitySpirit* mural is a landmark in the southwest Detroit community Mexicantown. As an active member of this community, I am proud to claim collective ownership of this historical work of art. This mural has survived for more than 30 years, and has become a landmark and destination point for tour groups and visitors who are always interested in hearing of its historic relevance, its thematic significance, and its painstaking restoration. *CitySpirit* demonstrates the power of public art to inspire and affect change within a community and beyond.

NORA CHAPA MENDOZA

PAINTER AND MURALIST, MAJOR ORGANIZER IN THE MICHIGAN ART SCENE

Every time I pass the mural site, I am reminded of the artists who have been present in the history of our barrio. It also reminds me of the losses of such artists like Martin Moreno and George Vargas; by loss, I mean that both have moved on to other areas of our country where they continue to enrich Hispanic arts and culture.

The tree of life in that mural represents to me our culture blossoming year after year. Although some of the branches have fallen off, they did not fall far from the tree (our barrio) and it is a constant reminder of where we were, where we are going, and that we will remain long after we are gone—for our future, Chicanito artists, and children to remember how deep our roots go.

VITO VALDEZ

PUBLIC ARTIST, ART TEACHER, ACTIVIST

Returning to Detroit early spring 1996, after living in Montreal and abroad for three years, I was an independent artist looking for work. I came back with a renewed interest in my roots, identity, and a project that would cultivate them. I found it in the streets I grew up in. At the corner of Ste. Anne and Bagley, a celebrated work of art had fallen into decay and was hardly visible. It could not be lost to history; it had to be saved. I knew one of the artists who helped conceive its design—Vargas. I asked him to contact Martin Moreno for photos and permission to undertake this restoration project.

As planning and funding came along, the enormous task of piecing it together began. With the help of an apprentice, we cleaned, marked, and began to work from the original surface. The community embraced us for taking on such an ambitious undertaking, and we again received help from local businesses. During the spring and very hot summer months that followed, many tourists, students, and interested public from all walks of life visited our work site. A great many questions were asked: What does it mean? Who is it for? Why is it here?

Public art is a visual language—a soundboard for reaction and response. This piece speaks of the rich history and culture of the Americas and its place here on the border—a border barrio called Mexicantown. *CitySpirit* has its place in history as the oldest Chicano mural still extant in Detroit from *el movimiento* ("the movement") that came out of the late 1960s. In the tradition of the great Mexican muralists, it is filled with universal symbols that can be understood by people from around the globe. It continues as a testament to the power, strength, and magic of an image on the wall—a mural.

Conclusion

The public mural *CitySpirit* is a true living monument to the Mexicantown neighborhood it serves, and to the city of Detroit, for it is more than a painting; it is a living testament dedicated to the heart and soul of an American people. The mural has weathered sun, snow, and rainstorm, as well as a total renovation of the building that it decorates. Over time, the mural itself was restored, and presently it needs a new restoration, because of a massive urban construction project in the area surrounding Mexicantown and the Ambassador Bridge. The mural has lasted more than three decades simply because the people see and feel their presence resonating within the mural itself, a precious mirror that no one can break!

NOTES

1. I, George Vargas, am the author of this essay and one of the artists of the *CitySpirit* mural. Herein as historian and artist, from time to time I will present firsthand recollections of events surrounding the mural's creation and preservation, as well as my personal perspective regarding its importance as public art.

2. "The Dying God is always killed on a tree," states Cooper (1978, 176, 178). Consider Jesus Christ as an archetypal mythic hero whose exploits have been replicated in many lands throughout history (Campbell 1988, 134).

3. Leonardo da Vinci's 1487 *Vitruvian Man* is a small pen-and-ink drawing that "visualizes [Roman architect] Vitruvius' notion that the human body may be used to derive the perfect geometrical forms of the circle and the square." "The power image" served as "a [carrier] of profound meaning as well as visual form," symbolizing the "place of man in the world" (Davies 2007, 255–56).

4. For more information on the ancient Mexican concept of time see Leon-Portillo 1963; 1990; Kay 1998.

REFERENCES

Campbell, E. T. 2007. "Bridge Project Misses Connection." *Michigan Citizen,* December 28. Available online: www.michigancitizen.com.

Campbell, J. 1988. *The Power of Myth.* New York: Doubleday.

Cooper, J. C. 1978. *An Illustrated Encyclopedia of Traditional Signs and Symbols.* London: Thames and Hudson.

Davies, P. J. 2007. *Janson's History of Art.* Upper Saddle, NJ: Pearson, Prentice Hall.

Farmer, S. 1890. *History of Detroit, Wayne County and Michigan.* New York: Munsell and Company.

Hall, J. 1974. *Dictionary of Subjects and Symbols in Art.* New York: Harper & Row.

Herbeck, M. L. 2007. "Re: My Short Essay." Email to author, December 23.

Kay, A. R. 1998. *Time and Sacrifice in the Aztec Cosmos.* Bloomington: Indiana University Press.

Leon-Portillo, M. 1963. *Aztec Thought and Culture.* Norman: University of Oklahoma Press.

————. 1990. *Time and Reality in the Thought of the Maya.* Norman: University of Oklahoma Press.

Lurker, M. 1974. *The Gods and Symbols of Ancient Egypt.* London: Thames and Hudson.

Mendoza, N. C. 2007. "Re: Mural." Email to author, December 20.

Michigan Department of Transportation. 2007. "Connecting Neighbors: MDOT I-75 Ambassador Bridge Gateway Project Newsletter." October.

Miller, M. A. 1986. *The Art of Mesoameria from Olmec to Aztec.* London: Thames and Hudson.

Valdes, D. N. 1982. *El Pueblo Mexicano en Detroit y Michigan: A Social History.* College of Education, Wayne State University.

Valdez, V. J. 2007. "Re: Mural." Email to author, December 21.

Vargas, G. 1988. *Contemporary Latino Art in Michigan, the Midwest and the Southwest.* Ph.D. diss., University of Michigan.

Walker, B. G. 1983. *The Woman's Encyclopedia of Myths and Secrets.* San Francisco: Harper & Row.

Conclusion

THE STUDIES AND ESSAYS IN THIS VOLUME SHED LIGHT ON SOME ASPECTS OF THE experiences and dimensions of Latinos in the Midwest. Although a robust body of scholarship is beginning to emerge, much research remains to be done both on the historical experience and current context of Latinos in midwestern communities, especially relative to ways by which they can be incorporated into societal institutions and how their socioeconomic status can be improved. The demographic shift that is currently under way portends many social, economic, and political consequences for the region and the nation, especially if the incorporation of this growing population segment into the fabric of core societal institutions is not addressed directly and systematically.

Zúñiga and Hernández-León (2005) point out that the "social situations, relations and contexts" of Latino newcomers are in a state of flux in their new communities. One factor that contributes to that flux is the conflict between political forces that seek to incorporate Latinos into the core institutions of U.S. society and those that seek to exclude them from full participation in society. This conflict seems to frame the context not only for newcomers but for all Latinos (Cafferty and Engstrom 2000). The forces of inclusion or incorporation are diverse in their rationales and philosophies for inclusion, but they recognize the importance that incorporating Latinos has for the future of the nation. The forces that pursue exclusion are nativist movements that seek to protect American culture and institutions from the impact of pluralistic forces and immigrants, especially Latino immigrants, who tend to be viewed either as unassimilable or unwilling to assimilate into American society. The struggles take place at the level of everyday life, where people come in contact with each other, whether on the street or inside organizations, and they take place at legal and policy levels, where success tends to have more general and enduring consequences. These may include local, state, and federal policies, many of which are constructed and challenged at the level of the electorate through referendums, in legislative arenas, and in the courts, depending on the forces at play.

Reactionary responses to the Civil Rights Movement of the 1960s set in motion a series of struggles between exclusionary and inclusionary forces that have persisted for decades. Indeed, as early as 1975, when Texas changed its education laws to deny a public education to undocumented school-age children, there have been organized efforts to limit public benefits to undocumented immigrants. Although the Texas law, Texas Education Code § 21.031, was found unconstitutional in *Plyler v. Doe* by the U.S. Court of Appeals for the Fifth Circuit and its decision was affirmed by the U.S. Supreme Court in 1982, efforts to deny public benefits to undocumented immigrants have persisted. In California, Proposition 187 (also known as the Save Our State Initiative) was passed by referendum in 1994, to limit public benefits to undocumented immigrants. And although it was found to be unconstitutional in 1997, the legal struggles persisted through appeals until it was finally killed in 1999, when Governor Gray Davis took the case to mediation and dropped the appeals process before the courts. Anti-affirmative action measures followed Proposition 187, and were passed in several states, including California, Washington, Nebraska, and Michigan. These measures targeted native-born Latinos and other minorities. In the wake of 9/11, frustration with the inability of the federal government to address immigration issues has resulted in a spate of additional anti-immigrant initiatives at state and local levels.

Most recently, the attacks tend to center on education. Perhaps among the many dimensions of incorporation (including civic engagement, entrepreneurship and economic development, community development, organizational leadership, and so on) education ranks among the most important because without a solid education members of subordinate groups are not likely to attain the knowledge and technical skill sets necessary for full participation in today's society. This is especially the case given that most new jobs tend to require some postsecondary education and the fact that good jobs require high-level cognitive skills (Carnevale and Fry 2002). Moreover, the education of minority males is a growing challenge across the country (Harris 2009).

These more recent attacks focus on abolishing out-of-state tuition exemptions for qualified undocumented students, although eliminating bilingual education and abolishing birthright citizenship for children born in the United States to undocumented immigrants are also part of the discourse. "In-state tuition laws" for undocumented immigrants, or "DREAM acts," as they have been dubbed, were passed initially in Texas and California in 2001, and were followed by several others states with substantial numbers of undocumented immigrants, including Illinois, Kansas, Nebraska, and Wisconsin in the Midwest. Other states include New Mexico, New York, Utah, and Washington. Similar bills were proposed in Arkansas and New Jersey but were not passed. Oklahoma passed a DREAM Act in 2003, but rescinded it in 2007.

California passed Assembly Bill 540 in 2001, and although it has been challenged in court, it has survived. According to AB 540, students must meet the following requirements to qualify for in-state tuition: (1) attend a California high school for three or more years; (2) graduate from a California high school or receive the equivalent general education diploma; (3) register or be enrolled in a public college or university in California, and (4) submit a signed statement with the college or university stating that the student has applied or will apply as soon as eligible to adjust their immigration status to be in compliance with immigration laws.

AB 540 has been challenged by the Federation for American Immigration Reform (FAIR), an anti-immigration organization based in Washington, DC, on the basis that it violates section 505 of the Illegal Immigration Reform and Immigration Responsibility Act of 1996 (IIRIRA), 8 U.S.C. § 1623. This section holds that persons who are not legally present in the United States are not eligible on the basis of residence within a state for any higher education benefit unless citizens or nationals of the country also are eligible for such a benefit without regard to whether they are residents. In 2006, the Superior Court of California, County of Yolo, decided that AB 540 is not in conflict with section 505 of IIRIRA because it does not confer a benefit on the basis of residency in California. However, in 2008, a California appeals court reversed the dismissal and remanded the case back to the trial court. The University of California appealed the decision to the California Supreme Court, which recently heard the case and decided that the provisions of AB 540 do not violate §1623 and neither do they violate the privileges and immunities clause of the 14th Amendment to the U.S. Constitution.

In a related matter, in 2008, the U.S. Immigration and Customs Enforcement (ICE) responded to a query from the Special Deputy Attorney General, North Carolina Department of Justice, regarding whether 8 U.S.C. § 1621 prohibited the North Carolina Community College System from enrolling "illegal aliens" in postsecondary education institutions in the absence of state legislation. The letter issued by ICE stated that IIRIRA does not regulate admission to postsecondary institutions as a benefit under the Personal Responsibility and Work Opportunity Reconciliation Act of 1996 (PRWORA), which, among other things, regulates monetary assistance for postsecondary education. In other words, providing tax-based financial aid would be seen as a monetary benefit, while admission would not. Thus, states and institutions can decide for themselves whether or not to provide admission to undocumented immigrants. Moreover, while PRWORA restricts undocumented immigrant eligibility for state or local benefits, it also provides states with the authority to grant benefits to undocumented immigrants should they decide to enact laws that affirmatively provide such eligibility (Ashford and Trout, n.d.).

In the Midwest, challenges have been brought forth in Kansas and in Nebraska. In 2004, soon after the law was enacted, a group of students classified as "nonresidents" of Kansas challenged the "in-state tuition law" that allowed undocumented students to pay in-state tuition rates if they met the requirements of the law. Similar to the requirements specified in California's AB 540, the Kansas law added a fourth requirement: that an individual could not be eligible for in-state tuition in another state on the basis of residence. The plaintiffs raised several claims, including violation of the IIRIRA and equal protection laws. The court dismissed the case for lack of standing, stating, among other things, that the plaintiffs did not have a private right of action to enforce the IIRIRA and did not meet the lawful, nondiscriminatory qualifications for the benefit. With regard to the latter, the plaintiffs did not demonstrate an injury on which to base their equal protection claim. The decision was upheld by the U.S. Court of Appeals for the Tenth Circuit, and in 2008, the U.S. Supreme Court declined to review the case.

Nebraska's legislature enacted LB 239 in 2006, overriding a veto of the bill by the governor, who argued that it would place the state in conflict with governing federal law. The provisions of LB 239 are similar to those of AB 540 in California, and specify the conditions under which individuals are deemed to have established residence in the state for purposes of in-state tuition rates at postsecondary education institutions. LB 239 provides eight conditions under which individuals may be seen as having established residence in the state. The eighth and final condition has the following requirements: An individual (1) resided in the state with parent, guardian or conservator while attending high school; (2) graduated from a high school in the state or obtained the equivalent of a high school diploma within the state; (3) resided in the state for at least three years before graduating from high school or receiving the equivalent of a high school diploma; (4) was not registered as an entering student at a public postsecondary education institution in the state prior to the fall of 2006; and (5) submitted an affidavit stating the he or she will file an application to become a permanent resident at the earliest opportunity. LB 239 was codified into law as Nebraska Revised Statute § 85-502. In January 2010, LB 1001 was introduced in the 101st Legislature of Nebraska by nativists who disagreed with the provisions of LB 239. However, after having been referred to the Education Committee, which held a hearing on education-related bills on February 1, 2010, LB 1001 was indefinitely postponed in April 2010. If passed, LB 1001 would have amended the statute by prohibiting resident status to persons who are not lawfully in the United States and by eliminating the provisions of section 8 of LB 239, which allows for students who may be undocumented to pay in-state tuition rates if they have met its requirements.

At the same time that struggles occur over the DREAM acts, a handful of states have passed legislation that denies in-state tuition rates to undocumented students. These are Arizona, Colorado, Georgia, Mississippi, Oklahoma, and Virginia. Other states, such as North Carolina and South Carolina, have also struggled over how to address the needs of undocumented students. North Carolina's Community College System has repeatedly changed its policy relative to enrolling undocumented students, waffling between barring them from enrolling to allowing them to do so. The latest North Carolina policy is to allow undocumented students to enroll, but they must pay out-of-state tuition irrespective of whether they live in the state or not. A similar policy is already in effect at the University of North Carolina. South Carolina has implemented the most extreme policy to date, that of barring undocumented students from public colleges and universities altogether.

Ultimately, restricting undocumented students from higher education will most likely have a negative impact on the economy of South Carolina and the nation as the demographic shift continues to unfold. The result is similar to that argued by the district court judge in *Plyler v. Doe:*

> If these already disadvantaged children are denied an education when they are young, they will be forever relegated to the lowest level of employment. If the state refuses to educate them now, even a future grant of amnesty by Congress will not prevent many of these children from having been permanently stigmatized and crippled by their former illegal status (*Plyler v. Doe* 1978, 592).

Such policies as the one enacted in South Carolina are based more on ideology than on a rational approach to serving the public good. The governor of South Carolina, upon signing the South Carolina Illegal Immigration Reform Act into law, praised legislators for putting forth legislation that cracks down on illegal immigration and affirming that the United States is a nation of laws. Apparently he was unaware that the Fourteenth Amendment to the U.S. Constitution is not limited to the protection of citizens but applies to all persons within the territorial jurisdiction. While anti-immigrant legislation by states may be viewed as laudable efforts, the matter of undocumented youth who have lived here for several years and have gone through the nation's schools is far more complex than merely cracking down on illegal immigration. In general, rounding up all undocumented persons in this country for purposes of deportation is neither feasible on political nor financial terms, which means they will most likely remain in this country, especially if they were raised and educated here. As a result, it becomes important to promote educational opportunities among all Latinos. Flores (2010) has provided results of a study that shows that in-state tuition policies significantly increase the college-going rates of "Latino foreign-born noncitizens," many of whom are undocumented. Having these young adults receive a college education is inherently good for the nation.

As the demand for college-educated workers increases over the coming years, it will likely be met by shortages that will negatively affect the economy. While some political leaders suggest that the demand for college-educated workers can be met by recruiting international students, especially those educated here in the United States, the demand will be too great to rely solely on this population segment. Moreover, this strategy raises important issues about promoting the public good and the basic values of this nation, as it still does not address the educational needs of native-born Latinos, who are the majority of the Latino population. To a great extent, the immigration issue has deflected attention away from the fact that the majority of Latinos, including children, are native-born and citizens of the United States. Therefore, as we move into the future, the educational needs of Latinos remain to be addressed, not just for their own good, but for the good of the country. The challenge is overcoming institutionalized patterns of intergroup relations.

At the local level in the Midwest, the contexts of reception include historical patterns of intergroup relations that frame how Latino newcomers are perceived and treated. They also include economic shifts that have prompted out-migration by local populations, forcing local employers to become more dependent on immigrant, low-wage labor (Flores 2010). The decline of the sugar beet industry in parts of the Midwest (Michigan and Ohio), for example, contributed to the movement of Latino agricultural labor into manufacturing and meatpacking and other food-processing industries (Rosenbaum 1996; Zúñiga and Hernández-León 2005). The result is that both native- and foreign-born Latinos, for the most part, are a subordinate group that is imbedded within the racial division of labor that limits their chances for upward mobility. Foreign-born Latinos are likely to experience a segmented assimilation process through which they are integrated into the bottom of the racial division of labor structure (see Portes and Zhou 1993, and Zhou 1997 for a conceptual view of segmented assimilation). Indeed, there is an American view that it is common for immigrants to enter the occupational structure at the bottom and work their way up over generations. For some groups, such as Mexican Americans or Chicanos, the traditional assimilation hypothesis does not apply. Forced entry into American society has engendered a set of intergroup relations that serve as structural barriers to full participation in society and perpetuate dominant/minority relations.

Studies have repeatedly shown that Latinos have been and continue to be subjected to prejudice, discrimination, and exploitation (San Juan Cafferty and McCready 1985; Rodríguez, Sáenz, and Menjívar 2008; Fraga et al. 2010). There are a multitude of factors that reproduce the stratification system of which Latinos are a part, irrespective of whether they are native or foreign born. At the level of policy there are variations in terms of enforcement that affect both native-born and foreign-born Latinos, including migrant labor flows and their points of destination. David Griffith (2005), for example, recounts an interaction with a labor contractor who spoke of his unwillingness to take agricultural crews north of the North Carolina –Virginia line because of the increased enforcement of labor laws that occurs north of the line. Griffith understood this to mean the greater enforcement of the Migrant and Seasonal Agricultural Workers Protection Act by the Philadelphia Regional Office of Labor than by the Atlanta Regional Office of Labor. Such variability is sure to occur not only in and across midwestern states but in other regions across the nation. Indeed, both lax and selective enforcement makes it easier to exploit migrant workers without having to provide even the minimum workplace requirements mandated by law.

Similarly, reactionary or anti-immigration policies that target Latino immigrants engender contexts in which they are more likely than usual to be harassed and to be targets of racial profiling. For example, in central Kentucky, where Latino migrant agricultural workers were recruited in significant numbers in 1987, local residents responded with fears that the migrant workers would increase crime rates and spread diseases (Denton 2002). In this case, fear of Latino migrant workers was coupled with resentment toward perceived labor market and community changes that would occur as a result of their presence. Consequently, Latino workers experienced difficulties in obtaining housing, sometimes having to lead homeless lives (Denton 2002). How much of this goes on is neither well documented through research nor known by the public, but that it happens is unquestionable.

As documented in some of the chapters in this volume, ICE raids have had disturbing effects on midwestern communities. What have not been discussed are the negative effects of immigration enforcement on the children, the majority of whom are U.S. citizens, whose parents have been arrested by ICE (Capps et al. 2007). Raids were conducted both at the workplace and at homes, where children witnessed the arrests. Initial studies are showing that these children experience behavioral changes, at least in the short term (Chaudry et al. 2010). It may also be that the experience will have a significant impact over the course of their lives. In the short term, children exhibited multiple behavior changes, including changes in eating habits and sleep, and exhibited frequent crying, anxiety and fear. These behavior changes were still reported several months after the raids (Chaudry et al. 2010). The impact of the raids on the lives of these children still remains to be seen.

In April, 2010 the governor of Arizona signed into law the controversial Senate Bill 1070, titled Support Our Law Enforcement and Safe Neighborhoods Act, which, among other things, would engage local law enforcement agencies in identifying, prosecuting and deporting illegal immigrants. Identification would be facilitated in cases where lawful contact has been made and there is reasonable suspicion that an individual may be an "unlawful alien" by requiring that steps be taken to verify the person's immigration status. Provisions of the law were barred from going into effect on July 28, 2010, by the U.S. Federal District Court for the District of Arizona, which held that there was substantial likelihood that Arizona law enforcement officers would wrongfully arrest "legal resident aliens" and thereby impose extraordinary burdens on them that only the federal government has authority to impose. Moreover, the Court recognized that the federal government has primary authority in the arena of immigration law and that it was in the public interest to enjoin the State of Arizona from enforcing portions of SB 1070 until the federal government's own lawsuit seeking to overturn the law is settled. Earlier in July the Department of Justice filed an injunction against Arizona arguing that states cannot pass immigration laws that interfere with federal law and the objectives of the U.S. Congress. As these cases were unfolding, legislators in six other states introduced their own "copycat" bills of Arizona's SB 1070. One was introduced in Michigan, a state with one of the lowest numbers of undocumented workers, but where reactionary movements in recent years have been supportive of candidates with nativistic agendas.

How do the Midwest and the nation move from reactionary or indifferent attitudes toward Latinos to proactive incorporation efforts intended to benefit whole communities and the nation? Can the demographic shift and its attendant challenges for the nation be effectively communicated so that Americans understand the importance of incorporating Latinos into U.S. institutions? One of the great challenges is maintaining informed citizens. Democracies require informed citizenries, and both educational systems and the mass media are crucial for ensuring that the nation's citizens are well informed of the challenges facing the nation. Public systems of education are intended to maintain educated citizens at the same time that they promote skilled labor forces and prepare young people for careers (London 2003). Educated citizens understand the nature of democracies, their roles within them, and the importance of their involvement in civic and political activity. They understand the values of freedom, justice, and equality, and the importance of securing and affirming civil and human rights. They are able to seek information and to critically assimilate it, whether it is provided by political leaders or the media. The incorporation of Latinos into U.S. institutions will require, among other things, the education of Americans about the demographic shift and its implications. It will also require the education of Latinos and their transformation into a highly skilled labor force. This implies the transcendence, if not the destruction, of the stratification processes in this country that combine racial and class dynamics to reproduce isolation and marginalization among Latinos and other groups.

For example, Hirschman (2001), in a test of the segmented-assimilation hypothesis focusing on the educational experience of immigrant youth, found that increasing numbers of new immigrant populations are disadvantaged on several of the measures of family socioeconomic status and social resources. Moreover, he found that Latino adolescents tend to have the highest levels of school attrition. Unlike Asian immigrant youth, who do not have any indicators of newcomer disadvantage with regard to high school enrollment, Latino adolescents, especially those who started their formal education in their country of origin, are at higher risk of dropping out of high school than their native-born counterparts, who already have higher dropout rates than their dominant group counterparts. These low levels of educational attainment have long-term consequences for Latino youth both in terms of political engagement and socioeconomic status when they could be having positive effects on their lives and on the economy (Carnevale and Desrochers 2004). Moreover, these negative outcomes are reinforced by the mass media, which tend to provide negative stereotypes of young Latinos as criminals who are aggressive, dishonest, and unkempt (Mastro and Behm-Morawitz 2005).

Recently, Ron Unz (2010), a self-avowed conservative, argued against the myths of Latino and Latino immigrant lawlessness perpetuated by media sensationalists such as Rush Limbaugh, Lou Dobbs and Glenn Beck. Unz recounts his personal experiences living and working in areas with high Latino densities without experiencing hostility or crimes. Moreover, he provides analyses of official crime data and concludes that cities with high proportions of Latinos generally have low crime rates, with violence and homicide rates well below the national urban average. This occurs despite the link between crime and poverty. Moreover, crime rates in these cities are dropping, and are expected to continue to drop as Latinos experience upward economic mobility. This trend in the decline of crime, especially violent crime, holds for cities in Arizona and that state's border with Mexico. Despite these patterns, the governor of Arizona has repeatedly characterized Arizona as being under siege by undocumented immigrants who are making the crime rates skyrocket.

It is not only nativistic politicians who cast immigrants and Latinos as criminals, the mass media do it as well. Consequently, portrayal of Latinos by the mass media is a major concern among Latino communities. In a statewide summit on Latinos held in East Lansing, Michigan, in July 2009, by the Julian Samora Research Institute, participants identified negative portrayals of Latinos by the media as one of the top 10 issues facing Latino communities. Latinos understand that the media shape the sociopolitical contexts that affect their lives and the structures of opportunity that frame their life chances in this society. The sociopolitical context engendered by today's media is one in which negative images of Latino immigrants perpetuate the mobilization of public sentiments against them. One of the key areas in which nativists or anti-immigration forces are focused is education, which is most important for upward mobility.

Improving educational opportunities is a key vehicle for promoting economic mobility for Latinos and other disadvantaged populations. This will require closing the educational achievement gap through improved academic preparation, improved guidance for college matriculation, and appropriate financial aid and academic support at the postsecondary education level (Haskins, Holzer, and Lerman 2009). Indeed, if Latinos are to be incorporated into U.S. institutions in the coming decades, substantial investments of monetary and human resources will be required from all sectors of the nation, including public, private, and nonprofit entities. Before those investments can be made, however, leadership from all sectors must engage constituencies in becoming aware of the massive challenges the nation faces, first in overcoming the myopic, ideologically driven, political strategies of nativists, then in addressing the substantive demands of the social, political, and economic incorporation of Latinos through programmatic initiatives that will close the gaps between service delivery systems and the needs of Latino communities.

Americans simply are not aware of the challenges facing the nation as a result of the demographic shifts that are under way. They tend to believe that people can still get ahead in this economy (79%), that their economic circumstances will improve in the next decade (72%), and that their children will have a higher standard of living than they have (62%) (Pew Charitable Trusts 2009). Their approach, then, is to get a lock on educational opportunities to ensure access to good jobs. To a great extent, Americans remain ideological creatures at a time when realism is a must for coping with the challenges of the day. Americans must come to grips with the massive societal and economic changes that are under way and the fact that globalization will fundamentally transform all that was part of an international order based on national economies. On the horizon are continued economic restructuring, increases in transnational labor, the rise of macro regional economies, and the emergence of transnational citizenship—in short, global citizens.

As we look to the impending challenges that are on the horizon, repositioning the nation's economy in a context of massive demographic shifts requires a heavy dose of realism. Without it, the struggle that is going on regarding the inclusion and exclusion of Latinos will persist, and will continue to waste time, energy, and valuable resources (especially in the form of unrealized human potential). The dynamics inherent in the lives of Latinos in the Midwest are connected to social, political, and economic dynamics occurring across the country. In this context, beyond just working, they are engaged in place-making, entrepreneurial, and civic activities to build better lives and better communities for themselves and for others. Shedding light on these dynamics at the regional level, as the studies and essays in this volume do, also sheds light on those at the national level. The key to moving forward in a constructive manner is having an informed American citizenry, one that knows it stands on the eve of a new epoch in the history of humankind, and that the future of this nation is bound up with that of Latinos because of the particular demographic circumstances of the times. In this period of great societal change, scholars have a special responsibility of contributing to an informed citizenry by providing research studies that contribute to an objective understanding of the changes that are under way and potential approaches for adapting to the emergent environment. They can also contribute to an understanding of the interdependence of all peoples in this country and across the globe. It is in this spirit that this volume is presented.

NOTE

1. A copy of the letter is available on-line at http://www.nacua.org/documents/Admission
UndocAlien072008.pdf.

REFERENCES

Ashford, B., and S. Trout. n.d. "Review of State and Local Approaches to Immigration Policy by Senator Brad Ashford, Judiciary Committee Chairman and Stacey Trout, Legal Counsel to the Judiciary Committee." Available online: http://www.nlc.state.ne.us/epubs/L3750/B054-2008.pdf.

Carnevale, A. P., and D. M. Desrochers. 2004. "Benefits and Barriers to College for Low-Income Adults." In *Low-Income Adults in Profile: Improving Lives Through Higher Education*, ed. B. Cook and J. E. King, 31–45. Washington, DC: American Council on Education.

Carnevale, A. P., and R. A. Fry. 2002. "The Demographic Window of Opportunity: College Access and Diversity in the new Century." In *Condition of Access: Higher Education for Lower Income Students*, ed. D. Heller, 137–52. Westport, CT: American Council on Education and Praeger Publishers.

Chaudry, A., R. Capps, J. M. Pedroza, R. M. Castañeda, R. Santos, and M. M. Scott. 2010. *Facing*

Our Future: Children in the Aftermath of Immigration Enforcement. Washington, DC: Urban Institute.

Capps, R., R. M. Castañeda, A. Chaudry, and R. Santos. 2007. *Paying the Price: The Impact of Immigration Raids on America's Children.* A Report by the Urban Institute. Washington, DC: National Council of La Raza.

Denton, B. M. 2002. "Community Response to the Introduction of Hispanic Migrant Agricultural Workers into Central Kentucky." In *The Dynamics of Hired Farm Labour: Constraints and Community Responses,* ed. J. L. Findeis, A. M. Vandeman, J. M. Larson, and J. L. Runyan, 115–23. New York: CABI Publishing.

Flores, S. M. 2010. "State Dream Acts: The Effect of In-State Resident Tuition Policies and Undocumented Latino Students." *Review of Higher Education* 33(2): 239–83.

Fraga, L. R., J. A. Garcia, R. E. Hero, M. Jones-Correa, V. Martinez-Ebers, and G. M. Segura. 2010. *Latino Lives in America: Making it Home.* Philadelphia: Temple University Press.

Griffith, D. C. 2005. "Rural Industry and Mexican Immigration and Settlement in North Carolina." In *New Destinations: Mexican Immigration in the United States,* ed. V. Zúñiga and R. Hernández-León, 50–75. New York: Russell Sage Foundation.

Harris, L. 2009. "Higher Education Success Among Historically Marginalized Males." Indianapolis: Lumina Foundation. Available online: http://www.luminafoundation.org/publications/success-among-historically-marginalized-males.pdf.

Haskins, R., H. Holzer, and R. Lerman. 2009. "Promoting Economic Mobility by Increasing Postsecondary Education." Economic Mobility Project, An Initiative of the Pew Charitable Trusts. Available online: http://www.economicmobility.com/assets/pdfs/PEW_EMP_POST-SECONDARY_ED.pdf.

Hirschman, C. 2001. "The Educational Enrollment of Immigrant Youth: A Test of the Segmented-Assimilation Hypothesis." *Demography* 38(3): 317–36.

London, S. 2003. *Higher Education for the Public Good: A Report From the National Leadership Dialogues.* Ann Arbor, MI: National Forum on Higher Education for the Public Good.

Mastro, D. E., and E. Behm-Morawitz. 2005. "Latino Representation on Primetime Television." *Journalism & Mass Communications Quarterly* 82(1): 110–30.

Pew Charitable Trusts. 2009. "Findings from a National Survey & Focus Groups on Economic Mobility." Economic Mobility Project, An Initiative of the Pew Charitable Trusts. Available online: http://www.economicmobility.com/assets/pdfs/Survey_on_Economic_Mobility_Findings.pdf.

Portes, A., and M. Zhou. 1993. "The New Second Generation: Segmented Assimilation and Its Variants." *Annals of the American Academy of Political and Social Science* 530: 74–96.

Plyler v. Doe, 458 F. Supp. 569 (E.D. Tex.1978).

Rodríguez, H., R. Sáenz, and C. Menjívar, eds. 2008. *Latino/as in the United States: Changing the Face of América.* New York: Springer.

Rosenbaum, Rene P. 1996. "Migration and Integration of Latinos into Rural Midwestern Communities: The Case of 'Mexicans' in Adrian, Michigan." JSRI Research Report No. 19, Julian Samora Research Institute, Michigan State University.

San Juan Cafferty, P., and D. W. Engstrom. 2000. *Hispanics in the United States: An Agenda for the Twenty-First Century.* New Brunswick, NJ: Transaction.

San Juan Cafferty, P., and W. C. McCready. 1985. *Hispanics in the United States: A New Social Agenda.* New Brunswick, NJ: Transaction.

Unz, R. 2010. "His-Panic." *American Conservative.* Available online: http://www.amconmag.com/ article/2010/mar/01/00022/.

Zúñiga, V., and R. Hernández-León, eds. 2005. *New Destinations: Mexican Immigration in the United States.* New York: Russell Sage Foundation.

Zhou, M. 1997. "Segmented Assimilation: Issues, Controversies, and Recent Research on the New Second Generation." *International Migration Review* 31(4): 975–1008.

About the Contributors

FLAVIA C. D. ANDRADE is Assistant Professor at the University of Illinois at Urbana–Champaign. Her research focuses on the demography of health and aging. Current projects focus on the social, behavioral, economic, and biological determinants of population health over the life course, with a focus on Latin America and the Caribbean. She is currently collaborating with colleagues in Brazil, Costa Rica, and Mexico.

DAVID A. BADILLO is Associate Professor of Latin American and Puerto Rican Studies at Lehman College, City University of New York. His most recent book is *Latinos and the New Immigrant Church* (published by Johns Hopkins University Press, 2006). Other publications include *Latinos in Michigan* (MSU Press, 2003) and several book chapters and numerous scholarly articles in the field of immigrant history and sociology. His current book project focuses on a history of the Latino civil rights movement.

LYDIA P. BUKI is Associate Professor in the Department of Kinesiology and Community Health at the University of Illinois at Urbana-Champaign. She earned her doctorate in counseling psychology from Arizona State University in 1995. Her research interests include the psychosocial, cultural, individual, and institutional factors that contribute to health disparities in medically underserved Latina/o populations. She has conducted studies with funding from the National Cancer Institute, has served on the editorial board of various journals, and is currently Associate Editor for the journal *Cultural Diversity and Ethnic Minority Psychology*. She is a Fellow of the American Psychological Association.

JENNIFER TELLO BUNTIN is a Visiting Assistant Professor at the Julian Samora Research Institute at Michigan State University. She received her Ph.D. from the Department of Sociology at the University of Chicago. Focusing on Latinos and immigrants in the Midwest, her research examines the ways that receiving community institutions transform in response to the presence of a transnational immigrant population. Her work investigates the ways that assimilation and transnationalism may occur simultaneously and the implications of this for both immigrant and non-immigrant residents.

ANA CAMPOS-HOLLAND is a Ph.D. candidate in the Sociology Department in the University of Iowa. She specializes in criminology, law, substance/drug use, childhood, and adolescence. She is currently working on her dissertation project, concerned with children's lived experiences when a parent is in county jail.

ANTONIO CASTRO-ESCOBAR is originally from Guanajuato, Mexico, and currently resides in Lansing, Michigan. He has been employed with the Michigan Department of Agriculture, Pesticide and Plant Pest Management for over 15 years as Program Manager. He came to the United States in 1988, after graduating from college; his educational experience includes a BS in agronomy and plant pathology from the School of Agro-biology in Uruapan, Michoacán, Mexico, an English as a second language degree, an MS in herbicide physiology, an MS in integrated pest management and entomology, and a Business Management and Communication Skills Certificate, all from MSU.

FRANK DUNN is a city planner with the City of Des Moines, Iowa, and is finishing his master's degree in community and regional planning at Iowa State University. He has spent more than a decade planning leadership activities and conferences within the Latino community in Iowa. He offers a range of skills from commercial development visioning to community engagement and diversity training.

JAN L. FLORA is Professor of Sociology and Extension Community Sociologist at Iowa State University. His current research analyzes the relationship of community social capital to economic, community, and sustainable development. His Extension work focuses on involving Latino immigrants in the affairs of rural Iowa communities, and encouraging immigrants to rural Iowa to become farmers.

SANDRA M. GONZALES serves as Director of the TRiO Upward Bound program at Eastern Michigan University. She recently received her doctorate in International Education from Columbia University, Teachers College. Her research interests include alternative epistemologies, particularly the use of story to explore Midwestern Chicano identity, history, and migration.

DONALD T. HUTCHERSON II, Ph.D., is an Assistant Professor of Sociology and Criminal Justice at Ohio University, Lancaster Campus. His research interests include the effect of extralegal factors on the criminal justice system and the collateral consequences of incarceration on individuals.

HANNAH LEWIS is the Midwest Regional Director for the National Center for Appropriate Technology. She has an MS from Iowa State University, where she co-majored in sustainable agriculture and sociology. She conducts collaborative research and program development to link immigrants with farming backgrounds to agricultural entrepreneurship opportunities in Iowa, including access to education, markets, and land. She has traveled widely in Mexico, Central America, and the Caribbean.

THEO J. MAJKA is Professor of Sociology at the University of Dayton. He is coauthor of Farmers' and Farm Workers' Movements and of Farm Workers, Agribusiness, and the State. His publications and research interests include immigration patterns and issues, in particular exploring how institutions facilitate or hinder the adaptation and integration of immigrants. He is chair of the Ethnic and Cultural Diversity Caucus, a local organization that focuses on eliminating practices that disadvantage minorities. The group organized two "Forums on Immigration" for the Dayton community that addressed issues of incorporation for immigrants and their children. He is part of a group of academics and community participants who are examining the experiences of local refugees in their new communities.

LINDA C. MAJKA is Professor of Sociology at the University of Dayton. She is coeditor of *Children's Human Rights: Progress and Challenges for Children Worldwide* and *Families and Economic Distress*, and coauthor of *Farm Workers, Agribusiness, and the State*. Her publications and research interests include labor and employment, families, and social inequality. She is active in her local community as part of the Ethnic and Cultural Diversity Caucus, a group involved in immigrant and refugee issues that is an initiative of the National Conference for Community and Justice. She contributes to the core curriculum of the Human Rights major at the university and is a council member for the Human Rights Section of the American Sociological Association.

RUBÉN O. MARTINEZ is Professor of Sociology and Director of the Julian Samora Research Institute at Michigan State University. He is editor of the book series *Latinos in the United States*. His areas of expertise include diversity and higher education, race and ethnic relations and diversity leadership. His research focuses on leadership and institutional change, education and ethnic minorities, youth development, and environmental justice.

JENNIFER B. MAYFIELD is a doctoral student in the Counseling Psychology Division at the University of Illinois at Urbana-Champaign. Her research interests focus on cultural and psychosocial determinants of health among racial/ethnic minority women, including the role health literacy in cancer screening behaviors of African-American women. Jennifer received her BS in psychology from Xavier University of Louisiana and her MS in Educational Psychology from the University of Illinois. She is currently working on her dissertation.

MARIA JOSEFA SANTOS has a Ph.D. in social anthropology from the Universidad Nacional Autónoma de México. She is a researcher at the Institute of Social Research at the UNAM. Her research interests include the social aspects of technology and the relationships between technology and culture. Thirty of her papers have been published in specialized journals and books.

CÉSAR P. MONTALVO has worked with immigrant populations in New Jersey, Iowa, and the Czech Republic. He received scholarships to study at the Universidad San Francisco de Quito and Manchester College in Indiana. He obtained his masters in economics at Iowa State University. Currently he is Director of the Department of Research in the Ministry of Production in Ecuador.

CLAUDIA PRADO-MEZA has her first degree in economics from the University of Colima, Mexico. She obtained her masters, and is now pursuing her Ph.D., in sustainable agriculture, at Iowa State University (ISU). Her research is on changes in local food systems in two transnational communities: Marshalltown, Iowa, and Villachuato, Michoacán, Mexico. Her other scholarly interests include social justice advocacy and sustainable development. She is President of ISU's Latino Heritage

Month committee, coordinator of the Latino Seminar Series, and Vice President of the campus-based Latinoamericanos.

ROGELIO SAENZ is Professor in the Department of Sociology at Texas A&M University. He has written extensively on topics related to Latina/os, demography, immigration, and social inequality. He is a coeditor of *Latinas/os in the United States: Changing the Face of América.*

TIA STEVENS is a doctoral student in the School of Criminal Justice at Michigan State University. She holds an M.A. from Bowling Green State University in sociology. Her research interests include female crime and delinquency, gender violence, and intersections of race, class, and gender. Her research has appeared in the *Australian and New Zealand Journal of Criminology* and *Violence Against Women.*

MIKE TAPIA is an Assistant Professor in the Department of Criminal Justice at the University of Texas, San Antonio. His research interests include race and ethnicity in juvenile justice, street gangs, and community corrections. His work has been published in the *Journal of Ethnicity in Criminal Justice* and the *Journal of Criminal Justice* and he has articles forthcoming in the *Journal of Research in Crime and Delinquency* and *Youth and Society.*

GEORGE VARGAS is Associate Professor of Art History at Texas A&M University, Kingsville. He was educated at the University of Michigan, where he earned his three degrees (BFA, MA, Ph.D.). He has an extensive background in Latin American and Latino Studies, film studies, public art, community development, and arts/education administration. He has received numerous awards and fellowships, including a Ford Fellowship and a Martin Luther King, Jr./Cesar Chavez/ Rosa Parks Fellowship. Vargas has organized national and international exhibitions, including Chicano shows featuring the art collection of Cheech Marin. His book *Contemporary Chicano Art: Color & Culture for a New America* documents the dramatic evolution of Chican@ art, from the 1960s to the present, within the broader context of American cultural history.

ARTURO VEGA is Director of the Public Administration Graduate Program and an Associate Professor in Political Science at St. Mary's University in San Antonio. He received his doctorate from the University of Oklahoma in 1990, where he was a Carl Albert Congressional Fellow. His research interests include Latino politics, urban affairs, and U.S. congressional politics.

FRANCISCO A. VILLARRUEL is a University Outreach and Engagement Senior Fellow and a Professor of Human Development and Family Studies. Villarruel has served as the Acting Director of the Julian Samora Institute. His research has focused on Latino youth and their development, and also addresses issues of youth in conflict with the law.